HANDBOOKS

# CLEVELAND

DOUGLAS TRATTNER

# Contents

# Maps

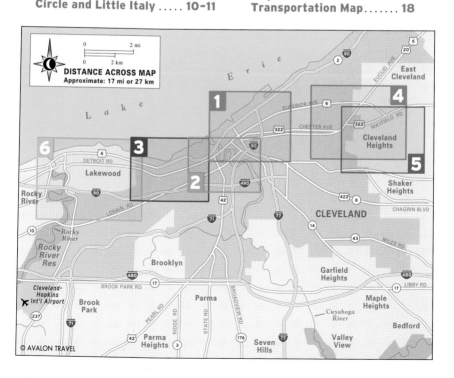

## ⊕ SIGHTS

3 GREAT LAKES SCIENCE CENTER
5 ⬛ ROCK AND ROLL HALL OF FAME AND MUSEUM
8 U.S.S. COD SUBMARINE
9 ⬛ WALKING TOURS OF CLEVELAND
10 CUYAHOGA COUNTY COURTHOUSE
11 ⬛ FREE STAMP
37 OLD STONE CHURCH
39 WAR MEMORIAL FOUNTAIN

40 OLD FEDERAL BUILDING
41 CLEVELAND PUBLIC LIBRARY, MAIN BRANCH
44 FEDERAL RESERVE BANK
51 TERMINAL TOWER
56 SOLDIERS AND SAILORS MONUMENT
57 ⬛ THE ARCADE
83 TROLLEY TOURS OF CLEVELAND
92 ⬛ HOPE MEMORIAL BRIDGE

## ⓡ RESTAURANTS

17 ⬛ SLYMAN'S DELI
18 SUPERIOR PHO
19 LI WAH
27 JOHNNY'S LITTLE BAR
29 BLUE POINT GRILL
31 XO PRIME STEAKS
32 METROPOLITAN CAFÉ
33 NAUTI MERMAID

35 CROP BISTRO
46 MARKET CAFÉ
62 ⬛ LOLA
65 SAIGON VIETNAMESE CUISINE
82 PONTE VECCHIO
91 JUNIPER GRILLE

## ⓝ NIGHTLIFE

13 SOMETHING DADA
24 ANATOMY
28 D'VINE WINE BAR
30 VELVET DOG
34 MERCURY LOUNGE
64 KEVIN'S MARTINI BAR
64 HILARITIES 4TH STREET

66 VIEW
69 WILBERT'S FOOD & MUSIC
75 PEABODY'S CONCERT CLUB
79 SHOOTER'S
80 METROPOLIS
84 THE IMPROV

0      300 yds
0      300 m

**DISTANCE ACROSS MAP**
Approximate: 3.2 mi or 5.1 km

Lake Erie

Walking Tours of Cleveland 9 ⊕

7 ⊕
Voinovich Bicentennial Park 6

8 ⊕ U.S.S. COD Submarine  South Harbor RTA

Rock and Roll Hall of Fame and Museum 5 ⊕  North Coast RTA

3 ⊕ⓐ 4
Great Lakes Science Center

2 ⓐ
Cleveland Browns Stadium

Free Stamp 11 ⊕

Cuyahoga County Courthouse 10 ⊕

War Memorial Fountain 39 ⊕

43 ⊕
44 45 Federal Reserve Bank 46

DOWNTOWN

322

47 ⊕
PLAYHOUSE SQUARE

West 3rd RTA

36 ⓐ
Old Federal Building 40 ⊕  Cleveland Public Library

37 ⊕
Public Square

57 58 59
The Arcade 56 ⊕
68

70 ⓝ
EUCLID

Flats East Bank RTA

30 31
28 ⓝ 29
23 ⓡ 32 Old Stone 33 Church 34
24 35
25 27
26 ⓐ
Terminal Tower 51 ⓐⓢ

50 53 54
55 ⓐ

60 61 62 63 64 65

66 ⓝ

69 ⓝ

Erie Street Cemetery

THE FLATS

MAIN AVENUE BRIDGE

Soldiers and Sailors Monument

Quicken Loans Arena

Progressive Field

79 ⓝ
Trolley Tours of Cleveland 83 ⓐ ⓝ 84
85 ⓢ Settler's Landing

Tower City Center RTA
Tower City-Public Square

88 ⓐ

89 ⓐ

90 ⓝ

80 ⓝ

82 ⓡ

81 ⓐ

86 ⓐ

Hope Memorial Bridge 92 ⊕

INDUSTRIAL VALLEY

87 ⓐ

90

SEE MAP 2

Cuyahoga River

SEE MAP 2

VETERANS MEMORIAL BRIDGE

WAREHOUSE DISTRICT

Burke
Lakefront
Airport

Kirtland
Park

ST. CLAIR
SUPERIOR

PAYNE/GOODRICH-
KIRTLAND PARK

Cleveland State
University

Cuyahoga Community
College - Metro Campus

CENTRAL

SEE MAP 4

## A ARTS AND LEISURE

| | | | |
|---|---|---|---|
| 1 | CLEVELAND NATIONAL AIR SHOW | 53 | TOWER CITY CINEMAS |
| 2 | CLEVELAND BROWNS | 55 | CLEVELAND WINTERFEST |
| 4 | OMNIMAX THEATER | 60 | THE BANG AND THE CLATTER |
| 6 | CLEVELAND PRIDE PARADE AND FESTIVAL | 61 | HOUSE OF BLUES |
| 7 | *GOODTIME III* | 63 | THE CORNER ALLEY |
| 7 | CLEVELAND SKATE PARK | 67 | FITWORKS |
| 12 | ST. PATRICK'S DAY PARADE | 71 | GREAT LAKES THEATER FESTIVAL |
| 14 | WOOLTEX GALLERY | 72 | BONFOEY GALLERY |
| 16 | ZYGOTE PRESS | 74 | CLEVELAND STATE UNIVERSITY VIKINGS |
| 20 | CONVIVIUM 33 GALLERY | 74 | WOLSTEIN CENTER |
| 21 | FRONT ROOM GALLERY | 76 | YMCA OF GREATER CLEVELAND |
| 26 | KARMA YOGA | 78 | CLEVELAND AGORA |
| 36 | CLEVELAND POLICE HISTORICAL SOCIETY AND MUSEUM | 81 | SPACES GALLERY |
| 42 | CLEVELAND PUBLIC LIBRARY EASTMAN READING GARDEN | 85 | BURNING RIVER FEST |
| | | 85 | PLAIN DEALER PAVILION AT NAUTICA |
| 45 | MONEY MUSEUM AT FEDERAL RESERVE BANK | 86 | WESTERN RESERVE ROWING ASSOCIATION |
| 47 | INGENUITY FESTIVAL | 87 | GREAT AMERICAN RIB COOK-OFF |
| 47 | DANCECLEVELAND | 87 | TASTE OF CLEVELAND |
| 47 | OPERA CLEVELAND | 87 | TIME WARNER CABLE AMPHITHEATER |
| 47 | PLAYHOUSESQUARE | 88 | CLEVELAND CAVALIERS |
| 48 | CLEVELAND CITY STARS | 88 | CLEVELAND GLADIATORS |
| 49 | ART GALLERY AT CLEVELAND STATE UNIVERSITY | 88 | LAKE ERIE MONSTERS |
| | | 88 | QUICKEN LOANS ARENA |
| 53 | CLEVELAND INTERNATIONAL FILM FEST | 89 | CLEVELAND INDIANS |

## S SHOPS

| | | | |
|---|---|---|---|
| 22 | CLEVELAND METROBARK | 54 | THE ONLY CLEVELAND STORE |
| 23 | STYLE LOUNGE | 54 | TOWER CITY CENTER |
| 25 | SURROUNDINGS HOME DÉCOR | 58 | MARENGO LUXURY SPA |

## H HOTELS

| | | | |
|---|---|---|---|
| 15 | FLEX BATHS | 68 | HOLIDAY INN EXPRESS HOTEL AND SUITES |
| 38 | MARRIOTT DOWNTOWN AT KEY CENTER | 70 | WYNDHAM CLEVELAND AT PLAYHOUSE SQUARE |
| 43 | CROWNE PLAZA CLEVELAND CITY CENTRE | 73 | COMFORT INN DOWNTOWN |
| 50 | RENAISSANCE CLEVELAND HOTEL | 77 | BROWNSTONE INN |
| 52 | THE RITZ-CARLTON | 90 | HILTON GARDEN INN |
| 59 | HYATT REGENCY AT THE ARCADE | | |

© AVALON TRAVEL

St. John's
Episcopal
Church

Jay Avenue
Homes

Franklin
Castle

Fairview
Park

St. Patrick's
Church

John
Heisman's
Birthplace

West Side
Market

West 25th-
Ohio City

St. Ignatius
High School

Carnegie
West Library

**OHIO CITY**

SEE MAP 3

SEE MAP 1

Monroe
Cemetery

St. Mary's
Cemetery

© AVALON TRAVEL

## SIGHTS

| | | | |
|---|---|---|---|
| 4 | ST. JOHN'S EPISCOPAL CHURCH | 24 | JAY AVENUE HOMES |
| 7 | FRANKLIN CASTLE | 34 | WEST SIDE MARKET |
| 12 | CARNEGIE WEST LIBRARY | 57 | LINCOLN PARK |
| 14 | ST. PATRICK'S CHURCH | 71 | ST. THEODOSIUS RUSSIAN ORTHODOX CATHEDRAL |
| 19 | ST. IGNATIUS HIGH SCHOOL | 72 | A CHRISTMAS STORY HOUSE |
| 20 | JOHN HEISMAN'S BIRTHPLACE | | |

## RESTAURANTS

| | | | |
|---|---|---|---|
| 2 | THE HARP | 43 | SOKOLOWSKI'S UNIVERSITY INN |
| 11 | NICK'S DINER | 44 | FAT CATS |
| 16 | LE PETIT TRIANGLE CAFÉ | 45 | PARALLAX |
| 17 | JOHNNY MANGO | 46 | SOUTH SIDE |
| 18 | MOMOCHO MOD MEX | 48 | A COOKIE AND A CUPCAKE |
| 25 | OLD ANGLE | 50 | LOLITA |
| 29 | BAR CENTO | 58 | DISH DELI |
| 30 | GREAT LAKES BREWING CO. | 59 | CIVILIZATION |
| 33 | NATE'S DELI | 62 | TREMONT SCOOPS |
| 35 | WEST SIDE MARKET CAFÉ | 65 | FAHRENHEIT |
| 37 | FLYING FIG | 67 | TY FUN THAI BISTRO |
| 39 | SOUPER MARKET | 68 | LUCKY'S CAFÉ |

## NIGHTLIFE

| | | | |
|---|---|---|---|
| 3 | UNION STATION/BOUNCE | 44 | VELVET TANGO ROOM |
| 27 | GARAGE BAR | 49 | 806 WINE & MARTINI BAR |
| 31 | MCNULTY'S BIER MARKT | 53 | TREMONT TAP HOUSE |
| 36 | MARKET AVENUE WINE BAR | 55 | LAVA LOUNGE |
| 41 | MAJOR HOOPPLES | 56 | PROSPERITY SOCIAL CLUB |
| | | 66 | FLYING MONKEY PUB |

## ARTS AND LEISURE

| | | | |
|---|---|---|---|
| 1 | WENDT PARK AT WHISKEY ISLAND | 13 | NEAR WEST THEATRE |
| 5 | VETERANS MEMORIAL BRIDGE TOUR | 52 | CONVERGENCE-CONTINUUM |
| 6 | OHIO CITY BICYCLE CO-OP | 61 | PAUL DUDA GALLERY |
| 9 | FAIRVIEW PARK/ KENTUCKY GARDENS | 63 | ASTERISK GALLERY |

## SHOPPING

| | | | |
|---|---|---|---|
| 10 | ANTIQUES IN THE BANK | 47 | EYE CANDY GALLERY |
| 15 | UNIQUE THRIFT | 51 | BANYAN TREE |
| 26 | GLASS BUBBLE PROJECT | 54 | POWTER PUFF BOUTIQUE |
| 28 | ELEGANSIA | 60 | VISIBLE VOICE BOOKS |
| 32 | SOMETHING DIFFERENT | 64 | PINKY'S DAILY PLANNER |
| 38 | HANSA IMPORT HAUS | 69 | LILLY HANDMADE CHOCOLATE |
| 40 | OPEN AIR IN MARKET SQUARE | | |

## HOTELS

| | | | |
|---|---|---|---|
| 8 | STONE GABLES BED AND BREAKFAST | 22 | CLIFFORD HOUSE BED AND BREAKFAST |
| 21 | GLENDENNIS BED & BREAKFAST | 23 | J. PALEN HOUSE |

TREMONT

Lincoln Park
57

St. Theodosius Russian Orthodox Cathedral

Tremont Valley Field

72 A Christmas Story House

DISTANCE ACROSS MAP
Approximate: 2.6 mi or 4.2 km

0    300 yds
0    300 m

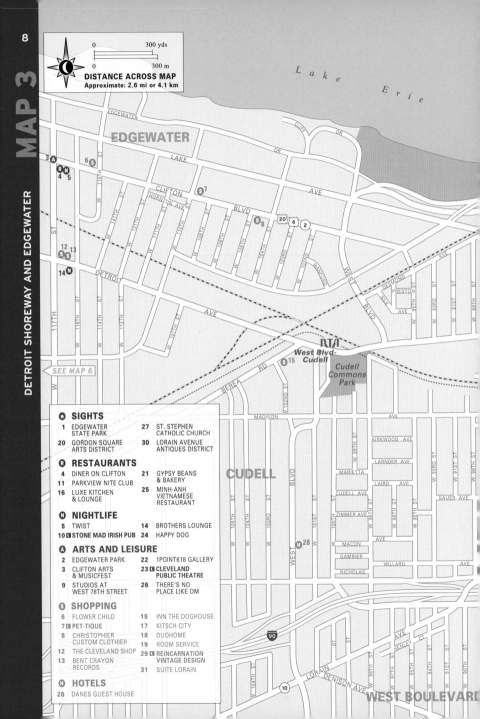

**DISTANCE ACROSS MAP**
Approximate: 2.6 mi or 4.1 km

0    300 yds
0    300 m

*L a k e   E r i e*

EDGEWATER

CUDELL

WEST BOULEVARD

SEE MAP 6

West Blvd-Cudell

Cudell Commons Park

## ● SIGHTS

| | | | |
|---|---|---|---|
| 1 | EDGEWATER STATE PARK | 27 | ST. STEPHEN CATHOLIC CHURCH |
| 20 | GORDON SQUARE ARTS DISTRICT | 30 | LORAIN AVENUE ANTIQUES DISTRICT |

## ● RESTAURANTS

| | | | |
|---|---|---|---|
| 4 | DINER ON CLIFTON | 21 | GYPSY BEANS & BAKERY |
| 11 | PARKVIEW NITE CLUB | 25 | MINH-ANH VIETNAMESE RESTAURANT |
| 16 | LUXE KITCHEN & LOUNGE | | |

## ● NIGHTLIFE

| | | | |
|---|---|---|---|
| 5 | TWIST | 14 | BROTHERS LOUNGE |
| 10 | STONE MAD IRISH PUB | 24 | HAPPY DOG |

## ● ARTS AND LEISURE

| | | | |
|---|---|---|---|
| 2 | EDGEWATER PARK | 22 | 1POINT618 GALLERY |
| 3 | CLIFTON ARTS & MUSICFEST | 23 | CLEVELAND PUBLIC THEATRE |
| 9 | STUDIOS AT WEST 78TH STREET | 26 | THERE'S NO PLACE LIKE OM |

## ● SHOPPING

| | | | |
|---|---|---|---|
| 6 | FLOWER CHILD | 15 | INN THE DOGHOUSE |
| 7 | PET-TIQUE | 17 | KITSCH CITY |
| 8 | CHRISTOPHIER CUSTOM CLOTHIER | 18 | DUOHOME |
| 12 | THE CLEVELAND SHOP | 19 | ROOM SERVICE |
| 13 | BENT CRAYON RECORDS | 29 | REINCARNATION VINTAGE DESIGN |
| | | 31 | SUITE LORAIN |

## ● HOTELS

| | |
|---|---|
| 28 | DANES GUEST HOUSE |

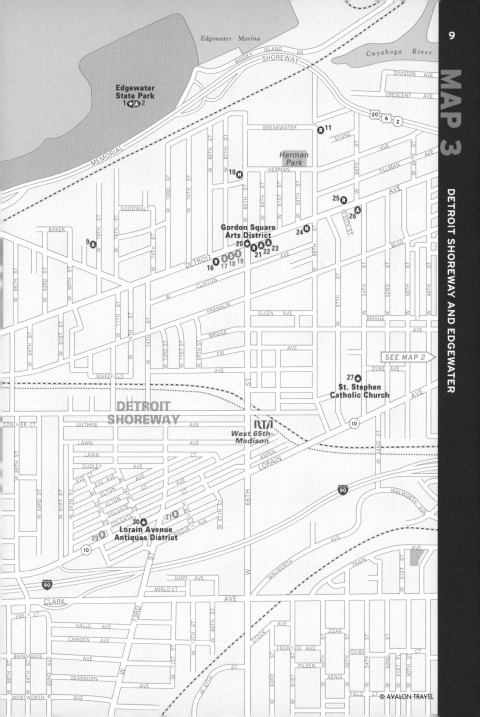

Edgewater Marina

Cuyahoga River

WHISKY ISLAND DR
SHOREWAY

DIVISION AVE
CRESCENT AVE

Edgewater
State Park
1 ★ Ⓐ 2

20 6 2

BREAKWATER

Ⓡ 11

STONE

AVE

Herman
Park

HERMAN

10 Ⓝ

MEMORIAL

GOODWALT

25 Ⓡ

Ⓐ 26

BAKER

9 Ⓐ

Gordon Square
Arts District

20 ★
Ⓡ Ⓐ

24 Ⓝ

21 22 23

DETROIT

16 Ⓡ
17 18 19

AVE

CLINTON

FRANKLIN

ELLEN AVE

BRIDGE

BRIDGE

AVE

FIR

AVE

WAKEFIELD

SEE MAP 2

DETROIT
SHOREWAY

27
St. Stephen
Catholic Church

CONVER CT

GUTHRIE

AVE

RTA
West 65th-
Madison

10

LAWN

AVE

LAWN

CT

DUDLEY

AVE

ASPEN

LORAIN

EVE AVE

EVE

AVE

90

WALWORTH

ELTON

CT

AVE

ELTON

COLGATE

30 ★

31 ★

Lorain Avenue
Antiques District

29 ★

10

AVE

90

WALWORTH

TRAIN

HOPE AVE

MIRLO CT

CLARK

AVE

EMILY CT

HALLE AVE

ZOAR

CAMDEN AVE

FRONTIER AVE

KOUBA

BRINSMADE

PILSEN

AVE

XENIA

DEARBORN

AVE

WENTWORTH
AVE

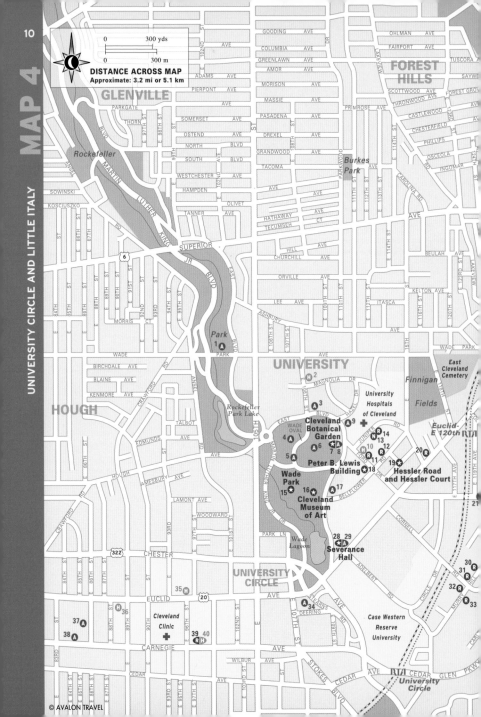

© AVALON TRAVEL

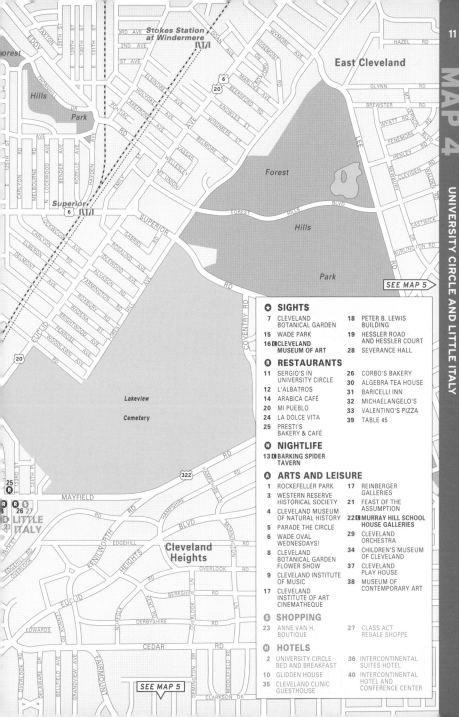

East Cleveland

Stokes Station at Windermere

Forest
Hills
Park

Superior

Lakeview
Cemetery

LITTLE
ITALY

MAYFIELD

Cleveland
Heights

SEE MAP 5

SEE MAP 5

### ✪ SIGHTS

| | | | |
|---|---|---|---|
| 7 | CLEVELAND BOTANICAL GARDEN | 18 | PETER B. LEWIS BUILDING |
| 15 | WADE PARK | 19 | HESSLER ROAD AND HESSLER COURT |
| 16 | CLEVELAND MUSEUM OF ART | 28 | SEVERANCE HALL |

### ® RESTAURANTS

| | | | |
|---|---|---|---|
| 11 | SERGIO'S IN UNIVERSITY CIRCLE | 26 | CORBO'S BAKERY |
| 12 | L'ALBATROS | 30 | ALGEBRA TEA HOUSE |
| 14 | ARABICA CAFÉ | 31 | BARICELLI INN |
| 20 | MI PUEBLO | 32 | MICHAELANGELO'S |
| 24 | LA DOLCE VITA | 33 | VALENTINO'S PIZZA |
| 25 | PRESTI'S BAKERY & CAFÉ | 39 | TABLE 45 |

### Ⓝ NIGHTLIFE

13 BARKING SPIDER TAVERN

### Ⓐ ARTS AND LEISURE

| | | | |
|---|---|---|---|
| 1 | ROCKEFELLER PARK | 17 | REINBERGER GALLERIES |
| 3 | WESTERN RESERVE HISTORICAL SOCIETY | 21 | FEAST OF THE ASSUMPTION |
| 4 | CLEVELAND MUSEUM OF NATURAL HISTORY | 22 | MURRAY HILL SCHOOL HOUSE GALLERIES |
| 5 | PARADE THE CIRCLE | 29 | CLEVELAND ORCHESTRA |
| 6 | WADE OVAL WEDNESDAYS! | 34 | CHILDREN'S MUSEUM OF CLEVELAND |
| 8 | CLEVELAND BOTANICAL GARDEN FLOWER SHOW | 37 | CLEVELAND PLAY HOUSE |
| 9 | CLEVELAND INSTITUTE OF MUSIC | 38 | MUSEUM OF CONTEMPORARY ART |
| 17 | CLEVELAND INSTITUTE OF ART CINEMATHEQUE | | |

### Ⓢ SHOPPING

| | | | |
|---|---|---|---|
| 23 | ANNE VAN H. BOUTIQUE | 27 | CLASS ACT RESALE SHOPPE |

### Ⓗ HOTELS

| | | | |
|---|---|---|---|
| 2 | UNIVERSITY CIRCLE BED AND BREAKFAST | 36 | INTERCONTINENTAL SUITES HOTEL |
| 10 | GLIDDEN HOUSE | 40 | INTERCONTINENTAL HOTEL AND CONFERENCE CENTER |
| 35 | CLEVELAND CLINIC GUESTHOUSE | | |

SEE MAP 4

East
Cleveland
Cemetery

Finnigan
Fields

University
Hospitals
of Cleveland

Euclid
E 120th RTA

Lake View
Cemetery
1

DISTANCE ACROSS MAP
Approximate: 3.2 mi or 5.2 km

0        300 yds
0        300 m

EAST
WADE
OVAL
BLVD

Wade

WADE OVAL

Park

Wade
Lagoon

105TH

322 CHESTER

UNIVERSITY
CIRCLE

20

DEERING

PARK LN

MAYFIELD          RD          322

LITTLE
ITALY

HEIGHTS

EUCLID

DERBYSHIRE

SEE MAP 4

Case Western
Reserve
University

EDWARDS

17 N    R 18

N 19

R

Fairmount
Boulevard
District

20

CEDAR

NOTTINGHILL

CEDAR GLEN PKWY

Shaker

FAIRHILL

BUCKEYE-
SHAKER

Lakes

W. ST. JAMES PKWY

BLVD

## ○ SIGHTS

| | |
|---|---|
| 1 ☾ LAKE VIEW CEMETERY | 39 SHAKER SQUARE |
| 15 CAIN PARK | 43 NATURE CENTER |
| 20 ☾ FAIRMOUNT | AT SHAKER LAKES |
| BOULEVARD DISTRICT | |

## ○ RESTAURANTS

| | |
|---|---|
| 2 PACIFIC EAST | 27 STONE OVEN |
| 10 ☾ TOMMY'S | 30 ☾ ON THE RISE |
| 13 INN ON COVENTRY | 31 FELICE URBAN CAFÉ |
| 18 LA GELATERIA | 32 BIG AL'S DINER |
| 24 DEWEY'S PIZZA | 38 SASA MATSU |
| 26 ANATOLIA CAFÉ | 42 ☾ FIRE FOOD & DRINK |

## ○ NIGHTLIFE

| | |
|---|---|
| 12 WINKING LIZARD | 14 GROG SHOP |
| TAVERN | 17 NIGHTTOWN |
| 14 ☾ LA CAVE DU VIN | 22 PARNELL'S PUB |

## ○ ARTS AND LEISURE

| | |
|---|---|
| 16 EVANS AMPHITHEATER | 37 SHAKER SQUARE |
| 21 CEDAR LEE THEATRE | CINEMAS |
| 23 HEIGHTS ARTS | 40 ☾ NORTH UNION |
| GALLERY | FARMERS MARKET |
| 28 THE ATMA CENTER | 44 HORSESHOE |
| | LAKE PARK |

## ○ SHOPPING

| | |
|---|---|
| 3 CLOTHING BRIGADE | 29 SUNBEAM, A SHOP |
| 4 UTRECHT | FOR CHILDREN |
| ART SUPPLIES | 33 FINE POINTS |
| 5 PASSPORT TO PERU | 34 HEIDE RIVCHUN |
| 6 COVENTRY CATS | CONSERVATION |
| 7 CITY BUDDHA | STUDIOS |
| 8 BIG FUN | 35 GENTLEMAN'S |
| 9 MAC'S BACKS BOOKS | QUARTERS/ |
| 11 RECORD REVOLUTION | FROG'S LEGS |
| 25 QUINTANA'S | 36 LOGANBERRY BOOKS |
| BARBER SHOP | 41 PLAYMATTERS TOYS |

## ○ HOTELS

| | |
|---|---|
| 19 THE ALCAZAR | |

LARCHMERE

BROWNING        AVE

HAMLEN        AVE

ROMWELL        AVE

BUCKINGHAM        AVE

WILLIAMS

87

SHAKER

32
R S 35
31 R S 33    S 34    36

OVERLOOK
AVE

Shaker
Square RTA

Shaker
Square

Shaker Square
Shopping Center    R 38    37 39 A 40
42
41 S    RTA

Cumberland
Park

COVENTRY
VILLAGE

Cain Park

Cleveland
Heights

Shaker
Heights

Lower
Shaker
Lake
Park

Nature Center
at Shaker Lakes

Horseshoe

Coventry

Southern
Park

Southington

Horseshoe
Lake

Park

Lake

44 © AVALON TRAVEL

## ❶ SIGHTS
1 OLDEST STONE HOUSE
2 LAKEWOOD PARK
9 THE BECK CENTER FOR THE ARTS

## ❶ RESTAURANTS
3 PIER W
5 TARTINE BISTRO AND WINE BAR
7 WEST END TAVERN
8 THREE BIRDS
12 MELT BAR AND GRILLED
18 BUCKEYE BEER ENGINE
19 MALLEY'S CHOCOLATES
20 PLAYERS ON MADISON
22 EL TANGO TAQUERIA

## ❶ NIGHTLIFE
6 AROUND THE CORNER SALOON
14 FIVE O'CLOCK LOUNGE
26 WINCHESTER TAVERN & CONCERT CLUB

## ❶ ARTS AND LEISURE
10 BECK CENTER FOR THE ARTS
15 41' NORTH KAYAK ADVENTURES
16 LAKEWOOD OFF-LEASH DOG PARK
17 POP SHOP GALLERY
23 LAKEWOOD CIVIC AUDITORIUM
25 MAHALL'S TWENTY LANES
27 SERPENTINI ARENA
30 HALLORAN ICE SKATING RINK

## ❶ SHOPPING
11 REAGLE BEAGLE
13 GEIGER'S CLOTHING & SPORTS
21 PLAY IT AGAIN, SAM
24 MY MIND'S EYE RECORDS
29 CAROL & JOHN'S COMIC BOOK SHOP

## ❶ HOTELS
4 DAYS INN
28 EMERALD NECKLACE INN

**Lakewood Park**
2

**Oldest Stone House**
1

EDGEWATER

HOMEWOOD DR

3

DISTANCE ACROSS MAP
Approximate: 4.3 mi or 7 km

0     500 yds
0     500 m

AVE

CLIFTON

LAKE

HARBOR VIEW DR

EDGEWATER DR

20  6  2     4

BLVD

JACKSON

CHASE AVE

CHARLOW AVE

Merl Park

MERL

AVE

uffman rk

COOK

Lakewood

12  13

NICHOLSON

THOREAU

COVE

FRY

116TH

114TH

112TH

AVE

14

FRENCH

CHARLES

AVE

AVE

ROD

ROSALIE

VICTORIA AVE

FRANKLIN

BELLE

MARLOWE

OLIVEWOOD

BLOSSOM PARK

CEDARWOOD

MADISON

AVE

AVE

AVE

WATERBURY

CLARENCE

GRACE

COHASSETT

ALAMEDA

LAKEWOOD

RIDGEWOOD

WINCHESTER

HOPKINS

COUTANT

23

19

20

22

25

26

West 117th-Madison

21

24

LEONARD

ARMIN

ATHENS

MARLOWE

RD

AVE

Madison Park

THRUSH

HALSTEAD

DOWD

ROBIN

PARK

MAGEE

CUDELL

SEE MAP 3

BAYES

AVE

BROWN

RICHLAND

BUNTS

WASCANA

WYANDOTTE

ELBUR

LEWIS

CHESTERLAND

CLARENCE

PLOVER

BEREA

117TH

WESTERN

GARFIELD

LINCOLN

AVE

AVE

LAKEWOOD HEIGHTS BLVD

SECTOR AVE

BELMONT AVE

Belmont Park

27

ROXBORO

Tuland Park

HAZELMERE AVE

ELMWOOD

90

121ST

120TH

112TH

ALGER

WARREN

BIRCHWOOD

BIDWELL

ARLIS

44TH

42ND

W 33RD

RTA
Triskett

TRISKETT

RD

GERALDINE

10

MONTROSE

ADRIAN

Mohican Park

BEREA

ORCHARD PARK AVE

HARLEY AVE

GRAPELAND AVE

GRAMATAN AVE

JEFFERSON

LORAIN

HOBART

BELDEN

120TH

HEADLEY

ELORIAN AVE

GOVENOR AVE

ST. MARK AVE

FORTUNE AVE

TRISKETT

TUCKAHOE

West Park
RTA

AVE

DALE AVE

W 148TH ST

W 143RD ST

W 140TH ST

W 137TH ST

W 135TH ST

W 134TH ST

130TH

126TH

127TH

123RD

LINNET

Jefferson Park

Halloran Park
30

WEST BOULEVARD

BERWYN

COOLEY

MILAN AVE

SAN DIEGO AVE

BRIGHTON AVE

WESLEY AVE

MARNE AVE

© AVALON TRAVEL

0          2 mi

0     2 km

**DISTANCE ACROSS MAP**
Approximate: 33 mi or 53 km

L  a  k  e      E  r  i  e

Bay Village

Ⓐ23

Lakewood

DETROIT RD

Ⓢ24

Rocky
River

Westlake

Avon

Fairview
Park

LORAIN RD

25 Ⓐ

Cleveland Metroparks
Zoo and Rainforest
29 Ⓐ

28 Ⓢ

Ⓢ24

Rocky
River
Res

27 Ⓐ
Memphis
Kiddie Park

Brooklyn

Ⓝ
30

Rocky
River

Ⓡ 26

NASA Glenn
Research Center

North
Olmsted

Ⓐ38
Brook
Park

BROOK PARK RD

17

39 Ⓢ

Ⓐ36
Cleveland-
Hopkins
Int'l Airport

37 Ⓐ

Parma

Ⓐ35

CUYAHOGA
COUNTY

Berea

42

Parma
Heights

3

STATE RD

237

Middleburg
Heights
Cuyahoga County
Fairgounds
Ⓐ45

Olmsted
Falls

176

LORAIN
COUNTY

North
Royalton

RIDGE RD

Broadview
Heights

BROADVIEW RD

Strongsville

82

Ⓐ46
Mill Stream
Run Reservation

CUYAHOGA
COUNTY

## ✪ SIGHTS

| | | | |
|---|---|---|---|
| **6** | HOLDEN ARBORETUM | **36** | NASA GLENN RESEARCH CENTER |
| **15** | MALTZ MUSEUM OF JEWISH HERITAGE | **48** | CUYAHOGA VALLEY NATIONAL PARK |
| **27** | MEMPHIS KIDDIE PARK | | |
| **29** | CLEVELAND METROPARKS ZOO AND RAINFOREST | | |

## Ⓡ RESTAURANTS

| | | | |
|---|---|---|---|
| **3** | GROVEWOOD TAVERN AND WINE BAR | **16** | CORKY & LENNY'S |
| | | **19** | MOXIE |

## Ⓝ NIGHTLIFE

| | | | |
|---|---|---|---|
| **1** | BEACHLAND BALLROOM | **30** | FIVE CENT DECISION |

MEDINA
COUNTY

3

To Medina

Brunswick

303

Wickliffe

LAKE COUNTY

To 6
Holden Arboretum

Richmond Heights

Mayfield

East Cleveland

Mayfield Heights

Lyndhurst

MAYFIELD RD

SUPERIOR AVE

CHESTER AVE

Cleveland Heights

CEDAR RD

Pepper Pike

Maltz Museum of Jewish Heritage

Shaker Heights

Beachwood

CHAGRIN BLVD

SHAKER BLVD

CLEVELAND

GEAUGA COUNTY

CUYAHOGA COUNTY

Moreland Hills

Garfield Heights

MILES RD

LIBBY RD

Maple Heights

Bedford Heights

Cuyahoga River

Bedford

Seven Hills

Valley View

Brecksville

Cuyahoga

SUMMIT COUNTY

Valley

Macedonia

National

Park

Richfield

To Akron

To 51 Blossom Music Center,
52 Century Cycles, and
53 Kendall Lake Winter
Sports Center

Hudson

## ⒶARTS AND LEISURE

4 POLKA HALL OF FAME MUSEUM
5 CLEVELAND ROCK GYM
7 ALPINE VALLEY SKI RESORT
9 KARAMU HOUSE
24 CLEVELAND KAYAK TOURS
25 ⒸRAY'S MTB INDOOR PARK
31 OHIO & ERIE CANAL RESERVATION MOUNTAIN BIKE TRAIL
32 THISTLEDOWN
35 BURNING RIVER ROLLER GIRLS
37 HOME AND GARDEN SHOW
38 CHENGA WORLD

41 CUYAHOGA VALLEY SCENIC RAILROAD
42 ⒸOHIO & ERIE CANAL TOWPATH TRAIL
43 SHAWNEE HILLS GOLF COURSE
44 NORTHFIELD PARK
45 OKTOBERFEST
46 MILL STREAM RUN RESERVATION
47 SLEEPY HOLLOW GOLF COURSE
50 BOSTON MILLS/BRANDYWINE
51 BLOSSOM MUSIC CENTER
52 CENTURY CYCLES
53 KENDALL LAKE WINTER SPORTS CENTER

## ⒼSHOPPING

2 ⒸMUSIC SAVES
8 $2 RARE BOOKS
10 ⒸRUSSIAN-TURKISH BATHS
11 HEATHER'S HEAT AND FLAVOR
12 LEGACY VILLAGE
13 BACI
14 BEACHWOOD PLACE
17 ⒸETON CHAGRIN BOULEVARD

17 ⒸNICKY NICOLE
17 KILGORE TROUT
18 KNUTH SHOES
20 FULL CIRCLE STUDIO
25 CROCKER PARK
28 THE SAUSAGE SHOPPE
33 BARKLEY PET HOTEL AND DAY SPA
39 B.A. SWEETIE CANDY COMPANY

## ⒽHOTELS

21 HAMPTON INN BEACHWOOD
22 HILLBROOK INN
26 CLEVELAND AIRPORT MARRIOTT

34 INN OF CHAGRIN FALLS
40 EMBASSY SUITES CLEVELAND ROCKSIDE
49 ⒸINN AT BRANDYWINE FALLS

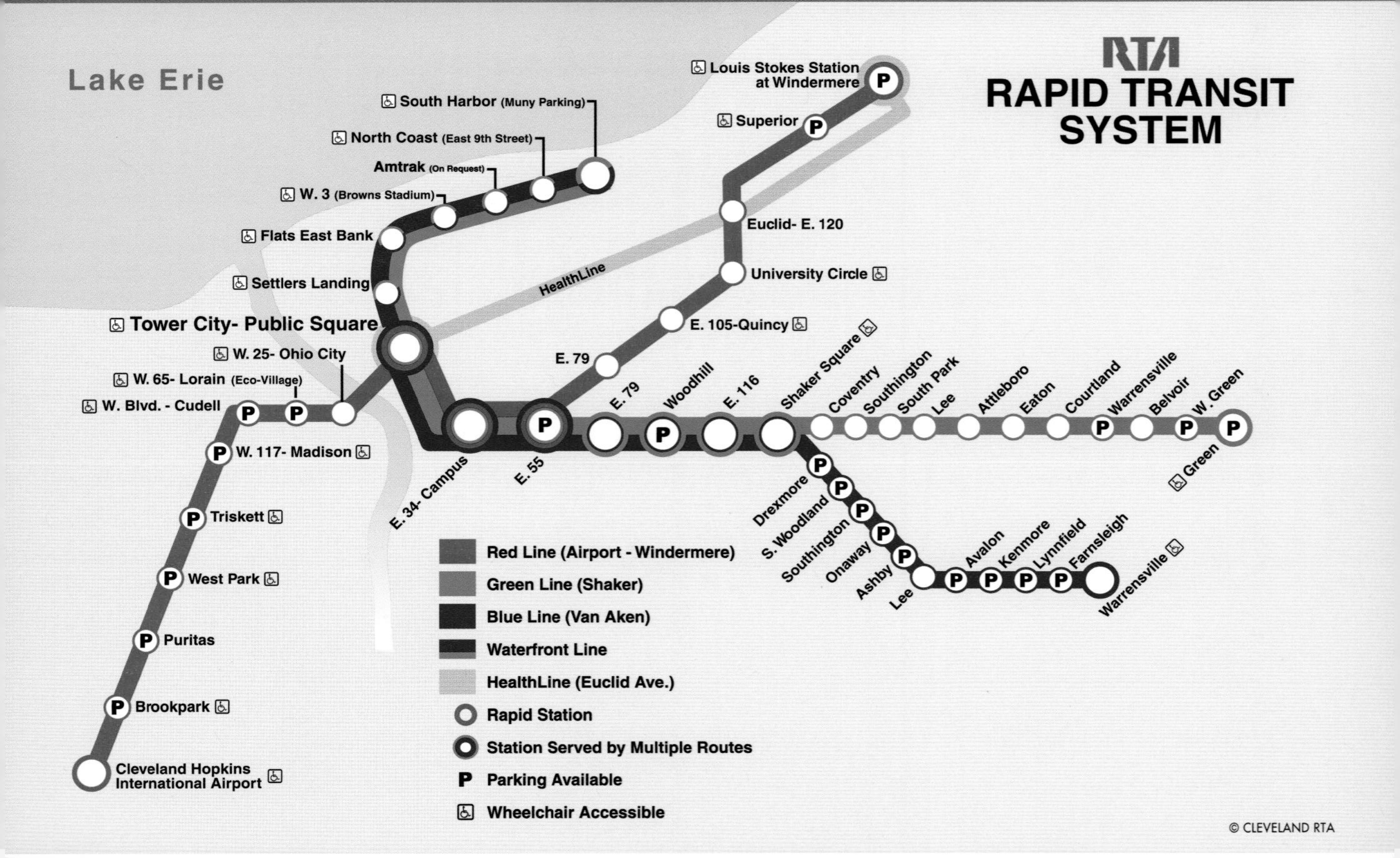

MAP 8

# RTA
# RAPID TRANSIT SYSTEM

© CLEVELAND RTA

Lake Erie

## Legend

- Red Line (Airport - Windermere)
- Green Line (Shaker)
- Blue Line (Van Aken)
- Waterfront Line
- HealthLine (Euclid Ave.)
- ◯ Rapid Station
- ◎ Station Served by Multiple Routes
- Ⓟ Parking Available
- ♿ Wheelchair Accessible

## Stations

- Louis Stokes Station at Windermere Ⓟ
- Superior Ⓟ
- Euclid- E. 120
- University Circle
- E. 105-Quincy
- Woodhill
- E. 79
- E. 116
- Shaker Square
- Coventry
- Southington
- South Park
- Lee
- Attleboro
- Eaton
- Courtland
- Warrensville
- Belvoir
- W. Green
- Green
- Drexmore
- S. Woodland
- Southington
- Onaway
- Ashby
- Lee
- Avalon
- Kenmore
- Lynnfield
- Farnsleigh
- Warrensville
- E. 55
- E. 34-Campus
- HealthLine
- South Harbor (Muny Parking)
- North Coast (East 9th Street)
- Amtrak (On Request)
- W. 3 (Browns Stadium)
- Flats East Bank
- Settlers Landing
- Tower City- Public Square
- W. 25- Ohio City
- W. 65- Lorain (Eco-Village)
- W. Blvd.- Cudell
- W. 117- Madison
- Triskett
- West Park
- Puritas
- Brookpark
- Cleveland Hopkins International Airport

# Discover Cleveland

After decades of serving as the nation's favorite punch line – "Mistake on the Lake" ring a bell? – Cleveland has blossomed into a vibrant world-class city with a heart of gold. Approachable, affordable, and overflowing with good Midwestern folk, this unpretentious town consistently exceeds visitors' expectations. That's why these days, as Alec Baldwin's character on *30 Rock* put it, "We'd all like to flee to the Cleve."

Is it any wonder Cleveland's two million residents are a contented lot? They have short commutes from reasonably priced homes in charming, tree-lined neighborhoods – neighborhoods that beg to be explored. In these ethnically diverse nooks, burgeoning art districts share space with century-old churches. Sprinkled throughout are chef-owned bistros, idiosyncratic dive bars, and avant-garde theaters.

Despite its Rust Belt roots, Cleveland is very much a modern city. Numerous universities and grad schools keep the area forever young, and eco-friendly transit zips people to and fro. And though Cleveland is modest in size, it is blessed with first-rate cultural attractions like the Cleveland Orchestra, Cleveland Museum of Art, and PlayhouseSquare, along with a robust dining scene. Less highbrow but no less enjoyable are the Rock and Roll Hall of Fame, three pro sports teams, and more than 50,000 acres of parkland, topped off with a Great Lake. A short drive away, you'll find wineries on the shores of Lake Erie; the world's largest Amish community; and "the Best Amusement Park in the World," Cedar Point.

Last but not least, this city is a fantastic place to get your groove on, with its multitude of live-music venues. Cleveland was, is, and will always be a rock-and-roll town.

# Planning Your Trip

## ▶ WHERE TO GO

### Downtown

From nine to five, downtown serves as the financial, legal, and governmental nucleus of the entire county. After dark, though, the vibrant **Warehouse District** and **East 4th Street** teem with restaurants, nightclubs, and live-music venues like the **House of Blues.** Downtown also is the place to enjoy live theater, cheer on professional sports teams, and explore the ephemera at the **Rock and Roll Hall of Fame and Museum.** Clean, compact, and walkable, downtown rewards urban hikers with an abundance of glorious classical architecture, and the largest stock of hotels can be found here as well.

### Ohio City and Tremont

The 19th-century homes in Ohio City make strolling its leafy lanes feel like a trip back in time, but the neighborhood's not stuck in the past. The celebrated **West Side Market** and fine eateries like Flying Fig and Bar Cento make the area ground zero for adventurous foodies. Nearby Tremont has the highest concentration of **chef-owned bistros,** like Lolita, Fahrenheit, and Parallax, but is better known for its creative energy, on display in the monthly **ArtWalks**; architecture fans enjoy the historic churches in this former university neighborhood, and shoppers come for the upscale boutiques.

Severance Hall is the gorgeous home of the Cleveland Orchestra.

the Glasshouse at the Cleveland Botanical Garden

## Detroit Shoreway and Edgewater

Some of Cleveland's most exciting changes are taking place in these near-west neighborhoods. Eco-conscious residents are moving here to live in green-built homes, and **trendy new boutiques** like Room Service and duoHOME are helping them furnish their nests. Building on the 20-year history of Cleveland Public Theatre, the up-and-coming **Gordon Square Arts District** is home to art galleries, design studios, and exciting bars and restaurants. Antiques hunters prowl the secondhand shops of **Lorain Avenue** in hopes of scoring a treasure.

## University Circle and Little Italy

Often referred to as "One Perfect Mile," University Circle is home to an unmatched concentration of educational, medical, and cultural institutions—the **Cleveland Museum of Art, Cleveland Botanical Garden,** and **Severance Hall,** to name just a few. The Old World is alive and well in neighboring **Little Italy,** a lively borough featuring redbrick lanes, authentic Italian eateries, and eclectic art galleries.

## Cleveland Heights and Shaker Heights

Incorporated in the early 1900s, the neighboring communities of Cleveland Heights and Shaker Heights developed as leafy streetcar suburbs on the fringes of town. Today, these popular inner-ring cities boast all the amenities of a self-sufficient town. The Main Street–like districts of **Shaker Square, Cedar-Lee,** and **Coventry** keep residents and visitors alike entertained with **restaurants, jazz clubs,** and **movie theaters,** and sightseeing drives allow one to explore the **impressive mansions** built by Cleveland's wealthy industrialists.

## Lakewood

The bulk of the commercial activity in this West Side neighborhood is found on the thoroughfares of Detroit, Madison, and Clifton, which are dotted with **funky shops, restaurants,** and **bars.** But one of the biggest draws here is the **Rocky River Reservation,** part of the Cleveland Metroparks system. Boasting a dog park, a web of trails, and a scenic strip of rushing river, this picturesque retreat attracts joggers, bicyclists, anglers,

the Beachland Ballroom

and picnickers. Lakewood is also home to the **Beck Center for the Arts,** a long-standing community arts beacon.

## Greater Cleveland

The Greater Cleveland area stretches for miles in every direction save for north, where it is stymied by Lake Erie. Much of that real estate is consumed by bedroom-community suburbs, but that doesn't mean you should just hole up downtown. The majestic **Cuyahoga Valley National Park** is located just south of town, while the equally verdant **Holden Arboretum** can be found out east. In the wintertime, mountain bike enthusiasts travel from throughout the Midwest to hit **Ray's MTB Indoor Park.** Meanwhile, shoppers flock to upscale boutiques in Beachwood, Rocky River, and Chagrin Falls, and live music fans venture to the **Beachland Ballroom** and **Blossom Music Center.**

# ▶ WHEN TO GO

Fall is the best time to visit Cleveland, to savor the vibrant fall foliage and crisp, dry air by hitting hike-and-bike trails, apple orchards, and football games. Autumn also signals the start of the abundant performing-arts calendar, filled with dance, theater, and musical productions.

If you really can't stand cold weather, it's best to avoid Cleveland from December through March—but you will be missing out on quite a bit. The winter holidays here can be Dickensian, with downy-white snow blanketing the region as residents make the rounds at museums, theaters, and restaurants.

Spring can be frustratingly wet, even snowy, but it also can offer glimpses of the warm days to come. Folks here take advantage of these rare days atop bikes, in gardens, and on restaurant patios.

Summer is filled with Indians baseball games, rounds of golf, neighborhood festivals, visits to farmers markets, and fishing trips on Lake Erie. Nearly every restaurant takes advantage of the season by offering alfresco seating.

# ▶ BEFORE YOU GO

Most visitors to Cleveland come through Hopkins International Airport, hich is a 25-minute drive from downtown. Sane and frugal travelers opt for the direct path of RTA's light rail (Red Line) when heading to the city center.

Those who don't fly here invariably arrive by car. Whether you'll need a car once in town depends greatly on activities planned and excursions intended. A vast majority of Cleveland's major attractions are located downtown and in University Circle, both of which are easy to navigate without wheels.

## What to Take

Common sense and a good umbrella go a long way in Cleveland: This city fully experiences all four seasons (sometimes in the course of a single day). If attending a Browns game, for instance, it might be wise to dress as if one were leading an Antarctic expedition—baseball games at Progressive Field, depending on the month, weather, and time of day, can be scorching hot, miserably wet, or, in early spring, even snowy. For much of the summer, the plan of attack is layers, a wide-brimmed hat, sunglasses, and sunscreen.

Appropriate footwear in C-Town can range from flip-flops to mukluks. Lightweight raingear is always nice to have on hand, as is a sweatshirt. In the fall, temps can plummet from a balmy 75 degrees to a chilly 55 degrees just a minute after sundown.

Upscale-casual dress will work at almost any Cleveland restaurant. Most do get dolled up, however, when attending concerts at Severance Hall or theater at PlayhouseSquare.

Golfers should really consider bringing their clubs when visiting between May and October. Northeast Ohio has some spectacular golf courses, with over 120 public courses reachable in under an hour's drive.

# Explore Cleveland

## ▶ BEST OF CLEVELAND WEEKEND

### Friday

▶ Kick the weekend off Friday evening with a culinary bang by snagging a table downtown at **Lola,** home to Cleveland-based food celeb Michael Symon. This **sophisticated bistro** showcases Symon's trademark style of transforming familiar dishes into contemporary showstoppers.

▶ After dinner, stroll down East 4th Street and take your pick from a host of entertainment options. **The Corner Alley** is a modern-day **bowling** venue that combines lane-side cocktail service and pencil-free scoring.

▶ Ditch the rental shoes and walk the short distance to **Pickwick & Frolic,** where a lower-level martini bar and **cabaret lounge** conjure images of Vegas.

### Saturday

▶ Visit the **West Side Market** on a Saturday morning and you'll swear every last Clevelander is present and accounted for. This bustling public market is a treat not just for cooks, but also for people-watchers and architecture buffs. Start your day with a sausage sandwich from **Frank's Bratwurst.** To keep the line moving, it helps to know the drill: hard or soft roll; kraut or plain; spicy-brown or yellow mustard. Those who prefer to restrict their pork consumption to afternoons should grab a Belgian waffle from **Crepes De Luxe** and a cup of joe from **City Roast.**

▶ If it's between Memorial Day and Labor

The Corner Alley

Day, set aside some time to prowl the knick-knacks at **Open Air in Market Square,** an outdoor flea market and block party that takes place across the street from the West Side Market.

▶ Stroll north on **West 25th Street** and check out the various shops that dot the eclectic urban strip. Hit **Elegansia** for glam vintage threads, **Glass Bubble Project** for original blown-glass art objects, and **Something Different** for, well, something different.

▶ When hunger sets in, try **Great Lakes**

# RAIN OR SHINE FAMILY FUN

## TOP CHOICES FOR SUN-SOAKED CLEVELAND FAMILY FUN

- Take in an **Indians** baseball game at **Progressive Field.** To snag player **autographs,** arrive up to 45 minutes before first pitch and head to sections 125-134 or 169-175.

- Hop aboard the *Goodtime III* for a **narrated cruise** on Lake Erie and the Cuyahoga River. Bring a camera to capture the amazing skyline.

- What child doesn't love monkeys? Go bananas at the **Cleveland Metroparks Zoo,** with its gorillas, chimps, lemurs, and baboons.

## RAINY DAY IN CLEVELAND? NO PROBLEM

- Space freaks will love the interactive exhibits at **NASA Glenn Research Center.** Extended tours are offered the first Saturday of the month (Apr.-Oct.).

- **The Museum of Natural History** is loaded with cool stuff: a Foucault pendulum, Tyrannosaurus and stegosaurus skeletons, and a **planetarium,** to name a few.

- Take the **Cuyahoga Valley Scenic Railroad** through the scenic forests, wetlands, and prairies of the lush Cuyahoga Valley National Park.

the Cuyahoga Valley Scenic Railroad

# FOODIE HEAVEN:
# BEST OF THE WEST SIDE MARKET

The West Side Market is a big, bustling bazaar, with more than 100 food stands. Here's a taste of what's inside.

- Diet-shattering baked goods are around every turn. For artisan-style European bread, hit **Mediterra Bakehouse.** If your tooth leans more sweet than savory, wander over to **Cake Royale,** where the luscious pastries are made from scratch.

- **Ohio City Pasta** supplies dozens of upscale restaurants with fresh pasta, ravioli, and gnocchi. At the ever-popular **Pierogi Palace,** dozens of varieties of stuffed Polish dumplings are sold frozen to go.

- Adventurous home cooks shop at **Urban Herbs** and **Narrin's Spice** to track down hard-to-find herbs, spices, grains, and chiles. Narrin's also stocks a wide assortment of hot sauces.

- Tucked into the corner of the market, **Mediterranean Imported Foods** is a jam-packed Italian grocery offering high-quality cheeses, olives, salamis, dried fruit, and nuts. To purchase Old World Hungarian-style meats, like double-smoked bacon, rice sausage, and cottage ham, stroll over to **Dohar Meats.**

- For a quick and tasty meal, try **Maha's Falafel** for fresh-fried falafel or **Kim Se** for prepared Thai and Cambodian dishes. Visit **Orale** for the city's best chips and salsa, empanadas, and corn husk–wrapped tamales.

- Fans of retro candy flock to **Candy Corner** for old-timey sweets like Dots, Flying Saucers, and Sugar Daddys. Over at **Campbell's Popcorn,** the sugary offerings include cotton candy, chocolate-covered pretzels, and amazing cheesy popcorn.

West Side Market

Asterisk Gallery

Brewing Co. for pub grub or **Bar Cento** for Neapolitan-style pizza.

▶ To see what Cleveland looked like 150 years ago, stroll down **Jay Avenue** to admire blocks of restored 19th-century homes.

▶ In the afternoon, make your way over to Nautica Entertainment Complex on the west bank of the Flats to hop aboard **Lolly the Trolley.** These fun and informative **sightseeing tours** wind through downtown, PlayhouseSquare, and University Circle.

▶ When the ride is over, travel to the North Coast Harbor for a visit to the **Rock and Roll Hall of Fame and Museum.** Though the iconic museum looks small from the outside, it can devour entire afternoons in a single visit.

▶ If kids are in tow, swap the Rock Hall for a visit to the adjacent **Great Lakes Science Center.**

▶ Spend Saturday evening in fun-spirited **Tremont.** Before dinner, pop into a few of the neighborhood's many galleries and boutiques, including **Asterisk Gallery, Paul Duda Gallery,** and **Banyan Tree.**

▶ For upscale pasta and pizza in a lively bistro setting, visit **Fahrenheit.** While not technically an Asian restaurant, **Parallax** has some of the city's finest sushi and seafood. Or go to Michael Symon's affordable **Lolita** for Mediterranean fare.

▶ After dinner, peruse the wonderful collection of art, film, and music books at **Visible Voice Books,** or grab a nightcap

Fire Food & Drink

at the quirky and comfortable **Prosperity Social Club.**

## Sunday

▶ Thousands of Clevelanders start their Sundays with a leisurely **dim sum brunch.** Make your way to AsiaTown, just east of downtown, to enjoy this popular weekend feast. For a great selection try **Li Wah.**

▶ If you prefer an American-style à la carte brunch, head to **Fire Food & Drink** at Shaker Square for refined seasonal cuisine in a casual atmosphere.

▶ For proof there is more to do in Cleveland than eat, head to **University Circle** for a day filled with art, architecture, and history. Though presently in the midst of a seven-year, $350 million construction and renovation project, the **Cleveland Museum of Art** is very much open for business. The original 1916 building has reopened, and new wings will open in the coming months and years.

▶ Science and history geeks would be wise to spend some time exploring the **Cleveland Museum of Natural History,** while the horticulturally minded might prefer the **Cleveland Botanical Garden.**

▶ Stroll over to the nearby campus of Case Western Reserve University to view the **Peter B. Lewis Building,** an avant-garde structure designed by famous architect Frank Gehry.

▶ And, for proof that even a "fly-over" state can serve sparkling sushi, grab dinner at **Sasa Matsu,** a sleek Japanese-style tapas bar at Shaker Square.

# SIGHTS

To rip off Dickens: Cleveland is a tale of two cities. By 1920, the city on a lake, a river, and a grand canal had grown to become the fifth most populous city in America. Cleveland's early successes in steel, rail, and automotive production, not to mention oil, banking, and chemical manufacturing, led to very prosperous times. As the city expanded, so too did its need for new local, county, and federal buildings. Fortuitously, that need happened to coincide with the City Beautiful movement, a progressive philosophy that a well-planned, visually appealing downtown could go a long way toward boosting the spirit of its inhabitants. Those heady times left a lasting legacy of monumental classical architectural, world-class cultural institutions, and idyllic residential suburbs on the fringes of town.

It would take Cleveland another 75 years to match its building boom of the early 20th century. But in the mid-1990s, shaking off the chains of its Rust Belt reputation, the rebounding city pulled off a slew of massive public projects. The legacy of those giddy days continues to reward residents with sporty new baseball, basketball, and football venues, a state-of-the-art science and technology museum, and a glass-and-steel temple to the guitar riff, the Rock and Roll Hall of Fame.

In revitalized old neighborhoods like Ohio City and Tremont, the Gothic steeples of 100-year-old churches cast slender shadows across sleek new townhomes. Brick-paved lanes are dotted with decades-old ethnic restaurants, but also trendy chef-owned bistros. If you keep your eyes open at the West Side Market, you'll

# HIGHLIGHTS

LOOK FOR **(●** TO FIND RECOMMENDED SIGHTS.

**(●** **Most Amazing Old Mall:** When it was built in 1890, The Arcade came with a price tag of $875,000. Today, it would be impossible to replicate. This absolutely breathtaking Victorian-style atrium flaunts a 300-foot-long, 100-foot-high skylight comprised of 1,800 panes of glass. A well-executed $60 million renovation in 1999 repurposed much of the space into the **Hyatt Regency at The Arcade** (page 31).

**(●** **Most Controversial Pop Art:** Love it or loathe it, the *Free Stamp* never fails to incite an opinion. Sure, artist Claes Oldenburg's 30-foot-tall faux rubber stamp is silly bordering on ridiculous. But the fact that we're still discussing it after all these years has to account for something (page 33).

**(●** **Most Iconic Bridge Art:** The art deco statues carved into the 43-foot sandstone pylons of the **Hope Memorial Bridge** are fondly referred to as the "guardians of traffic." Eight separate figures stand sentry at either end of the mile-long bridge, making even the worst commute a little bit easier to stomach (page 33).

**(●** **Best-Sounding History Lesson:** If all school was as entertaining as this "school of rock," there would be no more truancy. The **Rock and Roll Hall of Fame and Museum** boasts a dizzying kaleidoscope of rock memorabilia, both familiar and obscure (page 34).

**(●** **Best Way to Get to Know Cleveland:** Longtime guide and gregarious host Karl C. Johnson makes a living showing curious visitors the ins and outs of C-Town. His enlightening and entertaining two-hour **Walking Tours of Cleaveland** (named for Moses Cleaveland, the city's founder) cover all facets of local history, architecture, politics, and sports (page 37).

**(●** **Most Famous Church:** Tremont is well known for its panoply of architecturally stunning churches, but only one was prominently featured in the Academy Award–winning film *The Deer Hunter*. The 13 onion-shaped domes atop **St. Theodosius Russian Orthodox Cathedral** hover like a battalion of faded copper weather balloons (page 40).

**(●** **Best Old World Grocery Store:** Other cities have grand old public markets; too bad most of them have replaced the actual food stalls with shops selling T-shirts and candles. At Ohio City's beloved **West Side Market,** people actually shop – for pork, halibut, sausage, pierogies, tomatoes, and everything in between. Look up at the barrel-vaulted ceiling and you'll forget everything on your shopping list (page 41).

**(●** **Most Extreme Makeover:** Art fans pretty much had to go cold turkey waiting for the **Cleveland Museum of Art** to reopen following a three-year renovation of its 1912 main building. The lovingly restored space somehow manages to make the impressive art collection look even better (page 44).

**(●** **Best Show of Homes:** In the early 1900s, Cleveland's rich and famous employed the architect hotshots of the day to build stately homes in the **Fairmount Boulevard District** in Cleveland Heights. Park your ride and take a stroll past Georgian mansions, terra cotta-clad Italian villas, and wildly asymmetrical Tudor Revivals (page 46).

**(●** **Finest Final Resting Place:** Yes, people are dying to get into **Lake View Cemetery,** and you should be, too. This 290-acre oasis on the border of Cleveland Heights is equal parts botanical garden, history lesson, and alfresco art gallery. Approximately 400,000 people visit the grounds each year, many to gander at Wade Chapel's Tiffany interior (page 47).

spot Polish pierogies and Hungarian sausage along with wild Alaskan salmon and squid-ink pasta. And if you keep your ears open, you'll pick out a dozen different native tongues along the way.

That happy juxtaposition between new-fangled and old-fashioned, contemporary and classical, punk and polka seems to permeate the whole of Cleveland. With one foot pleasantly planted in the present, the other stubbornly stuck in the past, this city has a knack for surprising visitors of all stripes.

## Downtown — Map 1

### ☾ THE ARCADE

420 Superior Ave., 216/696-1408,
www.thearcade-cleveland.com

**COST:** Free

Easily one of the most glorious Cleveland interiors, this Victorian-style atrium flaunts a 300-foot-long, 100-foot-high skylight comprised of 1,800 panes of glass. Fabricated in 1890, and modeled after a similar structure in Milan, Italy, the building holds the dubious distinction of being this country's first indoor shopping mall. The staggering-for-its-time price tag of $875,000 was covered by John D. Rockefeller and other wealthy Cleveland industrialists. Five years after it was built, the grand space hosted the National Republican Convention. While lost on many of the commuters who routinely navigate its corridors, the Arcade's intricate brass and iron detail can stop a visitor dead in his or her tracks. Especially appealing is the cadre of cast-iron griffons and gargoyles that rings the skylight. A well-executed $60 million renovation of the historic structure in 1999 repurposed much of the upper floors into hotel rooms for the **Hyatt Regency at The Arcade.** Shops, services, and restaurants occupy the lower levels of this five-story gem.

© DOUGLAS TRATTNER

You don't find malls like the Arcade anymore.

# GROUP PLAN OF 1903

In the late 1800s, as city populations continued to rise, so too did the levels of crime, poverty, and disease. Fresh on the heels of the 1893 Chicago World's Fair, the City Beautiful movement began to creep across the land. Advocates behind this civic-minded movement believed that a beautiful city could go a long way toward improving the moral spirit and caliber of its inhabitants. In cities like Chicago, Washington, D.C., and Cleveland, the initiative took the form of architectural "group plans" – cohesive arrangements of like-minded structures positioned around a great public mall.

The movement reached the shores of Lake Erie at an opportune time as federal, county and municipal governments all were planning to erect sizeable new structures. Cleveland's Group Plan of 1903, supported by Ohio governor George Nash and executed by New York and Chicago architects Daniel Burnham, John Carrere, and Arnold Brunner, planned for a monumental grouping of civic buildings around a mall. Built in the Beaux Arts style, which emphasizes symmetry, uniformity, and harmony, the structures all share similar scale and design. Six of the classically designed buildings were completed: the **Old Federal Building, Cleveland Public Library, City Hall, Cuyahoga County Courthouse, Public Auditorium,** and **Board of Education building.** A rail station, proposed for the northern boundary of the plan, was abandoned in favor of the **Terminal Tower.**

Sitting like near-identical twins to the south are the Old Federal Building and Cleveland Public Library. To the north, the Cuyahoga County Courthouse and City Hall are similar in height and mass, but not identical. Classic design, comparable scale, and the use of noble material like granite and marble in the whole of the buildings created a unified sense of dignity and order. But these reserved exteriors belie the grandeur of the interiors within, most featuring soaring vaulted ceilings, polished marble staircases, intricate ironwork, and original commissioned artwork. Linking all the buildings is an expanse of green space known as the Mall, which forms a corridor from Public Square to Lake Erie. Eventually, height limitations and "grand plans" gave way to modern skyscrapers. But the Group Plan, an ambitious schematic hatched over a century ago, still serves as the backbone of this city.

## CLEVELAND PUBLIC LIBRARY, MAIN BRANCH

325 Superior Ave. NE, 216/623-2800, www.cpl.org
**HOURS:** Mon.-Sat. 9 A.M.-6 P.M., plus Sun. 1-5 P.M. Sept.-May only

The main branch of the Cleveland Public Library, one of the nation's most respected urban library systems, is comprised of two buildings linked by a subterranean passageway. Built in 1925 by the noted architecture firm Walker & Weeks, the talent behind Severance Hall, the main library is a neoclassical citadel. This building sits in stark contrast to the Louis Stokes Wing, a striking postmodern tower added in the mid-1990s as part of a $90 million expansion. Look closely, however, and a nexus can be found. With a nod to the original structure, the annex features a facade of the same height and stone. Rising from that six-story marble frame, the 10-story glass tower matches the height of the neighboring Federal Reserve Bank. Inside the glorious old frame, a magnificent globe-shaped chandelier greets visitors, and grand marble stairs lead to upper floors. Vaulted ceilings, some 44 feet high, contain vivid geometric patterns and paintings of historical figures. Leaded glass windows flood the reading rooms with light. Decorative friezes, original paintings and sculpture, and New Deal–commissioned murals are sprinkled throughout.

## CUYAHOGA COUNTY COURTHOUSE

1 Lakeside Ave., 216/443-8800

A county courthouse must possess a certain amount of charm for it to become popular with brides as a wedding site. Photographers love this historic building because the Beaux Arts interior serves as the most dramatic backdrop a shutterbug could hope for: sweeping marble staircases, soaring three-story vaulted ceilings, jaw-dropping stained glass, and art-deco light fixtures. Along with city hall, the building serves as the northern terminus of the 1903 Group Plan, which arranged local and federal buildings around a public mall.

## FEDERAL RESERVE BANK

1455 E. 6th St., 216/579-2000, www.clevelandfed.org
**HOURS:** Mon.-Thurs. 10 A.M.-2 P.M., closed holidays
**COST:** Free

Headquarters of the Fourth Federal Reserve District, the Federal Reserve Bank of Cleveland is an opulent palace of prosperity, security, and wealth. Designed by the noted Cleveland firm of Walker & Weeks, the 12-story granite and marble fortress resembles a Medici-style palazzo. The gilded interior features hand-painted vaulted ceilings, polished marble walls and pillars, and intricately detailed ironwork. Surprisingly, visitors are free to enter the bank's lobby, Learning Center, and **Money Museum.** Tours, offered Tuesday at 2 P.M. and Thursday at 10 A.M., fill up fast, so it is wise to reserve a spot well in advance.

## ◖ FREE STAMP

Williard Park, E. 9th St. and Lakeside Ave.

The *Free Stamp* has placed Cleveland squarely on the pop-art map. Located on an expanse of green just east of city hall, the comically large aluminum-and-steel sculpture of a rubber office stamp was created by artist Claes Oldenburg for Standard Oil (SOHIO). When Standard Oil was purchased by BP, new management wanted nothing to do with the modern sculpture, so it was relegated to storage out of state. Tired of paying storage fees for years, BP ultimately offered the work to the City of Cleveland—for free. A new site was selected, the artist modified the design to better suit the locale, and the *Free Stamp* was officially dedicated in 1991. To this day many abhor its design—but just count the number of folks scrambling for a picture.

## GREAT LAKES SCIENCE CENTER

601 Erieside Ave., 216/694-2000, www.glsc.org
**HOURS:** Daily 10 A.M.-5 P.M., closed Thanksgiving and Christmas
**COST:** $9.50 adult, $7.50 youth, $8.50 senior

Along with the Rock Hall and Cleveland Browns Stadium, the Great Lakes Science Center commands a prominent spot along the lakefront in North Coast Harbor. With the stated goal of making science, technology, and the local environment fun and accessible, this modern steel-and-glass structure boasts some 400 hands-on activities on three floors of exhibits. One of the largest science centers in the country, the 165,000-square-foot museum lures school-children and adults with an edifying roster of permanent, temporary, and traveling exhibits. Favorites include the indoor twister, static generator, and photoluminescence shadow wall. The "Great Lakes Story" explores the physical characteristics, geography, and geology that make the Great Lakes region unique. The complex is also home to a 320-seat Omnimax theater and the Science Store, a great source for science-related books, games, and kits. Out front, a single 150-foot wind turbine generates enough juice to satisfy 7 percent of the center's electrical needs. Open May through October, the adjacent Steamship *William G. Mather* is a retired Great Lakes freighter that offers a glimpse of life aboard a commercial vessel.

## ◖ HOPE MEMORIAL BRIDGE

connects Carnegie Ave. and Lorain Ave. where they cross the Cuyahoga River
**COST:** Free

Bridges typically are utilitarian affairs, elevated roadways designed to move commuters from here to there. But the Hope Memorial Bridge, also known as the Lorain-Carnegie, is beautiful to behold. Built in 1932, the gently arched span over the Cuyahoga River connects the East and West sides of town. For most commuters, the highlight of each crossing is not safe arrival on the other side, but the epic sculptures that sit sentry on either end. Carved into the bridge's 43-foot sandstone pylons, the art-deco figures are known fondly as the "guardians of traffic."

© DOUGLAS TRATTNER

**This masterpiece (and seven others like it) watches over the Hope Memorial Bridge.**

Like bookends, the monuments stand back-to-back, for a total of eight unique designs. Cradled in the hands of each is a mode of transportation, from covered wagon and stage coach to automobile and truck. The mile-long bridge features generous walkways on either side, offering easy passage from downtown to Ohio City, as well as fantastic vantage points for skyline photos.

## OLD FEDERAL BUILDING

201 Superior Ave. NE, 216/615-1235
**HOURS:** Mon.-Fri. 7 A.M.-5 P.M.
**COST:** Free

Originally constructed as a U.S. post office, customs house, and courthouse, the so-called Old Federal Building was the first structure built under the 1903 Group Plan (see sidebar), setting the tone for the five buildings that followed. Today, the building is known as the Howard M. Metzenbaum U.S. Courthouse, housing district and bankruptcy courts, as well as Departments of Homeland Security and Agriculture. The inspiration for this classical Beaux Arts beauty is said to be the Place de la Concorde in Paris. Clad

in gray granite, and mirroring in size and scope the nearby public library, the majestic landmark occupies a full city block. Artist Daniel Chester French created two monumental sculptures for the exterior, *Jurisprudence* and *Commerce,* which flank the Superior Avenue entrance. Climb the stone steps and enter the magnificent marble lobby, taking in its grand vaulted ceiling, turn-of-the-20th-century chandeliers, and original postal windows.

## OLD STONE CHURCH

91 Public Sq., 216/241-6145, www.oldstonechurch.org

This church is formally called First Presbyterian Society, but because it is the oldest surviving structure on Public Square, and because it was constructed of hand-hammered native sandstone, the church has become known simply as the Old Stone Church. Twice ravaged by fire, the Romanesque Revival structure was thrice built—in 1855, 1858, and 1884. The awe-inspiring interior boasts a barrel-vaulted ceiling, handsome oak pews, and a 3,000-pipe Cleveland-built Holtkamp organ. Perhaps more impressive are the four Louis Comfort Tiffany stained-glass windows, all of which have undergone complete restoration. But this building is not relegated to forgotten-museum status; it is a contemporary place of worship for its congregants, and families gather for weekly prayer, attend free organ concerts (row 77 center is the sweet spot), or practice yoga. Dwarfed by modern skyscrapers, this elegant old church also serves as a gentle reminder that sanctuary is never too far away.

## ◖ ROCK AND ROLL HALL OF FAME AND MUSEUM

1100 Rock and Roll Blvd., 216/781-7625, www.rockhall.com
**HOURS:** Thurs.-Tues. 10 A.M.-5:30 P.M., Wed. 10 A.M.-9 P.M., closed Thanksgiving and Christmas
**COST:** $22 adult, $13 child, $17 senior, free 8 and under

They say you can't cage an animal like rock and roll, but this iconic shrine does a laudable job of telling the story of rock's gritty past, present, and future. Some 150,000 square feet of space is crammed with permanent and temporary

# HOW CLEVELAND LANDED THE ROCK HALL

Since opening its doors in 1995, the Rock and Roll Hall of Fame has become such a symbol of Cleveland that the notion of it being located anywhere else seems absurd. Yet, despite the fact that "Cleveland Rocks" – thank you very much, Ian Hunter – this city had to pull off nothing short of a miracle to land the big prize.

When the Rock and Roll Hall of Fame Foundation was established in New York in 1985, with the aim of creating a museum to honor the legends of rock and roll, Cleveland wasn't even considered as a potential site. It took heroic efforts by Cleveland-based rock historian Norm N. Nite to convince the board to humor a contingent of city boosters. Those in attendance, including Ahmet Ertegun of Atlantic Records and Jann Wenner of *Rolling Stone*, were impressed enough by the presentation to schedule a fact-finding mission to C-Town.

Cleveland certainly had the rock chops to warrant that trip. This is where celebrated deejay Alan Freed and Record Rendezvous owner Leo Mintz first popularized the phrase "rock and roll." The Moondog Coronation Ball, considered the world's first rock concert (and subsequent rock-concert fracas), took place in the Cleveland Arena in 1952. Groundbreaking deejays like Bill Randle, Pete "Mad Daddy" Myers, Casey Kasem, and Kid Leo all worked the turntable and microphone here. The region has a proven track record for delivering stars, from Joe Walsh and Chrissie Hynde to Eric Carmen and Nine Inch Nails. All the biggest names in rock made certain to stop and say "Hello, Cleveland" when touring, including Elvis, the Beatles, Rolling Stones, David Bowie, Led Zeppelin, and the Who. Those big names performed, and their successors continue to do so, in some of the best live-music venues in the land, like Public Music Hall, Cleveland Agora, Peabody's, Beachland Ballroom, Grog Shop, and House of Blues. Ahead of its time, the album-oriented WMMS – Home of the Buzzard – was one of the most important rock-and-roll radio stations in the country. Jane Scott, one of the greatest, and most unlikely, rock reporters of anybody's generation made her living at the Cleveland *Plain Dealer*.

But ultimately it was the good people of Cleveland who tipped the scales in their own favor. When a *USA Today* telephone poll asked its readers to cast a vote for their choice of home for the Rock Hall, Cleveland trounced the competition, garnering 15 times the votes of second-place Memphis. When the foundation did eventually make that fact-finding tour to Cleveland, it was an impromptu pit stop at the original (now gone) Record Rendezvous that sealed the deal for some decision makers.

Cleveland officially won the Hall in 1986, but it would take an additional nine years and $90 million to see it through to completion. Today, the iconic I. M. Pei-designed glass-and-steel pyramid is a globally recognized affirmation of this city's rock-and-roll clout. And the museum has been a smash hit: Drawing more than six million guests since its opening, the Rock Hall is the most-visited hall of fame in the world.

Despite all the success, Cleveland was far from content. The Rock and Roll Hall of Fame Foundation's most prominent event, the annual induction ceremony, maintained a permanent residence at New York's Waldorf-Astoria hotel. Lobbying, it seems, has once again paid off: Starting in 2009, Cleveland will host the Hall of Fame induction gala every three years, a fitting tribute to a city that has proven that the Rock Hall belongs on the shores of Lake Erie.

exhibits, interactive displays, and live-performance spaces. An incredible array of memorable costumes, instruments, personal effects, and ephemera provide visitors with a unique perspective on rock's roots and culture. Sure, the entry fee is a bit steep. And, yes, it stinks that you can't take photographs inside the building. But where else are you going to see a Janis Joplin blotter acid sheet drawn by comic-book artist Robert Crumb and the hand-written lyrics of "Lucy in the Sky with Diamonds" in one afternoon? To take a little bit of rock home with you, stop by the well-stocked museum store, which is loaded with music-themed books, CDs, and genuine memorabilia. This pyramidal building on Lake Erie's shore may look modest from the outside, but like a Grateful Dead concert, it will devour entire portions of one's day.

## SOLDIERS AND SAILORS MONUMENT

3 Public Sq., 216/621-3710, www.soldiersandsailors.com

**HOURS:** Mon.-Sat. 9 A.M.-4 P.M., closed Thanksgiving, Christmas, and New Year's Day

**COST:** Free

Since 1894, this stately bronze-and-granite statue has served to commemorate the men and women of Cuyahoga County who served their country during the Civil War. Situated in the heart of Cleveland's Public Square, the monument features a 125-foot spire, four exterior sculptural groupings, and an interior Memorial Hall. A walk around the base reveals arresting scenes of the four principal branches of service—Infantry, Artillery, Cavalry, and Navy—in the throes of battle. Wander inside to see the carved names of 9,000 Civil War veterans, some stained-glass windows, and the base of the spire, which bears bronze panels of Abraham Lincoln proclaiming emancipation.

## TERMINAL TOWER

50 Public Sq., 216/623-4750, www.towercitycenter.com

When it was completed in 1930, this graceful skyscraper was the second-tallest building in the world. Rising 710 feet above Public Square, the building was the crown jewel of the Terminal Tower Complex, an ahead-of-its-time mixed-use development that included Cleveland Union Terminal rail station, hotels, department stores, and a post office. While it no longer competes for height records, Terminal Tower still serves as a beautiful reminder of this city's once-lofty status as the nation's fifth-largest city. Belying its neoclassical exterior, the building's interior spaces ooze with Beaux Arts and art deco details. Today, the complex houses hotels, office towers, a modern mall with restaurants, shops, and movie theaters, and a terminal for Cleveland's light rail system, RTA. Tunnels and pathways connect to Progressive Field and Quicken Loans Arena. A five-year $40 million restoration, due to finish in 2010, has repaired damaged exterior portions, restored the cupola

to its original golden hue, modernized the tower's 21 elevators, and replaced 2,050 windows. When the ambitious project is completed, the 42nd-floor observation deck, which has been closed since September 11, 2001, finally may reopen to the public. *Life* magazine photographer Margaret Bourke-White's famous black-and-white shot of Terminal Tower is said to have launched her noteworthy career. Bird-watchers should keep an eye out for peregrine falcons, which nest high on the tower and occasionally swoop down for a meal of fresh pigeon.

## TROLLEY TOURS OF CLEVELAND

2000 Sycamore St., 216/771-4484, www.lollytrolley.com

**COST:** One-hour tour $11 adult, $8 child, $10 senior; two-hour tour $17 adult, $12 child, $16 senior

The clang, clang, clang of Lolly the Trolley is a familiar sound for locals, who for years have observed these bright-red open-air carriages shuttling the curious about town. Despite the hokeyness factor, these trolleys provide a wonderful perspective on a city that often obscures its assets, with seasoned guides weaving historical, architectural, cultural, and political tidbits into a memorable excursion. General one- and two-hour tours hit the major sights of North Coast Harbor, the Warehouse District, Ohio City, PlayhouseSquare, Millionaire's Row, and University Circle, while numerous specialty tours focus on Little Italy and Lake View Cemetery, ethnic markets of Cleveland, unique churches about town, and the trail of Eliot Ness. Tours, which leave from the **Powerhouse at Nautica Entertainment Complex** in the Flats, run year-round, but leave more frequently from Memorial Day to Labor Day. All customers are required to call to reserve a spot in advance. Children under five are not permitted on the two-hour tour.

## U.S.S. *COD* SUBMARINE

E. 9th St. and N. Marginal Rd., 216/566-8770, www.usscod.org

**HOURS:** May-Sept. daily 10 A.M.-5 P.M.

**COST:** $6 adult, $3 student, $5 senior, free for military in uniform

Launched in 1943, this 312-foot fleet submarine

made seven war patrols in the South Pacific during World War II. She is credited with sinking a Japanese destroyer, mine sweeper, several cargo ships, and troop transports with her steam-powered torpedoes. The *COD* also performed the only international sub-to-sub rescue in history, saving 56 Dutch sailors before destroying their grounded ship. A popular tourist attraction since 1976, the *COD* is unique among restored display submarines in that visitors use the very same ladders and hatches employed by the crew (making it challenging for elderly and handicapped). On shore is a Mark 14 steam-driven torpedo, a five-bladed 2,080-pound bronze sub propeller, and a plaque honoring submariners who have lost their lives throughout the history of the United States. Military in uniform and wives and family of active-duty submariners are admitted free.

### ◖ WALKING TOURS OF CLEAVELAND

1501 N. Marginal Rd., Ste. 181, 216/575-1189, www.clevelandwalkingtours.com

**HOURS:** By appt.

**COST:** $60 up to four people, $15 additional person

For inquisitive groups large and small, longtime guide Karl C. Johnson answers a simple question: What's in Cleveland? Once this curious, gregarious host is through with them, participants will know plenty about Cleveland's rich history, architecture, politics, even sports. Johnson offers two separate three-mile, two-hour walking tours: one of downtown, the other through Ohio City. The downtown tour covers notable spots like the Arcade, Cuyahoga County Courthouse, Terminal Tower, and Old Stone Church in deeply intimate fashion. In Ohio City, Johnson not only guides folks past grand Victorian homes, he tells tales about occupants past and present. The tour works its way through the West Side Market, past old brewers' mansions, and along church-dotted lanes. Johnson also offers a Sedan Safari, a more sedate car-bound version in your coach or his.

### WAR MEMORIAL FOUNTAIN

Veterans' Memorial Plaza, St. Clair Ave. NE and W. Mall Dr.

Alternatively known as the Fountain of Eternal Life, Peace Arising from the Flames of War or, simply, the Green Guy, this regal statue enjoys prominent placement in a large open space called the Mall. The 35-foot granite-and-bronze sculpture depicts a stately male figure rising from the flames of war, his outstretched arm reaching toward the heavens. Illuminated fountains ring the base. Designed by a Cleveland Institute of Art graduate, the monument serves as a memorial to those who perished during World War II and the Korean War. During the planning stages, in the mid-1960s, conservative city officials insisted that the artist "cover up" his too-naked male form, which he did with strategically placed flames.

# Ohio City and Tremont                                   Map 2

### CARNEGIE WEST LIBRARY

1900 Fulton Rd., 216/623-6927, http://cpl.org/index.php?q=node/44

**HOURS:** Mon., Tues., and Thurs. 9:30 A.M.-8 P.M., Wed., Fri., and Sat. 9:30 A.M.-6 P.M.

Outside of philanthropist Andrew Carnegie's hometown of Pittsburgh, more Carnegie libraries were constructed in Cleveland than anywhere else. Of the 15 built here, all but three are still used as libraries. One of them is this graceful Renaissance Revival structure, a triangular-shaped edifice designed by Edward Tilton and completed in 1910. The interior of this Ohio City branch of the Cleveland Public Library boasts Corinthian columns, expansive windows, and room-illuminating skylights. Original Arts and Crafts touches can be found throughout the warm space, like the charming green-glazed Alice in Wonderland tiles, crafted by noted potter William Grueby, that frame the fireplace in the children's room. Set on a roomy and open green space, the library forms

## KEEPING THE CHURCH LIGHTS ON

Cleveland neighborhoods are graced with scores of architecturally stunning churches, their steeples and bell towers visible from area highways. And thanks to a generous donation by a retired dentist, many are visible day or night.

Before he died, Reinhold Erickson saw to it that his life savings of $370,000 would be used to improve his city's image to outsiders. His plan was specific: By illuminating church steeples along Cleveland interstates, he could give folks arriving via Cleveland Hopkins International Airport something beautiful to look at during their ride into the city. His goal was to light 20 churches along the oft-traveled I-90 and I-71 corridors.

Today, the Reinhold W. Erickson Fund is managed by the Cleveland Foundation and the Cleveland Restoration Society. So far, a dozen churches have participated in the ambitious Steeple Lighting Program. See how many you can spot along the way.

COURESTY OF POSITIVELY CLEVELAND

**Ralphie lived here:** *A Christmas Story* House in Tremont.

a graceful backdrop for impromptu strolls, neighborhood gatherings, and lazy Sunday mornings with coffee and the paper.

### A CHRISTMAS STORY HOUSE

3159 W. 11th St., 216/298-4919, www.achristmasstoryhouse.com

**HOURS:** Wed.-Sat. 10 A.M.-5 P.M., Sun. noon-5 P.M., closed Thanksgiving and Christmas

**COST:** $7 adult, $5 children, $6 senior

People thought Brian Jones, a West Coaster who had never stepped foot in Cleveland, was out of his mind when he purchased the house that served as the visual backdrop for the classic film *A Christmas Story*. A lifelong fan of the flick, Jones bought the 1895 Tremont structure site unseen, with plans of restoring the "Parker house" to its original movie splendor. Every effort was made to recapture the authentic look and feel of the times, including exchanging vinyl siding with real wood, ditching the replacement windows, and converting the building from a duplex back to a single-family home. Jones took pains to match the interior layout of the movie home, scouting out identical furnishings. Fans of the movie will recognize the familiar yellow-and-green of the building's exterior. Directly across the street from the house is a gift shop and museum, where film buffs can view original props, costumes, and memorabilia. Feel deserving of a "major award"? Pick up a full-size replica of the notorious leg lamp to take home and proudly display in the front window.

### FRANKLIN CASTLE

4308 Franklin Blvd.

**HOURS:** Not open to the public

This 9,000-square-foot Gothic carved-sandstone mansion is presently unoccupied—and some say that is a good thing. Host to many unspeakable acts, the house is long rumored to be haunted by unhappy spirits. Built in the late 1800s by a wealthy banker, the mansion boasts 26 rooms, five marble fireplaces, and some 80 windows. It is also, according to lore, the sight of a few grisly slayings, including that of a housekeeper who was murdered on her wedding day. Passersby regularly claim to see a ghost in the upstairs window, while others hear blood-curdling cries. Stroll by at night—if you dare.

### JAY AVENUE HOMES
Jay Ave. btwn. W. 25th and W. 30th Sts.

Jay Avenue can be viewed as a microcosm of the whole of Ohio City. Not long ago, this leafy tree-lined block in Cleveland's oldest neighborhood was a picture of despair, with once majestic Victorians inching ever closer to collapse and oblivion. Today, nearly every one of those homes has been thoughtfully restored, transforming each from eyesore to attraction. Stroll south on Jay from West 25th to its terminus at West 30th and explore the Archibald Willard House (2601 Jay), built in 1860 and once home to the famous painter of *The Spirit of '76,* and the Marquard Mansion (2920 Jay), built in 1903 by Philip Marquard, owner of the Marquard Sash and Door Co.

### JOHN HEISMAN'S BIRTHPLACE
2825 Bridge Ave.

Sports fans know that the Heisman (officially the Heisman Memorial Trophy) is awarded annually to the best athlete in college football. Most, however, do not know that John W. Heisman was born in Ohio City, and, according to many, in this very house. A commemorative plaque marks the site, but the house is not open to the public. Heisman was a wildly successful coach at Oberlin College, University of Akron, Auburn, Clemson, and Georgia Tech, where he guided his team to a mind-boggling 222–0 victory over the Cumberland College Bulldogs.

### LINCOLN PARK
Starkweather Ave. and W. 14th St.

Once part of Cleveland University, a short-lived mid-1800s college, this leafy green expanse is Tremont's version of Public Square. Ringed by bars, restaurants, and lovingly restored century-old homes, this park sees activity all day long. It is the site of numerous neighborhood festivals, alfresco summer concerts, and even Civil War encampments. Throughout the summer, free dance and music concerts attract large picnicking crowds at night, while the park's municipal swimming pool attracts overheated locals during the day. A stroll around the park's perimeter will unearth such haunts as Sanctuary (coffeehouse), Dish (deli), and Prosperity Social Club (neighborhood pub). Over on Starkweather Avenue, sharp modern townhomes occupy the Lincoln Park Bath building, which was constructed in 1921 as a public bathhouse for the many residents who still lacked modern plumbing.

### ST. IGNATIUS HIGH SCHOOL
2825 Bridge Ave., 216/651-6313, www.ignatius.edu

With 13 majestic buildings spread across a lush 16-acre campus, St. Ignatius High School looks more like a tony liberal arts college than a Catholic prep school for boys. Founded in the late 1800s by a group of German Jesuits, the school is both a neighborhood icon and a Cleveland educational institution. Along with the West Side Market's clock tower, St. Ig's 160-foot redbrick spire is one of the most recognizable skyline landmarks in the area. Respected equally for its athletics and academic excellence, this school has graduated both Olympic gold medalists and Ohio Supreme Court justices. Ohio City is often filled with the youthfully exuberant sounds of lacrosse, football, and track-and-field athletes as they compete on the pro-style turf field.

### ST. JOHN'S EPISCOPAL CHURCH
2600 Church Ave., 216/781-5546

Cleveland's oldest church, this Ohio City landmark was built by a Connecticut settler in 1836. Beloved for its Gothic Revival style and its facade of local sandstone, the building has survived both a devastating fire and a violent tornado. In the mid-1800s, Ohio offered safe passage for tens of thousands of slaves; St. John's was the last stop on the so-called Underground Railroad before arriving in Canada. The newest acquisition for this storied church is a fully restored 500-pipe organ, originally crafted in 1926, which has made its way through at least three separate places of worship.

## ST. PATRICK'S CHURCH

3602 Bridge Ave., 216/631-6872,
www.stpatrickbridge.org

The story of this church's construction in 1873 truly is an inspiring tale of commitment and allegiance. When parishioners outgrew their original place of worship, land at the present site was purchased, an architect was hired, and plans for a Gothic Revival structure were drawn up. And that was the easy part. Offered all the free blue limestone they could cut and carry, parishioners made weekly trips to a quarry 65 miles away, where they would cut stone for days on end before returning by wagon to Cleveland. The parishioners who remained onsite had the task of sizing and positioning the stone. This process continued for a full two years. These days, neighbors often gather and cheer as newlyweds make their way down the church steps.

## ◖ ST. THEODOSIUS RUSSIAN ORTHODOX CATHEDRAL

733 Starkweather Ave., 216/741-1310,
www.sttheodosius.org

Fans of *The Deer Hunter* will surely recognize the characteristic onion-shaped domes that dot the top of this magnificent cathedral, which served as the backdrop for that film's wedding scenes. The 13 copper-clad domes that rise above the structure represent Christ and the 12 apostles. At 112 years old, St. Theodosius is the oldest Russian Orthodox cathedral in Ohio, and it is considered one of the finest examples of traditional orthodox architecture in the country. Nearly every inch of the interior is adorned with vivid religious murals, icons, and holy pictures, the highlight of which is a

the glorious interior of the West Side Market

© DOUGLAS TRATTNER

screen bearing images of Christ, the Virgin Mary, the 12 apostles, and St. Theodosius. A 2001 renovation has breathed fresh life into the historic church.

### ◖ WEST SIDE MARKET

1979 W. 25th St., 216/664-3387,
www.westsidemarket.com
**HOURS:** Mon. and Wed. 7 A.M.-4 P.M., Fri.-Sat.
7 A.M.-6 P.M.

Though it looks like a grand railway station, the building that houses this historic public market was constructed expressly to sell food. Built in 1912, and added to the National Register of Historic Places in the mid-1970s, the West Side Market attracts food fans, architecture buffs, and campaigning politicians. But mostly it functions as the city's most fantastic supermarket, where residents buy their weekly eggs, meat, produce, and bread. Unlike prominent public markets elsewhere that stock everything from incense to T-shirts, this market is almost exclusively focused on food. Some 80 individually operated stalls hawk everything from Polish pierogies and Hungarian sausage to fresh pasta and exotic herbs and grains. There are multiple butchers for poultry, pork, beef, lamb, and goat, three separate fishmongers, and a handful of artisan bakers. Notice the conspicuous absence of fresh produce? That's because it's all next door in the fruit and vegetable annex, situated on the north and east sides of the complex.

# Detroit Shoreway and Edgewater     Map 3

### EDGEWATER STATE PARK

6500 Memorial Shoreway, 216/881-8141,
www.ohiodnr.com/parks
**HOURS:** Daily 6 A.M.-11 P.M.

Edgewater may not have the blushing pink sands of a Bahamas beach, or the jet-set crowds of the French Riviera, but it does have something only a handful of beaches in the world can claim: remarkable Cleveland skyline views. Amateur and professional shutterbugs flock to this urban sanctuary for breathtaking city, lake, and sunset views. This sprawling lakefront park is comprised of two main areas: an elevated bluff and a lake-level beach. On sweltering summer days, largely working-class families seek relief in the cool lake waters (despite the lake's less-than-stellar water quality). But most visitors don't come here to swim. Kite-flyers enjoy steady breezes nearly 12 months out of the year. Walkers, joggers, and bicyclists criss-cross the park on paved pathways. Anglers drop lines off a nearby fishing pier. Boaters launch their watercraft from various ramps. And winter at the park is just as spectacular thanks to the dramatic ice sculptures that form along the rocks. Wise Clevelanders know to flee this park before dark.

### GORDON SQUARE ARTS DISTRICT

Centered around Detroit Ave. and W. 65th St.,
www.gordonsquare.org
**HOURS:** Vary

When completed in late 2009, this arts-focused district will become the nucleus not only of the Detroit Shoreway neighborhood, but likely the entire near–West Side of Cleveland. Located two miles from downtown, with easy access to Lake Erie, the district is the site of ambitious new residential, commercial, and cultural development. Anchored by the 20-year-old Cleveland Public Theatre, the walkable area soon will feature a 250-seat community theater, a restored 1921 art-house movie theater, and a renovated streetscape. Already, the vibrant area is picking up steam. Shoppers are beginning to discover funky new boutiques like Room Service and duoHOME. Design studios and art galleries like 1point618 Gallery continue to sprout up in renovated storefronts. Sharp new cafés, restaurants, and bars keep the diverse streets peopled day and night.

# LOLLY THE TROLLEY'S CLEVELAND

For over 20 years, Sherrill Paul Witt has been leading narrated sightseeing tours through Cleveland on bright red vehicles called Lolly the Trolley. In that time, the company has grown from one trolley and one guide to eight trolleys and 10 guides. The clientele has shifted from mostly locals to mostly out-of-towners, including visitors from every U.S. state and most countries. We asked Witt some questions about the city she loves to show off.

**How did the trolley tours start?** I began giving tours of PlayhouseSquare theaters and loved it. Soon, I was leading walking and bus tours of Cleveland. When I went to Boston for a wedding and saw a trolley tour, I decided Cleveland needed one.

**What opinions do first-time visitors often have of Cleveland?** Some think we are provincial and have a rust-belt-city mentality. They don't know that Cleveland is a sophisticated multicultural city with all the big-city pluses and few of the minuses. There is a tremendous amount of quiet wealth in the area and people are generous to a fault.

**What are some of your favorite places to take visitors?** I love the Arcade. It is a Victorian delight that opened in 1890, and its huge glass ceiling and fabulous wrought-iron railings just stun people. Also, Lake View Cemetery has the Garfield Memorial, John D. Rockefeller's grave site, and Wade Chapel, the only Tiffany-designed interior in the United States.

**What do kids get a kick out of?** They love the lake, U.S.S. *COD* Submarine, and the jets on display at Burke Lakefront Airport. They also love all of our professional sports venues and bridges.

**What impression of Cleveland do your customers leave with?** People always say what a beautiful city we have. They love the classical downtown architecture and how clean our streets and Lake Erie are. Also, they like how affordable Cleveland is both for visitors and residents. You can go to Broadway shows for a fraction of the cost of the East Coast.

**What's the best excursion from town?** Pedaling along the Ohio & Erie Canal Towpath in Cuyahoga Valley National Park.

© DOUGLAS TRATTNER

**Take a sightseeing ride on Lolly the Trolley.**

## LORAIN AVENUE ANTIQUES DISTRICT

Lorain Ave. btwn. W. 65th St. and West Blvd.,
www.discoverlorainave.com

**HOURS:** Vary, see website for more information

This rag-tag collection of thrift, consignment, antiques, and restoration shops has long been a magnet for steely-eyed bargain hunters. Loosely centered around West 78th Street, the stores range from filthy dustbins to New York–style lofts. There is never a dearth of architectural salvage, from stately wooden fireplace mantels and stained-glass windows to porcelain pedestal sinks and claw-foot tubs. Don't miss Suite Lorain for vintage collectibles, Antique Gallery at the Bijou for Arts and Crafts furnishings sold in an old theater, and Reincarnation Vintage Design for everything from farmhouse chic to mid-century modern. Hours vary from store to store, but many are open only Wednesday–Sunday, noon–5 P.M. This urban landscape is better suited to the self-assured explorer than the high-maintenance mall-walker. For the truly adventurous, a stop at Steve's Lunch for cheap, delicious, and potentially addictive chili dogs is an absolute must any time of day or night.

## ST. STEPHEN CATHOLIC CHURCH

1930 W. 54th St., 216/631-5634,
www.saintstephenchurch.org

This stunning Gothic-style church was built in 1881 to serve the West Side's large contingent of German-speaking Catholics—by 1900 there were nearly 40,000. Many of the original parishioners agreed to mortgage their homes to insure that construction was completed. What distinguishes a German Catholic church from, say, a Roman Catholic one? For starters, the interior features a blond Virgin Mary, the hand-carved altars and statuary were imported from Munich, and the image of the Lord is a bearded one. Mass is still held in the Germanic tongue on the first Sunday of each month. The freestanding hand-carved oak pulpit, a 25-foot tower of ornamental figurines, was initially exhibited at the Chicago World's Fair. Basket-weave marble tiles cover the sanctuary floor. St. Stephen's imported stained-glass windows were shattered by a tornado in 1999 and have since been replaced.

# University Circle and Little Italy    Map 4

## CLEVELAND BOTANICAL GARDEN

11030 East Blvd., 216/721-1600, www.cbgarden.org

**HOURS:** Mon.-Sat. 10 A.M.-5 P.M., Sun. noon-5 P.M., open late Wed.

**COST:** $7.50 adult, $3 child

With origins in a converted boathouse on nearby Wade Park Lagoon, the botanical garden moved to its current site in 1966. The facility's most conspicuous asset is the 18,000-square-foot Glasshouse, which contains faithful re-creations of two fragile ecosystems, a Costa Rican cloud forest and the desert of Madagascar. Inside, visitors glide from biome to biome, immersed in environments rich with magical fauna and flora. Some 400 varieties of plants and animals take up residence in the conservatory, including 20 species of butterfly, the world's most diminutive orchids, and an

COURTESY OF CLEVELAND BOTANICAL GARDEN

**It's always balmy inside the Cleveland Botanical Garden Glasshouse.**

army of hungry leaf-cutter ants. Perhaps even more spectacular are the 10 acres of award-winning outdoor gardens. Among them are a traditional Japanese dry garden, a show-stopping rose garden, perennial and woodland gardens, and an herb garden with 4,000 distinct plants. The Hershey Children's Garden caters specifically to the littlest green thumbs in the bunch with mini forests, caves, worm bins, and a wheelchair-accessible tree house. An on-site library houses one of the largest repositories of gardening information in the country, with more than 17,000 garden-related books and periodicals. All gardens are open year-round except the Children's Garden, which closes during winter.

### ◖ CLEVELAND MUSEUM OF ART

11150 East Blvd., 216/421-7340, www.clevelandart.org

**HOURS:** Tues., Thurs., and Sat.-Sun. 10 A.M.-5 P.M.,
Wed. and Fri. 10 A.M.-9 P.M.

**COST:** Free

The Cleveland Museum of Art has always been regarded as one of the nation's finest repositories of art and antiquities. Thanks to a massive, and some might say long overdue, expansion and renovation, future visitors will enjoy a much improved art-viewing experience. The first phase of the $350 million project saw the reopening of the original 1916 building following three years of construction; the entire project, which includes two new wings, is expected to be completed in 2012, and one of the wings is scheduled to open June 2009. Forthcoming phases will replace outmoded additions with two new wings, uniting all with a large central atrium. Restored to its original glory, the classical marble-clad main building now gives the art a wider berth and gives visitors an easier path to navigate. Restored skylights create optimal lighting conditions for viewing the work, while state-of-the-art mechanicals provide a more comfortable environment. Until the next phases of the project are completed, just a fraction of the museum's permanent collection of 43,000 works of art is on display. Still, the 1,000 or so works that presently hang in the 19 renovated galleries contain

COURESTY OF POSITIVELY CLEVELAND

Cleveland Museum of Art

innumerable gems. Currently on display are European and American works from 1600 through 1900, including Reni's *Adoration of the Magi,* Caravaggio's *The Crucifixion of St. Andrew,* Canova's *Terpsichore* and Bellow's *Stag at Sharkey's.* Long a favorite of young and old, the Armor Court contains one of the largest and finest compilations of medieval and Renaissance arms and armor. Set on a picturesque bluff in University Circle, the museum presides over a sweeping landscape designed by Frederick Law Olmsted Jr., whose father created New York's Central Park. Photography without a flash is permitted.

### HESSLER ROAD AND HESSLER COURT

Ford Dr. and Hessler Rd.

It may not look like much at first blush, but these two tiny lanes in University Circle have been the site of many battles, protests, and celebrations. The buildings here date back to the early 1900s, so it's understandable that folks didn't take too kindly to the notion of their neighborhood being demolished to make room for parking lots. A vigilant street association formed in 1969 and managed to fight off the proposed development. Before long, the neighborhood was declared a historic district and was placed on the National Register of Historic Places. Hessler Court is just 300 feet long and is the only street in Cleveland that is paved with wood blocks. Held each May, the Hessler Street Fair is a spirited block party that unites friends and neighbors through art, music, food, and dance.

## PETER B. LEWIS BUILDING

Bellflower Rd. and Ford Dr., 216/368-4771, www.weatherhead.case.edu

**COST:** Free

Set amid the tranquil tree-lined streets that make up the campus of Case Western Reserve University, the Peter B. Lewis Building doesn't just stand out, it explodes onto the landscape. Home to the Weatherhead School of Management, the Frank Gehry–designed building is precisely what one would expect from the acclaimed avant-garde architect. Seemingly lacking even a single right angle, the twisting brick structure corkscrews out of the ground. There is no roof, per se, but rather a riot of stainless steel ribbons that festoon the top, reflecting whatever the sky happens to be doing at any given moment. Like the coiling tail of a rambunctious fish, the scaly steel tiles provide a flurry of movement and whimsy. Visible for blocks and blocks, the architectural landmark has become an attraction all to itself. Group tours can be arranged by calling ahead two weeks in advance.

## SEVERANCE HALL

11001 Euclid Ave., 216/231-1111, www.clevelandorchestra.com

**COST:** Varies by performance

The saga of Severance Hall is a love story. One month after tycoon and Cleveland Orchestra president John Long Severance committed to building the concert hall, his wife, Elisabeth, died suddenly of a stroke. Vowing to dedicate the venue to the memory of his beloved partner, Severance went on to build a performance hall that rivals in beauty and sound any found in Vienna, Boston, or New York. Severance Hall was designed by Walker & Weeks, Cleveland's leading architecture firm throughout the 1920s and 1930s, and it mimics a Greek temple. The majestic building's neoclassical facade, with its Ionic column–supported pediment, harmonizes with the nearby Cleveland Museum of Art. Tributes to Mrs. Severance can be found throughout the hall. Silvery shapes high above the main concert floor are reported to be modeled after the lace from her bridal veil. Lotus blossoms, Elisabeth's favorite flower, appear in the grand foyer's terrazzo floor and elsewhere. Entering the Grand Foyer, visitors are immersed in an opulent environment of two-story red marble columns, art-deco chandeliers, decorative metalwork, and dazzling floors. A $40 million renovation and restoration has updated the facility while remaining faithful to the original design. Severance Hall is, and always has been, a fitting home for the "Best Band in the Land." Concerts and tours are held year-round except during the summer months, when the orchestra performs at Blossom Music Center.

## WADE PARK

Bordered by East Blvd. and Martin Luther King Jr. Blvd.

Not just any ordinary park, Wade is the epicenter of arts, culture, and education in Cleveland, surrounded by the city's finest museums, performing-arts venues, and universities. It is also the site of Wade Oval and Wade Lagoon. Whether one is off to a museum, concert, or lunch date—or none of the above—time should be set aside for a leisurely stroll through this urban oasis. The grounds are dotted with alluring public art, architecturally stunning buildings, and meticulously tended gardens. On sunny spring, summer, and fall days, it isn't uncommon to see numerous newlywed couples roaming the green space with photographer in tow. During a random stroll, a visitor might encounter Rodin's *The Thinker,* a garden designed by Frederick Law Olmsted Jr., and a colorful neighborhood parade. Wade Oval is the site of WOW!, weekly free outdoor concerts held on Wednesday from June through August.

# Cleveland Heights and Shaker Heights   Map 5

## CAIN PARK

Superior Ave. at Lee Rd., 216/371-3000,
www.cainpark.com

The crown jewel of this 22-acre urban park is the Evans Amphitheater, a 1,200-seat covered venue with accompanying open-air lawn for outdoor seating. Despite its meager size, the stage attracts top-talent touring acts who appreciate the intimacy of the setting. Pick a show, pack a picnic, and spend a glorious summer night under the stars. Varied performances on either of the two stages include dance, cabaret, singer-songwriters, and Broadway musicals. In addition to some modest biking and hiking trails, the wooded parkland contains basketball and tennis courts, a toboggan hill, and a skate park. Every July, Cain Park hosts one of the most impressive arts festivals in the region. For three full days, thousands gather to shop the wares of some 150 artists, covering a broad swath of disciplines.

## THE COMMERCIAL DISTRICTS OF CLEVELAND HEIGHTS

Cleveland Heights is a progressive and diverse inner-ring suburb of about 45,000 residents. The area's unique physical layout and history as a "streetcar city" caused the creation of various commercial districts within its environs, each boasting its own look, feel, and flair. Cedar-Lee (Lee Rd. between Superior and Dellwood), so named for the major intersection in its midst, acts as "Main Street" for Cleveland Heights. This walkable mile-long strip of shops, services, restaurants, and bars serves the students, young professionals, and families who call the neighborhood home. Running south from Cain Park to the public library, the street includes the Cedar Lee Theatre, a local hardware store, a yoga studio, numerous galleries and boutiques, and countless bars and restaurants. There is rarely a time of day or night that finds the street totally deserted. Coventry Village (Coventry Rd. between Mayfield Rd. and Euclid Heights Blvd.) is perhaps best known for its counter-culture past, a time when underground cartoonists R. Crumb and Harvey Pekar made the street their living room. Sadly, the strip has succumbed to more than a few national chains, causing a slow and steady erosion of its infamous indie spirit. But all is not lost; Coventry still deserves attention thanks to a quirky amalgam of shops, restaurants, bars, and clubs. This is the only place in the world you'll find Big Fun, the Grog Shop, and Tommy's restaurant. We'll forgive Cedar-Fairmount its Starbucks, mainly because this picturesque gathering of Tudor-style buildings looks today much as it did in 1920. Known as the "Gateway to the Heights," the district sits at the pinnacle of Cedar Hill. That aforementioned coffeehouse teems with activity all day long, while world-renowned jazz club Nighttown bops all night. A spirited mix of independent shops includes a bookstore, wine shop, pilates studio, gelato parlor, pool hall, and martini bar. The nearby professional buildings are filled with architects, lawyers, psychiatrists, and doctors.

## ◖ FAIRMOUNT BOULEVARD DISTRICT

Fairmount Blvd. from Cedar Rd. to Wellington Rd.

In the early 1900s, industry tycoons began migrating from the city core to the eastern suburbs. At the time, Cleveland Heights still was considered far out in the country despite being a mere nine miles from Public Square. Serviced by the Cleveland Electric Railway, which traveled from downtown up Cedar Hill, the area quickly became home to the city's wealthiest residents. Employing the architect hotshots of the day, those businessmen built some of the finest homes of the 1910s and 1920s. Today, Fairmount Boulevard in Cleveland Heights is dotted with stately Georgian mansions, terra cotta–clad Italian villas, and wildly asymmetrical Tudor Revivals. Park your car on any of the side streets and make the trek on foot in order to enjoy architectural details like original copper gutters, leaded glass windows, steeply pitched slate roofs, and wrought-iron balconies. The annual Heights

Heritage Home Tour, held in September, offers participants intimate access to some of these homes and their magnificent gardens.

### ◖ LAKE VIEW CEMETERY

12316 Euclid Ave., 216/421-2665,
www.lakeviewcemetery.com
**HOURS:** Daily 7:30 A.M.-5:30 P.M.
**COST:** Free

This 290-acre plot of land is much more than just a final resting place for loved ones; it is an outdoor museum visited by approximately 400,000 people each year. Botanical garden, history lesson, and art gallery all in one, Lake View is a tranquil oasis in the middle of a congested urban environment. Best known as the burial site for many of this city's movers and shakers, the cemetery is "home" to John D. Rockefeller, Eliot Ness, and 22 Cleveland mayors. The most notable resident, perhaps, is president James A. Garfield, whose stately memorial provides views clear to Lake Erie. Hidden behind the simple, classical lines of the Jeptha Wade Memorial Chapel is a fairy-tale interior designed by Louis Comfort Tiffany. Four-ton bronze doors protect a deliriously beautiful stained-glass window, worthy of a cross-town visit itself. A few hours spent wandering the grounds and viewing the architecturally appealing markers and headstones is time well spent. Numerous walking tours are offered during spring and summer. Both the Garfield Monument and Wade Chapel are open 9 A.M.–4 P.M. April 1–November 19.

### NATURE CENTER AT SHAKER LAKES

2600 South Park Blvd., 216/321-5935,
www.shakerlakes.org
**HOURS:** Mon.-Sat. 10 A.M.-5 P.M., Sun. 1-5 P.M., trails open dawn to dusk
**COST:** Free

Armed with the slogan "Better ducks than trucks," a vigilant ladies garden club managed to save this bucolic 200-acre preserve from becoming another four-lane superhighway. That was in the late 1960s. Today the Shaker Lakes, and the single-minded Nature Center that serves as their environmental steward, attract thousands of eco-conscious visitors each year thanks to an absolute embarrassment of wildlife riches. The parklands encompass lakes, streams, marshes, fields, and dense forest, providing natural habitats for a host of native flora and fauna. Two trails—one wheelchair-accessible, the other

© DOUGLAS TRATTNER

Stop by Shaker Square for shopping and a bite.

more rugged—wind through this incredible landscape, providing the day-tripper an up-close and immersive experience. Die-hard bird-watchers flock here for regularly scheduled walks, ticking off warblers, thrushes, catbirds, juncos, red-tailed hawks, and barred owls from their checklists. Innovative programs held throughout the year inspire visitors to live greener lives.

### SHAKER SQUARE
Shaker Blvd. and N. and S. Moreland, www.shakersquare.net

More an octagon than a square, Shaker Square is the heart of a spirited and diverse neighborhood six miles east of downtown. Built in the late 1920s, and connected to downtown via the Rapid Transit line, the square is considered the second-oldest outdoor shopping district in the nation. But more than just a collection of shops, the square is a public space, where neighbors meet over coffee, take in a summer concert, or simply wander the circumference with a baby stroller. On warm nights, the roomy front patios of the numerous restaurants fill with diners. A movie theater shows both the latest releases as well as more off-beat indie flicks. Coffee, ice cream, and popcorn, all available on the square, provide the perfect post-movie nosh. A smattering of galleries, boutiques, and shops make for entertaining window shopping. Held every Saturday morning from mid-April through fall, the North Union Farmers Market attracts a massive sampling of small growers and producers, making it the largest fresh-food bazaar in the region.

# Lakewood Map 6

### THE BECK CENTER FOR THE ARTS
17801 Detroit Ave., 216/521-2540, www.beckcenter.org

The Beck is the largest nonprofit performing-arts and arts-education organization on the West Side of Cleveland. In addition to professional theatrical productions, which take place on two stages, the center offers comprehensive arts-education programming in dance, music, theater, and visual arts. Lead by artistic director Scott Spence, Beck's productions of musicals, dramas, and comedies consistently draw rave reviews from area critics and fans. The center's ambitious schedule of offerings attracts 100,000 people per year. Folks looking to try something new scramble for spots in classes that range from hip-hop to nude life drawing. Two on-site art galleries regularly feature the works of local, regional, and nationally recognized artists.

### LAKEWOOD PARK
Belle and Lake Aves., 216/529-4081, www.ci.lakewood.oh.us/pw_parks.html

One of 15 city parks in neighboring Lakewood, Lakewood Park is a 31-acre lakefront recreational area with eight tennis courts, three sand volleyball courts, two softball fields, outdoor swimming pool, picnic pavilions, skateboard park, and a kid-friendly playground. The park's band shell offers free Friday-night movies and Sunday-night concerts throughout the summer. On or around the Fourth of July, thousands gather here for a celebration of games, food, music, and fireworks. The Oldest Stone House is also located within the confines of this park.

### OLDEST STONE HOUSE
14710 Lake Ave., 216/221-7343, www.lakewoodhistory.org
**HOURS:** Feb.-Nov. Wed. 1-4 P.M., Sun. 2-5 P.M., closed major holidays
**COST:** Free

In the 1830s, Lakewood was a densely forested hamlet populated by a handful of rugged pioneer types. Back then, now-busy Detroit Road was a dusty Indian trail dotted with log-cabin homes. In 1838, John Honam built this small stone house out of locally quarried sandstone, pretty much signaling the end for log-cabin construction. The building, which served at various times as a residence, post office, and barbershop, remained at its original location for 117 years. In the mid-1950s, at a cost of around $10,000, the solidly built stone house was moved to its current location and established as the home of the Lakewood Historical Society and Museum. Though tiny, the museum boasts a rich tapestry of pioneer relics, including a preserved pioneer kitchen, four-harness loom, furnished parlor with horsehair sofa, and bedrooms with roped beds and homespun sheets. The museum also displays samplers, quilts, and folk art. An on-site herb garden is representative of those pioneer families would maintain as a source of scents, dyes, and food seasonings. Tours of the museum are conducted by costumed hostesses on Wednesday and Sunday 2–5 P.M.

# Greater Cleveland                            Map 7

## CLEVELAND METROPARKS ZOO AND RAINFOREST

3900 Wildlife Way, 216/661-6500, www.clemetzoo.com
**HOURS:** Daily 10 A.M.-5 P.M., Memorial Day through Labor Day until 7 P.M. Sat., Sun., and holidays
**COST:** Apr.-Oct. $10 adult, $6 child,
Nov-Apr. $7 adult, $5 child

With more than a million visitors each year, the zoo continues to be one of the region's top draws. Spread across 170 acres, the park contains 3,000 animals representing 600 different species. The most popular attraction is the RainForest, a two-acre, two-story steam bath jammed with a cornucopia of plants and animals, including birds, monkeys, and odd-smelling beasts. A simulated tropical rainstorm washes over the room every few minutes. 'Roo fans will hop over the Australian Adventure, home to parrots, koalas, and kangaroos. Like an African safari in Ohio, the Savannah teems with lions, rhinos, giraffes, zebras, and gazelles. Black bears and grizzlies take up residence in the Northern Trek, while tortoises and cheetahs race behind the Primate Building. In 2008, the zoo broke ground on a $25 million elephant habitat due to be completed in 2011. There are numerous fast and casual food options at the park, but guests are free to bring in a packed lunch to save money. Avoid nearby Fulton Road Bridge when visiting the park; it is closed for repairs.

## CUYAHOGA VALLEY NATIONAL PARK

7104 Canal Road, Valley View, 216/524-1497,
www.nps.gov/cuva
This 33,000-acre national park follows the twists and turns of the Cuyahoga River for 22 miles. Thanks to a wide range of habitats, from deep ravines and wetlands to open prairie and grasslands, the park is home to a great diversity of wildlife. Bird-watchers routinely spot great blue herons, short-eared owls, bobolinks, even bald eagles. Anglers pluck from the rushing waters steelhead trout, bullhead, bluegill, and bass. White-tailed deer seem to be everywhere, coyotes prowl the hillsides, and spring peepers provide the evening soundtrack. Bicycling is likely the most popular activity in the park, taking place along four major trails, including the perennially popular Towpath Trail, which follows the path of the historic Ohio & Erie Canal for 20 miles. Over 125 miles of hiking trails wend and weave their way through the park, offering treks of varying degrees of difficulty. In wintertime, folks don snowshoes, cross-country skis, and ice skates for some blustery fun. The Cuyahoga Valley Scenic Railroad provides a decidedly more passive park experience, giving riders an eagle's-eye view of the landscape from the comfort of a vintage rail car. Cyclists hop the train with bicycle in tow to get to or from favorite paths.

## HOLDEN ARBORETUM

9500 Sperry Rd., Kirtland, 440/946-4400,
www.holdenarb.org
**HOURS:** Daily 9 A.M.-5 P.M., closed Thanksgiving and Christmas
**COST:** $6 adult, $3 child, $5 senior
This nature preserve east of Cleveland began as a modest 100-acre parcel of land. Today it

encompasses 3,500 acres and includes more than 120,000 diverse plants, making it one of the largest arboretums and botanical gardens in the country. The lush and rambling landscape features a vast array of natural habitats, including bogs, gulches, ponds, lakes, rivers, meadows, and forests, combining to create a wildlife lover's paradise. Various display and specimen gardens specialize in trees, shrubs, and herbaceous perennials, colorful butterfly-attracting plants, even nut-bearing trees. Classes are offered in a range of disciplines, from utilizing native plants at home to propagating deciduous woody perennials. Winter is no time to shun the arboretum; it evolves into an absolute wonderland punctuated by bounding deer, frozen-in-time waterfalls, and a downy blanket of snow. Numerous guided tours (held largely from spring through fall) focus on various regions of the park, while 20 miles of pathways offer visitors a host of self-guided treks through easy, moderate, and rugged terrain.

## MALTZ MUSEUM OF JEWISH HERITAGE

2929 Richmond Rd., Beachwood, 216/593-0575, www.maltzjewishmuseum.org

**HOURS:** Tues.-Sun. 11 A.M.-5 P.M., until 9 P.M. Wed., closed Rosh Hashanah, Yom Kippur, and Thanksgiving

**COST:** $7 adult, $5 senior and student, free under 12

Jewish or not, visitors to this East Side museum typically leave moved beyond words: This museum tells the story of 200 years of Jewish-American history, but it could just as easily be recounting the experience of every American immigrant. Opened in 2005, the Maltz Museum is modern, well planned, and thoughtfully executed. It was created by the folks behind the International Spy Museum in Washington, D.C., and like that highly immersive facility, it relies on cutting-edge interactive exhibits to tell its tales. Through oral histories,

Maltz Museum of Jewish Heritage is fascinating for people of all faiths.

artifacts, and films, visitors experience what it might be like to leave everything behind to start life anew in a foreign place. Yes, there is reference to the dark days of the Holocaust, but there are also humorous examinations into the contribution of Jews to the world of entertainment. The museum's Temple-Tifereth Israel Gallery is a treasure trove of significant Judaica, including scrolls and documents of antiquity, European silverwork, and 18th-century tapestries.

## MEMPHIS KIDDIE PARK

10340 Memphis Ave., 216/941-5995,
www.memphiskiddiepark.com
**HOURS:** Apr.-Sept. daily 10 A.M.-9 P.M.
**COST:** No admission fee, but rides require a ticket

This is the amusement park where little ones get revenge on all those other parks—you know, the ones that say you have to be "this tall" to ride the rides. At Memphis, children must be *under* 50 inches tall to enjoy most rides. Not far from the zoo, this cherished Cleveland landmark has been putting smiles on kids' faces for over 50 years. Pint-size thrill-seekers scramble for seats on trains, in boats, aboard spaceships, and high (well, not so high) atop the Ferris wheel. For something both young and old can get behind, consider an 18-hole round of championship mini golf. Good clean fun abounds at this tidy family-friendly park. Memphis runs on tickets, with each ride a pay-as-you-go affair; a book of 25 tickets costs $21.50.

## NASA GLENN RESEARCH CENTER

21000 Brookpark Rd., 216/433-2000,
www.nasa.gov/centers/glenn/home
**HOURS:** Mon.-Fri. 10 A.M.-4 P.M., Sat. 10 P.M.-3 P.M., Sun. 1-5 P.M., closed holidays
**COST:** Free

With its work in the fields of fluids, combustion, and zero gravity, Glenn supports all NASA space missions. But top secret the facilities aren't. Space and science geeks are free to visit the NASA Glenn Visitor Center, with 6,000 square feet of interactive exhibitswhere guests will discover the unique challenges behind aircraft propulsion, examine a bona fide moon rock, and learn all about the center's namesake astronaut, John Glenn, the first American to orbit the Earth. A flight simulator buckles visitors into the pilot's seat of a prop plane, high-performance jet, or commercial airliner. True space nuts book spots well in advance for Glenn's popular "First Saturday" tours, which are held on the first Saturday of each month between April and October. Also free, these tours take visitors deep into the NASA campus, hitting facilities such as the propulsion lab, wind tunnel, and zero-gravity chamber. Call 216/433-9653 up to one month in advance to reserve a spot. All visitors to NASA Glenn must be U.S. citizens with proper photo ID (except children). Cars are subject to search, so limit their contents for a speedy entrance.

# RESTAURANTS

The Cleveland dining scene has received loads of positive national attention lately. Glossy magazines such as *Gourmet, Esquire,* and *Bon Appétit* have all singled out area restaurants for inclusion in articles. A number of high-profile food and travel shows have made pit stops here to film recent episodes. And the local visitors and convention bureau is seeing a steep rise in food-focused visits by out-of-towners. Certainly, Food Network star Michael Symon gets and deserves much of that interest, but there are dozens of other talented chefs who are making waves and drawing praise.

For a city its size, Cleveland boasts a disproportionately high number of independent chef-owned restaurants. Sure, the suburbs are littered with the identical national chains that exist in most metro areas, but alongside those repetitive

eateries are scores of ambitious one-of-a-kind bistros, gastropubs, and trattorias. Nestled in the fertile Cuyahoga Valley, Cleveland is well ahead of the national curve when it comes to its sophisticated system of farmers markets. In turn, chefs here are able to offer their customers farm-to-table cuisine crafted from local, seasonal, and sustainable ingredients. In fact, that progressive stance is quickly undoing Cleveland's reputation as a conservative meat-and-potatoes burg.

Not that there is anything wrong with meat and potatoes, mind you. Cleveland's unique charm lies in the very juxtaposition of new and old, classic and cutting-edge. It is a place where tony bistros rub shoulders with old-school cafeterias and mom-and-pop ethnic eateries. Folks here are just as zealous about butter-poached wild salmon as mile-high corned beef

COURTESY OF POSITIVELY CLEVELAND

# HIGHLIGHTS

LOOK FOR ◖ TO FIND RECOMMENDED RESTAURANTS.

◖ **Best Place to Glimpse an Iron Chef:** When he's not at Lolita in Tremont or Roast in Detroit, or off filming some Food Network show, food celeb Michael Symon is at **Lola.** Book your table well in advance and you'll enjoy progressive American fare in a knock-out restaurant. Say hi to Mike on your way out (page 56).

◖ **World's Best Corned Beef Sandwich:** We know the term "best" gets tossed around a lot when discussing corned beef, but **Slyman's Deli** really is the best around. Don't take our word for it – visit this always-popular diner to see what mile-high perfection tastes like (page 57).

◖ **Tastiest Hangover Cure:** Head to **Lucky's Café** for a brunchtime Shipwreck, bound to cure any ailment – including those self induced. This mad jumble of scrambled eggs, bacon, cheddar, and fried potatoes seems to have magical healing powers. Either that, or the dish leaves diners too stuffed to notice (page 60).

◖ **Slowest Food:** Chef-owner Karen Small is an ardent supporter of the slow food movement, so much of the cuisine served at **Flying Fig** is prepared with local, seasonal, and organic ingredients. Small's frequent trips to the farmers market translate into delicious – and sustainable – meals for diners (page 60).

◖ **Best Cafeteria Meal:** Clevelanders of all stripes – young and old, white collar and blue, East Side and West – can't seem to get enough of **Sokolowski's University Inn.** This institution dishes up old-school Eastern European classics like stuffed cabbage, potato pierogies, and chicken *paprikash* in a tchotchke-filled cafeteria setting (page 63).

◖ **Best Late-Night Chow:** Bar Cento serves food until 2 A.M. every single day of the year, including Christmas, New Year's, and Arbor Day. The hardworking chefs here turn out approachable Mediterranean fare like charcuterie, warm herbed olives, Neapolitan-style pizza, and grilled Ohio lamb at this lively wine bar (page 64).

◖ **Best French Baguette:** Fine restaurants around town call on the services of artisan baker Adam Gidlow to fill their bread baskets. At **On the Rise,** his East Side bakery, customers can purchase fresh-baked muffins, scones, croissants, focaccia, and olive bread – but it is the baguettes that seem to fly out the door the fastest (page 69).

◖ **Best Hope for a Vegetarian:** Tommy's began in the 1970s as a hippie-run soda fountain. Today, it is the most popular eatery on Coventry Road. While not solely a vegetarian restaurant, Tommy's has a wildly eclectic menu with loads of delicious meat-free options for herbivores (page 69).

◖ **Best Non-Indian Use of a Tandoor:** Except in Indian restaurants, these clay ovens are not typical kitchen appliances in the United States. But at **Fire Food & Drink** chef-owner Doug Katz uses the atypical cooking implement to quick-bake flatbreads, seal in the juices in pork chops, and flash roast delicate fish (page 72).

◖ **Most Picturesque Patio:** Set back from busy Detroit Road and cradled between adjoining buildings, the garden courtyard at **Three Birds** can feel like Earth's last Eden. Mature trees, winding paths, and seasonal plantings all add to the unrivaled charm of this beloved patio (page 74).

**RESTAURANTS**

## PRICE KEY

⑤ Entrées less than $10
⑤⑤ Entrées $10-20
⑤⑤⑤ Entrées more than $20

sandwiches. The region's diverse immigrant population bestows culinary gifts in the form of Lebanese falafel, Slovenian pierogies, Polish kielbasa, and Jewish matzo-ball soup. Cleveland has an entire neighborhood of Chinese, Korean, and Vietnamese markets and restaurants.

The only reason a visitor to Cleveland would ever need to eat at Cheesecake Factory is if he or she really, really wanted to.

# Downtown
Map 1

## ASIAN
### LI WAH ⑤
2999 Payne Ave., Asia Plaza, 216/696-6556,
www.liwahcleveland.com
**HOURS:** Mon.-Thurs. 10 A.M.-midnight, Fri.-Sun.
10 A.M.-1:30 A.M.

Dim sum is a popular weekend brunch activity in Cleveland, and not just for Asian Americans. Hit Li Wah on a Saturday or Sunday morning to join entire families feasting on steamed dumplings, crispy duck, turnip cakes, and scores of other exotic dishes. Get here early for a table; the cavernous hall fills up fast. Once seated, you simply point to the items that interest you as they roll past on countless steam carts. Items are ridiculously inexpensive, so be adventurous. When the teapot runs dry, prop open the lid so your server knows to refill it.

### SAIGON VIETNAMESE CUISINE ⑤⑤
2061 E. 4th St., 216/344-2020,
www.saigoncleveland.com
**HOURS:** Mon.-Thurs. 11 A.M.-10 P.M., Fri. 11 A.M.-11 P.M.,
Sat. 5-11 P.M., Sun. 5-10 P.M.

Thanks to the opening in 2008 of this polished East 4th Street restaurant, fans of Vietnamese cuisine needn't travel all the way to AsiaTown to enjoy their favorites. The lengthy menu includes dozens of noodle soups, rice vermicelli dishes, and flavorful stir-fries. Best among them are the Vietnamese crepes, lettuce-wrapped chicken, and clay-pot shrimp. While the *pho* lacks the depth of those found east of

town, the convenient location, swank setting, and sidewalk seating more than make up for it. There is a full beer, wine, and cocktail list.

### SUPERIOR PHO ⑤
3030 Superior Ave., 216/781-7462
**HOURS:** Tues.-Sat. 10 A.M.-8 P.M., Sun. 11 A.M.-7 P.M.

Long before *pho* became a fixture on the Cleveland culinary landscape, there was Superior Pho. This low-profile restaurant is tucked away in Golden Plaza, a small collection of shops and services. Park in back and take a seat in this clean but spare eatery to enjoy the city's best bowl of *pho,* bar none. To round out the meal order one of their amazing *bahn mi,* a Vietnamese sandwich stuffed with sliced roast pork, grated radish, jalapeño, fresh cilantro, chicken-liver pâté, and mayo.

## BREAKFAST
### JUNIPER GRILLE ⑤
1332 Carnegie Ave., 216/771-1334
**HOURS:** Mon.-Fri. 7 A.M.-3 P.M., Sat. 8 A.M.-2 P.M.,
Sun. 9 A.M.-2 P.M.

As one of downtown's few breakfast joints, Juniper Grille would be popular even if it did merely a so-so job. But this sharp-dressed diner pulls out all the stops in crafting its upscale breakfast and lunch items. The quality of ingredients and attention to detail are what you would expect to find at pricier restaurants, and the setting is as cool as a cucumber. Juniper opens early with all the usual egg-and-batter suspects. Lunch brings bounteous salads, gourmet

# DIM SUM AND THEN SOME: A GUIDE TO ASIATOWN

Over 30,000 Asians call Cuyahoga County home, making them one of the larger ethnic populations. Many reside in AsiaTown, an area just east of downtown that is loosely bordered by East 30th and 40th Streets, and St. Clair and Payne Avenues. This vibrant, diverse neighborhood is teeming with Asian-owned shops, restaurants, and markets. A visit here is a must for ethnic-food fans, adventurous home cooks, and lovers of all things exotic.

The Chinese are Cleveland's oldest Asian immigrant group, dating all the way back to the 1860s, but the area that used to be called Chinatown is now referred to as AsiaTown to better reflect the residents that call the area home. Recent decades have welcomed arrivals from Korea, Vietnam, and Thailand, and immigrants from each of these countries have established restaurants and markets in this area.

*Pho* has become an absolute food craze all over the country – and for good reason. This Vietnamese meal in a bowl features noodles, beef, broth, and veggies in a plentiful, affordable, and delicious package. Two of Cleveland's best versions can be found in AsiaTown. Many locals prefer to hit **Superior Pho** for their bowl despite the spare, modest setting. For those who prefer a little more flash, there is **#1 Pho** (3120 Superior Ave., 216/781-1176), an attractive Vietnamese restaurant less than a block away. Both menus travel well beyond noodle soup.

Dim sum is a popular weekend brunch in Cleveland, and not just for Asians – the practice of selecting food as it rolls by on carts is pretty much a universal pleasure. Some Chinese restaurants are designed specifically with dim sum in mind, with cavernous dining rooms capable of handling hundreds of guests at once. Two local dim sum institutions are **Bo Loong** (3922 St. Clair Ave., 216/391-3113) and **Li Wah**. Both have wonderful selections, efficient service, and reasonable prices. Try the barbecue pork buns, turnip cakes, shrimp dumplings, crisp-skinned duck, and, if you're brave, chicken feet.

One of the best Asian restaurants in all of Northeast Ohio is **Siam Café** (3951 St. Clair Ave., 216/361-2323), a large, relatively attractive space. The sprawling menu covers traditional and creative Chinese dishes (plus some Thai and Vietnamese), but this restaurant excels at seafood. Live lobster, crab, eel, and shrimp are pulled from tanks and cooked up in dishes like shrimp in black bean sauce, lobster in garlic sauce, and salt-baked shrimp.

There are few greater culinary joys than grilling up garlicky beef *bulgogi* at a Korean restaurant such as **Seoul Hot Pot** (3709 Payne Ave., 216/881-1221) – it doesn't look like much from the outside, but is cute and comfy inside. This restaurant also has a few grill tables (ask for one when booking a reservation) that turn a *bulgogi* meal into a festive event. **Korea House** (3700 Superior Ave., 216/431-0462) is more spacious and modern, but *bulgogi* is cooked on a tabletop hot plate. Both restaurants put out respectable arrays of *banchan*, those pungent condiments such as kimchi that accompany every meal.

AsiaTown is blessed with great ethnic markets that transform an everyday shopping trip into a culinary expedition. These bustling groceries stock exotic live seafood items like frogs and eels, hard-to-find herbs and spices, and even dirt-cheap cookware. One of Cleveland's oldest and best is **Tink Holl** (1735 E. 36th St., 216/881-6996), a large, bright space crammed with interesting stuff. For a treat, purchase half a roasted duck. Hacked into pieces, this bird blows away the Colonel's. One of the newest additions to the area is **Koko Bakery** (3710 Payne Ave., 216/881-7600), a contemporary shop that sells an amazing selection of Asian baked goods. Come here for sweet and savory buns, Chinese cakes, egg custards, and bubble tea.

RESTAURANTS

sandwiches, and comfort classics. The location is as close to Progressive Field as one could get.

## CAFÉS
### MARKET CAFÉ $

1801 E. 9th St., AmTrust Building, 216/394-0124, www.cafebonappetit.com/market

**HOURS:** Mon.-Fri. 7 A.M.-8 P.M.

Within the diverse family of food establishments, cafeterias rarely earn props. And why should they, with their steam tables, gray vegetables, and hairnets? But this cafeteria is different. For starters, it's beautiful, thanks to Amish-built communal tables, chandeliers made from recycled milk jugs, and honey-jar accent walls. Various food stations offer seasonal soups, custom salads, fresh-baked calzones, grilled-to-order burgers, kebabs and fish, and hot pressed sandwiches. Better still, much of the product is locally sourced, and the kitchen uses only sustainable seafood, cage-free eggs, BGH-free dairy products, antibiotic-free beef and poultry, and trans fat–free cooking oils. Great pre-packaged food items are on display for convenient carry-out.

## CONTEMPORARY AMERICAN
### CROP BISTRO $$$

1400 W. 6th St., 216/696-2767, www.cropbistro.com

**HOURS:** Tues.-Fri. 11 A.M.-2 P.M. and 5-10:30 P.M., Sat. 5-10:30 P.M., Sun. 5-9 P.M.

Foodies have fallen in love with this fun-spirited Warehouse District bistro. Chef-owner Steve Schimoler keeps the mood light while crafting big-flavored American bistro fare. Approachable, delicious, and at times whimsical, the food rarely fails to put a smile on diners' faces. Here, old standards like deviled eggs, roast chicken, and shrimp and grits are reimagined into contemporary showstoppers. (Do yourself a favor and order the Cherry Bomb.) Occasionally on weekend nights the crew trades in their kitchen utensils for musical instruments and jams late into the night. Don't pass up Crop's inventive cocktails, many of which use infused spirits made in-house.

### ◖ LOLA $$$

2058 E. 4th St., 216/621-5652, www.lolabistro.com

**HOURS:** Mon.-Thurs. 11:30 A.M.-2:30 P.M. and 5-10 P.M., Fri. 11:30 A.M.-2:30 P.M. and 5-11 P.M., Sat. 5-11 P.M.

This uber-cosmopolitan restaurant is the nucleus of food celeb Michael Symon's ever-growing empire. Along with Lolita in Tremont and Roast in Detroit, Lola is where Symon spends his time satisfying fans one forkful at a time. In addition to having a winning personality, the dude can cook. Come here to sample creative Midwestern fare constructed from local, seasonal, and artisanal ingredients. Pierogies are stuffed with slow-braised beef cheeks; crisp pork belly is gilded with warm poached egg; a well-marbled rib eye gets an over-the-top push from buttery bone marrow. Sweets fans will doubtless swoon over this restaurant's dessert selections. Even if you can't score a dinner reservation (check www.opentable.com), grab a stool at the glowing alabaster bar for a cocktail and an appetizer. Wherever you sit, you might hear Symon's trademark laugh.

### METROPOLITAN CAFÉ $$$

1352 W. 6th St., 216/241-1300, www.hydeparkrestaurants.com/metro

**HOURS:** Mon.-Fri. 11:30 A.M.-11 P.M., Sat. 4-11 P.M., Sun. 4-9 P.M.

When you want a splash of fashion with your fare, head to this flashy crowd pleaser in the heart of the Warehouse District. It isn't uncommon to spot Cleveland's movers, shakers, and high-paid ball players at this ebullient American brasserie. On tap are bracing martinis, creative pizzas, lush pastas, and thick grilled USDA Prime steaks. On warm evenings, Metro's high-profile sidewalk seating is the best perch in town from which to enjoy the lively parade of downtown fun-seekers.

### XO PRIME STEAKS $$$

500 W. St. Clair Ave., 216/861-1919, www.xoprimesteaks.com

**HOURS:** Mon.-Thurs. 11 A.M.-3 P.M. and 5-11 P.M., Fri. 11 A.M.-3 P.M. and 4 P.M.-midnight, Sat. 4 P.M.-midnight, Sun. 4-9 P.M.

No surprise here: XO deals in high-quality USDA Prime beef. But like the latest herd of modern steakhouses popping up across the prairies, this one is sleek, contemporary, and loaded with creative twists. Siding those superlative steaks are dozens of delicious accompaniments, like to-die-for truffled creamed corn. Fish fans can swap the cow for super-fresh sushi-grade tuna, meaty grouper, or buttery sea bass. Start with an order of the ever-popular fried rock shrimp, which is presented in a Chinese take-out box with spicy chili sauce. This spot is popular with Cavs players after home games.

## DELIS
### 🍴 SLYMAN'S DELI ●
3106 St. Clair Ave., 216/621-3760, www.slymans.com
**HOURS:** Mon.-Fri. 6:30 A.M.-2:30 P.M.

According to such definitive sources as *Esquire* magazine and the Barenaked Ladies, Slyman's really does have the best corned-beef sandwich in America. (*Esquire*'s Scott Raab wrote, "I've noshed deli across the globe, and no corned-beef sandwich anywhere knuckles up to this.") Just before noon on weekdays, a line begins forming at the deli counter. Soon, that line is snaking down the sidewalk. But don't worry, it moves quickly, and waiting at the other end is a fat, buttery, gut-busting beauty about which you too might pen songs. Order your sammy "natural" if you like it plain, "original" for mustard only, and "all the way" for Swiss, mustard, and horseradish.

## ITALIAN
### PONTE VECCHIO ●●●
2100 Superior Via, 216/556-8200, www.pontevecchioristorante.com
**HOURS:** Mon.-Thurs. 11 A.M.-2 P.M. and 5-10 P.M., Fri. 11 A.M.-2 P.M. and 5-10:30 P.M., Sat. 5-10:30 P.M.

This restaurant's setting on the old Superior-Detroit viaduct, a sandstone bridge completed in 1878 and made obsolete in 1920, gives it one of the most unique (and cryptic) locations in town. It also affords diners with some of the most striking city views. A polished interior serves as an appropriate backdrop for upscale regional Italian fare, including amazing pastas, hearty grilled chops, and fresh fish and seafood. Thanks to white granite tabletops, twinkling candlelight, and those million-dollar views, Ponte Vecchio is often ranked among the city's most romantic dinner destinations.

Slyman's serves the best corned beef sandwich around.

## PUBS
### JOHNNY'S LITTLE BAR ●
614 Frankfort Ave., 216/861-2166, www.johnnyscleveland.com
**HOURS:** Mon.-Fri. 11 A.M.-2:30 A.M., Sat. 5 P.M.-2:30 A.M., Sun. 7 P.M.-2:30 A.M., opens at 10 A.M. for Browns Sunday home games

The Little Bar is indeed little, tucked away as it is in an alley off the main drag. But what this popular watering hole lacks in stature it makes up for in attitude. During the day, downtown suits duck in here for iceberg wedge salads, matchless burgers, and hearty home-style entrées. After work, the genial bar takes on a more neighborly vibe as downtown residents pop in for happy hour beers and upscale pub grub. If the Browns are on the small screen, Little Bar becomes game central.

## SEAFOOD
### BLUE POINT GRILL ●●●
700 W. St. Clair Ave., 216/875-7827, www.hospitalityrestaurants.com
**HOURS:** Mon.-Thurs. 11:30 A.M.-3 P.M. and 5-10:30 P.M., Fri. 11:30 A.M.-3 P.M. and 4-11:30 P.M., Sat. 4-11:30 P.M., Sun. 5-10 P.M.

Ask a random Clevelander where to go for

upscale seafood and you'll invariably be directed here. In the business of fish since 1998, this Warehouse District mainstay serves up some of the most consistently delicious seafood in the city. The drop-dead gorgeous warehouse space boasts soaring ceilings, castle-thick brick walls, and modest nautical accents. Blue Point is famous for its crab cakes, chowders, surf and turf, and grouper with lobster mashed potatoes. Meat lovers are in good hands here too, since this small restaurant group also operates a wonderful steakhouse. For a more affordable way to savor the atmosphere, grab seats at the bar and enjoy the best oyster selection around. Reservations are recommended for weekends.

## NAUTI MERMAID ⑤⑤
1378 W. 6th St., 216/771-6175,
www.thenautimermaid.com
**HOURS:** Daily 11 A.M.-10 P.M.

Often the best places to enjoy seafood are the most casual, and this lively fish-shack tavern is proof of that. Equal parts bar and restaurant, this unpretentious Warehouse District eatery serves raw-bar items, fried fish, and whole Maine lobsters. Favorites here include spicy fish

# RESTAURANT WEEK

Every fall, typically during the early part of November, Cleveland Restaurant Week encourages diners to try new restaurants by offering incredible dining deals. The 40 or so restaurants that participate usually serve special three-course prix fixe dinners for around $30; some proffer even better bargains. By and large, the event applies to dinner only, but some eateries extend the promotion to lunches. If you are visiting the area in fall, visit the Cleveland Independents website (www.clevelandindependents.com) to see a complete listing of participating restaurants. Some years, the event runs for two weeks, excluding Saturdays.

tacos, fried lake-perch sandwiches, and hush puppies. If you're looking for a fun, reasonably priced, and atypical place to grab a quick bite, consider a visit to the Mermaid. This is also a great spot to enjoy a craft beer and watch the Cavs, Indians, or Brownies on the telly.

# Ohio City and Tremont                    Map 2

## BREAKFAST
### LE PETIT TRIANGLE CAFÉ ⑤
1881 Fulton Rd., 216/281-1881,
www.lepetittrianglecafe.com
**HOURS:** Tues.-Thurs. 11 A.M.-10 P.M., Fri.-Sat.
11 A.M.-11 P.M., Sun. 10 A.M.-3 P.M.

As the name suggests, this café is a wee wedge of a place, with scarcely two dozen seats in all. On balmy days, that capacity jumps considerably thanks to a grouping of bright-red bistro furniture that tumbles out onto the sidewalk. Inside or out, this charming neighborhood spot captures the carefree insouciance of a Parisian café, complete with sweet and savory crepes, fluffy omelets, and ethereal café au laits. On wintery nights, this tiny spot is like a warm embrace,

made all the balmier thanks to French onion soup, piping-hot cassoulet, and red wine. Get here early on weekend mornings to enjoy an authentic slice of Ohio City life along with your fluffy smoked-salmon omelet.

### NICK'S DINER ⑤
4116 Lorain Ave., 216/631-7757
**HOURS:** Mon.-Fri. 7 A.M.-3:30 P.M., Sat.-Sun.
7 A.M.-4 P.M.

This diner may not look like much, but if you're in the market for a good, cheap breakfast, this laid-back spot will do the trick. An otherwise plain space is brightened up by posters of comic-book heroes and quirky embellishments. A full breakfast of three eggs, bacon, home fries, and toast can be had for less than $3. Nick's house specialties are the "skillets," earthenware platters stuffed with everything but the kitchen sink. The Mr. Speedy Gonzalez, for example, is piled high with hash browns, spicy ground chorizo, onions, peppers, cheese, and three eggs, any style.

### WEST SIDE MARKET CAFÉ $

1995 W. 25th St., 216/579-6800, www.westsidemarketcafe.com

**HOURS:** Mon.-Thurs. 7 A.M.-4 P.M., Fri.-Sat. 7 A.M.-9 P.M., Sun. 9 A.M.-3 P.M.

On Saturday, the busiest shopping day at the West Side Market, this café is absolutely buzzing with activity as folks fuel up on eggs Benedict, corned-beef hash, and righteous blueberry pancakes. Weekday mornings, lunches and dinners are decidedly calmer affairs, but still worth a visit thanks to quality ingredients and consistent attention to detail. Fans of stick-to-your-ribs diner fare will dig this café not only for its food but also its decor, which features original fixtures and historic photos of the market's earliest days.

# CAFÉS
## CIVILIZATION $

2366 W. 11th St., 216/621-3838, www.cityroastcoffee.com/civil

**HOURS:** Mon.-Thurs. 7 A.M.-7 P.M., Fri. 7 A.M.-11 P.M., Sat. 8 A.M.-11 P.M., Sun. 8 A.M.-6 P.M.

This European-style coffeehouse is located right on Lincoln Park and features a generous sidewalk patio for enjoying a post-dinner espresso. The beans are locally roasted by the owner, who also runs the City Roast Coffee stand at the West Side Market. The rustic 100-plus-year-old storefront feels like a general store from days gone by. The fare here is light and simple, such as pastries, soups, and sandwiches.

### JOHNNY MANGO $

3120 Bridge Ave., 216/575-1919, www.jmango.com

**HOURS:** Mon.-Thurs. 11 A.M.-10 P.M., Fri. 11 A.M.-11 P.M., Sat.-Sun. 9 A.M.-10 P.M.

Ohio City's other pie-shaped café, the Mango is as lovably quirky as its setting. With its rattan ceiling fans and vividly hued walls, the interior looks as if it was plucked from a Mexican beer

**RESTAURANTS**

© DOUGLAS TRATTNER

Johnny Mango in Ohio City serves global cuisine at wallet-friendly prices.

commercial. That seems to suit the locals just fine, as many of them are sporting flip-flops and tattoos as bright as the surroundings. Borrowing elements from Caribbean, Mexican, and Asian kitchens, the menu melds widely disparate food-stuffs into a seamless global cuisine. Vegetarians dig the juice bar and fried tofu, while carnivores tuck into Jamaican jerk chicken and gaucho steak. Toss in pad Thai, shrimp-fried rice, and a robust weekend brunch, and you end up with an eclectic neighborhood hangout.

### ( LUCKY'S CAFÉ $

777 Starkweather Ave., 216/622-7773,
www.luckyscafe.com
**HOURS:** Mon.-Sat. 7 A.M.-5 P.M., Sun. 8 A.M.-5 P.M.

In addition to being the de facto java stop for many Tremont residents, Lucky's features one of the most popular weekend brunches in town. Chef-owner Heather Haviland scours the countryside in search of local eggs, sustainable produce, and eco-friendly meats. Hearty breakfast here means big plates of Ohio sweet-corn waffles with strawberry-rhubarb compote, fresh-baked cheddar-scallion scones topped with scrambled eggs and sausage gravy, and a delicious disaster dubbed the Shipwreck featuring scrambled eggs, bacon, white cheddar, and fried potatoes. Haviland is also a prominent pastry chef, so you can count on phenomenal sweets, tortes, brownies, and cakes.

### SOUPER MARKET $

2528 Lorain Ave., 216/737-7687,
www.thesoupermarket.com
**HOURS:** Mon.-Fri. 11 A.M.-7 P.M., Sat. 11 A.M.-6 P.M.

Located around the corner from Ohio City's main drag, this tiny soup house is worth finding. The attraction here, of course, is the hand-crafted soup, made daily with house-brewed stocks, wholesome ingredients, and ladlefuls of patience. An ever-rotating roster keeps fans coming back time and again for beautiful bisques, broths, and bouillabaisses. There are always veggie options like chunky mushroom and tomato-ginger, hearty stews like jambalaya and mulligatawny, and, in the summer, refreshing chilled soups such as gazpacho and strawberry bisque. Most diners get their soup to go, as there's only enough room for a few people to stand at a window-facing counter.

## CONTEMPORARY AMERICAN

### FAHRENHEIT $$$

2417 Professor Ave., 216/781-8858,
www.fahrenheittremont.com
**HOURS:** Mon.-Thurs. 5-11 P.M., Fri.-Sat. 5 P.M.-1 A.M.

Chef Rocco Whalen picked up his pizza-making skills directly from Wolfgang Puck, so you can assume the gourmet pies here are superlative. But this hopping Tremont bistro goes well beyond pizza, venturing into Asian-inspired starters, seasonal pastas, hearty chops, and, perhaps, the city's finest short ribs. Seafood fans will have no difficulty enjoying a meal here; the menu usually features oysters, scallops, and walleye. Or, enjoy a cocktail in Fahrenheit's sharp lounge before or after having dinner elsewhere. Reservations are highly recommended for weekends.

### ( FLYING FIG $$$

2523 Market Ave., 216/241-4243, www.theflyingfig.com
**HOURS:** Mon.-Thurs. 5-11 P.M., Fri.-Sat. 5-11:30 P.M., Sun. 5-10 P.M.

Located on a charming brick-paved lane in Ohio City, this bistro is among the city's very best places to dine. Frequented by fawning locals and well-heeled travelers alike, the Fig's crowd is an eclectic blend of young and old, tattooed and suited, liberal and conservative. Chef-owner Karen Small works closely with local farmers, farmers markets, and artisanal producers to craft a menu that changes nearly as frequently as the calendar. Savory starters include crispy sweetbreads and chorizo-stuffed dates. Entrées run the gamut from braised and grilled short ribs to pristine halibut. Hit this restaurant's famous happy hour for heavily discounted drinks, nibbles, and house-made chips. Reservations are recommended for weekends.

### PARALLAX $$$

2179 W. 11th St., 216/583-9999,
www.parallaxtremont.com
**HOURS:** Mon.-Thurs. 5-11 P.M., Fri.-Sat. 5 P.M.-midnight

While not technically an Asian restaurant,

Parallax is beloved for its sparkling sushi. The selection of raw fish is not as extensive as one might find at a Japanese restaurant, but what is prepared here is beyond reproach. Operated by noted chef and restaurateur Zachary Bruell, Parallax is an elegant and stylish bistro that specializes in impeccable fish and seafood, whether served raw, poached, fried, grilled, or roasted. The Alaskan black cod with miso glaze is an absolute winner of a dish, but the menu might also include monkfish, salmon, tuna, and lobster. Meat eaters can choose from grilled hanger steak, braised short ribs, and Bruell's famous chicken *pommes frites* with beurre blanc. Reservations are a necessity on weekends.

## SOUTH SIDE $\$\$$
2207 W. 11th St., 216/937-2288,
www.southsidecleveland.com
**HOURS:** Mon.-Sat. 11 A.M.-2 A.M., Sun. 10 A.M.-2 A.M.
Besides having the absolute largest patio in Tremont, South Side has a great bar scene. Upscale comfort food, a rambunctious atmosphere, and friendly bartenders keep this joint jumping most hours of the day. For something different, try the chicken and waffles, a Tremont take on the Harlem classic. The menu also features fresh salads, tasty burgers, and quality pastas. The South Side can get extremely loud and crowded, especially during important televised sporting events or when there is live music. But if you snag a seat at the bar early enough, you should be in for a great night. The genial neighborhood vibe makes this pub a popular meet-and-greet spot.

## DELIS
### DISH DELI $\$$
1112 Kenilworth, 216/523-7000, www.dishtremont.com
**HOURS:** Mon. 10 A.M.-6 P.M., Tues.-Fri. 10 A.M.-7 P.M., Sat. 11 A.M.-5 P.M.
Chef and former restaurateur Donna Chriszt has focused her considerable culinary talents on this adorable storefront deli bursting with fresh, globally inspired fare. Stop in and fashion a meal from the colorful prepared items displayed in coolers. There are Asian-inspired noodle bowls, Middle Eastern vegetable salads, creative deli

sandwiches, and house-baked stromboli. If you are planning a picnic in nearby Lincoln Park or are looking for a mobile feast, come here for a well-packaged meal with all the fixings. Seating is very limited, so most guests opt for takeout.

### NATE'S DELI $\$$
1923 W. 25th St., 216/696-7529
**HOURS:** Mon.-Fri. 10 A.M.-5 P.M., Sat. 10 A.M.-4 P.M.
A local institution, Nate's is reflective of Cleveland's rich ethnic diversity, and the city's love for all things delicious. Possessing a sort of edible split personality, this austere café serves traditional deli-style breakfast and lunch alongside Middle Eastern specialties. This means that while diners at one table are enjoying pastrami on rye and char-grilled burgers, their neighbors are cooing over a platter of hummus, tabbouleh, and stuffed grape leaves. On Saturdays this deli buzzes with shoppers fueling up for their trip to the nearby West Side Market.

## DESSERT
### A COOKIE AND A CUPCAKE $\$$
2173 Professor Ave., 216/344.9433,
www.acookieandacupcake.com
**HOURS:** Mon.-Sat. 11 A.M.-7 P.M.
Wendy Thompson, long an executive pastry chef, opened up this boutique bakeshop in 2008, next to Eye Candy Gallery. Wander in for hand-crafted cookies, brownies, macaroons, cupcakes, and vintage-style cakes. The signature cupcakes come in a dozen flavors that mirror those of the cakes: red velvet, German chocolate, carrot cake, and grasshopper, to name a few. Thompson also creates one-of-a-kind cakes for weddings and other special occasions; you can watch her decorate them in the shop's open kitchen.

### TREMONT SCOOPS $\$$
2362 Professor Ave., 216/781-0352,
www.tremontscoops.com
**HOURS:** Sun.-Thurs. noon-9 P.M., Fri.-Sat. noon-10 P.M., extended hours in summer
This great neighborhood ice-cream shop serves hand-dipped cups, cones, and sundaes in a wide variety of flavors. Delicious creations like

banana splits, dirt sundaes, and turtle delights are sold in two sizes so the little ones can have their own. There are also shakes, malts, floats, and smoothies.

## EASTERN EUROPEAN AND MEDITERRANEAN

### FAT CATS ⑤⑤

2061 W. 10th St., 216/579-0200,
www.coolplacestoeat.com

**HOURS:** Mon.-Thurs. 11 A.M.-3 P.M. and 4-10 P.M., Fri. 11 A.M.-3 P.M. and 4 P.M.-midnight, Sat. 4 P.M.-midnight

Along with Michael Symon's original Lola locale, Fat Cats was one of the first restaurants to set up shop in Tremont. Today, thanks to pioneering eateries such as these, Tremont has blossomed into a gourmand's playground. Fat Cats is tucked into an old house on the far end of a residential block, and this cozy bistro never fails to delight first-time visitors. Guests might come for the charm, but they invariably return for the delicious, eclectic comfort food. The seasonal Mediterranean offerings might include steamed mussels, roasted monkfish, grilled skirt steak, or braised veal shank. Copious portions, hospitable service, and modest prices make this restaurant a popular destination for both lunch and dinner.

### LOLITA ⑤⑤

900 Literary Rd., 216/771-5652,
www.lolabistro.com

**HOURS:** Tues.-Thurs. 5-11 P.M., Fri.-Sat. 5 P.M.-1 A.M., Sun. 4-9 P.M.

Michael Symon's downtown restaurant Lola may garner most of the national accolades, but many local Symon fans actually prefer this more inviting neighborhood bistro. Dimly lit and tragically hip, this place feels more like a wine bar than a restaurant. But the food, a well-executed blend of Mediterranean small, medium, and large plates, is far beyond what you'd ever find in an enoteca. Start with platters of house-cured charcuterie before moving on to wood-fired pizzas topped with roast suckling pig, duck prosciutto, or plump white

Michael Symon's more neighborhoody restaurant, Lolita.

COURTESY OF LOLA/LOLITA

anchovies. Amazing pastas, fresh fish, and wood-fired meats are good enough to leave even a politician speechless. Hit Lolita for happy hour 5–6:30 P.M. or 10 P.M. to close, when a half-pound Kobe burger topped with cheddar, bacon, and a fried egg costs just $5.

## 🄲 SOKOLOWSKI'S UNIVERSITY INN 💲💲

1201 University Rd., 216/771-9236,
www.sokolowskis.com
**HOURS:** Mon.-Thurs. 11 A.M.-3 P.M., Fri. 11 A.M.-3 P.M. and 5-9 P.M., Sat. 4-9 P.M.

There may be no more uniquely Cleveland restaurant than Sokolowski's, which opened in 1923 on the edge of Tremont. What makes this restaurant unique is the cafeteria-style dining. What makes it "Cleveland" is the smorgasbord of Eastern European delicacies. All manner of folks work their way down the chow line, loading up trays with heaping portions of stuffed cabbage, potato pancakes, pierogies, chicken *paprikash,* and rice pudding. This is comfort food in its purest form. The homey lodge-like dining room features a fireplace, live piano music, and a curious collection of ephemera that 90 years in business inevitably generates. Fans of the Travel Channel's *No Reservations* will undoubtedly recall the Cleveland episode where Tony Bourdain swooned over this place.

# MEXICAN
## MOMOCHO MOD MEX 💲💲

1835 Fulton Rd., 216/694-2122, www.momocho.com
**HOURS:** Tues.-Sat. 5 P.M.-2 A.M., Sun. 4-9:30 P.M.

Not your typical chips-and-salsa Mexican joint, this dark, clubby eatery elevates south-of-the-border cuisine to a delicious art form. Set in a two-story colonial, Momocho features a lively 1st-floor lounge and a more serene upstairs dining room. Locals stop in for a festive meal of appetizers and margaritas, starring smoked-trout guacamole and the rightly famous duck tamales. The smart ones stick around for the adobo braised pork or the *pepita*-crusted trout. When the weather is cooperating, this restaurant's lush and leafy patio comes alive with drinkers, diners, and daters.

# PUBS
## GREAT LAKES BREWING CO. 💲💲

2516 Market Ave., 216/771-4404,
www.greatlakesbrewing.com
**HOURS:** Mon.-Thurs. 11:30 A.M.-10:30 P.M., Fri.-Sat. 11:30 A.M.-11:30 P.M.

Housed in the former home of a seed and feed company, this saloon-style pub is equally famous for its world-class beer and the bullet holes in the vintage bar rumored to have come from Eliot Ness's pistol. To go with those wonderful suds is a menu of hearty pub classics like sausage samplers, burgers, fish-and-chips, and pot roast. Start with an order of the barley pretzels, which are made from spent grains leftover from the brewing process. Beer fans will want to visit on Friday or Saturday afternoon when free brewery tours are offered. Great Lakes operates a biodiesel bus (dubbed the Fatty Wagon) that shuttles diners to Indians games for $1 round-trip. If you're looking for a nice outdoor roost, this place has a great (doggie-friendly) sidewalk patio.

## THE HARP 💲💲

4408 Detroit Ave., 216/939-0200, www.the-harp.com
**HOURS:** Mon.-Thurs. 11 A.M.-10 P.M., Fri.-Sat. 11 A.M.-11 P.M., Sun. 11 A.M.-9 P.M.

Clevelanders have been coming to The Harp for years to enjoy hearty Irish fare, wonderful drink, and a great patio with Lake Erie views. Best sellers, apart from the Guinness and Jameson, include the corned beef and sauerkraut rolls, shepherd's pie, and the salmon boxty, a large potato pancake folded around salmon, veggies, and pesto cream sauce. Most of the items are made from the owner's traditional family recipes. There is festive live Irish music on Wednesday, Friday, and Saturday.

## OLD ANGLE 💲

1848 W. 25th St., 216/861-5643,
www.oldangletavern.com
**HOURS:** Mon.-Thurs. 4 P.M.-2:30 A.M., Fri.-Sun. 11:30-2:30 A.M.

Set in a former hardware store, this is not your typical shot-and-a-beer Irish pub. An ambitious renovation of the 100-year-old building resulted in a sleek, contemporary space

RESTAURANTS

boasting tin ceilings, tile flooring, and a lengthy mahogany bar. The food, too, rises above standard pub fare with an eclectic mix of appetizers, sandwiches, and entrées. Best among them are the fried ravioli, lamb stew, falafel, and hot ham sandwich. With plenty of hard surfaces, this joint can get rather loud when there is a band playing or a can't-miss sporting event on the large screen.

## THAI
### TY FUN THAI BISTRO $$

815 Jefferson Ave., 216/664-1000,
www.tyfunthaibistro.com
**HOURS:** Mon.-Thurs. 5-10 P.M., Fri.-Sat. 5-11 P.M.,
Sun. 5-9 P.M.

We wouldn't go so far as to say Ty Fun is the most authentic Thai restaurant in town, but it may be the sharpest. This petite urban bistro is tastefully decorated, with long banquettes dotted with vivid fabric and silky cushions. Food is presented on dramatic tableware, with intricately carved vegetable garnishes adorning each dish. The kitchen does wonders with soups and starters, like the perfectly balanced coconut chicken soup, moist chicken *satay*, and spicy fried fish cakes. Ty Fun also serves wonderful curries and a more than respectable pad Thai.

## WINE BARS
### ( BAR CENTO $$

1948 W. 25th St., 216/274-1010, www.barcento.com
**HOURS:** Sun.-Fri. 4:30 P.M.-2 A.M., Sat. noon-2 A.M.

The lively, mostly youthful staff at this bustling enoteca keep the mood buoyant. But that playfulness belies the serious culinary talent in the kitchen. Meals here can be as delightfully uncomplicated as carafes of house wine and plates of thin-sliced charcuterie, or as substantial as grilled Ohio lamb with white beans or olive oil–poached wild salmon. Picture-perfect Neapolitan-style pizzas fly out of the brick ovens topped with clams, pancetta, or locally foraged ramps (wild leeks). Daily specials like lasagna, meatballs, or sausage and peppers cost around $10. Open every day of the year until 2 A.M., Bar Cento is the favored late-night hangout for chefs and night owls.

# Detroit Shoreway and Edgewater    Map 3

## CAFÉS AND DINERS
### DINER ON CLIFTON $

11637 Clifton Blvd., 216/521-5003,
www.dineronclifton.com
**HOURS:** Mon.-Fri. 7 A.M.-11 P.M., Sat. 9 A.M.-11 P.M., Sun.
8 A.M.-11 P.M.

Since it opened in 1998, the Diner on Clifton has quietly become a Cleveland landmark. In the beginning it seemed the place had the feel of one of those flashy urban diners that focused more on beauty than bacon. Fortunately, that could not have been further from the truth. On top of a full slate of genuinely crafted and generously portioned diner classics (Greek salad, hot roast turkey, patty melt), Clifton offers wonderful breakfast items, some served all day long. Try the great stuffed omelets, corned-beef hash, pancakes, and French toast.

### GYPSY BEANS & BAKERY $

6425 Detroit Ave., 216/939-9009,
www.gypsybeans.com
**HOURS:** Sun.-Thurs. 7 A.M.-9 P.M., Fri.-Sat. 7 A.M.-11 P.M.

Situated at the epicenter of the burgeoning Detroit Shoreway neighborhood, and serving as its unofficial community center, Gypsy Beans is an independently owned and operated café. Open from early morning until late in the evening, the attractive double storefront serves coffee drinks, fresh-baked muffins and croissants, pasta salads, thick-crust pizza by the slice, and over-stuffed sandwiches. This is a great place to meet up before or after a show at Cleveland Public Theater.

## MEDITERRANEAN
### LUXE KITCHEN & LOUNGE 💲💲
6605 Detroit Ave., 216/916-8732,
www.luxecleveland.com
**HOURS:** Tues.-Sat. 5 P.M.-1 A.M., Sun. 11 A.M.-3 P.M.
With a wide range of small plates, shared plates, pizzas, and prix fixe dinners, this super-cool Mediterranean restaurant satisfies just about every taste, mood, and budget. A couple can sit in the lounge and nibble on a charcuterie plate and cheese board and split a bottle of wine for about $25. Small plates include pork and chicken kebabs, bacon-wrapped shrimp, and veal-stuffed peppers. For the main event there are thin-crust pizzas, pastas, and fun-spirited family-style meals. The stylish space features a salvaged art-deco bar, shabby-chic chandeliers, and a wine cellar built into an old bank vault. A DJ plays an amazing mix of retro and contemporary tunes. All bottles on the wine list are sold at $10 over retail. You can also grab wine to go at retail prices.

## PUBS
### PARKVIEW NITE CLUB 💲
1261 W. 58th St., 216/961-1341,
www.parkviewniteclub.com
**HOURS:** Mon.-Sat. 11 A.M.-11 P.M., Sun. 11 A.M.-10 P.M.
You won't find a cooler old-school Cleveland watering hole than the Parkview. Hidden away at the end of a block, this rowdy club pretty much has its own neighborhood. The crowd is as agreeably disparate as one can find, with rough-and-tumble blue collars, musicians, reporters, and politicians all seeking shelter from more conspicuous spots. This tavern's age and history are evident in the photos, memorabilia, and detritus that plaster the weathered walls. Come here for great burgers, fried walleye sandwiches, house-smoked pulled pork, and the ever-popular Sunday brunch featuring eggs Benedict and Bloody Marys. On Wednesday night, the Parkview hosts a rousing live blues jam.

## VIETNAMESE
### MINH-ANH VIETNAMESE RESTAURANT 💲
5428 Detroit Ave., 216/961-9671, www.minh-anh.com
**HOURS:** Mon.-Thurs. 11 A.M.-9:45 P.M., Fri. 11 A.M.-10:45 P.M., Sat. noon-10:45 P.M., Sun. noon-8:45 P.M.
What you won't find at Minh-Anh are swanky table settings and gregarious servers. What you will find is authentic home-style Vietnamese cuisine. This simple restaurant serves lacy crepes loaded with shrimp, vegetables, and fresh herbs. There are nearly a dozen soups, best of which is the cinnamon beef soup with rice noodles. Numerous vermicelli noodle dishes come topped with egg rolls, shrimp on sugar cane, or grilled pork. After dinner, walk next door to the Asian market to load up on ingredients like Sriracha hot sauce, fresh lemongrass, and fermented shrimp paste.

RESTAURANTS

# University Circle and Little Italy    Map 4

## BAKERIES
### CORBO'S BAKERY 💲
12210 Mayfield Rd., 216/421-8181, www.corbos.com
**HOURS:** Tues.-Sat. 8 A.M.-10 P.M., Sun. 8 A.M.-8 P.M.
Not to name-drop, but super-chef Mario Batali said, "Corbo's Bakery has the best *cassata* [cake] I have tried in the U.S.A." This long-standing Little Italy bakery is known far and wide as the source for delectable Italian sweets, treats, and classic desserts. If there is an Italian wedding happening within 100 miles of the shop, chances are good the bride and groom will be slicing into a Corbo's *cassata*. A move down the block has sacrificed a bit of the old-school charm in favor of space, comfort, and modernity, but there has been no loss in quality.

### PRESTI'S BAKERY & CAFÉ 💲
12101 Mayfield Rd., 216/421-3060,
www.prestisbakery.com
**HOURS:** Mon.-Thurs. 6 A.M.-9 P.M., Fri.-Sat. 6 A.M.-10 P.M., Sun. 6 A.M.-6 P.M.
In Little Italy, Presti is a name that carries some clout. To foodies, it is a name synonymous

with killer cannoli. This airy corner café is busy morning, noon, and night thanks to a full range of necessities, delicacies, and delights. Espresso and cappuccino attract the early-morning set, who on nice days take their cups outside to enjoy along with the newspaper. At lunch, students from nearby Case Western Reserve University pop in for slices of pizza, sandwiches, and soda. After work, folks drop by to pick up tidy white boxes laden with buttery cookies, flaky pastries, and those amazing cannoli.

## CAFÉS

### ALGEBRA TEA HOUSE $

2136 Murray Hill Rd., 216/421-9007, www.algebrateahouse.net
**HOURS:** Daily 10 A.M.-11 P.M.

As much a funky living collage as it is a teahouse, Algebra is the de facto bohemian hangout in Little Italy. The inside of this whimsical gypsy den is filled with original furniture, wall hangings, and paintings. The floor is a one-of-a-kind mosaic; the ceiling is hand-painted; the cups and saucers are the handiwork of artist-owner Ayman. Tea fans will find dozens of superior-quality flavors, including house blends. Light eats run mainly to salads, Lebanese dishes, and desserts. Try the hummus and pita platter or the toasted pita sandwich with cheese and veggies.

### ARABICA CAFÉ $

11300 Juniper Rd., 216/791-0300
**HOURS:** Mon.-Fri. 7 A.M.-10 P.M., Sat.-Sun. 7:30 A.M.-8 P.M.

The Arabica name has been a symbol of quality coffee in Cleveland for decades, with numerous outposts scattered about town. This café can be considered the headquarters if for no other reasons than size and location. Built into an old mansion on University Circle, the rambling coffeehouse features rooms of various shapes and sizes, plus a lovely patio. Popular with students from nearby Case Western Reserve University, who sip in the constant company of their laptops, Arabica serves salads, sandwiches, and desserts along with hot and cold caffeinated beverages.

© DOUGLAS TRATTNER

Arabica Café in University Circle satisfies the coffee crowd.

## EUROPEAN

### BARICELLI INN $$

2203 Cornell Rd., 216/791-6500, www.baricelli.com
**HOURS:** Mon.-Thurs. 5-10 P.M., Fri.-Sat. 5-11:30 P.M., open for lunch during holiday season

Set inside a 110-year-old mansion, the lovely Baricelli Inn is a special-occasion restaurant that doesn't have to be saved for special occasions. Long one of the priciest bistros in town, recent changes to the menu have softened the blow on pocketbooks by offering a more diverse range of options. Nationally recognized chef and owner Paul Minnillo still uses only the finest ingredients available, but he does so from a more casual frame of mind. Charcuterie and artisanal cheese boards, half orders of pasta, heritage cuts of meat, and fresh fish and seafood are some of the reasons why this place is so popular.

### L'ALBATROS $$

11401 Bellflower Rd., 216/791-7880, www.albatrosbrasserie.com
**HOURS:** Mon.-Wed. 11:30 A.M.-11 P.M., Thur.-Sat. 11:30 A.M.-12 A.M.

Situated inside a completely modernized 19th-century carriage house, L'Albatros is a contemporary French brasserie with loads of style. Set against this ultra-sleek backdrop is a menu overflowing with bistro classics, like onion soup gratinee, escargot, pork terrine and cassoulet. For those who prefer less far-flung tastes, there are pasta, fish and poultry dishes that satisfy just as heartily. Popular with the pre-theatre and orchestra set, the lively restaurant features items specifically selected for rapid enjoyment. In warm weather, in-the-know folks flock to this restaurant's idyllic tree-shaded patio for fine food and drink.

### LA DOLCE VITA $$

12112 Mayfield Rd., 216/721-8156,
www.ladolcevitacleveland.com
**HOURS:** Mon.-Thurs. 5-10 P.M., Fri.-Sat. noon-11 P.M.,
Sun. noon-10 P.M.

On pleasant days and nights, the prime sidewalk space surrounding this popular Little Italy restaurant is flooded with diners. The attitude is festive and light-hearted; the food is flavorful and unfussy. Consistently satisfying salads, pizzas, pastas, and Italian classics are dished up in large portions. Try the clams Tarantino, a pasta dish with clams and fresh zucchini, or the veal Pavarotti, made with portabella mushrooms and marsala wine. Visit on a Monday night and you'll enjoy live opera with your pizza.

### MICHAELANGELO'S $$$

2198 Murray Hill Rd., 216/721-0300,
www.mangelos.com
**HOURS:** Mon.-Thurs. 5:30-10 P.M., Fri.-Sat. 5:30-11 P.M.,
Sun. 5-9 P.M.

In a neighborhood that often dumbs down Italian food to match tourists' expectations, Michaelangelo's is a magnificent exception. Authentic and ambitious northern Italian cuisine is the order of the day at this elegant, well-appointed trattoria. Run by a Piedmont-trained chef, the restaurant serves cold and hot antipasti, handmade pastas in luxurious cream sauces, wine-braised meats, including boar, rabbit, and lamb, and fresh fish specials. If the veal cannelloni is on the menu, get it. Ethereal crepes are filled with ground veal and ricotta cheese and topped with a mascarpone cream sauce.

### VALENTINO'S PIZZA $

2197 Murray Hill Rd., 216/795-0463
**HOURS:** Mon.-Fri. 11 A.M.-11 P.M., Sat. 3-11 P.M.

You might expect a neighborhood called Little Italy to be crawling with amazing pizza joints, but in Cleveland you'd be wrong. Fortunately, there's Valentino's, the closest thing to a New York pie this side of Manhattan's West Side Highway. Thin-crusted yet floppy enough to fold, the pepperoni pizza is the real deal. But unlike in New York, you can enjoy your slice on a leafy outdoor patio. This small takeout-only shop also sells salads, meatball sandwiches, and above-average pasta dishes.

## MEDITERRANEAN
### SERGIO'S IN UNIVERSITY CIRCLE $$$

1903 Ford Dr., 216/231-1234,
www.sergioscleveland.com
**HOURS:** Mon.-Thurs. 11:30 A.M.-2:30 P.M. and
5-9:30 P.M., Fri. 11:30 A.M.-2:30 P.M. and 5-11 P.M.,
Sat. 5-11 P.M.

Sergio Abramof is one of Cleveland's most admired chefs and restaurateurs. To see why, make reservations at this sophisticated little restaurant next door to the Glidden House. Once a carriage house, the intimate space now serves fresh Mediterranean-inspired dishes with an emphasis on seafood. Occasional live music and a delightful patio overlooking the buildings of Case Western Reserve University make this spot popular with the pre-orchestra crowd.

### TABLE 45 $$$

9801 Carnegie Ave., 216/707-4045,
www.tbl45.com
**HOURS:** Sun.-Fri. 11 A.M.-11 P.M., Sat. 3-11 P.M.

In addition to Tremont's popular Parallax and nearby L'Albatros, chef Zack Bruell also operates this ultra-contemporary restaurant located inside the InterContinental Hotel. Relying on influences as varied as Moroccan, Indian, Asian, and Latin American, Table 45's eclectic menu might feature green-tomato gazpacho, naan pizza, five-spice short ribs, and tandoor-roasted chicken. Despite the range, these dishes have amazing focus and the flavors

**RESTAURANTS**

RESTAURANTS

© DOUGLAS TRATTNER

Have your pre-show supper at Sergio's in University Circle.

come across like a bolt of genius. Architecture and design fans will undoubtedly get a kick out of the minimal digs, which embrace white like no other.

## MEXICAN
### MI PUEBLO ⑤
11611 Euclid Ave., 216/791-8226
**HOURS:** Mon.-Wed. 11:30 A.M.-10 P.M., Thurs.-Sat. 11:30 A.M.-11 P.M., Sun. noon-9 P.M.
This laid-back Mexican restaurant serves some of the best chips and salsa, authentic soft tacos, and boozy margaritas in town. If you can steer yourself away from the chorizo tacos, try an order of the amazing enchiladas *suizas* (chicken-stuffed tortillas topped with creamy tomatillo sauce). Mole fans will want to try Mi Pueblo's version, which is dark, stormy, and sufficiently complex. On weekends, specials like *menudo* (tripe soup) and goat stew are available, and a strolling mariachi band adds a festive note.

# Cleveland Heights and Shaker Heights    Map 5

## BAKERIES
### 🌙 ON THE RISE ⑤
3471 Fairmount Blvd., 216/320-9923

**HOURS:** Tues.-Fri. 7 A.M.-6 P.M., Sat. 8 A.M.-5 P.M., Sun. 8 A.M.-2 P.M.

Cleveland Heights is blessed to have a trio of fantastic bakeries, and this charming little shop is one of them. Artisan baker Adam Gidlow crafts everything by hand in the old-fashioned European way, and eager fans arrive every morning to grab their daily bread and coffee. Come here for buttery scones and cookies, flaky croissants, dense and chewy focaccia and sourdough, and the best French baguette in Cleveland, if not Ohio. There is very limited seating inside, but on nice days you can sit outside.

## BREAKFAST
### BIG AL'S DINER ⑤
12600 Larchmere Blvd., 216/791-8550

**HOURS:** Mon.-Sat. 6:30 A.M.-2:30 P.M., Sun. 8 A.M.-2:30 P.M.

Greasy spoon? Neighborhood diner? Workingman's lunch spot? Whatever you call it, Al's is a cherished East Side institution. Get here before church lets out on weekends and you'll score one of the coveted booths, which offer room enough for both a newspaper and a plate of corned-beef hash. Located on the border of Cleveland and Shaker Heights, this popular diner is as diverse as they come, with progressive politicians rubbing shoulders with hungover hipsters and oil-stained auto mechanics. The draws here are monster portions of hearty home-style grub, like biscuits and gravy, blueberry pancakes, three-egg omelets, and the aforementioned corned-beef hash. Pay at the counter when you're done.

### INN ON COVENTRY ⑤
2785 Euclid Heights Blvd., 216/371-1811

**HOURS:** Mon.-Thurs. 7 A.M.-2:45 P.M., Fri. 7 A.M.-8:30 P.M., Sat.-Sun. 8 A.M.-2:45 P.M.

This homey café is *the* place to go on Coventry Road for hearty home-cooked breakfast fare.

Ricotta pancakes, over-stuffed omelets, and delish French toast are just a few of the reasons this place gets slammed most weekend mornings. The intimate place fills up fast and there is often a wait for a table, so once served and sated, a diner might feel rushed to move on. But take your time and enjoy creative wholesome and fresh breakfast fare before exploring the shops of Coventry.

## CAFÉS
### STONE OVEN ⑤
2267 Lee Rd., 216/932-3003, www.stone-oven.com

**HOURS:** Mon.-Thurs. 7 A.M.-9 P.M., Fri. 7 A.M.-10 P.M., Sat. 8 A.M.-10 P.M., Sun. 8:30 A.M.-8 P.M.

This other fine Cleveland Heights bakeshop is one of the most popular spots on Lee Road for a quick, casual lunch or dinner. This bright, airy contemporary café specializes in soups made daily, fresh salads, and gourmet sandwiches. Built atop wonderful house-baked bread, the sandwiches include egg salad and chive, chicken curry salad, and roast beef and Swiss with horseradish mayo. There is also a wonderful selection of pastries, cookies, and cakes. Outdoor dining is available behind the restaurant.

### 🌙 TOMMY'S ⑤
1824 Coventry Rd., 216/321-7757, www.tommyscoventry.com

**HOURS:** Sun.-Thurs. 9 A.M.-9 P.M., Fri. 9 A.M.-10 P.M., Sat. 7:30 A.M.-10 P.M.

What started out in the 1970s as a hippie-run soda fountain has become the anchor not only of Coventry Road, but of Coventry Village. Multiple locations and incarnations later, this bustling family-friendly café now commands a large and lovely space in the middle of the action. A lengthy menu features an amazing range of vegan, vegetarian, and meaty options, many of which are named after the owner's friends and customers. Soups are made daily from scratch, an entire page is devoted to fresh and inventive salads and meat and spinach pies, falafel sandwiches come with fillings too numerous to list, and the hand-dipped milk shakes are the best in the city.

**RESTAURANTS**

# DESSERT
## LA GELATERIA $

12421 Cedar Rd., 216/229-2636,
www.lagelateriacleveland.com
**HOURS:** Tues.-Sun. noon-10 P.M.

On balmy summer nights, many in the Heights make their way to this cheery little shop for out-of-this-world gelato. Made right here, the Italian version of ice cream is the preferred dessert for couples, families, and wandering souls in search of a sweet ending to the day. A wide range of milk- and fruit-based versions are available on a rotating basis. Flavors such as grapefruit, pistachio, tiramisu, and chocolate are sold in various sizes, from a diminutive cup to a half gallon. La Gelateria also has an authentic wood-burning pizza oven, which crisps up fine pies on most days.

# JAPANESE
## PACIFIC EAST $$

1763 Coventry Rd., 216/320-2302,
www.pacificeastcoventry.com
**HOURS:** Mon.-Fri. 11 A.M.-10 P.M., Sat. noon-11 P.M., Sun. 3-10 P.M.

When it comes to sushi, diners have two choices in this area for wonderful quality and construction. Pacific East lacks the polished decor of Sasa Matsu, and the sushi bar is small by comparison, but the à la carte sushi selection here is much more diverse. Sample crunchy freshwater crabs, monkish liver, tuna belly, and broiled yellowtail collar along with standards like salmon, sea urchin, and eel. The Japanese menu also offers the usual host of Asian salads, tempuras, yakitori, noodle bowls, and creative rolls. Unique to this locale is the region's only Malaysian menu.

## SASA MATSU $$

13120 Shaker Sq., 216/767-1111, www.sasamatsu.com
**HOURS:** Mon.-Sat. 5 P.M.-midnight, Sun. 5-10 P.M.

Cleveland's first and only *izakaya,* or Japanese-style tapas bar, Sasa is a treat for adventurous diners. In addition to wonderful sushi, sashimi, and specialty rolls, this contemporary lounge at Shaker Square boasts pages of out-of-the-ordinary small and medium-size plates. Dishes can be as simple as fresh-steamed edamame with sea salt or as elaborate as marinated sliced beef cooked tabletop on a heated river rock. Try the Kobe beef *gyoza,* addictive Sasa fries, or the best grilled mackerel around. For dessert, try the house-made chai ice cream. Sasa also has the largest sake selection in town, with approximately 40 imported and domestic varieties that range from crisp and cold to unfiltered and sweet.

# PIZZA
## DEWEY'S PIZZA $$

2194 Lee Rd., 216/321-7355,
www.deweyspizza.com
**HOURS:** Mon.-Thurs. 11 A.M.-10 P.M., Fri.-Sat. 11 A.M.-11 P.M., Sun. 4-10 P.M.

Kids love visiting Dewey's because they can watch through the glass as the pizza chefs toss, twirl, and stretch the dough. Parents love Dewey's because it is attractive, contemporary, and serves good beer and wine. The menu here is delightfully uncomplicated, featuring just fresh salads, hand-tossed pizzas and calzones, and a few desserts. Diners can design their own pies from a list of sauces, cheeses, and toppings, or simply select from a dozen gourmet pizzas.

# TURKISH
## ANATOLIA CAFÉ $$

2270 Lee Rd., 216/321-4400,
www.anatoliacafe.com
**HOURS:** Mon.-Fri. 11 A.M.-11 P.M., Sat. noon-11 P.M., Sun. noon-10 P.M.

This roomy upscale Turkish restaurant does a brisk business in refreshing dips, flavorful spit-roasted meats, and aromatic stews. Start with fresh-baked pita and platters of hummus and smoky baba ghanoush, a wonderfully aromatic lentil soup, lemony sautéed calf's liver, or fried phyllo fingers stuffed with feta and parsley. For dinner, choose from numerous grilled meat and fish kebabs. Better yet, order anything made with Anatolia's delicious *doner,* thin-shaved spit-roasted meat. In the *iskender,* the *doner* is stacked on pita chips, topped with tomato sauce, and served with creamy yogurt.

# CLEVELAND'S ETHNIC SMORGASBORD

Cleveland's melting-pot past and present means that fans of ethnic food have their pick of delicious, adventurous options. For those who prefer to stay at home, the region is blessed with extraordinary markets and groceries that cater to individual ethnicities and tastes.

To say that the Greater Cleveland area is home to a lot of ethnic eateries is a major understatement. For every bland national chain there are a dozen mom-and-pop shops dishing up authentic foods from the homeland. Scattered like mustard seeds across the landscape, these gems are just waiting to be discovered by adventurous eaters.

For an appetizer, consider the fact that Cleveland has restaurants devoted to Italian, Greek, German, Irish, Lebanese, Turkish, Hungarian, Slovenian, Ethiopian, Indian, Mexican, Central American, and Jewish foods, to name a few. Some neighborhoods, like Little Italy and AsiaTown, are densely populated with restaurants serving a specific cuisine. And for some reason, the West Side is disproportionately endowed with Mexican eateries.

So how do you choose? Consider beginning with something you've never tried before, like Ethiopian food at **Empress Taytu** (6125 St. Clair Ave., 216/391-9400). Meals here are served family-style at traditional basket tables, and silverware is replaced with spongy flatbread called *injera*. Ever tried Turkish food? It's a lot like Lebanese, only tastier. Visit **Anatolia Café** to see how good shish kebab can be. For more traditional Middle Eastern food pencil in a trip to **Nate's Deli** in Ohio City.

There may be no finer comfort food than Polish stuffed cabbage, and there may be no finer version than the one served at **Sokolowski's University Inn.** Folks come here for not just the rib-sticking food but also the quirky cafeteria arrangement and the cozy lodge-like dining room. As much a part of the Cleveland landscape as the Cuyahoga River, **Frank Sterle's Slovenian Country House** (1401 E. 55th St., 216/881-4181, www.sterlescountryhouse.com) attracts folks by the busload with made-from-scratch Eastern European delicacies like liver and onions, roast pork, and heavenly strudel. Hungarian food includes veal *paprikash*, beef goulash, and roast duck, but one out of four diners at **Balaton Restaurant** (13133 Shaker Sq., 216/921-9691) orders the Wiener schnitzel. These platter-size cutlets are pounded thin, breaded, and fried, and served with spaetzle and applesauce.

To sample some Brazilian food you can head either to **Brasa Grill**(1300 W. 9th St., 216/575-0699, www.brasagrillsteakhouse.com) or **Sarava** (13225 Shaker Sq., 216/295-1200, www.sergiosinthecircle.com). The former is a Brazilian steakhouse specializing in grilled and roasted meats served tableside by spit- and saber-wielding servers. The latter is a festive restaurant with Latin beats, tropical cocktails, and Brazilian street foods like fried smelt and spicy shrimp. When shopping at Eton, stop into **Paladar** (28601 Chagrin Blvd., 216/896-9020, www.paladarlatinkitchen.com) for creative, ambitious, and totally delicious Nuevo Latino fare.

If you've never tried a Cuban sandwich, you'll want to pay a visit to **Lelolai Bakery & Café** (1889 W. 25th St., 216/771-9956, www.lelolaibakery.com). The combination of pork, ham, Swiss cheese, pickles, and mustard might sound odd, but it all comes together when smooshed in a hot sandwich press. For some of the best and most authentic tacos, head west to **Mi Pueblo Taqueria** (12207 Lorain Ave., 216/671-6661)--sister to University Circle's Mi Pueblo--where warm corn tortillas are stuffed with carne asada, chorizo, beef tongue, and chicken. Next door to the restaurant is a fantastic Latin grocery where you can score some fresh-fried pork rinds.

Indian-food lovers come in one of two categories: vegetarians or omnivores. **Udupi Café** (6339 Olde York Rd., 440/743-7154) caters to the first group with vegetarian-only fare from southern India. Meat lovers might want to bypass Udupi in favor of **Café Tandoor** (2096 S. Taylor Rd., 216/371-8500, www.cafetandoorcleveland.com), a comfortable East Side restaurant serving mildly spiced northern Indian food.

© DOUGLAS TRATTNER

Felice Urban Café is like home away from home.

# UPSCALE
## FELICE URBAN CAFÉ $$
12502 Larchmere Blvd., 216/791-0918,
www.coolplacestoeat.com
**HOURS:** Tues.-Thurs. 4-10 P.M., Fri.-Sat. 4 P.M.-midnight

When it comes to curb appeal, Felice pretty much has a lock on the competition. Set in a restored Craftsman-style home, this intimate eatery is as cozy as they come. Arriving here for dinner feels more like dropping in on a friend than entering a public restaurant. Inside, diners discover the original leaded glass windows, warm wooden fixtures, and historic hearth. The eclectic menu features Mediterranean-inspired treats like grilled baby octopus, chorizo-spiked mussels, lamb sliders, and skirt steak with *chimichurri*. Out back there is a beautiful flagstone courtyard set beneath a towering oak.

## ◖ FIRE FOOD & DRINK $$$
13220 Shaker Sq., 216/921-3473,
www.firefoodanddrink.com
**HOURS:** Tues.-Thurs. 5-10 P.M., Fri.-Sat. 5-11 P.M., Sun. 10 A.M.-2 P.M. and 5-10 P.M.

Relying almost exclusively on local, seasonal, and sustainable ingredients, widely praised chef Doug Katz is well ahead of the national curve when it comes to "slow food." Located at Shaker Square, just steps from the largest farmers market in the region, this snazzy bistro serves simply prepared and robustly flavored American fare. Sit at the poured-concrete bar and enjoy a glass of wine and a clay-oven pizza. Or sit in the industrial-chic dining room and tuck into crispy chicken livers, tandoor-roasted pork chops, or diver scallops with Ohio sweet corn. Fire has an incredible Sunday brunch and boasts an expansive sidewalk patio overlooking the square.

# Lakewood

Map 6

## BREAKFAST
### WEST END TAVERN ❸

18514 Detroit Ave., 216/521-7684

**HOURS:** Daily 11 A.M.-2 A.M.

This comfortable neighborhood tavern has been a fixture in the western 'burbs for over two decades. You know the type: repurposed old storefront, creaky wood floors, tin ceilings, uncomfortable booths, gregarious bartenders, amazing wings. In addition to the great vibe, cold beer, and decent jukebox, the West End dishes up some mighty fine pub grub. Come on weekends for the beloved brunch starring the infamous Bloody Mary bar, where diners get to doctor up their hair of the dog any way they choose. There's food, too, like great eggs Benedict, stuffed French toast, roast-beef hash, and big-as-a-dinner-plate omelets.

## CASUAL AMERICAN
### BUCKEYE BEER ENGINE ❸

15315 Madison Ave., 216/226-2337,
www.buckeyebeerengine.com

**HOURS:** Mon.-Sat. 11 A.M.-midnight,
Sun. 10 A.M.-midnight

Artificially carbonated kegs, which essentially dispense themselves, rendered old-fashioned beer engines obsolete. But because this West Side tavern serves unfiltered, unpasteurized, and naturally carbonated cask-conditioned ale, that antiquated beer pump isn't so obsolete after all. Co-owned by the brewmaster of a local craft brewery, the Beer Engine takes suds seriously. Hopheads will find dozens of spectacular and hard-to-find drafts here, all served in style-appropriate glassware. And to go with those brews is a menu crammed with some 20 different half-pound burgers, with toppings that include pulled pork, smoked bacon, and fried eggs. The kitchen also offers hearty platters of pot roast, Wiener schnitzel, and fish-and-chips.

### MELT BAR AND GRILLED ❸❸

14718 Detroit Ave., 216/226-3699,
www.meltbarandgrilled.com

**HOURS:** Mon.-Thurs. 11 A.M.-11 P.M., Fri.-Sat.
11 A.M.-midnight, Sun. 10 A.M.-10 P.M.

In the relatively brief period since this restaurant opened in 2006, it has received props from *Esquire, USA Today,* and dozens of drooling food bloggers. What's all the fuss about? Grilled cheese—nearly three dozen wild and wonderful versions are currently on the menu. At this cool rock-fueled tavern, everybody's favorite childhood comfort food is contorted into tasty variations on the bread-and-cheese theme. Fillings range from crab cakes to peanut butter and banana. The Wake & Bacon is loaded with bacon, egg, and cheese; the Parmageddon is an intimidating stack of potato pierogies, kraut, onions, and cheese; and the Lake Erie Monster nets a diner deep-fried walleye, jalapeno tartar sauce, and—wait for it—*cheese!* Melt also has a superb beer selection.

## CONTEMPORARY AMERICAN
### PIER W ❸❸❸

12700 Lake Ave., 216/228-2250,
www.selectrestaurants.com

**HOURS:** Mon.-Thurs. 11:30 A.M.-2:30 P.M. and 5-10 P.M.,
Fri. 11:30 A.M.-2:30 P.M. and 5-11 P.M., Sat. 5-11 P.M.,
Sun. 4:30-9 P.M.

Despite being situated on the shores of a Great Lake, Cleveland is woefully underserved when it comes to lakeside restaurants. But having this sparkling West Side gem seems to make up for that deficiency. Located in a ritzy highrise west of town, the restaurant offers stunning views of the lake and Cleveland skyline. A tiered dining room means that none are left out on the fun. Unlike most "view" restaurants, this one actually serves great food. Diners can expect contemporary seafood dishes, like updated versions of crab Louis, bouillabaisse, and surf and turf. A great lounge offers a smallplate menu with mini-halibut tacos, Kobe sliders, and shrimp tempura. Come for the Sunday brunch; it's a bit pricey, but you won't be disappointed.

RESTAURANTS

### PLAYERS ON MADISON ❶❸

14523 Madison Ave., 216/226-5200,
www.playersonmadison.com
**HOURS:** Mon.-Thurs. 5-10 P.M., Fri.-Sat. 5-11 P.M.,
Sun. 5-9 P.M.

Housed in a light-filled double storefront, this bistro has a decidedly California feel to it. Blond hardwood flooring, a copper-top bar, and lemony walls give this popular date-night restaurant a cheery vibe. Diners can create their own pizza, calzone, or pasta dish by mixing and matching from a lengthy list of noodles, sauces, and gourmet toppings. There are also a number of creative appetizers, salads, and entrées, such as chipotle braised short ribs, pear-and-walnut-stuffed pork chops, and pumpkin ravioli. Players has a charming enclosed garden patio for outdoor dining, weather permitting.

### ◖ THREE BIRDS ❶❸❸

18515 Detroit Ave., 216/221-7480,
www.3birdsrestaurant.com
**HOURS:** Mon.-Thurs. 5-10 P.M., Fri.-Sat. 5-11 P.M.

The West Side has a reputation for trailing the East Side when it comes to high-quality chef-owned bistros; Three Birds is one of the few reasons East Side food snobs travel west of the Cuyahoga River. The interior is hip-industrial, with open kitchen, exposed HVAC systems, and massive floor-to-ceiling windows. Folks settle into comfortable booths to enjoy progressive ingredient-driven American cuisine. Seasonal foodstuffs are crafted into popular items like a salad with watermelon, radish, and feta, Maine lobster pizza with Manchego cheese, fried sweet-corn croquettes, and foie gras–topped duck breast. Three Birds has a dramatic garden courtyard set well back from the road, making it one of the loveliest places to dine alfresco in Cleveland.

## DESSERT
### MALLEY'S CHOCOLATES ❸

14822 Madison Ave., 216/529-6262, www.malleys.com
**HOURS:** Mon.-Thurs. 10 A.M.-10 P.M., Fri.-Sat.
10 A.M.-11 P.M., Sun. noon-10 P.M.

The Malley family has been making and selling fine chocolates in and around Cleveland since 1935. At this old-fashioned ice-cream parlor, guests can sit at a real soda fountain and pig out on amazing cones, shakes, and sundaes. This being a chocolate company, anything with hot fudge pretty much rules the night. Kids just love the decor, a pink-hued playground reminiscent of Grandma's kitchen. The candy counter is stocked with unique bars, holiday sweets, chocolate-covered cookies, dark chocolate–covered marshmallow, pecan-and-caramel clusters called Billy Bobs, and many others. Malley's is so popular in Cleveland that the store's characteristic "CHOC" stickers can be spotted on car bumpers throughout the city.

## FRENCH
### TARTINE BISTRO AND WINE BAR ❶❸

19110 Old Detroit Rd., Rocky River, 440/331-0800,
www.tartinebistro.com
**HOURS:** Mon. 4:30-11 P.M., Tues.-Thurs.
11:30 A.M.-2:30 P.M. and 4:30-11 P.M., Fri.-Sat.
11:30 A.M.-2:30 P.M. and 4:30 P.M.-midnight

This welcoming bistro and wine bar feels like an authentic slice of Paris in sleepy Rocky River, Ohio. Exposed-brick walls, a blood-red tin ceiling, and a sturdy old bar give this place its charm. A tightly constructed menu of French-inspired small plates and entrées is designed to pair well with the appealing Old World wine list. A tiny kitchen offers charcuterie plates, *tartines* (open-faced sandwiches), hearty mains, and really good pizza. A facade of French doors opens on warm evenings, uniting the outside and inside.

## MEXICAN
### EL TANGO TAQUERIA ❸

14224 Madison Ave., 216/226-9999
**HOURS:** Mon.-Sat. 11 A.M.-10 P.M.

The owner of this small, quirky, and undisputedly delicious taco shop hails from New Mexico, and the cornucopia of peppers he imports from there are roasted and ground on-site. Falling somewhere between Mexican and Southwestern, the menu features both authentic and creative Latino-style dishes. A fresh

Mexican salad is topped with salsa and chipotle cream dressing. The beef, chicken, pork, and veggie tacos, made with soft corn tortillas, are wonderful. Chicken burritos are stuffed with long-simmered meat and spices. If the green chile stew is available, get it.

# Greater Cleveland                                    Map 7

## CONTEMPORARY AMERICAN

### GROVEWOOD TAVERN AND WINE BAR ❸❸

17105 Grovewood Ave., 216/531-4900,
www.grovewoodtavern.com

**HOURS:** Sun.-Thurs. 5-10 P.M., Fri.-Sat. 5-11 P.M.

This unassuming tavern, slipped into a blue-collar neighborhood east of town, has consistently exceeded the expectations of diners who travel here for a delicious change of pace. The unpretentious saloon looks like any other buffalo wing–flinging bar, except this one serves upscale grub like barbecue fried crawfish, prosciutto-wrapped scallops, and honey-and-lavender-glazed chicken. And unlike any corner tavern we've experienced, this one offers over 100 wines by the bottle, with most of those also available by the glass. Pair a visit here for dinner with a show at nearby Beachland Ballroom.

### MOXIE ❸❸❸

3355 Richmond Rd., Beachwood, 216/831-5599,
www.moxietherestaurant.com

**HOURS:** Mon.-Thurs. 11:30 A.M.-10 P.M., Fri. 11:30 A.M.-11 P.M., Sat. 5:30-11 P.M.

Despite its suburban digs, this progressive American bistro has the contemporary feel of a downtown hotspot. And when the editors of *Gourmet* magazine pieced together their 2004 list of the best places to eat in America, Moxie made the cut. Praising chef Jonathan Bennett's dedication to quality ingredients and practiced technique, the magazine announced to the nation what Clevelanders have known for years: Bennett has a knack for assembling inventive, forward-thinking dishes that remain exceedingly approachable. Think artisanal cheese plates, roasted chicken livers with squash puree, house-smoked duck breast, and butter-roasted lobster knuckle with parsnip risotto. An in-house pastry chef crafts some of the finest desserts on the East Side.

## DELIS

### CORKY & LENNY'S ❸❸

27091 Chagrin Blvd., Beachwood, 216/464-3838,
www.corkyandlennys.com

**HOURS:** Sun.-Thurs. 7 A.M.-9:30 P.M., Fri.-Sat. 7 A.M.-11 P.M.

For over 50 years, this Jewish delicatessen has supplied Cleveland with its matzo-ball soup, smoked sable fish, potato knishes, and hearty stuffed cabbage dinners. Come early for busy breakfasts of lox, onions, and eggs, challah French toast, and Western omelets with corned beef. Lunches are all about mile-high deli sandwiches, hot turkey and mashed potatoes, and patty melts. For a real Cleveland treat, order your corned-beef sandwich on potato latkes instead of rye bread. You won't be able to stand afterwards, but you won't soon forget the experience either. Corky's has a great deli counter for quick take-out orders, deli trays, and baked goods.

**RESTAURANTS**

# NIGHTLIFE

Cleveland didn't score the Rock and Roll Hall of Fame because it is a snoozer of a town. The Moondog Coronation Ball, considered the world's first rock concert, was held here in 1952. Along with Record Rendezvous owner Leo Mintz, DJ Alan Freed promoted the concert that attracted tens of thousands of music fans to the old Cleveland Arena. (Granted, the fun was fleeting—the first rock concert quickly devolved into the first rock-concert riot.

Countless performers have emerged from Cleveland garages to go on to fame, including Screamin' Jay Hawkins, Glenn Schwartz, Michael Stanley, and Tracy Chapman. Today, music is as much a part of daily life as it was in the late 1950s. Countless venues are sprinkled throughout town, beckoning fans with live jazz, rock, blues, metal, and alt-country lineups.

Cleveland's long, cold winters seem to spawn new bars by the shovelful. Locals elect to hibernate in snug taverns with warm fireplaces, good wine, and hearty grub. While corner bars are far and away the most prevalent dens, Cleveland also is chock-full of wine bars, beer halls, martini lounges, and dance clubs. The city has a robust and proud GLBT community, and as such there is no shortage of gay-friendly bars, restaurants, and events.

If and when spring does finally arrive, locals are eager to move the party outdoors. Restless from a long, slothful season and an ample dose of cabin fever, folks scramble to bars with patios, courtyards, sidewalks, and rooftop decks and stay there until the first snowfall forces them back indoors.

COURTESY OF POSITIVELY CLEVELAND

# HIGHLIGHTS

LOOK FOR  TO FIND RECOMMENDED NIGHTLIFE.

**( Best Place to Drink with Fido:** Scattered beneath a cluster of old-growth trees, the picnic tables at **Barking Spider Tavern** fill up fast on warm summer nights. Many people come with their well-behaved pooches to enjoy pitchers of beer and live acoustic music emanating from an old carriage house (page 78).

**( Sweetest Jukebox:** Thanks to Internet jukeboxes, bar patrons have access to nearly limitless music catalogues. If that is progress, why do so many rock fans swoon over the vintage Rock-Ola at **Beachland Ballroom**? Because it's loaded with 80 hand-picked vinyl 45s – one of the most beautiful things a rock-and-roller will ever see (page 78).

**( Best Place to Drink on a Chilly Night:** **Prosperity Social Club** is always a welcoming place to enjoy a cocktail. But thanks to a free-standing wood-burning stove that fills the room with warmth, fragrance, and cheer, wintertime might be the best time of all (page 83).

**( All-time Best Bar Game:** While we have nothing against pool, darts, or pinball, isn't it time for a change of pace? Folks looking for the new game in town visit **Stone Mad Irish Pub,** where a full-size sunken bocce court keeps them pleasantly amused all year long. (Runner-up: the Cornhole boxes at Around the Corner Saloon.) (page 84)

**( Best Underground Wine Bar:** Located 15 feet below Coventry Road, **La Cave du Vin** is a grotto-like wine bar with a spectacular 500-bottle list. If wine isn't your bag, select from nearly 200 beers in the self-serve display coolers (page 86).

**( Most Picturesque Sidewalk Patio:** By definition, sidewalk patios are situated alongside streets, and as such are exposed to noise, dust, and unwelcome finger gestures. **Market Avenue Wine Bar** is located on Market Avenue, a short tree-lined cobblestone lane that sees

**The cool kids take a break from the bands at the Beachland Ballroom.**

very little auto traffic. Views here are of people, dogs, and a tony urban bistro (page 86).

**( City's Finest Cocktail:** The Ramos Gin Fizz, as constructed by the pros at **Velvet Tango Room,** tastes like clouds and sunshine. Built gram by gram on a chemist's scale to ensure consistency, the drink contains small-batch gin, orange blossom water, fresh cream, and egg whites. Shake it all together and you get the most delicious taste ever (page 90).

**( Funniest Seat in the House:** Nick Kostis is a brilliant judge of up-and-coming comedic talent, and his club, **Hilarities 4th Street Theater,** is the place to catch them. This upscale 425-seat comedy club attracts the very best touring comics, and the theater is as nice as they come (page 90).

NIGHTLIFE

# Live Music

### ◖ BARKING SPIDER TAVERN

11310 Juniper Rd., 216/421-2863,
www.barkingspidertavern.com

**HOURS:** Mon.-Sat. 2 P.M.-1 A.M., Sun. 1 P.M.-midnight

**Map 4**

Located in an alleyway in the middle of the Case Western Reserve University campus, this laid-back venue requires more than an address and a good map to find. Look for Arabica Café, then listen for the live acoustic music emanating from a converted carriage house. Performing nightly at this small tavern are singer-songwriter, folk, blues, and bluegrass acts. There is never a cover charge, but guests are encouraged to add to the tip jar as it makes its rounds. On balmy nights, the outdoor picnic tables are filled with well-behaved locals sharing pitchers of beer, many with their dogs in tow.

### ◖ BEACHLAND BALLROOM

15711 Waterloo Rd., 216/383-1124,
www.beachlandballroom.com

**HOURS:** Vary depending on show

**Map 7**

What once served as a Croatian social hall is now one of the coolest places to catch live music in Ohio. The popular concert venue is comprised of an intimate tavern and a large ballroom, both original to the 1950 structure. Attracted by an eclectic roster of local, regional, and national acts, not to mention the unique setting, live-music fans travel here from as far away as Columbus, Pittsburgh, and Detroit. Grab a bite to eat before shows in the tavern. While you're in there, check out the vintage 80-record Rock-Ola jukebox that *Blender* magazine labeled in 2008 as the best in the country.

The Barking Spider Tavern is hard to find but worth the effort.

© DOUGLAS TRATTNER

NIGHTLIFE

# HOUSE OF SWING

Cleveland music fans have their pick of awesome clubs for catching live acts. Tops among them are **Beachland Ballroom, Grog Shop,** and **Nighttown.** But for over three decades, a tiny East Side club has been packing in die-hard jazz, blues, and swing fans.

In 1977, Lou Kallie opened the **House of Swing** (4490 Mayfield Rd., 216/382-2771) simply to give his massive record collection a permanent home. His 15,000 vintage jazz and swing platters are crammed into the rear of the club, serving as a backdrop to the bands that perform. Those bands – electrifying R & B and swing groups – often attract so many people that this House becomes standing room only.

During set breaks, a staffer or very privileged regular will walk back to the impressive stacks, reach for an obscure Krupa or Coltrane, and gingerly place it on the turntable. Watching it all transpire is Lou Kallie, whose ashes are part of the ephemera that bedecks every square inch of the joint.

## BROTHERS LOUNGE

11607 Detroit Ave., 216/226-2767, www.brotherslounge.com
**HOURS:** Mon.-Fri. 11:30 A.M.-2 A.M., Sat.-Sun. 3 P.M.-2 A.M.
**Map 3**

A multimillion-dollar renovation of this historic blues club has transformed it into a sleek entertainment complex with neighborhood pub, wine bar, and concert hall. Amish oak flooring, mahogany bars, and a high-tech sound system conspire to create an upscale musical experience not found at most clubs. There is a nightly lineup of local, regional, and national acts, and a great house band that plays every Sunday. Open-mic nights and jam sessions allow others to get in on the action. Don't bother eating elsewhere before or after the show—this place also dishes up some mighty fine grub.

## GROG SHOP

2785 Euclid Heights Blvd., 216/321-5588, www.grogshop.gs
**HOURS:** Daily 7 P.M.-2 A.M.
**Map 5**

The original Grog Shop smelled foul, sounded worse, and looked as if it was designed by a blind architect. Still, when the gritty Grog lost its lease and was forced to start anew, musicians and fans cried in their beers. These days, nobody misses that old club too much thanks to bigger, better, and sweeter-sounding digs. But it's a rock-and-roll club, and this joint is by no means posh. Cement floors, concrete columns, and a growing collection of promo photos and band stickers keep this place real. Owner Kathy Simkoff has a knack for spotting talent early on, and the rock, grunge, and garage bands that break here often move on to greatness.

## NIGHTTOWN

12387 Cedar Rd., 216/795-0550, www.nighttowncleveland.com
**HOURS:** Daily 11:30 A.M.-1 A.M.
**Map 5**

Reminiscent of the old-school jazz clubs one used to be able to find in Manhattan, Nighttown is a one-stop shop for killer music, great grub, and sparkling conversation. Named by *Down Beat* magazine as one of the 100 Great Jazz Clubs in the world, this joint snags the biggest names in music as they travel between Chicago and New York. Cleveland Heights is known for its diverse and progressive populace, and this club acts as the neighborhood's living room. An eclectic crowd gathers for dinner shows, cocktails at the bar, or to enjoy a warm night on the roomy patio. Seating for shows is on a first-come, first-served basis, and it's always wise to reserve your ticket in advance.

## PEABODY'S CONCERT CLUB

2083 E. 21st St., 216/776-9999, www.peabodys.com
**HOURS:** Vary depending on show
**Map 1**

When this storied Cleveland club was located in the Flats, it welcomed every big name that traveled between New York and Chicago, including Pearl Jam, the Red Hot Chili Peppers, and

**NIGHTLIFE**

R.E.M. A new location and new management bode well for the venue, now located downtown by the Cleveland State University campus. The two-story concert club has three performance stages that range from small and intimate to big and loud. Up-and-coming rock bands still make stops here, and the line-up can include some real gems. This venue is also a favorite of legendary local acts who never fail to attract a following.

### WILBERT'S FOOD & MUSIC
812 Huron Rd. E., 216/902-4663,
www.wilbertsmusic.com
**HOURS:** Vary depending on show
`Map 1`

Another club with deep Cleveland roots, Wilbert's has seen its share of superstars. Jeff Buckley, Ryan Adams, Buckwheat Zydeco, and Buddy Guy have all played either here or at the club's previous site. Performing in the modern, spacious, and comfortable club are mainly local and regional blues, jazz, reggae, and roots-rock acts. The venue's location right by Progressive Field makes it a convenient post-game stop for live music. Wilbert's serves food with a Mexican and Southern slant, with items such as quesadillas, burritos, and barbecue ribs.

### WINCHESTER TAVERN AND CONCERT CLUB
12112 Madison Ave., 216/226-5681,
www.thewinchester.net
**HOURS:** Vary depending on show
`Map 6`

The Winchester is a special place. Formerly a bowling alley, the neighborhood tavern and ballroom were designed to emphasize comfort, value, and musical enjoyment. There are seats enough for all who want them and the bands sound amazing. If you enjoy screeching metal, mosh pits, and beer-soaked fans, the Winchester might not be for you. But if great old acts like Leon Russell, Howard Jones, the Fixx, and the English Beat, served up in a sweet old room, sound like your thing, this place will feel like nirvana. Musicians seek this place out because of its size, sound, and appreciative audience. Check the website frequently to see which legends of jazz, rock, rockabilly, alt-country, and bluegrass will be gracing the stage.

# Bars

### AROUND THE CORNER SALOON
18616 Detroit Ave., 216/521-4413, www.atccafe.com
**HOURS:** Mon.-Thurs. 3 P.M.-2 A.M., Fri.-Sat. 11 A.M.-2 A.M.,
Sun. 10 A.M.-2 A.M.
`Map 6`

As the crowds at this meet-and-greet tavern continued to grow, so too did the bar's footprint. What started out as a one-room corner saloon has ballooned into a multidimensional hotspot with the largest and best drinking patio in Lakewood, graced with a full bar, flat-screen TVs, and amusing Midwestern yard games so there's rarely a good reason to head inside (snow included, thanks to protection and heating). Come on Monday for two-for-one hamburgers or any weekday 3–7 P.M. for $5 pitchers. A profusion of single guys and girls makes this place hook-up central.

### FIVE O'CLOCK LOUNGE
11904 Detroit Ave., 216/521-4906
**HOURS:** Mon.-Sat. 2 P.M.-2:30 A.M.,
Sun. 8 P.M.-2:30 A.M.
`Map 6`

Like any great neighborhood dive, the Five offers cheap beer, uncomfortable seats, and well-spun rock and roll. Come around happy hour and the crowd is strictly gin-blossomed regulars, noses firmly ensconced in beer mugs. But like the hands on an analog timepiece, the atmosphere here is always shifting. On weekend nights, the better-dressed set scuttles into large round booths, the padding flattened by 70 years of abuse, to while away the night gripping and sipping PBR tallboys. DJs spin a tasty mix of rock, punk, and new wave, and the occasional live band hits the small stage.

# PUB CRAWL, ANYONE?

Clevelanders love themselves a good pub crawl. Maybe it's the gray skies, chilly night air, or the fact that their pro sports teams always find a way to blow it – locals here spend a lot of time in bars.

Cleveland is blessed with old-fashioned neighborhoods, the kind with a Main Street densely populated with pubs, taverns, saloons, and corner bars. One of the best ways to experience the local color is by working one's way down the block, popping into every single drinking establishment along the way. Better yet, just pick a few that look inviting.

A great way to get to know Tremont is from the inside of a bar. People come from all over to soak up this district's café culture, hitting a procession of galleries, bistros, and bars. Start your trek at **Edison's Pub** (2373 Professor Ave., 216/522-0006, www.edisonspub. com), a cozy den serving great imported beers. Friendly folks, knowledgeable bartenders, and decent pizza make this place a must-crawl. Next up is the **Flying Monkey Pub,** a handsome tavern filled with hand-crafted wood furnishings. The only gimmick here is the monkey mascot that pops out of his hidey-hole late at night. Dive-bar fans will swoon over **Hotz Café** (2529 W. 10th St., 216/771-7004), an old-school Cleveland bar that's been around since 1919. One block west is **Prosperity Social Club,** a retro saloon popular with every demographic. Folks here take seats at the 1930s bar or, on cold nights, around the blazing wood-burning stove.

What's the sense in paying one's tab and heading to an identical bar down the block? Diversity is precisely what makes Ohio City the pinnacle of pub-crawl locales. Beer aficionados have the one-two punch of **Great Lakes Brewing Co.** and **McNulty's Bier Markt.** The former brews and serves matchless American suds in a woodsy pub setting. The latter specializes in Belgian and Belgian-style ales on tap and in bottles. Wine lovers are treated to **Market Avenue Wine Bar,** a European-like jewel with an amazing by-the-glass and bottle selection of wine. If a contemporary Irish bar sounds tempting, pop into **Old Angle.** Set in a renovated hardware store,

Grab a glass of wine at Market Avenue Wine Bar during your Ohio City pub crawl.

this pub is not your typical shamrock shack. One of the liveliest places to go for last call is **Garage Bar,** a high-energy bar with loud rock, interesting people, and cheap shots.

Lee Road in Cleveland Heights is a pub-crawler's dream. Packed into a short 1,500-foot strip is a wide array of welcoming watering holes. Start at the intersection of Cedar and Lee Roads, near the glowing movie marquee, and work your way south. **Parnell's Pub** is an Irish-themed sports pub with Guinness on tap, darts in back, and a map of Europe that conspicuously omits England. If it's Tuesday or Thursday, cross the street and head to **Lopez** (2196 Lee Rd., 216/932-9000, www. lopezonlee.com), a trendy Southwestern restaurant. Thanks to half-price margaritas and tequila drinks, this place fills up fast. On the same side of the street a little further south is **Tavern Co.** (2260 Lee Rd., 216/321-6001). This place changes from family-friendly tavern to locals-only bar as the night progresses. Cap off the night at **Brennan's Colony** (2299 Lee Rd., 216/371-1010), a neighborhood institution that has attracted crowds for decades. On warm nights, make sure to check out the secluded courtyard and bar.

### FLYING MONKEY PUB

819 Jefferson Ave., 216/861-6659,
www.flyingmonkeypub.com
**HOURS:** Daily 4 P.M.-2:30 A.M.
**Map 2**

This welcoming Tremont pub is one of the most handsome drinking establishments around. Two lengthy bars were constructed in mosaic fashion from a variety of attractive hardwoods. Tables are hand-crafted from fine woods too, but these familiar patterns do double duty as chess, checkers, and backgammon boards. A unique belt-driven system spins every ceiling fan in the house with a single motor. Despite the luxe touches, the Monkey is as low-key as they come. That is, until the pleas for the monkey force the little (faux) mascot from his hidey hole, causing the room to erupt in cheers.

### GARAGE BAR

1859 W. 25th St., 216/696-7772, www.thegaragebar.net
**HOURS:** Daily 4 P.M.-2:30 A.M.
**Map 2**

If it wasn't such a blast, Garage Bar might be taken for a grease monkey–themed gimmick. Shiny diamond plate lines the walls, vintage gas pumps dispense cold beer, and glossy racing stripes scream down the bar top. But this rock-and-roll bar has the street cred to back it up, as demonstrated by the number of motorcycles that rumble up to its door. Granted, many of those bikes are ridden by pony-tailed lawyers and tattooed accountants, but still. On any given night, the turntables might be spinning rockabilly, grunge, or '80s hair metal. In summer, a massive back patio erupts into a rowdy block party complete with hot dogs, hamburgers, and trucker caps.

### HAPPY DOG

5801 Detroit Ave., 216/651-9474,
www.happydog58.com
**HOURS:** Mon.-Sat. 4 P.M.-2 A.M., Sun. 10 A.M.-2 A.M.
**Map 3**

Happy Dog is a prime example of what makes Cleveland special. While developers in other cities take pride in knocking down the old to make room for the new, folks here cling to the past with stubborn determination. You just don't find bars like this elsewhere, save for those ironic replicas built to satisfy urban hipsters. Happy Dog's most impressive feature is its august wooden bar, a 45-stool elliptical behemoth that commands a full third of the room. Original wood-fronted coolers chill the beverages; walls are wrapped in genuine wood paneling; shabby (not shabby-chic) linoleum blankets the floor. This neighborhood tavern stays true to its ethnic roots by serving up pierogies, Polish beer, and family-appropriate behavior. Stop by on Friday afternoons for the lively polka happy hours.

### MAJOR HOOPPLES

1930 Columbus Rd., 216/575-0483, www.hoopples.com
**HOURS:** Mon.-Sat. 11:30 A.M.-2:30 A.M.
**Map 2**

There are a handful of things every Clevelander must do before they die or move to Florida. One of them is to catch a walleye on Lake Erie. Another is to make a Thursday-night pilgrimage to Hoopples to watch the Schwartz brothers perform. Glenn Schwartz was the founding guitarist of the Cleveland-based James Gang, and he plays off-the-hook blues and rock sets each week at this tiny club. But the truth is, many come just to watch Schwartz's completely unhinged rantings on women, modern life, and the end of time, which occur with alarming regularity. Even if it isn't Thursday, this out-of-the-way workingman's tavern is worth a visit. Rock-bottom prices, sweet views of the industrial Flats, and salt-of-the-earth folks keep this legend rocking decade in and decade out.

### MCNULTY'S BIER MARKT

1948 W. 25th St., 216/344-9944, www.bier-markt.com
**HOURS:** Sun.-Fri. 4:30 P.M.-2:30 A.M., Sat. noon-2:30 A.M.
**Map 2**

Don't know your *lambics* from your *saisons*? Try them all in this dimly lit beer hall that dispenses some 20 varieties of Belgian and Belgian-style ales on tap—with the appropriate glassware to match—plus an additional 80 or so in bottles. A favorite among hip Ohio City residents, suburbanite pub-crawlers, and the odd bachelorette party, the atmosphere tends to reflect the occupants. Depending on the day or hour, the scene can be quiet and sleepy or bawdy and raucous. But what never seems to change is the top-flight service, matchless beer selection, and super-cool setting. With Bar Cento located in the same building, good food is just an order away.

© DOUGLAS TRATTNER

## PARNELL'S PUB

2167 Lee Rd., 216/321-3469,
www.myspace.com/parnellspub
**HOURS:** Mon.-Thurs. 6 P.M.-2 A.M., Fri. 5 P.M.-2 A.M.,
Sat.-Sun. 4 P.M.-2 A.M.
`Map 5`

You can't pen a St. Patrick's Day story in Cleveland without including this perennially popular Irish pub. As if the perfect pints of Guinness, bona fide Irish ownership, and a real bristle dartboard weren't enough, this is also the place to go to watch World Cup soccer, regardless of the hour when games are televised. Located directly next door to the Cedar Lee Theatre, this pub makes an ideal pre- or post-flick meet-up spot. A simple menu of deep-fried tidbits offers drinkers enough sustenance to endure a long night of liquid recreation.

Prosperity Social Club in Tremont is retro-cool and cozy.

## 〖 PROSPERITY SOCIAL CLUB

1109 Starkweather Ave., 216/937-1938,
www.prosperitysocialclub.com
**HOURS:** Mon.-Sat. 4 P.M.-2:30 A.M., Sun. 4-10 P.M.
`Map 2`

If you're looking for a laid-back neighborhood bar with decades-old authenticity, look no further than Prosperity. Owner Bonnie Flinner took a 75-year-old shot-and-beer joint and transformed it into a rustic-chic tavern with good food and better drink. There are no hokey themes here, just real folks meeting up for some conversation, occasional live music, and above-average pub grub. A freestanding wood stove adds wintertime charm to the barroom, while a rec room with pool table, antique bowling machine, and classic board games adds a bit of wholesome fun. Come on weekdays 4–7 P.M. for great deals during happy hour. A garden-style patio is furnished with mid-century modern chairs.

## SHOOTER'S

1148 Main Ave., 216/861-6900, www.shootersflats.com
**HOURS:** Daily 11:30 A.M.-close
`Map 1`

Thanks to a massive commercial and residential development project, much of the Flats is inaccessible to diners and drinkers. Fortunately, there's Shooter's, a long-loved riverside bar and eatery. During the summer, there are few better places to unwind with a cocktail and watch the boat traffic cruise up and down the Cuyahoga. An outdoor bar and stage for live music keep this place hopping most nights, but especially so on weekends. To go with the nautical theme, a seafood-centric menu with items like shrimp cocktails, crab legs, and lobster rolls is available all year long. During the off-season, the place slows down considerably, and the patio is all but put to bed.

NIGHTLIFE

## ◖ STONE MAD IRISH PUB

1306 W. 65th St., 216/281-6500
**HOURS:** Daily 11 A.M.-2:30 A.M.
**Map 3**

It took owner Pete Leneghan three years and untold dollars to construct this new Irish bar in Detroit Shoreway. What took so long? A stickler for quality craftsmanship, Leneghan made certain that every single element in the place was constructed using the finest materials and methods possible. From the hand-laid cobblestone parking lot and oil-rubbed walnut bars to the stained-glass windows and intricately carved ironwork, this stunningly attractive space is loaded with eye candy. The sizeable pub boasts two separate barrooms, a casual dining room with sunken bocce court, and an outdoor courtyard featuring stone-slab tables and a towering four-sided fireplace.

## TREMONT TAP HOUSE

2572 Scranton Rd., 216/298-4451,
www.tremonttaphouse.com
**HOURS:** Mon.-Sat. 4 P.M.-2 A.M., Sun. 10 A.M.-2 A.M.
**Map 2**

This great gastropub is a few blocks away from the more heavily trafficked areas of Tremont, so it requires a special effort to get here. But hopheads have been doing just that once they stumbled across the matchless draft beer selection available here. Some two dozen craft beers, many rare and exclusive to this locale, are on tap. Loads more are sold by the bottle. A scrupulous beer menu lists each variety's style, alcohol level, glassware, and price. This being a gastropub, guests can count on a menu loaded with well-executed upscale comfort foods. Visit the pub-side patio in the summer.

## WINKING LIZARD TAVERN

1852 Coventry Rd., 216/397-8380,
www.winkinglizard.com
**HOURS:** Mon.-Thurs. 11 A.M.-1 A.M., Fri.-Sat. 11 A.M.-2 A.M., Sun. noon-midnight
**Map 5**

This local chain of taverns has grown to over a dozen locations in about 20 years. Following a formula for success that includes great food and drink served in a comfortable, quirky setting, the Lizard can always be counted on to satisfy a crowd. This homegrown restaurant group also deserves props for electing to reuse vacant properties instead of knocking down and building anew. That means each location has its own unique feel (and a live lizard mascot). This setting once housed the famous Turkey Ridge Tavern, so it's nice to see it getting good use. Expect the bar and dining room to be filled with large parties of college students, sports-obsessed professionals, and buffalo-wing connoisseurs. If you plan on sticking around Northeast Ohio, sign up for the Lizard's legendary World Tour. Simply drink all 100 beers on the list in one calendar year and you'll be the proud owner of a, ahem, jacket vest.

# Wine Bars

### D'VINE WINE BAR

836 W. St. Clair Ave., 216/241-8463,
www.dvinewinebar.com

**HOURS:** Mon.-Thurs. 4 P.M.-1 A.M., Fri.-Sat. 4 P.M.-2 A.M.,
Sun. 6 P.M.-midnight

**Map 1**

At times it feels like the staff here is more serious about wine than the clientele, but to each his or her own. This trendy Warehouse District boîte offers a great selection of wine flights, each with four two-ounce pours that adhere to a theme. Grouped by varietal, wine-growing region, or style, the flights are like personal tastings. Exposed brick walls, flickering candlelight, and lofty warehouse ceilings attract couples looking for a romantic getaway. Come early on warm afternoons to snag one of the coveted sidewalk tables. An interesting tapas menu is comprised of enough tasty wine-friendly bites to cobble together a decent meal.

### 806 WINE & MARTINI BAR

806 Literary Rd., 216/862-2912,
www.806martinibar.com

**HOURS:** Tues.-Sat. 4 P.M.-2 A.M.

**Map 2**

To find this swanky Tremont wine and martini bar, simply look for the building-size mural of a high-stepping flapper. Like the speakeasies of the late 1920s, 806 strives for sophisticated but under-the-radar appeal. Behind a plain brick facade is a luxurious interior boasting cherrywood walls, black granite bar tops, and 12-foot molded ceilings. The largely affluent crowd sips martinis, classic cocktails, or glasses of wine before scurrying off to dinner at any of the nearby bistros.

NIGHTLIFE

© DOUGLAS TRATTNER

**Lofty flights of wine are on tap at D'Vine Wine Bar.**

# THE FLATS: PAST, PRESENT, AND FUTURE

Clevelanders are often surprised when they hear out-of-towners still asking about the Flats. While the area once was widely recognized as a nightlife mecca, it hasn't been that way for years. Most of the bars, nightclubs, and restaurants that once lined Old River Road are long gone. But soon, the Flats will enter a brand-new chapter in its long and colorful history.

The wide, flat floodplain on either side of the Cuyahoga River known as the Flats has played a prominent role in the history of Cleveland. The area's first settlers called it home, followed by boat docks, flophouses, shipyards, rail stations, steel mills, lumberyards, and chemical factories.

In the late 1980s and early 1990s, the east and west banks of the Flats had become a playground for adults from throughout the Midwest. The old warehouses that lined the streets were transformed into bars, live-music venues, seafood restaurants, dance clubs, and brewpubs. Fancy boats docked three deep along the piers. Water taxis shuttled partiers from one side of the river to the other. In short, it was one of the most popular entertainment districts in the country.

Crime, mismanagement of clubs, and the development of the Warehouse District ultimately shuttered most businesses on the east bank of the Flats, but the west bank has done considerably better. This is where you'll find **Shooter's, Improv, Howl at the Moon Saloon** (2000 Sycamore St., 216/771-4695, www.howlatthemoon.com), **Rock Bottom Brewery** (2000 Sycamore St., 216/623-1555, www.rockbottom.com), and **Plain Dealer Pavilion** (now called **Nautica Pavilion**). This is also where folks catch a ride on **Lolly the Trolly** and board the **Nautica Queen** (216/696-8888, www.nauticaqueen.com) riverboat dinner cruise. Sharp glass-and-steel condos have been built and filled, and there appear to be more on the way.

But the news is not all grim for the east bank. The Wolstein Group has begun a massive development project that will include residential and commercial properties, restaurants and entertainment venues, retail shops and markets. After some significant holdouts, all the property has been acquired and demolished to make room for the project, which is scheduled for completion in 2010.

During the summer, an equally well-appointed courtyard opens for alfresco refreshments.

## ( LA CAVE DU VIN

2785 Euclid Heights Blvd., 216/932-6411, www.lacaveduvin.com

**HOURS:** Mon.-Sat. 5 P.M.-2 A.M., Sun. 7 P.M.-2 A.M.

**Map 5**

This subterranean cave satisfies both grape and grain lovers thanks to a stellar beer and wine selection. Who needs natural light when you've got a well-selected 500-bottle wine list to brighten the spirits? This dimly lit grotto is frequented by of-age college kids, young professionals on dates, and wine-loving service-industry types who know a good thing when they trip over it. For beer fans, much of the fun comes from plucking one's own from a convenience store–style cooler filled with 200

varieties of fine ale (sorry, Budweiser fans). A small but pleasant menu of wine-friendly snacks is offered to satisfy light appetites.

## ( MARKET AVENUE WINE BAR

2521 Market Ave., 216/696-9463, www.marketavewinebar.com

**HOURS:** Sun.-Fri. 4 P.M.-1 A.M., Sat. 2 P.M.-1 A.M.

**Map 2**

Cleveland's oldest and best wine bar succeeds because it is a comfortable neighborhood joint that just happens to have an amazing wine selection. The understated charm of the place, with its exposed brick walls, ancient wood floors, and shimmering candlelight, only serves to heighten the appeal of the wine selection. The well-chosen 500-bottle list is loaded with obscure gems, evergreen chestnuts, and drinkable deals, and thanks to their encyclopedic knowledge the staff can tell you a story about each and every one of them. On any given night, some 75 varieties are available by the glass. There is no hard booze sold here, but there is a small but wonderful list of craft beers.

Market Avenue is the picturesque cobblestone alley in Ohio City where Flying Fig and Great Lakes Brewing are located. Absorb the charm from Market Avenue Wine Bar's expansive sidewalk patio.

# Gay and Lesbian

## FIVE CENT DECISION
4365 State Rd., 216/661-1314,
www.myspace.com/thenickelbar
**HOURS:** Daily 6 P.M.–close
`Map 7`

The Nickel, located a few miles south of downtown, is where women go to meet other women. And they have been doing so for about 20 years, making this one of the oldest lesbian bars around. Known equally for its karaoke nights, cheap food, and laid-back atmosphere, the Nickel is a fun, casual joint. Apart from the all-gal landscape, the tavern would fit right in on the end of any block. The beer's cold, the pool table works, and the company is as agreeable as they come.

## TWIST
11633 Clifton Blvd., 216/221-2333
**HOURS:** Mon.–Sat. 11:30 A.M.–2:30 A.M.,
Sun. noon–2:30 A.M.
`Map 3`

You don't have to be gay to enjoy this diverse neighborhood bar. While gay men definitely make up the majority of the crowd, many in the house are simply there for the good times. Located at the epicenter of Cleveland's gay-friendly district, Twist is more laid-back than

many other boy bars. A large main room features a central bar, some soft-seating areas, and loft balconies. A sleek subterranean lounge offers a quiet hideaway for guests hoping to escape the upstairs action. On warm nights, two overhead garage doors are raised high, spreading the party out onto the sidewalk. Affordable martinis, upbeat tunes, and welcoming employees have kept Twist popular for over 15 years.

## UNION STATION/BOUNCE
2814 Detroit Ave., 216/357-2997,
www.columbusnightlife.com
**HOURS:** Daily 5 P.M.–3 A.M.
`Map 2`

This gender-bending entertainment complex features a restaurant, dance club, and cabaret. Union Station is an at-times raucous video café that dishes up tasty pub grub, camp-filled TV, and wall-to-wall show tunes. Bounce is the lively dance club, where a diverse crowd shakes it on an elevated circular dance floor. In the cabaret, drag queens keep gay and straight audience members in stitches with over-the-top performances that include stand-up comedy, lip-synching melodies, and spot-on impersonations. A fenced-in parking lot makes coming and going a snap (until it fills up, that is).

# Dance Clubs and Lounges

### ANATOMY
1299 W. 9th St., 216/363-1113,
www.anatomycleveland.com
**HOURS:** Thurs.-Sat. 9 P.M.-2:30 A.M.
**Map 1**

If pulsing beats, roped-off VIP seating areas, and A-List crowds sound appealing, this weekend-only nightclub should be on your list. The sharp Warehouse District space attracts sought-after DJs, who in turn attract the well-dressed set. But fickle as club kids are, this place can go from busy to bust on any given night. The best suggestion is to peek through the large front windows to see just what's shaking inside.

Regardless, one can always plop down at the sweeping curved bar for a glass of bubbly and wait for the action to come to them.

### KEVIN'S MARTINI BAR
2035 E. 4th St., 216/241-7425,
www.pickwickandfrolic.com
**HOURS:** Tues.-Sat. 5:30 P.M.-close
**Map 1**

Tucked into the basement of **Pickwick & Frolic,** a multidimensional entertainment complex, Kevin's is a Vegas-style lounge with a G-rated personality. Tuxedoed bartenders and kicky cocktail waitresses serve up classic martinis in a

## GLAM IT UP, GIRLS!

You and your group of girlfriends needn't travel far to put together an engaging night on the town. When it comes to the all-important three Ds – drinks, dinner, and dancing – downtown's Warehouse District has all the bases covered. Best of all, the trip back to the hotel is likely a short one.

### Primping in the Afternoon
Why not leave the primping to the pros at **Marengo Luxury Spa,** downtown's only full-service day spa. Located at the **Hyatt Regency at The Arcade,** the spa offers facials, massages, manicures, and pedicures. While many of the finest apparel shops are located in the 'burbs, Chic et Mode in nearby **Tower City Center** is a wonderful boutique stocking fine fashions and accessories from around the globe.

### Drinks at Dusk
The Warehouse District is jam-packed with bars, restaurants, and nightclubs. Start the evening on a high note with flights of wine at **D'Vine Wine Bar.** If it's nice out grab a table on the sidewalk patio and watch the show. D'Vine offers over a dozen themed wine flights, from light and bubbly to dark and stormy. Pair the

wine with a cheese plate or charcuterie board to bridge the gap until dinner.

### Dinner at Dark
Deciding where to eat in the Warehouse District is all a matter of taste. For fresh-shucked oysters and tasty seafood, head to the beautiful **Blue Point Grill.** If innovative American comfort food sounds more appealing, make tracks to the fun-spirited **Crop Bistro.** Sometimes the scene is as important as the food, and at the always-happening **Metropolitan Café** that's certainly the case.

### Dancing the Night Away
There are only a precious few spots in town that offer views from a rooftop patio. The **Velvet Dog** provides not only great views, but also great dancing on its 3rd-floor deck. Typically, the youthful crowd is as picturesque as the views, with sharp-dressed party girls flirting with buff, if buzzed, boys. This club is just as fun on a rainy or snowy night when the patio is closed, though it can get loud, steamy, and sultry inside. If you're looking for a slightly more mature crowd and better music in a glam lounge setting, skip the Dog and visit **Mercury Lounge** instead.

retro-chic setting. Bouncy red banquettes, plush drapery, and a glowing bar top make this joint a feast for the senses. Kevin's also features a champagne bar with one of the largest catalogues of bubble bottles in the city. Bartenders here have a few tricks up their sleeves, which, depending on your mood, can be amusing or corny.

## LAVA LOUNGE

1307 Auburn Ave., 216/589-9112,
www.coolplacestoeat.com
**HOURS:** Mon.-Sat. 11 A.M.-2:30 A.M., Sun. 7 P.M.-2:30 A.M.
Map 2

When this low-key lounge opened a decade ago, it was known only to the coolest of cats. These days, it is on most people's radar, but in no way has it lost its cool. More of an anti-club, Lava is for folks who enjoy great tunes without the sweaty gyrations and personal advances. Dark, clubby, and candlelit, the small lounge features martinis, a great beer and wine selection, and vinyl-spinning DJs. There is a 2nd-floor bar and lounge, a small back patio, and

a surprisingly good menu that is available late into the night.

## MERCURY LOUNGE

1392 W. 6th St., 216/566-8840,
www.themercurylounge.com
**HOURS:** Mon.-Fri. 5 P.M.-2 A.M., Sat. 8 P.M.-2 A.M., Sun. 9 P.M.-2 A.M.
Map 1

Half dance club, half ultra lounge, Mercury has been at the top of the Cleveland cocktail heap for almost a decade. Surviving where many others have failed, this cosmopolitan nightclub provides a swank environment suitable for both dancing and lounging. Cozy nooks for kicking back, open areas for dancing, and some of the best local, national, and international DJ talent keep the Mercury consistently busy most nights of the year. Many here dress to the nines, so keep that in mind when staring into the closet for an outfit. Check the website to keep track of the various shows and events.

## METROPOLIS

2325 Elm St., 216/241-1444,
www.metropolis-cleveland.com
**HOURS:** Fri. 9 P.M.-3 A.M., Sat.-Sun. 10 P.M.-3 A.M.
Map 1

The Flats used to be teeming with clubs like Metropolis, cavernous old warehouse spaces given new life as raging dance halls. This one holds on thanks mostly to decent crowds, good DJs, and an interesting setting. Numerous rooms, spaces, and bars offer guests a variety of atmospheres and environments. But the club's size can conspire against itself, making crowds look smaller than they are. Check the website for the events schedule, which can include house, techno, and hip-hop nights.

## VELVET DOG

1280 W. 6th St., 216/664-1116,
www.velvetdogcleveland.ypguides.net
**HOURS:** Wed. 9 P.M.-2 A.M., Thurs.-Fri. 4 P.M.-2 A.M., Sat. 8 P.M.-2 A.M., Sun. 9 P.M.-2 A.M.
Map 1

Men and women of a certain age (young, that is) can't seem to make it through a single weekend

© DOUGLAS TRATTNER

Hit Mercury Lounge for cocktails and house music.

NIGHTLIFE

without doing the Dog. The Velvet Dog has deservedly earned a reputation as the best place to boogie, and as such, it welcomes the largest and most fashionable crowds. West 6th Street is the Warehouse District's party strip, and this nightclub acts like a beacon for fun-seekers. The high-tech multilevel club features a Top-40 dance floor, a dimly lit lounge, and the best party roof in town. The place can definitely feel like a meat market at times, but isn't that the point?

### ☾ VELVET TANGO ROOM

2095 Columbus St., 216/241-8869,
www.velvettangoroom.com
**HOURS:** Mon.-Fri. 4:30 P.M.-1 A.M., Sat. 6 P.M.-1 A.M.
**Map 2**

Long considered Cleveland's most exclusive speakeasy, Velvet Tango Room is no longer an undiscovered gem. Featured in glossy national magazines, major dailies, and spirits blogs the world over, it is safe to say that the cat is officially out of the bag. No matter: This '40s-style lounge is as compelling today as it was yesterday. Tucked inside a plain brick wrapper is an anachronistic world of gentlemanly behavior, professional service, and upscale furnishings. Labor-intensive classic cocktails are constructed gram by gram on a scale to ensure consistency. Ingredients are all top-flight, including house-made mixers, fresh-squeezed fruit juices, and cut-to-order garnishes. These drinks require time to create, and they cost twice what one might pay elsewhere, but the finished product makes it all worthwhile. Call ahead to reserve a spot in the private back room.

### VIEW

618 Prospect Ave. E., 216/664-1815,
www.viewnightclub.com
**HOURS:** Vary by night and show
**Map 1**

One of Cleveland's glitziest ultra-lounges, View features posh digs, VIP rooms, and bottle service. Just around the corner from the East 4th Street action, this club can be hit or miss with respect to crowds, but later is usually better. One of the best features of the club, apart from the light show, sound system, and dance floor, is the rooftop patio. South Beach–style cabanas, killer skyline views, and hot tunes keep this place in business during good weather.

# Comedy Clubs

### ☾ HILARITIES 4TH STREET THEATER

2035 E. 4th St., 216/736-4242,
www.pickwickandfrolic.com
**HOURS:** Showtimes Tues.-Thurs. 8 P.M., Fri.-Sat. 7:30 and 10:15 P.M., Sun. 7:30 P.M.
**Map 1**

This is the premier comedy club in Cleveland, featuring the best talent in the best setting. Located inside Pickwick & Frolic, a $5 million entertainment complex on East 4th Street, Hilarities attracts every big name in the biz. Owner Nick Kostis has been running comedy clubs in this town for 20 years, and he has earned a reputation as a brilliant judge of up-and-coming talent. Shows take place in a sharp 425-seat theater, the backdrop of which is a brick wall left over from the old Euclid

## SMOKING BAN

On election day in 2006, Ohio voters passed Issue 5, putting into effect a sweeping indoor smoking ban that extends to all public places and places of employment. This ban applies to all bars, restaurants, and bowling alleys. It may seem strange to walk into a dimly lit corner tavern and not be greeted by a cloud of cigarette smoke, but that's the new reality in Cleveland. If you prefer a cigarette in one hand, many bars have patios that are used simultaneously by puffers and non-puffers alike. Short of that, sidewalks, rooftops, and even fire escapes appear to work just fine.

Opera House. Before the show, hit the rustic American restaurant upstairs. After, visit Kevin's Martini Bar for cocktails.

## THE IMPROV

2000 Sycamore St., 216/696-4677,
www.improvupcoming.com
**HOURS:** Showtimes Wed.-Thurs. 8 P.M.,
Fri.-Sat. 8 and 10:15 P.M., Sun. 7 P.M.
**Map 1**

With venues in about 20 U.S. cities, The Improv is a well-known comedy club and restaurant. Top touring comedians, rising-star talent, and local favorites confront audiences most nights of the week. Those who want to secure the best seats in the house must make dinner reservations, but the wiser choice may be to dine elsewhere and take your chances on seating. Like every other comedy club in the world, The Improv charges a little more than they probably should for drinks. To take a crack at the laugh craft yourself, come on the first Tuesday of the month for open-mic night (auditions are held at noon).

## SOMETHING DADA

1900 Superior Ave., 216/696-4242,
www.somethingdada.com
**HOURS:** Showtimes Fri. 8 P.M., Sat. 8 and 10:30 P.M.
**Map 1**

This fast-paced improvisational comedy troupe formed in 1994, making it the longest-running improv show in town. These days, the team operates out of Tower Press, a live-work warehouse populated by artist types. Fueled by audience suggestions, however lame they might be, Dada manages to manufacture a roller-coaster ride of laughs. Shows cost about $10 and are never the same experience twice.

**NIGHTLIFE**

# ARTS AND LEISURE

Cleveland is not a mini New York City. Clevelanders do not expect to wake up one morning to learn that their town has become the new Second City. Cleveland sports fans will always envy the teams of Boston, Denver, and Pittsburgh, despite what they say in crowded bars. But when one considers the abundance of arts, culture, and recreational pursuits available to residents and visitors of Northeast Ohio, it is clear that nobody here has cause to complain.

Talent trickles down. And rainmakers like the Cleveland Orchestra, Cleveland Museum of Art, Cleveland Institute of Music, and Cleveland Institute of Art help to create an absolute embarrassment of riches that even towns like New York and Chicago can begrudge. With its five stunning vaudeville-era theaters, plus scores of smaller stages, PlayhouseSquare is the second-largest performing-arts center in the country. (Sorry, Chicago.) The Cleveland Orchestra has been labeled by some foreign critics as the finest symphony in the world. (Don't feel bad, New York.) The Cleveland Museum of Art always has been regarded as one of the nation's finest repositories of art and antiquities; thanks to a present-day $350 million renovation project, it will only get better.

In neighborhoods like Tremont, Little Italy, Detroit Shoreway, and Ohio City, independent galleries seem to pop up like concertgoers during a standing ovation. Adventurous art fans flock to these lively urban districts for regularly scheduled art walks and gallery hops. These same neighborhoods fill up the social calendar with seasonal block parties, food festivals, and home tours.

Few American cities can support more than

# HIGHLIGHTS

LOOK FOR ◖ TO FIND RECOMMENDED ART AND ACTIVITIES.

◖ **Most Macabre Art:** In the 1930s, 13 people were brutally murdered in a crime spree dubbed the Torso Murders. Because most of the victims were unknown, police made plaster casts of their faces called death masks in hopes of identifying them. Four of these chilling masks are on display at the **Cleveland Police Historical Society and Museum** (page 94).

◖ **Best Reuse of a Schoolhouse:** Once the bane of youngsters, a schoolhouse in Little Italy is now **Murray Hill School House Galleries,** a warren of small art galleries, boutiques, and incubator-sized studios. Best part: You don't need a pass to wander these halls (page 98).

◖ **Best Damn Band in the Land:** It isn't just locals who fawn all over the **Cleveland Orchestra**; critics in London, Salzburg, and Vienna all have hailed the symphony as one of the very best in the world. Check them out at either Severance Hall or Blossom Music Center to hear what the world is talking about (page 102).

◖ **Finest Experimental Theater:** For 30 years, **Cleveland Public Theatre** has produced innovative and adventurous original theater. In fact, the success of this very outfit has in large part triggered the revival of the entire Detroit Shoreway neighborhood (page 103).

◖ **Sweetest Summer Concert Spot:** Tucked into the densely forested Cain Park in Cleveland Heights, **Evans Amphitheater** is invisible to the casual passersby. Beneath the stars and surrounded by nature, the gently pitched lawn is a magical place to enjoy a summer performance (page 106).

◖ **Broadest Assortment of Indie Flicks:** Over the course of 11 days in March, the **Cleveland International Film Fest** screens roughly 140 feature-length films and 170 short subjects from over 60 different countries. See how many you can cram into a workday (page 109).

◖ **Where to Find the Ripest Tomato:** The **North Union Farmers Market** at Shaker Square runs pretty much all year, but it really hits its peak from June through September. Bring a cooler to this bustling Saturday market and load it up with local fare (page 112).

◖ **Where to Ride When the Snow Falls:** Mountain bikers flock to **Ray's MTB Indoor Park** because it truly is one-of-a-kind. Located in a 100,000-square-foot warehouse, this remarkably wild indoor bike park is almost as good as the real thing (page 118).

◖ **World's Greatest Outdoor Jogging Track:** The **Ohio & Erie Canal Towpath Trail** is a 75-mile gem that winds its way through the beautiful Cuyahoga Valley National Park. With a mostly smooth limestone surface, the path attracts millions of walkers, joggers, and cyclists each year (page 119).

◖ **Best Place to Catch a Foul Ball:** Jacob's Field is now Progressive Field, but this urban ballpark is still tops with local and traveling baseball fans. Home of the Cleveland Indians, **Progressive Field** is consistently ranked among the best places in the major league to watch a game (page 120).

one professional sports team. Cleveland is blessed with three (four if you count Arena Football), not to mention a handful of exciting minor-league organizations. And the courts, diamonds, and fields on which they play are exemplary in the world of sports. Cleveland sits on a Great Lake, is threaded with rushing waterways, and boasts a backyard dotted with dozens of leafy parks and reservations. Just down the road is a 33,000-acre playground called Cuyahoga Valley National Park. If you are an outdoors enthusiast, Northeast Ohio isn't such a bad place to set up a tent.

Cleveland may not be the richest town in terms of wealth, but when it comes to things that really matter, the town is one of the most prosperous in the Midwest.

# The Arts

## MUSEUMS

### CHILDREN'S MUSEUM OF CLEVELAND

10730 Euclid Ave., 216/791-7114,
www.clevelandchildrensmuseum.org
**HOURS:** Daily 10 A.M.-5 P.M.
**COST:** $6 adult, $7 student
Map 4

More than just a rainy-day activity, this hands-on museum will keep the little ones cheerfully engaged come rain or shine. Exhibits endeavor to teach children about science, weather, and Earth's natural water cycle. A tableau walks young urban pioneers through basic skills of the grocery store, gas station, bank, and public transportation system. Children under the age of four will enjoy just horsing around in the Big Red Barn–inspired playhouse. Visit Elf Corner, the museum's gift shop, for fun educational toys, books, and games.

### CLEVELAND ACCORDION MUSEUM

Rocky River, 440/895-9223, jackathy@ameritech.net
**HOURS:** By appt.
**COST:** Free
Map 7

Polka used to be king, and Cleveland's own Frankie Yankovic was known as "America's Polka King." Visit the Rocky River home of Jack and Kathy White and you'll discover not only a shrine to the greatest Slovenian-style polka player of all time, but also a bona fide button-box museum. Granted, this museum is in somebody's basement, and viewings are by appointment only, but polka fans need to come here. On display are over 400 accordions, 400 accordion-personality photos, and 10,000 sheets of accordion music. Looking for a good home for your aging instrument? The Whites will gladly take it off your hands.

### CLEVELAND MUSEUM OF NATURAL HISTORY

1 Wade Oval Dr., 800/317-9155, www.cmnh.org
**HOURS:** Mon.-Sat. 10 A.M.-5 P.M., Wed. 10 A.M.-10 P.M.,
Sun. noon-5 P.M., closed major holidays

**COST:** $9 adult, $7 child and senior, planetarium tickets
$4 with general admission
Map 4

History is on display at this fine institute of scientific education. From the moment folks cross the threshold, they are immersed in a world of past, present, and future wonder. Both permanent and visiting exhibits seek to shed light on the mysteries and truths at work in our universe. A mesmerizing Foucault pendulum demonstrates in dramatic, albeit slow, fashion the Earth's rotation on its axis. A 270-pound bob swings on a 32-foot wire, covering six inches of real estate per hour. Fallen dominos mark the passage of time and space. As one might expect of a natural-history museum, there are bones, and lots of them. *Australopithecus afarensis,* a.k.a. "Lucy," is our three-million-year-old aunt. A cast of the original skeleton is on display. Dino fans will also discover a tyrannosaur, stegosaurus, and "Happy," one of the most complete mounted sauropods on display in the world. A domed planetarium features the amazing Skymaster ZKP3/S projector, which can show the positions of more than 5,000 stars, nebulae, and galaxies. Outside the building's walls, visitors can explore a two-acre wildlife center that highlights native Ohio flora and fauna, including bobcats and bald eagles, river otters, and owls. The Blue Planet café serves healthy and delicious lunch every day. Before you leave, stop by the Museum Store to pick your very own "Evolution Happens" T-shirt.

### ◖ CLEVELAND POLICE HISTORICAL SOCIETY AND MUSEUM

1300 Ontario St., 216/623-5055,
www.clevelandpolicemuseum.org
**HOURS:** Mon.-Fri. 10 A.M.-4 P.M.
**COST:** Free
Map 1

Cleveland was a city gripped by fear in the mid-1930s as a result of the Kingsbury Run Murders, better known as the "Torso Murders." Over the course of four years beginning in 1934, 13 people were brutally murdered, all of them

# CLEVELAND PLUS PASS

For those who plan on visiting a number of Cleveland's major cultural attractions in a short period of time, it might make financial sense to pick up a Cleveland Plus Pass. This one ticket is good for admission to 10 Northeast Ohio attractions. Here's how it works: Sightseers purchase a pass good for either a two-, three-, or five-day stay. During that time period, they can use the pass to get into as many of the included museums and attractions as they want. Passes are priced according to the number of days they remain valid ($25/two days, $35/three days, $50/five days). Passes are activated at the first stop.

Included in the package is admission to the Children's Museum of Cleveland, Cleveland Botanical Garden, Cleveland Metroparks Zoo, Cleveland Museum of Natural History, Museum of Contemporary Art, Western Reserve Historical Society, Maltz Museum of Jewish Heritage and Holden Arboretum. The Cleveland Museum of Art has free general admission, but the pass shaves 10 percent off purchases at its gift shop. Admission to the **Rock Hall** is not included, but again, the pass saves on purchases while there. Discounts to other attractions and restaurants are rolled into the price as well.

You really have to crunch the numbers to determine if the pass makes sense for you. If it does, visit **Positively Cleveland** (100 Public Sq., 800/321-1001, www.positivelycleveland .com) to get yours.

---

decapitated, most while they were still breathing. Because most of these victims were unidentified transients, plaster casts, or "death masks," were made of the faces for public viewing in hopes of putting a name with the deceased. Four of these chilling masks are on display at this law-enforcement museum, which chronicles the history of the Cleveland Division of Police from its inception in 1866. Roughly 4,000 square feet of space contain thousands of photos, scrapbooks, and old police blotters. Visitors will discover the first police call box, first bank closed-circuit camera, and the black box of a U.S. Air Force Thunderbird that crashed during the 1981 Cleveland Air Show. Learn about Safety Director Eliot Ness and other achievements of the Cleveland Police Department during one of two guided tours. Stop by the Cop Shop to snag your very own CPD T-shirt or a book about the gruesome Torso Murders.

## MONEY MUSEUM AT FEDERAL RESERVE BANK

1455 E. 6th St., 216/579-2000,
www.clevelandfed.org
**HOURS:** Mon.-Thurs. 10 A.M.-2 P.M.,
closed bank holidays
**COST:** Free
`Map 1`

How did we buy things before we had money? Who makes money? Why is a dollar worth a dollar? Answers to these and other cash conundrums are answered most days of the week at this fortress of funds. Designed to teach students and, perhaps, spendthrift adults about what money is, where it comes from, and how to manage it, this museum doesn't exactly sound like a thrill ride, but interactive exhibits help deliver the message in a fun way. For instance, a display on ancient currency shows us that stones, shells, and even cows were once traded as cash (imagine sticking a cow in your purse!). One of a dozen Federal Reserve Banks, the Cleveland office is worth a visit solely to gander at the 12-story Medici-style palazzo designed by the noted firm of Walker & Weeks.

## MUSEUM OF CONTEMPORARY ART

8501 Carnegie Ave., 216/421-8671,
www.mocacleveland.org
**HOURS:** Tues.-Sun. 11 A.M.-6 P.M.,
closed major holidays
**COST:** $4 adult, $3 student and senior
`Map 4`

Drawn like a moth to a sweater, MOCA is preparing for a monumental move in 2010 to University Circle, where it will inhabit a

**ARTS AND LEISURE**

contemporary new structure designed by an innovative London firm. Until then, this risk-taking and provocative visual-art organization will continue to operate from its current locale, adjacent to the Cleveland Playhouse. Hosting ambitious exhibitions from emerging and established artists, MOCA consistently raises the arts bar in Cleveland. Stunning installations, sculptures, paintings, photography, and video are just some of the works that routinely make layovers here. Lectures, readings, films, and performances round out the arts-education programming.

### POLKA HALL OF FAME MUSEUM
605 E. 222nd St., Euclid, 216/261-3263, www.clevelandstyle.com
**HOURS:** Tues.-Fri. noon–5 P.M., Sat. 10 A.M.–3 P.M.
**COST:** Free
Map 7

Fans of the "happiest sound around" will want to make the short journey to Euclid to visit this museum dedicated to all things polka. Cleveland-style polka has its roots in Slovenian folk music, which was popularized by local musicians such as Frankie Yankovic and Johnny Vadnal. Inside you'll find memorabilia and artifacts from past and present polka stars, including accordions, stage outfits, and photographs. Learn about not just the Cleveland style, but also Chicago, Czech, Slovak, and German. Prominent placement is also devoted to the winners of the annual Polka Hall of Fame awards.

### WESTERN RESERVE HISTORICAL SOCIETY
10825 East Blvd., 216/721-5722, www.wrhs.org
**HOURS:** Mon.-Sat. 10 A.M.–5 P.M., Sun. noon–5 P.M.
**COST:** $8.50 adult, $5 student, $7.50 senior
Map 4

Chronicling the history of the Western Reserve, this University Circle institution is comprised of a cultural history museum, an auto and aviation museum, and a research library. Cleveland Indians fans will get a kick out the 35-foot-tall Chief Wahoo sign, which was rescued from the old Municipal Stadium and now holds a prominent position in the front lobby. In addition to high-profile touring exhibits, the museum holds a bounty of local artifacts, treasures, and tales from the area once known as the Western Reserve. The Chisholm Halle Costume Collection is one of the top-ranked costume collections in the nation, with some 30,000 garments on rotating display. The Crawford Auto-Aviation Museum displays historically significant automobiles, aircraft, bicycles, motorcycles, and spacecraft, paying special attention to the significant contribution of Northeast Ohio companies. Nearly 200 unique vintage models are on hand. As the principal repository for documents relating to Western Reserve history, the library at WRHS is a popular and important research facility. The fee to park in the museum lot is $8, so consider taking public transport.

## GALLERIES

### ART GALLERY AT CLEVELAND STATE UNIVERSITY
2307 Chester Ave., 216/687-2103, www.csuohio.edu/artgallery
**HOURS:** Mon.-Fri. 10 A.M.–5 P.M., Sat. noon–4 P.M.
Map 1

Though this great exhibition space is located on the ground floor of the CSU Art Building, the exhibits are not limited to student shows. In addition to the annual juried student art show, these three galleries present five or six shows per year that explore contemporary political and social themes. The thematically curated exhibits cover a broad range of mediums and styles from local, national, and international artists. They are recognized by critics as some of the most visually stimulating in town.

### ASTERISK GALLERY
2393 Professor Ave., 330/304-8528, www.asteriskgallery.com
**HOURS:** Second Fri. of the month and by appt.
Map 2

To find this under-the-radar gallery, look for the illuminated "*" sign that hangs above the door. Known as one of the city's most cutting-edge art venues, Asterisk focuses solely on the

# TREMONT ARTWALK

Tremont, the Soho of Cleveland, is loaded with artist studios, galleries, boutiques, and bistros. The only problem is, many of the galleries close early or are open only by appointment. That's why the second Friday of each month is a popular day to hit this diverse, walkable neighborhood. Running 6-10 P.M., the Tremont ArtWalk (www.tremontartwalk.org) is an opportunity to hit dozens of locations in a single visit. Numerous shops and galleries open their doors and stay open until late. Better still, many offer free wine and hors d'oeuvres with which to ply customers. If you didn't get enough to eat, stop by any of the trendy restaurants for a proper meal.

work of young, progressive, and emerging local artists. Following the schedule of the monthly Tremont ArtWalks, the gallery launches 12 exhibits per year, always on the second Friday of the month. Unswerving quality and strong narratives keep art fans coming back month after month. Owner, curator, and artist Dana Depew tracks down engaging, contemporary, and thought-provoking work in mediums that span painting, sculpture, photography, video, and beyond. This is not your typical turtleneck crowd. If possible, check out Depew's untamed basement workshop.

## BONFOEY GALLERY

1710 Euclid Ave., 216/621-0178, www.bonfoey.com
**HOURS:** Mon.-Fri. 8:30 A.M.-5 P.M., Sat. 9 A.M.-noon
**Map 1**

The Bonfoey has rightfully earned a reputation as one of Cleveland's largest and finest art galleries. Established in 1893, it is certainly the most venerable. Located near PlayhouseSquare, the large space is filled with original 19th-century paintings, signed lithographs, photographs, pastels, glass, and sculpture. Rotating exhibits throughout the year bring in fresh merchandise. The shop also maintains a great

selection of original art priced under $500, making it a must-stop on any home-design outing. Come here, too, for appraisals, art restoration, framing, packing, shipping, and installation.

## CONVIVIUM33 GALLERY

1433 E. 33rd St., 216/881-7838,
www.josaphatartshall.com
**HOURS:** By appt.
**Map 1**

Set in the nave of a former Roman Catholic church, Convivium33 Gallery at Josaphat Arts Hall is a unique and beautiful space. The architecturally stunning building provides an appropriate backdrop for the works of established local artists. Like the church before it, the gallery and arts center serves to unite the community by presenting meaningful exhibits, hosting important events, and offering studio space to artists. Exhibits are often kicked off with popular Dinner with Art events, where guests feast on gourmet food alongside the artist and his or her work. The gallery keeps regular hours during exhibits; call or check the website for details.

## FRONT ROOM GALLERY

3615 Superior Ave. 4203A, 216/534-6059,
www.frontroomcleveland.com
**HOURS:** Thurs., Sat., and Sun. 1-4 P.M.
**Map 1**

Located on the 3rd floor of an industrial-park building complex, Front Room is not front and center in terms of visibility. But this artist-run gallery is ahead of the pack when it comes to finding talented emerging artists on the rise. Seemingly without boundary when it comes to geography and medium, the co-op exhibits work from local, regional, and national artists in disciplines as varied as collage, painting, video, and drawing on found paper. Shows can be solo runs or multi-artist affairs, but they tend to be fresh, current, relevant, and trendy. The lofty space is also the site of some great music shows that, like the art on the walls, lean to the indie and experimental.

**ARTS AND LEISURE**

## GALLERY Ü HAUL

Streets of Tremont, 216/323-0085
**HOURS:** Second Fri. of the month during summer
**Map 2**

When Cleveland Institute of Art graduate Patsy Kline was forced to shutter her successful Gallery Ü Cleveland, she decided to take her show on the road—literally. Using the back of a rented moving truck as her exhibition space, Kline transferred her creative energies from Gallery Ü to Gallery Ü Haul. Her mobile gallery is often on the road, as trucks are wont to be, but it is always parked in Tremont during the summer ArtWalks. Usually interactive and highly engaging, Kline's installations have an uncanny ability to bring people together to discuss and question art. It just so happens that they are doing so in the back of a truck.

## HEIGHTS ARTS GALLERY

2173 Lee Rd., 216/371-3457, www.heightsarts.org
**HOURS:** Wed.-Sat. noon-9 P.M., Sun. 1-5 P.M.
**Map 5**

Small but mighty describes this East Side gallery. Run by Heights Arts, a nonprofit community arts organization, the exhibition space focuses largely on the work of local artists. And when it comes to creative talent, residents of Cleveland Heights tend to be unfairly gifted. The gallery puts on four exhibitions a year plus two very popular seasonal events: "A Holiday Store" features affordable art gifts from local artists only, while "Collector's Choice" opens up the room to artists from beyond the neighborhood. Located next to the Cedar Lee Theatre, the gallery is a popular pre- and post-film stopover.

## ◖ MURRAY HILL SCHOOL HOUSE GALLERIES

2026 Murray Hill Rd., www.littleitalycleveland.com
**HOURS:** Vary
**Map 4**

Once a neighborhood schoolhouse, this warren of redbrick buildings now houses upscale apartments, condos, offices, and galleries. The numerous and ever-evolving roster of shops ranges from tiny incubator-sized studios to full-on retail and exhibition spaces. Juma Gallery (216/721-3773, www.jumagallery.com) displays hand-crafted functional art, plus paintings,

The Murray Hill School House is now filled with galleries and boutiques.

ARTS AND LEISURE

ceramics, glass. and jewelry. Beautiful and stirring figurative paintings are available at Tricia Kaman Studio (216/559-6478, www.triciakaman.com). Artemis Herber (216/707-0263, www.artbox.usa) crafts graceful cardboard sculpture and acrylic paintings. Sobella Paper Boutique (216/229-1333, www.so-bella.com) sells stationery, greeting cards, and custom invitations. These and the other galleries and boutiques in the schoolhouse keep varied hours. Find more information at Little Italy, Cleveland (www.littleitalycleveland.com).

## 1POINT618 GALLERY

6421 Detroit Ave., 216/281-1618,
www.1point618gallery.com
**HOURS:** During openings and by appt.
`Map 3`

This architecturally stunning storefront in the Gordon Square Arts District contains a 1st-floor art gallery and the offices of an award-winning architect. The gallery, 1point618, holds approximately six to eight shows per year, focusing on contemporary art from regional, national, and international talents. The symbiosis between art and space here serves to somehow elevate both, creating an atmosphere teeming with artistic tension. Stop here before or after dinner at fabulous Luxe Kitchen & Lounge.

## PAUL DUDA GALLERY

2342 Professor Ave., 216/589-5788,
www.pauldudagallery.com
**HOURS:** Second Fri. of the month 6-11 P.M.,
call for other hours
`Map 2`

When you fall in love with this town as deeply as have the locals, come to Paul Duda. This sleek Tremont gallery sells remarkable art photographs of ruggedly handsome Cleveland. Printed in dreamy giclée, an archival ink-jet printing process, images of the Guardians of Transportation, Lake Erie shoreline, and Terminal Tower are mantel-worthy mementos of a fine visit. Vibrant and full-color shots of the skyline, PlayhouseSquare, and Progressive Field will serve as permanent reminders of fun days and nights gone by.

## POP SHOP GALLERY

17020 Madison Ave., 216/227-8440,
www.popshopgallery.com
**HOURS:** Tues.-Sat. noon-7 P.M.
`Map 6`

Lakewood, and specifically this stretch of Madison Avenue, has always been an artistically inclined neighborhood. With galleries like the Pop Shop, the future once again looks bright for a grassroots West Side art community to take hold. Owner and artist Rich Cihlar does a great job tracking down a great and varied selection of locally grown art, from paintings and sculpture to clothing and jewelry. But don't expect a sad assortment of starving-artist oil paintings; the shows at this live and lively gallery are hip, relevant, and tinged with rock and roll. In fact, the gallery feels a lot like an indie record shop. Shows rotate every four to six weeks and are typically kicked off by raucous opening bashes. If you're looking for unique, affordable, and high-quality art, stop at the Pop Shop.

## REINBERGER GALLERIES

11141 East Blvd., 216/421-7407, www.cia.edu
**HOURS:** Tues.-Sat. 10 A.M.-5 P.M.
`Map 4`

The Reinberger Galleries are located in the Gund Building at the Cleveland Institute of Art, which is among the country's top art and design colleges. Billed as the largest college art gallery in Ohio, this 5,000-square-foot exhibition space often features the work of established artist graduates. In addition to displaying the graduate theses of BFA students, and the popular CIA Faculty Exhibition, the galleries present thousands of art and design objects, plus film, video, animation, and art installations. Visitors can look forward to approximately eight shows per year, including the often whimsical and always brash Student Independent Exhibition.

## SPACES GALLERY

2220 Superior Viaduct, 216/621-2314,
www.spacesgallery.org
**HOURS:** Tues.-Thurs. 11 A.M.-5:30 P.M., Fri. 11 A.M.-7 P.M.,
Sat. 11 A.M.-5:30 P.M., Sun. 1-5 P.M.
`Map 1`

**ARTS AND LEISURE**

Visitors to this 30-year-old artist-run gallery will feast on wildly creative experimental and non-commercial art exhibits from local, regional, and national artists. Through approximately four major shows a year, and spanning every conceivable medium, this leader in contemporary art showcases the talent of emerging and mid-career artists. Much of the art attempts to tackle the most important issues of the day, including political, social, and cultural themes. All events are free and open to the public, and the gallery's lively opening-night parties are some of the best in town. The spaces at SPACES are often rented out for private events, so it is always wise to phone before stopping by.

### STUDIOS AT WEST 78TH STREET
Lake Avenue between W. 78th and W. 80th Sts.
**HOURS:** Vary
Map 3

Just west of the Gordon Square Arts District, this out-of-the-way complex of redbrick buildings has for years attracted artistic types. It is home to *Alternative Press* magazine, as well as a highly sought-after recording studio. Now it is becoming a rather impressive congregation of art galleries, artist studios, and art-services businesses. Kenneth Paul Lesko Gallery (216/631-6719, www.kennethpaullesko.com) is a sharp contemporary space that shows fine art, sculpture, and photography. Kokoon Arts Gallery (216/832-8212, www.wgsproductions.com) shows the work of "Cleveland School" artists Frank Nelson, Paul Travis, and William Sommer, as well as contemporary American paintings, sculpture, and arresting 2-D computer graphics prints. Tregoning & Co. (216/281-8626, www.tregoningandco.com) displays important works of art from notable and established artists

### WOOLTEX GALLERY
Tower Press Bldg., 1900 Superior Ave., 216/241-4069, www.thewooltexgallery.com
**HOURS:** Mon.-Sat. 11 A.M.-3 P.M.
Map 1

One of the newer and better visual-art galleries in the city, Wooltex is roomy, contemporary, and easy to find. Located in an old warehouse that has been converted to live-work space for artists, the gallery never has to search far for talent. The large space serves as a backdrop for high-quality painting, sculpture, video, and installations from largely local artists. Exhibits come and go every month and half or so. Like many other galleries in town, this one is used for private events, so it is always smart to call before visiting.

### ZYGOTE PRESS
1410 E. 30th St., 216/621-2900, www.zygotepress.com
**HOURS:** Tues. 11 A.M.-3 P.M., Sat. noon-4 P.M., and by appt.
Map 1

In its formative stage, this gallery was merely a small printmaking studio for its owners. In little more than a decade, it has developed into the most important nonprofit fine-art printmaking collaborative in the region. Located in an old warehouse in the artistically blossoming Quadrangle District, Zygote Press exhibits a full panoply of printed works of art, including letterpress, waterless lithography, etchings, relief, screen printing, and photo-crossover. Their exhibits feature the work of local, national, and international artists and printmakers.

## PERFORMING ARTS
### APOLLO'S FIRE
216/320-0012, www.apollosfire.org

The *Boston Globe* called Apollo's Fire one of America's leading baroque orchestras. When they are not touring the nation or recording, this professional ensemble moves listeners at home through its calendar of performances. Concerts are held from fall through spring at various locations in and around Cleveland and Akron, primarily in large churches. For a bite-size portion of baroque, check the schedule for one of the popular matinee concerts, 45-minute programs geared to young children and antsy adults. Tickets for these and other programs can be purchased by phone or online.

# SPARED FROM THE WRECKING BALL: CLEVELAND'S GREAT THEATERS

Like all cities, Cleveland has blown it by demolishing buildings with great architectural merit. Only in hindsight do civic leaders and city residents typically grasp the value of what's been lost in the name of progress. If not for the work of a few visionary preservationists in the 1970s, Cleveland's PlayhouseSquare would have vanished like so many other architectural gems.

PlayhouseSquare's five opulent theaters opened between 1921 and 1922. Built in the classical style, the Ohio, State, Palace, Allen, and Hanna Theaters boasted expanses of marble, lush hardwoods, hand-painted murals, and extravagant lobbies. For decades these houses entertained pleasure-seekers with a variety of vaudeville acts, cinema, and dramatic performances.

In the late 1960s, downtown suffered from a disastrous cocktail of economic distress, suburban flight, and racial disquiet. Shops closed, people fled, and the theaters went dark. Vandals, thieves, and inattention so damaged the shuttered theaters that demolition was all but assured.

Led by Ray Shepardson, a nonprofit called Playhouse Square Association campaigned to save the theaters. Thanks to public and private partnerships, money was raised to not only save the theaters from destruction, but also to begin repairing and restoring them. By the late 1990s, four of the five theaters had been restored to their former glory. In 2008, the last of the five theaters reopened as the stunning new home of the **Great Lakes Theater Festival.** These days, every year over a million visitors see performances at these theaters and scores of smaller performance spaces concentrated in the two-block zone, and the economic overflow can be observed at area restaurants, shops, and hotels.

Walk through PlayhouseSquare on a brisk fall night and it's easy to see what Shepardson worked so hard to preserve. After all, without the arts, where is the beauty of life?

## THE BANG AND THE CLATTER
224 Euclid Ave., 330/606-5317, www.bnctheatre.com
`Map 1`

This small experimental theater in the East 4th Street District is making waves with its high-quality productions of off-beat American plays. Like its sister theater in Akron, this Cleveland outpost stirs the collective pot of discussion with its calendar of provocative performances. Depending on the play, seating capacity can range from just 50 to well over 100. All tickets cost $15, unless you can't afford that: BNC offers a Pay-As-You-Can program for students, seniors, and anybody else who needs it.

## BECK CENTER FOR THE ARTS
17801 Detroit Ave., 216/521-2540, www.beckcenter.org
`Map 6`

In addition to its impressive arts-education programming, the Beck produces a full season of professional theater, including comedies, musicals, and contemporary drama. Roughly eight performances per year are presented from fall through late spring on one of two stages. Recent productions include ambitious takes on *Urinetown, Peter Pan,* and *The Farnsworth Invention.* An equally impressive roster of youth theater is performed by Beck drama students. Make sure you leave a little extra time to wander through the Beck's art gallery, which often is filled with pulsating exhibits.

## CLEVELAND INSTITUTE OF MUSIC
11021 East Blvd., 216/791-5000, www.cim.edu
`Map 4`

Gifted classical musicians from all over the globe come to Cleveland to study at this world-class conservatory. Those of us who can only dream about such talent flock to this school's matchless concert series. Students, faculty (including 35 Cleveland Orchestra members), and visiting luminaries perform year-round on the

ARTS AND LEISURE

Dramatic Mixon Hall at the Cleveland Institute of Music is the site of free classical music concerts.

stages of this University Circle institution. Concerts range from solo guitar recitals to full-on string quartets. These days, concertgoers have it better than ever thanks to the stunning new Mixon Hall, a 250-seat rectangular glass recital hall. All concerts are free unless otherwise noted. Seating for free concerts is generally on a first-come, first-served basis, though some passes may be reserved one week ahead of time by phone. Cameras and recording devices are prohibited.

### ◖ CLEVELAND ORCHESTRA

11001 Euclid Ave., 216/231-1111,
www.clevelandorchestra.com
**Map 4**

There is little contention that the Cleveland Orchestra, under the leadership of music director Franz Welser-Möst, is one of the finest orchestras playing anywhere today. Audiences and critics from New York to Vienna routinely praise the band as sheer musical triumph. From late September through May, the orchestra performs at breathtaking Severance Hall. From early July through Labor Day, the orchestra performs weekend concerts at their summer home, Blossom Music Center. On a fine summer night, there is nothing better than spreading out a blanket on the lawn at Blossom to enjoy some classical music. In addition to performing major symphonies from the world's finest composers, the orchestra has announced the introduction of fully staged operas. Utilizing stage sets and costumes from the Zurich Opera, and with the orchestra relocated to Severance's orchestral pit, Welser-Möst will present Mozart's *The Marriage of Figaro* (2009), *Cosi fan tutte* (2010) and *Don Giovanni* (2011). For nearly 20 years, the Cleveland Orchestra has performed a free concert in downtown's Public Square in honor of Independence Day. The annual event takes place the week of the Fourth of July, attracts some 80,000 people, and is capped off with a rousing performance of Tchaikovsky's 1812 overture followed by a fireworks display. Get there early, bring a picnic dinner, and enjoy one of Cleveland's finest moments.

© DOUGLAS TRATTNER

Professional contemporary theater is onstage at the Cleveland Public Theatre.

## CLEVELAND PLAY HOUSE

8500 Euclid Ave., 216/795-7000,
www.clevelandplayhouse.com

Map 4

If you're looking for big names and bright lights, this is the theater for you. Established in 1915, the Play House is one of America's longest-running professional theater companies. Producing a full lineup of popular plays from well-established playwrights, this house is packed from September through May. While it's not the most adventurous programming in town, there is no denying that under artistic director Michael Bloom, the theater is currently enjoying a renaissance of both quality and commercial viability. Designed by star architect (and Cleveland native) Philip Johnson, the 12-acre compound consists of three buildings and four theaters. The annual production of *A Christmas Story,* which is based on the movie set in Cleveland, has become a holiday-season tradition. Backstage tours are available on weekends year-round. Tickets are available through the Play House website or by phone.

## ◖ CLEVELAND PUBLIC THEATRE

6415 Detroit Ave., 216/631-2727, www.cptonline.org

Map 3

There may be no more important stage in Ohio for experiencing innovative and adventurous original theater. Anchoring the burgeoning Gordon Square Arts District, this public theater opened in 1981 offers so much more than just modern drama. CPT's groundbreaking performances entertain and inspire an entire community, and, in the process, propel it to a better place. From fall through early summer, the calendar is loaded with theatrical gems, many of which are Ohio and regional premiers. On top of the regular roster, special events might include a festival of 10-minute plays, readings of new works by emerging playwrights, and the popular Big Box series of new resident-produced work. And though David Sedaris cringes every single time he hears the title, *The Santaland Diaries* is performed most winters. Tickets may be purchased by phone or by stopping by the box office Wednesday–Sunday.

ARTS AND LEISURE

## CONVERGENCE-CONTINUUM

2438 Scranton Rd., 216/687-0074,
www.convergence-continuum.org

**Map 2**

Shattering theater's fourth wall since 2002, this oddball theater company is anything but traditional. But with success comes a little more convention—a good thing considering that until recently, the company rarely announced its roster of plays ahead of time. Its stage, called the Liminis, is set in a former garage on the fringes of trendy Tremont and accommodates only 50. Many of the ambitious productions, which run spring through late fall, are performed for the first time in Ohio.

## DANCECLEVELAND

PlayhouseSquare, 216/241-6000,
www.dancecleveland.org

**Map 1**

Dedicated to bringing the very best of modern and contemporary dance to town, DANCECleveland presents the works of nationally and internationally recognized troupes. Performances are held in Akron and in PlayhouseSquare and feature the best touring companies out there, including those of Merce Cunningham, Alvin Ailey, and Lar Lubovitch. Approximately four to six bookings take place each season, which runs from fall through spring. Tickets are available at the State Theatre box office or by phone.

## GREAT LAKES THEATER FESTIVAL

1501 Euclid Ave., 216/241-6000,
www.greatlakestheater.org

**Map 1**

These are exciting times for the Great Lakes Theater Festival, a company that has been around since the early 1960s and has seen talent the likes of Tom Hanks, Piper Laurie, Hal Holbrook, and Olympia Dukakis. A high-tech overhaul of the historic Hanna Theatre has given this company a striking new home. The reconfigured theater is now an intimate 550-seat space featuring a flexible thrust stage that brings the action right into the laps of audience members. The futuristic stage is appropriate for a company renowned for reimagining classic productions. Unique, too, is the diversity of seating options, ranging from traditional theater chairs and private boxes to more casual lounge and bar seating. Plays are performed in rotating repertory, with shows alternating every few nights. Scheduled performances run from September through May and feature works by Shakespeare, Chekhov, and Sondheim, to name but a few. Charles Dickens' holiday classic *A Christmas Carol* is performed from late November through Christmas. Adult ticket prices range $15–70 and are available by phone.

## GROUNDWORKS DANCETHEATER

216/691-3180,
www.notsoobvious.com

GroundWorks breaks ground by taking risk. The small but professional company's repertory of contemporary dance includes pieces choreographed by artistic director David Shimotakahara as well as works created by various guest choreographers. Performances are scattered about town throughout the year, with appearances at PlayhouseSquare, Trinity Cathedral (2230 Euclid Ave.), and an Akron venue called the Ice House. Tickets range $15–25.

## KARAMU HOUSE

2355 E. 89th St., 216/795-7077,
www.karamu.com

**Map 7**

Formerly the Playhouse Settlement, Karamu is the nation's oldest African-American cultural arts institution. The famous interracial theater company was the site of many Langston Hughes premiers. Under the artistic direction of Terrence Spivey, Karamu is once again electrifying and edifying new generations of theatergoers. While there is no shortage of knee-slapping comedies and musicals, many of the works are serious and thought-provoking examinations of race and culture. The regular schedule runs from fall through spring. Tickets cost around $20 and are available by phone or at the theater's box office.

## NEAR WEST THEATRE

3606 Bridge Ave., 216/961-9750,
www.nearwesttheatre.org

Map 2

It's amazing what a few footlights can do for a person. Since 1978, this community theater has changed the lives of over 15,000 children, teens, and adults, many from poverty-stricken families and neighborhoods. By committing to a schedule that is intense, difficult, and ultimately rewarding, participants come out on the other end more confident and with a stronger sense of self. But don't let the grassroots cause delude you; the productions here are as good as any amateur youth theater around. Good news is around the bend, too, as plans to build a new 300-seat theater in the emerging Gordon Square Arts District come to fruition in the coming years.

## OPERA CLEVELAND

1519 Euclid Ave., 216/241-6000,
www.operacleveland.org

Map 1

The merger of Lyric Opera and Cleveland Opera has lead to a best-of-all-worlds situation for opera fans. Performed at the State Theatre in PlayhouseSquare, the full-scale productions are professionally produced, each costing upwards of $500,000. Seasons typically consist of three operas, each performed on three separate dates. Operas are sung in their native language with projected English supertitles. Forget everything you think you know about opera and come with an open mind. You will more than likely leave with a song in your heart and a spring in your step. Single-seat ticket prices range from as little as $25 up to $130 and are available at the State Theatre box office or by phone.

## PLAYHOUSESQUARE

Euclid Ave., 216/241-6000, www.playhousesquare.org

Map 1

Comprised of five 1920s-era theaters plus numerous smaller performing spaces, PlayhouseSquare is the nation's largest performing-arts center outside of New York City. Over 1,000 shows take place every year, including the best of

---

# SMART SEATS

Looking for an affordable way to catch a show in PlayhouseSquare? Many performances set aside a number of discount tickets that can be purchased ahead of time. These Smart Seats cost just $10 apiece, roughly the cost of going to a movie. Simply surf over to www.playhousesquare.org and search for a show that interests you. If the play, concert, or dance listing has the Smart Seats logo under the ticket information, that means there are cheap seats available. You likely will be seated in the rear of the balcony, but at a savings of up to 80 percent off the primo seats, there is little to complain about.

---

Broadway, musical acts, opera, literary presentations, and comedy shows. In the 1970s, the five grand vaudeville-era theaters—the Palace, State, Ohio, Allen, and Hanna—were literally moments from the business end of a wrecking ball. Public outcry and strong community involvement not only saved each and every one of them, it eventually brought about the largest theater restoration project of its kind. Saving the best for last, the Hanna has just received a $20 million makeover to transform it into the high-tech home of the Great Lakes Theater Festival, the company that gave Tom Hanks his first big break. PlayhouseSquare is more than just a collection of performance spaces; it is the creative backbone of a district that includes hotels, bars, restaurants, offices, and the new home of Cleveland's public radio and television stations. Tickets are available by phone or at the box office in the lobby of the State Theatre, which is open daily 11 A.M.–6 P.M. Smart Seats are available for some performances at a heavily discounted price (see sidebar)—ask for them if you don't care where you sit. A nearby parking garage is located at the corner East 15th St. and Chester Avenue. Free two-hour tours are typically offered the first Saturday of the month, leaving the State Theatre lobby every 15 minutes 10–11:30 A.M.

ARTS AND LEISURE

## VERB BALLETS

216/397-3757, www.verbballets.org

This contemporary dance company maintains a deep repertory of pieces, many choreographed by former artistic director Hernando Cortez. A self-described curator of expressive movement, Verb "discovers, collects, interprets, and stages choreography that matters." Performances are scattered about town throughout the year, from PlayhouseSquare and Cain Park to Tremont's Lincoln Park and points south in Akron. Tickets range from free to $70.

## CONCERT VENUES

### BLOSSOM MUSIC CENTER

1145 W. Steels Corners Rd., Cuyahoga Falls,
888/225-6776, www.clevelandorch.com
**Map 7**

Built in the late 1960s as the summer home of the Cleveland Orchestra, this amphitheater sees a full range of live-music action from spring until fall. Tucked into Cuyahoga Valley National Park, the setting is one of dense forests, leafy hillsides, and wide-open skies. On a warm summer evening, there is no greater joy than tossing down a blanket and enjoying a picnic under the stars while the orchestra or your favorite band performs. Then again, that night can sour quickly if the clouds darken and the rain falls. Be prepared with tarps, rain gear, and an extra set of dry clothes for the long drive home. Or do what many regulars do: Spring for seats in the covered pavilion as insurance. Traffic in and out of the park can be brutal, so leave plenty of extra travel time.

### ◖ EVANS AMPHITHEATER

Superior at Lee, 216/371-3000, www.cainpark.com
**Map 5**

This gem of an urban amphitheater is nestled into a wooded Cleveland Heights park. Wholly invisible to drivers and passersby, the concert venue always delights first-timers (though this is not to say that it doesn't tickle second- and third-timers as well). While small—1,200 under cover, 1,200 on the lawn—Evans Amphitheater draws top-talent artists who crave more intimate settings. The venue is a favorite of singer-songwriters like Lyle Lovett, k.d. lang, and Bruce Hornsby, who seem to make stops here most years. Concerts run from about the middle of June through August. Specials like $2 Tuesdays and free jazz in the afternoon offer amazing shows at amazing prices. The smaller 300-seat Alma Theater is the site of musicals, cabarets, and local acts. Pack a blanket and a picnic, or buy snacks at the concession stand. Though you can't bring in alcohol, you can buy beer and wine inside. Tickets are available through Ticketmaster (www.ticketmaster.com), but to save on fees hit the Cain Park box office. This park is also the site of the popular **Cain Park Arts Festival.**

### CLEVELAND AGORA

5000 Euclid Ave., 216/881-6700,
www.clevelandagora.com
**Map 1**

The Cleveland Agora has a rich history that dates all the way back to the 1960s. The live-music club has been an important force not only in the Cleveland music scene, but also the national one, breaking bands too numerous to list. All the great performers have graced its stages, from Bruce Springsteen and Bob Marley to the Clash and U2. Today the acts are largely metal, punk, and hard rock. The music hall is comprised of one large and one small room, with room for 1,700 and 500 fans respectively. Seating is always general admission, so get there early if you want to secure a specific spot. There are plans to renovate the club, so a brief closure may or may not be in the cards. Tickets for shows can be obtained through Ticketmaster (www.ticketmaster.com), or at the box office Monday–Friday 10 A.M.–5:30 P.M., later on show nights.

### HOUSE OF BLUES

308 Euclid Ave., 216/523-2583,
www.hob.com/cleveland
**Map 1**

One of a dozen or so HOBs sprinkled across the United States, the Cleveland venue was built in 2004. With its considerable might, the company snags most of the biggest acts that sweep through town. The large main hall accommodates approximately 1,200 guests, while the more intimate Cambridge Room, with its modest 300-seat capacity, is better suited to smaller attractions. The compound boasts numerous bars, a full-service restaurant, gift shop, and the exclusive members-only Foundation Room. Sundays at the House are all about the popular Gospel Brunch, which features a mile-long buffet and rousing live gospel performance. Tickets for shows can be obtained by phone, online through Ticketmaster (www.ticketmaster.com), or by stopping by the box office between 10 A.M. and 6 P.M.

## LAKEWOOD CIVIC AUDITORIUM
14100 Franklin Blvd., 216/529-4081, www.lkwdpl.org/schools/civicaud
**Map 6**

When bands, comics, and other entertainers graduate from clubs to theaters, they perform at a place like Lakewood Civic Auditorium. The 2,000-seat hall is not too big, not too small, but just right, as Goldilocks might say. Despite its plain-Jane appearance, the venue has quite a laudable reputation. It was where Tom Hanks got his theatrical start while performing with the Great Lakes Shakespeare Festival (now the Great Lakes Theater Festival). These days, the hall sees the likes of Wilco, Alice Cooper, and comedian Brian Regan. On a more local level, the auditorium is used for numerous high school graduations and concerts. The sober truth: Lakewood Civic Auditorium is attached to a high school, therefore no adult refreshments are served.

## NAUTICA PAVILION
2014 Sycamore St., 440/247-2722, www.livenation.com
**Map 1**

Pretty as a picture, this sharp urban amphitheater is located on the West Bank of the Flats, adjacent to Nautica Entertainment Complex, and boasts great views of the river, the bridges, and the passing ships. Largely covered, the roughly 5,000 seats are spread among general-admission floor seats, bleachers, and standing-room areas. Approximately 10 shows per summer come here, ranging from megastars like Dylan to jam bands like Widespread

Panic. This snug venue also is ideal for local legends like First Light and Michael Stanley.

## QUICKEN LOANS ARENA
One Center Court, 216/420-2000, www.theqarena.com
**Map 1**

Known simply as the "Q," Quicken Loans Arena is the permanent home of the Cleveland Cavaliers and Lake Erie Monsters and the temporary home of touring musicians, professional wrestlers, and Olympic gymnasts. Since 2000, the Q has also been the site of the Mid-American Conference (MAC) Men's & Women's Championship Tournaments. Located in the Gateway District, the 20,000-seat arena sits on the southwestern edge of downtown, directly adjacent to Progressive Field. LeBron James fans can stop by the Cavaliers Team Shop to grab a #23 jersey or shoot-around shirt. In nasty weather it's good to know that both the Q and Progressive Field can be reached from Tower City and the RTA via underground walkways.

## TIME WARNER CABLE AMPHITHEATER
351 Canal Rd., 216/522-4822, www.livenation.com
**Map 1**

This riverside concert venue accommodates roughly 5,000 concertgoers. While it is indeed outdoors, the main concert area is covered by a large circus tent–like roof. Depending on the show, tickets are either reserved or general admission. Performances run from early May through September and typically involve second-tier touring acts. Located behind Tower City Center, this is also the site of the Great American Rib Cook-Off.

## WOLSTEIN CENTER
2000 Prospect Ave., 216/687/9292, www.csuohio.edu/wolsteincenter
**Map 1**

Cleveland's other main arena is actually part of the Cleveland State University campus. This 14,000-seat venue is home to the CSU Vikings, men's and women's Division I basketball teams. It is also used year-round for major performers like Carrie Underwood, and touring spectacles

**ARTS AND LEISURE**

like the Wiggles. Tickets are available through Ticketmaster (www.ticketmaster.com) or at the box office (Prospect Ave. entrance) Monday–Friday, 10 A.M.–6 P.M.

## CINEMA

### CEDAR LEE THEATRE

2163 Lee Rd., 216/321-5411, www.clevelandcinemas.com

**Map 5**

The Cedar Lee shows the very best in first-run independent film. If it played well at Sundance, chances are good you'll see it on the marquee of this Cleveland Heights landmark. But it isn't only esoteric head-scratchers on the schedule; Oscar-worthy Hollywood fare is also screened here. Cult-movie fans have been coming here to catch the midnight showing of *The Rocky Horror Picture Show* for 20 years. At the better-than-average concession stands, you'll find fresh pastries, wraps, coffee drinks, herbal tea, imported beers, and wine—and popcorn, of course. Some of the six theaters are roomier than others. Like Tower City Cinemas and Shaker Square Cinemas, this theater hosts Bargain Mondays, with $5 tickets and free popcorn.

### CLEVELAND INSTITUTE OF ART CINEMATHEQUE

11141 East Blvd., 216/421-7450, www.cia.edu/cinematheque

**Map 4**

If it weren't for the Cinematheque, obsessive Cleveland film fans would never lay eyes upon some of the finest foreign, classic, and independent movies of our time—or any other, for that matter. As the name suggests, this 600-seat paean to alternative film is located on the campus of the CIA, in the Gund Building to be exact. Utilizing deluxe 35-mm projectors, approximately 250 different feature films are shown per year, mostly Thursday through Sunday nights. Admission to most films is $8, or $13 for two on the same day.

### OMNIMAX THEATER

601 Erieside Ave., 216/694-2000, www.glsc.org

**Map 1**

That big brown sphere on Lake Erie's shore is not a large egg waiting to hatch; it's the exterior of the Great Lakes Science Center's OMNIMAX Theater. While IMAX films are praised for their scale and richness, OMNIMAX takes the experience to another plane. A six-story wraparound screen surrounds the viewer, creating an extraordinarily immersive experience. The movies shown here are largely the science-museum type, focusing more on education than sheer enjoyment. Also, most are shown only in the middle of the day, making them difficult to schedule around. Still, taking a virtual ride in an F-15 is pretty sweet, especially tilted back at 30 degrees.

### SHAKER SQUARE CINEMAS

13116 Shaker Sq., 440/564-2032, www.clevelandcinemas.com

**Map 5**

This renovated art-deco movie house now features six state-of-the-art theaters that screen major Hollywood releases plus some independent and foreign fare. Located on Shaker Square, the theater is near numerous bars and restaurants, making a dinner-date a breeze. In addition to the typical sugary and crunchy provisions, the concession stand also sells pastries, beer, and wine. Like Tower City Cinemas and Cedar Lee Theatre, this theater hosts Bargain Mondays, with $5 tickets and free popcorn.

### TOWER CITY CINEMAS

Tower City Center, 230 W. Huron Rd., 440/564-2031, www.clevelandcinemas.com

**Map 1**

Downtown's only multiplex, this 11-screen theater shows popular first-run fare. While you won't likely catch the latest Woody Allen drama here, you will find slapstick, horror, and superhero mega-hits. Every March, Tower City Cinema is the site of the wonderful Cleveland International Film Fest, an 11-day, 140-film extravaganza. Like Cedar Lee Theatre and Shaker Square Cinemas, this theater hosts Bargain Mondays, with $5 tickets and free popcorn. Present your ticket stub and parking voucher at the Tower City Customer Service Desk to get free parking.

# Festivals and Events

## WINTER

### ☾ CLEVELAND INTERNATIONAL FILM FEST

Tower City Cinemas, 866/865-3456,
www.clevelandfilm.org
**COST:** Varies
`Map 1`

With about 50,000 people attending some 300 films over an 11-day period, the Cleveland International Film Fest is an absolute whirl of activity. Screenings take place all day in multiple theaters at Tower City Cinemas. Bona fide film-fest fans know to get their program guide well in advance so as to map out a plan of attack. The March event always kicks off with an opening-night film and gala, followed by approximately 140 feature-length films and 170 short subjects from over 60 different countries. Numerous filmmakers are personally on hand to lead post-flick Q-and-A sessions. Attending the festival for the first time can be a little overwhelming. The best strategy is to look over the program guide, select the movies you'd care to see, and buy tickets in advance. Short of that, it is wise to get to the cinema early to avoid being shut out. Tickets can be purchased in the lobby of Tower City Cinemas or by phone and cost $12, less for six-packs and members of the Cleveland Film Society. If you self-parked in the Tower City lot, make sure to get your parking voucher validated at the Festival Store kiosk.

### CLEVELAND WINTERFEST

Public Sq., www.cleveland.com/winterfest
**COST:** Free
`Map 1`

Thousands choose to get into the holiday spirit by attending this annual downtown celebration. Festivities take place in Public Square on the first Saturday after Thanksgiving. A number of family-friendly events occur throughout the day in and around the square, but the real party kicks off with the holiday tree lighting at dusk. Depending on the weather, the parade of

Cleveland celebrates the holidays at WinterFest.

vintage horse-drawn carriages that follows can look like a scene ripped from a Currier and Ives print. Fire trucks, fife and drum corps, and marching bands also boisterously work their way around the square. The night is capped off by a spectacular fireworks display.

### HOME AND GARDEN SHOW

I-X Center, 6200 Riverside Dr., 800/600-0307,
www.homeandflower.com
**COST:** $13 adult, $4 child
`Map 7`

At the tail end of winter, when it feels like spring will never arrive, the annual Home and Garden Show is a welcome reprieve. Close to a quarter of a million people make the trip to Cleveland's International Exposition Center over the course of one week in February to dream about what's just around the bend. The event is over 65 years old and is considered one of the largest indoor home and garden shows in the nation. A massive convention floor is filled with dazzling flower and garden displays, fully decorated model homes, home improvement vendors, and live cooking demonstrations. The popular closing-night plant sale is an opportunity to snag loads of plant material for a bargain. Be prepared to pay an infuriating $8 to park in addition to the entrance fee. Look for discounted tickets at Home Depot.

### ST. PATRICK'S DAY PARADE
Superior Ave., www.clevelandsirishparade.org
COST: Free
Map 1

The Cleveland Irish community is large and proud. How else do you explain an outdoor parade in the middle of March attracting upwards of 375,000 people? With roots stretching clear back to 1867, Cleveland's St. Patrick's Day Parade is one of the largest and oldest of its kind in the nation. The parade steps off at 1 P.M. on March 17th; if the holiday falls on a Sunday start time is 2 P.M. Over 10,000 participants take part in the march, which works its way down Superior Avenue from East 18th to Public Square. Get to the parade route early to secure a good vantage point to watch the seemingly never-ending line of marching bands, Irish dancers, drill teams, military units, civic clubs, waving politicians, and local celebrities. Because this event is held in March, the weather can be wildly unpredictable. As the Boy Scouts say, "be prepared."

## SPRING

### CLEVELAND BOTANICAL GARDEN FLOWER SHOW
11030 East Blvd., 216/721-1600, www.cbgarden.org
COST: $20 adult (less in advance), $6 child
Map 4

Every two years, the Cleveland Botanical Garden presents the largest outdoor garden show in North America. Its lofty reputation approaches that of England's RHS Chelsea Flower Show. In addition to the CBG's permanent-collection gardens, a dozen or so new themed gardens are constructed specifically for the five-day event. In all, some 30 stunning gardens covering approximately 10 acres

are on display. Rounding out the rain-or-shine event are expert lectures, flower arranging and photography exhibits, and an enormous marketplace filled with plants, garden accessories, and clothing. Look for the event on Memorial Day weekend.

### GREAT AMERICAN RIB COOK-OFF
Time Warner Cable Amphitheater, 888/761-7469, www.cleveland.com/rib
COST: $7 adult, free child under 12
Map 1

A Memorial Day tradition for close to 20 years, the Great American Rib Cook-Off kicks off summer with a carnivorous celebration of smoke, fire, meat, and music. For four days in May, some of the nation's best pit masters gather at Time Warner Cable Amphitheater to show off their barbecue prowess and compete for the titles of "Greatest Ribs," "Greatest Sauce," and "People's Choice." Wander the festival and sample St. Louis–style ribs, pulled pork, and barbecue chicken from some serious talent. Keep an eye out for former Cleveland Browns star Al "Bubba" Baker, who smokes the real deal at his popular Avon restaurant Bubba's Q. Admission price does not include food and beverage tickets, which are swapped for the real deal. Keep in mind that prices for ribs and other food items can be steep. Admission does include loads of free entertainment, including local, regional, and national music acts.

### RITE AID CLEVELAND MARATHON
800/467-3826, www.clevelandmarathon.com
COST: Free

Started in 1978, the Cleveland Marathon is one of the oldest continuously held foot races in the nation. Over $15,000 in prize money is awarded to the winners of the men's and women's marathon, half-marathon, and 10K races. Of course, the 10,000 or so athletes who compete each year do so for bragging rights, not cash. The relatively flat 26.3-mile course takes runners past such notable landmarks as the Rock Hall, Great Lakes Science Center, Cleveland Browns Stadium, and through Ohio

City, PlayhouseSquare, and University Circle. Even if you've never donned a pair of sneakers in your life, consider coming down for the party. In good weather, massive and enthusiastic crowds gather along the course and at the finish line (E. 9th St. and St. Clair Ave.) to cheer on the runners.

### TRI-C JAZZFEST
216/987-4400, www.tricjazzfest.com
**COST:** Varies
This annual two-week event is the largest music festival in Ohio and the largest educational jazz festival in the country. The popular event, now 30 years in the making, begins in late April and takes place at numerous venues throughout town. Local, national, and international jazz artists not only perform, but teach, compose, and inspire the next generation at workshops, clinics, and lectures. Tickets for the concerts, which take place at libraries, bars, clubs, PlayhouseSquare, and Severance Hall, range in price. Check the Tri-C website for schedules, performance, events, and ticket information.

### WEEKEND IN OHIO CITY
Market Ave. and W. 25th St., 216/781-3222, www.ohiocity.com
**COST:** $110 Evening in Ohio City, $20 Ohio City Home Tour
**Map 2**
For 20 years, this popular springtime event has showcased the slow, steady, and undeniable renaissance of this blossoming urban neighborhood. The umbrella event entitled Weekend in Ohio City is comprised of Evening in Ohio City, a progressive food- and wine-tasting that moves guests from house to house, and Ohio City Home Tour, the main event. Art, architecture, and history buffs—not to mention the unabashedly nosey—have the opportunity to snoop into a dozen or so lovingly restored late-19th-century Victorians, Italianates, and Colonials. Spread across a sizeable distance, attendees can either stroll from home to home or hop aboard one of the ever-circulating trolleys. Many in attendance make the wise decision to take a midday break at one of the local eateries for a quick bite and much-earned refreshment. Evening in Ohio City tickets move quickly, but Ohio City Home Tour tickets can be purchased the day of the event.

## SUMMER
### BURNING RIVER FEST
Nautica Entertainment Complex, 216/771-4404, www.burningriverfest.org
**COST:** $8 pre-sale, $12 day of event, free child under 8
**Map 1**
Stewarded by the green-tinged Great Lakes Brewing Co., the Burning River Fest is more than just another occasion to party. Held annually during the second weekend in August, the Fest is all about living responsibly. Important issues such as ecological conservation, environmental protection, historic preservation, and sustainable use of waterways are tackled through numerous exhibits, discussions, and demonstrations. Despite the lofty message, some 11,000 folks find plenty of reasons to smile at this bio-minded block party. Top chefs are on hand to whip up sustainably harvested meals. Bands play on two separate stages. Kids are entertained by face painting and biodegradable balloon animals. And for thirsty adults, there are always buckets of ice-cold locally brewed beer.

### CAIN PARK ARTS FESTIVAL
Superior Rd. at Lee Rd., 216/371-3000, www.cainpark.com
**COST:** $2
**Map 5**
Held annually the second full weekend in July, this top-rated juried arts festival runs Friday through Sunday and features the visual art of some 150 artists. Over the course of a weekend, over 60,000 visitors will stroll the wooded grounds of Cain Park exploring original works of art, including paintings, watercolors, photography, sculpture, ceramics, and jewelry. Accompanying the art show is a full complement of adult and family entertainment at nearby Evans Amphitheater and Alma Theater. Local restaurants also set up shop and provide the fuel for an afternoon of delicious spending.

ARTS AND LEISURE

## CLEVELAND PRIDE PARADE AND FESTIVAL

Voinovich Bicentennial Park, 216/371-0214,
www.clevelandpride.org
**COST:** Free, donations welcome
Map 1

In 2008, the Cleveland Pride Parade and Festival celebrated its 20th anniversary, making it one of the longest-running Pride events in the country. You certainly needn't be lesbian, gay, bi, or transsexual to enjoy this fantastically festive day. Normally held in late June, the event kicks off with a wild parade to Voinovich Park, where an all-day party ensues. Multiple stages feature top-talent musicians and entertainers, while rallies and speeches preach messages of tolerance and acceptance. Revelers can quench their thirst in a lakeside beer garden and sate their hunger at numerous food stands. Also, look for Pride-related events all weekend long at area gay bars such as Twist. Step off takes place at noon from West 3rd Street and Rockwell Avenue. The party at Voinovich Park kicks off at 1 P.M.

## CLIFTON ARTS & MUSICFEST

Clifton Blvd. at W. 117th St., 216/228-4383,
www.cudell.com/artsfest.asp
**COST:** Free
Map 3

What started as a small neighborhood block party some 20 years ago has blossomed into a full-fledged arts and music festival attracting close to 40,000 revelers per year. Only slightly smaller than the renowned Cain Park Art Festival, Clifton Arts features the works of about 120 different artists in every conceivable genre. Long regarded as one of the more free-spirited neighborhoods, Clifton knows how to throw a bash. A full lineup of live music covers most tastes, from rock and blues to reggae and funk. Scores of restaurants dish up local specialties and community and civic organizations offer craft activities for the little artists in the group. Look for this event around the third Saturday in June.

## FEAST OF THE ASSUMPTION

Mayfield Rd. at Murray Hill Rd., 216/421-2995,

www.littleitalycleveland.com
**COST:** Free
Map 4

Technically, the Feast celebrates the ascension of the Virgin Mary. Practically, it is an occasion to party like the characters on the *Sopranos*. This annual four-day blowout begins solemn enough, with Mass followed by a procession of the Blessed Virgin through Little Italy. The real party hits the streets at night, when literally thousands descend upon the narrow lanes of this Old World neighborhood. Main attractions, apart from the booze, include authentic Italian treats like sausage-and-pepper sandwiches, creamy gelato, and delicious cannoli. Back-alley charity casino games tucked into smoky tents have a delightfully illicit feel to them. The festivities end with a bang thanks to a rousing fireworks display. Look for the Feast in mid-August.

## INGENUITY FESTIVAL

PlayhouseSquare, 216/241-6000,
www.ingenuitycleveland.com
**COST:** $10 per day, $15 for the weekend
Map 1

This festival is billed as the fusion of art and technology. That's as precise a definition as one is likely to get when it comes to this free-flowing, high-concept avant-garde celebration of interactive art. As far from a stodgy museum experience as one can possibly get, Ingenuity takes place in numerous urban locations over the course of three summer days. Centered in PlayhouseSquare, the myriad performances that occur on stages, in theaters, and around every bend transform a portion of downtown into a vastly different place. With surprises at every turn, even in the darkest of back alleys, Ingenuity is an interactive feast for a creativity-starved mind. Look for it in July.

## ◖ NORTH UNION FARMERS MARKET

216/751-7656, www.northunionfarmersmarket.org
**COST:** Free

The North Union Farmers Market operates approximately eight seasonal markets throughout Greater Cleveland, mostly between July and

© DOUGLAS TRATTNER

heirloom tomatoes from the North Union Farmers Market

October (see a complete listing of locations, dates, and times on the website). All are authentic producer-only markets, meaning that all food sold is actually grown, raised, or produced in the region by those who peddle it. Depending on the time of year, shoppers are likely to find fresh greens, radishes, garlic, tomatoes, corn, grass-fed beef, foraged wild mushrooms, homemade goat cheese, honey, bread, farm-raised shrimp, free-range poultry, and edible flowers. Without question, the oldest and best market in the bunch is the one held on Saturday mornings at Shaker Square, beginning around the middle of April and lasting well into December. A smaller indoor market even lasts through winter. In midsummer, the Shaker market teems with activity. Young couples sip coffee purchased from one of the nearby cafés, and casually shop for dinner. The city's top chefs, including Doug Katz from Shaker Square's fabulous Fire Food & Drink, shop for the evening's specials. Other chefs give demonstrations on how to cook with local ingredients. Performers provide a musical

backdrop. To get the best selection, it is always wise to go early; many items sell out well before the noon closing time. Always make a complete lap before purchasing anything, as another producer may have something slightly better, cheaper, or sweeter. Bring cash, preferably small bills, and bags to cart your items home. Oh, and leave the dogs at home; they aren't welcome here.

## PARADE THE CIRCLE

216/707-5033, www.clevelandart.org
**COST:** Free
Map 4

University Circle's signature summer event is not focused around a specific holiday, but on artistic expression, creativity, and the rich diversity of the neighborhood. The centerpiece of the event is the parade, which begins at noon and features a psychedelic pageant of whimsical costumed marchers. Approximately 2,000 people take part, some dressed as giant puppets, some towering over the crowd on stilts, and others taking spots on imaginative floats. Entertainment before and after the parade ranges from African dance and classical music to storytelling and puppet shows. The Circle Village area on Wade Oval is loaded with family-appropriate arts and crafts, food, and festivities. Typically held the second Saturday in June, the parade and subsequent activities can attract 60,000 people in nice weather. Grab your spot along East Boulevard or Wade Oval Drive by noon to enjoy the show.

## TASTE OF TREMONT

Professor Ave., 216/575-0920,
www.tremontwestdevelopment.com
**COST:** Free
Map 2

Of all the summer neighborhood festivals, Taste of Tremont pretty much has a lock on the "best food" category. Tremont is home to many of Cleveland's best restaurants, and most are on full display at this boisterous block party. Cordoned off from Literary Road to Jefferson Avenue, Professor Avenue turns into a blocks-long street party, capped off with a celebratory open-air beer garden. Sample the specialties of over a dozen local restaurants, most of which are dished up by the chefs personally. Live bands perform throughout the day, as do various and sundry roaming entertainers. Many of the super-cool galleries and boutiques extend their hours to coincide with the festival. The Taste of Tremont usually runs 1–8 P.M. around the third Sunday in July.

### WADE OVAL WEDNESDAYS!
Wade Oval, 216/707-5033, www.universitycircle.org
**COST:** Free
Map 4

On Wednesday evenings from June through August, folks gather on beautiful Wade Oval for free outdoor concerts and entertainment. This family-friendly event features local bands that play reggae, jazz, blues, and rock. Food, beer, and wine are sold on-site, and local artisans set up booths to sell their crafts. Many of University Circle's major cultural attractions offer extended evening hours that coincide with WOW! events, making it easy to plan a civilized night on the town. Bike riders can stow their carriages for free in the attended bike corral. Concerts usually run 6–9 P.M.

## FALL
### CLEVELAND NATIONAL AIR SHOW
Burke Lakefront Airport, 216/781-0747, www.clevelandairshow.com
**COST:** Varies
Map 1

If it's Labor Day in Cleveland, you can be sure to hear the roar of the U.S. Navy's Blue Angels F/A-18s as they prowl the skies. As the show's headline act, the Angels perform a one-hour choreographed flight presentation each day of the show. Other major tactical demonstrations include those of the Air Force's F-15 Eagle, F-16 Fighting Falcon, Navy's F/A-18F Super Hornet, and the Ohio Air National Guard's C-130 Hercules support aircraft. Look skyward, too, for amazing airborne acts like Cold War dogfights, biplane barnstorming, and the Army's Golden Knights precision parachute team. Other attractions on the grounds

include an F/A-18 flight simulator, numerous planes for viewing and cockpit picture-taking, and educational displays from NASA Glenn Research Center. Expect also the typical assortment of overpriced fair food and beer. Gates open Saturday morning, with shows running 10 A.M.–5 P.M. Saturday, Sunday, and Monday. Parking at the Municipal Parking Lot is expensive, so consider carpooling or taking RTA's Waterfront Line to East 9th Street, which leaves a relatively short walk to the area. Or simply do as thousands of others do: Find a spot along the shoreline and watch the action for free. General admission and reserved box seating is available at the gates the day of the show, by phone, or online.

### OKTOBERFEST
Cuyahoga County Fairgrounds, 164 Eastland Rd., Berea, 440/250-8600, www.bereaoktoberfest.com
**COST:** $8 adult, free child under 12
Map 7

Fans of German food, beer, music, and even dogs will want to set aside some time over Labor Day weekend for this celebration of all things Deutschland. From the ceremonial tapping of the keg to the very last "pa" of the oom-pa-pa bands, this popular seasonal attraction really does have something for everybody. Massive tents are erected to house the steady stream of performers, making this a rain-or-shine event. Music spans the generational divide, with polka, swing, disco, and rock. Food is provided by some of the most authentic German restaurants in the region. Beer is free-flowing and plentiful in the Bier Garden. One of the most eagerly anticipated events is the wiener-dog race, where vertically challenged dachshunds lumber their way down a 35-foot track in hopes of snagging the trophy. Parking is free all weekend.

### SPARX GALLERY HOP
216/736-7799, www.cleveland.com/sparx
Billed as Ohio's largest art walk, Sparx unites the efforts of over 50 independent galleries into a weekend-long celebration of art and culture. Typically held around the third weekend of

September, Sparx organizes a network of trolleys to link the major art districts in Tremont, Little Italy, University Circle, and Downtown. Not only is the goal to spark interest in local art, but to stimulate excitement about these urban neighborhoods on a smaller, more intimate level. Over the Saturday and Sunday events, galleries and nearby retail shops extend their hours of operation. Satellite art exhibits, mini-festivals, and musical performances also take place at various locations over the course of the weekend. Brightly marked bike paths were recently added to the proceedings, making it easier to pedal one's way from gallery to gallery.

### TASTE OF CLEVELAND

Time Warner Cable Amphitheater, 888/761-7469, www.cleveland.com/tasteofcleveland

**COST:** $7 adult, free child under 12

Map 1

Labor Day's annual food, music, and family-fun celebration, Taste of Cleveland is a long-standing North Coast tradition. Each year, over 30 different restaurants vie for the coveted Best Restaurant and Best Entrée awards. While you won't find Cleveland's best restaurants here, you will find a somewhat decent cross-section of the local food scene augmented by generic fair food and national-chain fare.

Admission prices do not cover food, beer, or wine, but they do cover entertainment. Many people come strictly for the live bands, which can range from has-beens to strong national acts. In nice weather, approximately 90,000 people attend over the Friday, Saturday, and Sunday dates.

## YEAR-ROUND

### POP UP CITY

www.popupcleveland.com

Like the proverbial Jell-O on a wall, Pop Up City is tough to pin down. But this arts-centric organization's wild and spontaneous pop-up experiences are well worth the investigation. Temporarily plugging the idle gaps in a shrinking city, Pop Up uses abandoned structures and vacant spaces as its canvas of choice. A neglected downtown storefront is transformed into a bustling bazaar filled with eager shoppers seeking artsy wares. The roof of an industrial building is transformed into an elegant open-air restaurant serving local sustainable cuisine. A pedestrian overpass is inhabited by storytellers, artists, and musicians. One particularly exuberant mid-winter event took place on a barren stretch of riverbed and featured ice art, snowboarding, and a bonfire. Check the website periodically for updates.

# Sports and Recreation

## PARKS

### CLEVELAND METROPARKS

216/635-3200, www.clemetparks.com

Fortunately for the residents of Greater Cleveland, early city and county leaders had the foresight to set aside some ground for conservation, education, and recreation. Cobbling together patches of land, the park board ultimately assembled a remarkable chain of parks and connecting boulevards that encircled the whole of Cuyahoga County. This ribbon of green space largely follows the waterways of the Rocky River, Chagrin River, Big Creek, Chippewa Creek, Tinkers Creek, and Euclid Creek. On a map, this patchwork of parks looks like a leafy necklace around the neck of Lady Cleveland, hence the Metroparks' nickname, the Emerald Necklace. Combined, the Metroparks' 16 reservations cover over 22,000 acres of dense forest, wetland, prairie, ravines, lakes, and streams. The activities available within the park system are seemingly endless, including (just to name a few) hiking, biking, swimming, fishing, golfing, cross-country skiing, birding, tobogganing, and geocaching, not to mention visiting the Zoo and RainForest. In addition to all the standard recreational opportunities, Metroparks' ambitious Institute of the Great Outdoors offers skill-based courses in survival, fly-fishing, backpacking, canoeing, kayaking, and so much more. Throughout the entire year, captivating events are held at the reservations' various lodges, shelters, and nature centers. Folks assemble for moonlit owl walks, fall foliage strolls, and marshy reptile hunts. It would not be hyperbole to claim that one could spend the rest of his or her life taking advantage of the park's gifts without ever tapping them out. Begin to explore them on the Metroparks website.

### CLEVELAND PUBLIC LIBRARY EASTMAN READING GARDEN

325 Superior Ave. NE, 216/623-2800, www.cpl.org

**Map 1**

This semi-secluded urban park has the feeling of a secret garden. Wedged between the broad shoulders of the Main Library and the Louis Stokes Wing, the space is buffeted from wind, noise, and prying eyes. Yet open to the busy main streets on either end, the garden is still connected to the city around it. Beyond a pair of heavy bronze gates, the lovely open-air park unfolds gradually. Leafy trees and sturdy sculpture provide the bones, while a graceful fountain, designed by the Ohio-born artist behind Washington, DC's Vietnam Veterans Memorial, cascades gently in the background. On warm summer days, the garden is a favorite lunch spot for office workers itching to escape their desks.

### EDGEWATER STATE PARK

6500 Memorial Shoreway, 216/881-8141, www.ohiodnr.com/parks

**Map 3**

A magnet for walkers, joggers, bicyclists, kite-flyers, sun-bathers, and anglers, Edgewater is many things to many people. That it is located just a couple miles from the hustle and bustle of downtown is a boon for all pleasure seekers. This lakefront park is comprised of two main areas, an elevated bluff and a lake-level beach. Amateur and professional shutterbugs

© DOUGLAS TRATTNER

gates to the tranquil Eastman Reading Garden

flock to the bluff for unrivalled city, lake, and sunset views. Walkers, joggers, and bicyclists crisscross the park on paved pathways, while fishermen drop lines off nearby piers and break walls. Don't ignore this park in winter, when frozen ocean spray creates dramatic natural sculptures along the shore. As fun as this park can be during the day, it's best to hightail it on out come dusk.

### FAIRVIEW PARK/KENTUCKY GARDENS

Franklin Blvd. at W. 28th St., 216/621-0449

**HOURS:** Dawn-dusk

**Map 2**

This two-acre patch of organic earth is home to some 130 community gardens, each no larger than 20 feet by 20 feet. For nearly six decades, Ohio City residents have provided food for their families by tilling in this urban oasis. Neighbors pay as little as $5 a year for their plots, but must work to maintain common spaces, which include mature fruit trees, working beehives, and ripening compost piles. It's best to visit this park in summer and fall, when gardeners are busy tending to their pint-size farms, absolutely teeming with colorful life.

### HORSESHOE LAKE PARK
South Park Blvd. at Park Dr., www.shakeronline.com
`Map 5`

Some of the many assets that attract residents to Shaker Heights are its green spaces. Deliberately laid out in the early 1900s as a garden community, the East Side suburb boasts numerous recreational gems, and Horseshoe Lake Park is one of them. Located near the preservation-minded Nature Center at Shaker Lakes, this park shares a similar stance on the environment. Elevated boardwalks fashioned from recycled materials weave through wetlands, simultaneously protecting the natural habitats while providing visitors a keen vantage point. Paved trails offer walkers, joggers, and bicyclists a safe route around the park, while nearby dirt paths wind their way through forests, ravines, and fields. Bird-watchers come here for the rich diversity of songbirds, waterfowl, and predators. Stone-clad shelters feature fireplaces and plenty of space to celebrate.

### LAKEWOOD OFF-LEASH DOG PARK
1299 Valley Pkwy., www.lakewooddogpark.com
`Map 6`

This great off-leash doggie park is located off Valley Parkway, in the Rocky River Reservation of the Cleveland Metroparks. The fenced-in area takes up two-thirds of an acre and features mature trees, gravel surfaces, waste-bag dispensers, and water stations for both canines and humans. A double-gated entrance gives owners an opportunity to unleash the hounds safely. So they don't harass the big guys, dogs smaller than 20 pounds have their own fenced-in area. No aggressive dogs—or people—are welcome.

### ROCKEFELLER PARK
690 East 88th Street, www.city.cleveland.oh.us
`Map 4`

Tucked into an otherwise unforgiving neighborhood, Rockefeller Park is a leafy 200-acre swathe that links University Circle and Lake Erie. Mostly hugging Martin Luther King Jr. Boulevard, the park contains walking paths, tennis courts, picnic areas, playgrounds, and basketball courts. Gorgeous arched bridges move city traffic from one side to the other. The park is perhaps most widely recognized as the home of the Cultural Gardens (www.culturalgardens.org), some three dozen sculptural gardens dedicated to ethnicities that have made Cleveland their home. In the India Garden, there is a striking bronze statue of Mahatma Gandhi mid-stride, clutching his walking stick. Time and poverty have not been kind to the many statues, monuments, and sculptures that form the centerpiece of the gardens. Some have been stolen for scrap, were tagged by gang members, or have fallen to the ravages of weather and neglect. But others are in the midst of repair, which is good news for fans of outdoor sculpture. Located here, too, is the Rockefeller Park Greenhouse (750 E. 88th St., 216/664-3103, www.rockefellergreenhouse.org), a year-round conservatory boasting lush tropical fruit plants, exotic orchids, and formal gardens. The greenhouse is also a great place to park when visiting the Cultural Gardens as it is free and close. It is important to note that while largely safe during the day, the area surrounding Rockefeller Park is nowhere to hang out after dark.

### WENDY PARK AT WHISKEY ISLAND
2800 Whiskey Island, www.wendypark.org
**HOURS:** Dawn-dusk
`Map 2`

Seductively elusive, this 20-acre park is so close you can practically touch it. But good luck actually getting there. Located where the Cuyahoga River spills into Lake Erie, this park is literally a mile from Public Square. To get here, though, requires a series of navigational machinations that seem to thwart most would-be visitors. That's perfectly fine with the regulars, however, who worship this tiny park as if it were the last unsullied strip of land in the world. Named after the whiskey distilleries that dotted the peninsula in the 1830s, the park has become one of the newest gems gracing the North Coast. Permanent volleyball courts draw local

ARTS AND LEISURE

sports clubs, while the Whiskey Island Marina's Sunset Grille (216/631-1801, www.whiskeyislandmarina.com) is beloved by boaters and landlubbers looking for a seaside restaurant. Bird-watchers come here for the wildlife and shutterbugs for the matchless views of the Flats, city skyline, and Lake Erie. Even architecture fans come here, to gaze at the fading shell of an abandoned Art Moderne–style coast-guard station. For detailed directions, visit the website.

## BICYCLING
### Mountain Biking
### OHIO & ERIE CANAL RESERVATION MOUNTAIN BIKE TRAIL
Grant Ave. at E. 49th St., www.camba.us
**HOURS:** Dusk-dawn
Map 7

Hats off to the Cleveland Area Mountain Bike Association, who built and maintains this single-track trail located minutes from town at the Ohio & Erie Canal Reservation of the Cleveland Metroparks. Although it is just a two-mile loop, riders swear it feels longer

thanks to a nice switchback pattern down the face of a wooded hillside. Given the terrain, which leaves little room for error, the trail is best for intermediate riders. This park connects with the Towpath Trail, making it easily accessible to riders. If it has recently rained and the trail is muddy, riding is forbidden.

### RAY'S MTB INDOOR PARK
9801 Walford Ave., 216/631-7433, www.raysmtb.com
**HOURS:** Oct.-Apr. Tues.-Fri. 5-10 P.M., Sat.-Sun. 9 A.M.-10 P.M.
Map 7

Ray's is the only attraction of its kind anywhere on the globe. Now approaching 100,000 square feet of indoor mountain-bike nirvana, this remarkable place just keeps growing and growing. Located in a cavernous warehouse about five miles west of downtown, Ray's features separate courses geared to beginner, intermediate, and expert riders. Race down narrow paths, around steeped embankments, through obstacle courses, over bumpity bridges, and into the air courtesy of vertical jumps. Riders

© FRANK DESSOFFY

**Hug the curves at the Ohio & Erie Canal Reservation Mountain Bike Trail.**

come from all over the country to check out the rad madness. The park is only open during the winter months. Weekday visits cost around $17, while weekends are $20.

## Trails

### CLEVELAND METROPARKS ALL-PURPOSE TRAILS

www.clemetparks.com

Cleveland Metroparks maintains over 60 miles of paved, all-purpose trails for bicycling, walking, jogging, and rollerblading. They have over a dozen different reservations scattered around town, so a trailhead is never too far away. A short drive from downtown is Rocky River Reservation, which features a scenic 13-mile stretch of all-purpose trails that sometimes follows the Rocky River. Though not directly connected, another nine miles of all-purpose trail through Mill Stream Reservation can easily be accessed by a short ride along Valley Parkway, adding up to a very enjoyable 22-mile route. Other particularly picturesque rides can be found at the North and South Chagrin Reservations.

### ◖ OHIO & ERIE CANAL TOWPATH TRAIL

www.nps.gov/cuva

**Map 7**

When completed, this monumental path will stretch 110 miles from downtown Cleveland to New Philadelphia, following the path of the historic Ohio & Erie Canal. Already, some 75 miles of level crushed-limestone path attracts millions of walkers, joggers, and bike riders per year. Pick up the trail south of town in Valley View and follow it as it winds its way through beautiful Cuyahoga Valley National Park. The scenery along the path, which hugs and at times crisscrosses the Cuyahoga River, is simply amazing. Old canal locks and mile markers can be spotted, as can dense forests, fertile wetlands, and varied wildlife. Stop off at numerous visitors centers along the way to view historical and natural exhibits. Riders of all skill levels can enjoy this smooth trail. For those who have bit off a bit too much and are now dreading the journey back, the Cuyahoga Valley Scenic Railway (www.cvsr.com) is a lifesaver. Flag down the train at any boarding station, hop on with your bike, and ride as far as you want for $2. Check the website for train times.

## Rentals

### CENTURY CYCLES

1621 Main St., Peninsula, 800/201-7433, www.centurycycles.com

**HOURS:** Mon.-Thurs. 10 A.M.-8 P.M., Fri.-Sat. 10 A.M.-6 P.M., Sun. noon-5 P.M.

**Map 7**

To experience as much of the scenic Ohio & Erie Canal Towpath Trail as possible, a bike is pretty much a necessity. Of course, most folks don't make a habit of traveling with their bikes in tow, and that's where Century Cycles comes in. Located in the heart of the Cuyahoga Valley National Forest, in the charming town of Peninsula, this great cycle shop rents bikes for use on the trail for about $8 per hour. Riders with little ones can also rent kiddie trailers that attach to the rear of the bike. Best of all, the shop is literally steps from the towpath. Credit card required for security deposit.

### OHIO CITY BICYCLE CO-OP

1823 Columbus Rd., 216/830-2667, www.ohiocitycycles.org

**HOURS:** Mon. 4-9 P.M., Thurs. noon-9 P.M., Sat. noon-6 P.M.

**Map 2**

For bike rentals close to downtown, you can't beat Ohio City Bicycle Co-Op. This great nonprofit organization awards free bikes to kids who spend a little time learning about bike repair and safe cycling. In addition to selling surplus bikes, the agency rents quality bikes, which helps fund their Earn-a-Bike program. Bikes for rent come in two classifications: normal and performance. For getting around town, the collection of older road and mountain bikes should fit the bill. Racers or off-roaders will want to go with a higher-end performance model. Rates are about $6 per hour, $20 per day, and $50 per week for the basic bike, and approximately twice that for a performance bike. Cash or check deposits are required and range from $50 to $2,000.

© PHOTO CREDIT

**ARTS AND LEISURE**

## GOLF
### SHAWNEE HILLS GOLF COURSE
18753 Egbert Rd., Bedford, 440/232-7184,
www.clemetparks.com
`Map 7`

Shawnee Hills offers golf for players of all skill levels, making it one of the most versatile of the Cleveland Metroparks' seven public courses. Beginners and pros alike can sharpen their short game on the zippy little 9-hole, par-3 course. More advanced players, meanwhile, will likely gravitate to the 18-hole 6,200-yard course that features rolling terrain and unforgiving water hazards. Perhaps the most difficult hole of all Metroparks courses, #13 is a tree-lined uphill 433-yard par 4 dogleg left that was converted from a par 5. The course also has a pro shop, snack bar, cart and club rental services, practice putting green, and driving range. It's located in the Bedford Reservation.

### SLEEPY HOLLOW GOLF COURSE
9445 Brecksville Rd., Brecksville, 440/526-4285,
www.clemetparks.com
`Map 7`

This great Stanley Thompson–designed course opened in 1925 as a private country club. Today it is a part of the Cleveland Metroparks system, which runs seven public courses in and around Cuyahoga County. Considered brutally challenging yet also surprisingly beautiful, this 18-hole 6,700-yard course plays downhill and uphill, with and against the prevailing winds. Some holes play easier than others for that reason. Hole #2 is a long 240-yard par 3. The longest hole, #4, is a 590-yard par 5. Golfers will find a pro shop, snack bar, cart and club rental services, practice putting green, and driving range. It's located in the Brecksville Reservation.

## SPECTATOR SPORTS
### Baseball
### ⓒ PROGRESSIVE FIELD
Corner of E. 9th St. and Carnegie Ave., 216/420-4487,
www.indians.com
`Map 1`

If there is anything better than spending a glorious summer afternoon at the ballpark,

---

## CHIEF WAHOO: A MASCOT CONTROVERSY

Go to the season's opening baseball game at Progressive Field and you'll likely encounter some angry folks. No, these are not fans grumbling over the price of a cold beer; they are Native Americans protesting the use of Chief Wahoo, the Cleveland Indians mascot. There is little doubt that this caricature, with its red skin, toothy grin, and feathery headgear, is an offensive stereotype to many people. Like that of the Washington Redskins mascot, the image stirs up a robust discussion about race, free speech, and the slippery issue of intent. Team history would have people believe that the character was meant to honor the first American Indian in pro baseball, not to disparage any particular group. Regardless, teams have so much tradition wrapped up in a name, logo, and merchandise that change is difficult to accomplish.

© DOUGLAS TRATTNER

Chief Wahoo is the cause of racial controversy.

---

kindly don't tell the 40,000 or so happy souls at Progressive Field. Consistently selected as one of the best places in major league to watch a game, this park, which is home to the Cleveland Indians, will make a baseball fan out of just about anybody. When it was unveiled in 1994, this park was known as Jacob's Field—or simply, "The Jake." In 2008, Progressive Insurance purchased the naming rights, leaving

# CLEVELAND SPORTS: HOPE, HEARTACHE, AND WAIT TILL NEXT YEAR

In the film *Annie Hall*, Woody Allen's character, Alvy Singer, says, "I feel that life is divided into the horrible and the miserable." Cleveland sports fans know exactly how he felt.

Year in and year out, Clevelanders pin their hopes and dreams on a championship run only to have their hearts torn asunder by a last-minute calamity. And those are the good years; most leave no hope for a championship run whatsoever. Despite having three professional sports teams, locals have had little to cheer about since 1964, when the Browns won a pre–Super Bowl championship. The Indians haven't clinched a national title since Harry Truman was president. And even with LeBron James – the Chosen One – the Cavaliers have not yet won it all.

It's not like Cleveland teams haven't been close. There have been times when the Browns, Indians, and Cavs each have put together such miraculous seasons that little stood between them and sweet, sweet victory. And even as Cleveland fans rooted on these teams each and every step of the way, they prepared themselves for the ultimate, inevitable disappointment. This might seem like pessimism, but to Cleveland sports fans, it's just the ugly reality.

Ask locals about "The Drive," "The Fumble," or "The Shot" and watch as their faces sag into a familiar contortion of woe. These phrases might sound like simple game plays, but in truth they represent the heartbreaking moments that shaped generations of Clevelanders.

All the 1987 Browns had to do to reach the Super Bowl was prevent John Elway and the Denver Broncos from scoring all the way from their own two-yard line with a little over five minutes left to play in the game. Instead, Elway managed to march his team in a 15-play drive all the way to the end zone to send the game into overtime. We know what happened then.

Against all odds, the Browns managed to make it back to the AFC Championship Game the following season, only to face off against the Denver Broncos. With less than two minutes to play in the game, Cleveland needed a touchdown to tie the game. No problem, since they drove the ball all the way down to the eight-yard line. Bernie Kosar's handoff to Ernest Byner was clean and it looked like the running back would take the ball in for a game-tying touchdown. Instead, he fumbled the ball on the goal line; Denver recovered it and went on to win the game.

Starring in "The Shot" was basketball superstar Michael Jordan. In Game 5 of the NBA Playoffs, Cleveland led the Chicago Bulls by one point. The series was tied 2–2, so whichever team won the game moved on to the Semifinals. With just 3.2 seconds left in the game, the ball was inbounded to Jordan for one quick shot. He made it, clinching both the game and the series.

While lacking a catchy tagline like the others, the Indians' 1997 loss to the Florida Marlins in the 11th inning of the seventh game of the World Series ranks up there with the saddest moments in Cleveland sports. Others include blowing a 3–1 lead over the Boston Red Sox in the 2007 ALCS, losing to the Oakland Raiders in the 1981 AFC Playoff Game, and the Cavs getting swept by the San Antonio Spurs in their first-ever NBA Finals appearance in 2007.

After decades of wrenching heartache, you'd expect Cleveland sports fans simply to abandon hope altogether. But that's not the case. After a few weeks of inconsolable crying, fans here stand up, brush it off, and say, "Wait till next year."

fans without a suitable nickname. Unlike the Indians' previous home at cavernous Cleveland Municipal Stadium, which they shared with the pro football team, Progressive Field is strictly a ballfield. Its location in the heart of downtown makes it a true urban field of dreams. And when they built it, people came. Cleveland fans filled the venue between 1995 and 2001, creating a sellout record of 455 home games in a row that remained unmatched until the Red Sox surpassed it in 2008. During those years the Indians ruled the Central Division, making it to the playoffs every year and the World Series twice. After disappointing seasons from

2001 to 2004, the Indians began rebuilding under the leadership of GM Mark Shapiro and skipper Eric Wedge. In 2007, the team beat the New York Yankees to become American League Division champs, only to come up one win shy of the World Series.

The fan-friendly facility features comfortable seats, generous legroom, and angled seating that provides unobstructed sight lines of the field. Spectators have great views not only of the players, but also the downtown skyline and the largest full-color video display in American professional sports. Tours of the park are offered throughout the season and numerous Team Shops sell all matter of official gear. Newly created Heritage Park, located in center field, is home to the Indians Hall of Fame and other historical exhibits. Fans who want to try to get autographs of their favorite players may attempt to do so up to 45 minutes before game time in Sections 125–134 and 169–175.

About 80 home games are played April–September. Tickets can be purchased at the Progressive Field box office, though Ticketmaster (www.ticketmaster.com), or from unofficial scalpers who prowl the area before and during every game.

## Basketball
### CLEVELAND CAVALIERS
One Center Court, 800/820-2287,
www.nba.com/cavaliers
`Map 1`

For their inaugural year in the NBA, 1970, the Cavs amassed the worst record in the league. Things wouldn't improve much until 1976, when the team made it to, but lost, the Eastern Conference Finals. Following a very sad period in Cavs history known as the "Ted Stepien Years," the team ultimately rebounded under new ownership, coaching, and talent. The late 1980s and early 1990s were good to Cleveland basketball fans, with a number of consecutive years of playoff appearances and a shot at the Eastern Conference Championship. This being Cleveland, we'll let you guess how that one turned out.

The basketball gods smiled upon Cleveland in 2003, when the Cavs' first-pick choice in the NBA Draft netted a high school phenom by the name of LeBron James. Under the leadership of coach Mike Brown, "King James" and company would make it all the way to the Eastern Conference Finals in just three years. It would take four years, however, for the team to claim the title of Eastern Conference Champions. That year, 2007, the Cavaliers reached the NBA Finals for the first time in it 37-year history only to be swept by the San Antonio Spurs in four games.

In Cleveland, the Cavaliers play about 40 games October–April at Quicken Loans Arena, a 20,000-seat arena located downtown. Tickets are available through Ticketmaster (www.ticketmaster.com), or, preferably, through Flash Seats (www.cavs.flashseats.com), an online ticket exchange.

### CLEVELAND STATE UNIVERSITY VIKINGS
Wolstein Center, 2000 Prospect Avenue,
http://csuvikings.cstv.com
`Map 1`

For those who prefer the unsullied action of college sports, the Cleveland State University Vikings play a full roster of men's and women's collegiate sports, including basketball, baseball, swimming, soccer, and softball. Men's basketball is without question the most closely followed. The Vikings, under the direction of coach Gary Waters, are fast becoming a team to watch in NCAA Division I ball, playing in the Horizon League. Meanwhile, in 2007 the women's basketball team made their first trip ever to the NCAA Tournament. Basketball games are played at the Wolstein Center and tickets are available through Ticketmaster (www.ticketmaster.com) or by calling 216/241-5555. For more information on all CSU sports action, visit the website.

## Football
### CLEVELAND BROWNS
100 Alfred Lerner Way, 440/891-5050,
www.clevelandbrowns.com
`Map 1`

Cleveland is a football town. If you don't believe it, head over to the Municipal Parking Lot

© DOUGLAS TRATTNER

**Catch the gridiron action at Cleveland Browns Stadium.**

early in the morning on a brutally cold winter day. The scene one is likely to find will look as if an entire Jimmy Buffet concert was airlifted from Key West to the North Pole. Tailgaters get up early, brave traffic, and fight for spots just for the privilege of pre-partying with like-minded fans before games. Sure, alcohol plays a big part. But even the most sober Clevelanders can't help but get swept up in the passion of the pigskin. Einstein said that the definition of insanity is doing the same thing over and over again and expecting different results. Einstein obviously wasn't a Browns fan. Despite backing a team that has never even made it to the Super Bowl, Browns fans, game after game, year after year, merrily return to the scene of the crime.

Apart from three years in the late 1990s when team owner Art Modell, a name uttered only in the darkest of corners, moved the Browns to Baltimore, Cleveland has had a football team to support since 1946. And at many times, a very good one at that. The Browns have 15 former players in the Pro Football Hall of Fame, a number that is around the fifth-highest in the league. Names like Jim Brown, Otto Graham, Paul Warfield, and Ozzie Newsome will be instantly recognizable to even the most casual of fans. In the late 1980s quarterback Bernie Kosar lead the team to the AFC Championship game, only to be defeated by John Elway and the Denver Broncos on a 98-yard march down the gridiron that will forever be known simply as "The Drive." As Cleveland fate would have it, the following year's AFC Championship game—*against the Broncos*—ended in a loss as the result of a fumble on the three-yard line. That play, by the way, is now called "The Fumble." It appears that the near future of the team will be in the hands of either Derek Anderson or heartthrob Brady Quinn, two quarterbacks vying for the top post.

Regardless of who ultimately gets the start, come rain, shine, or Lake Effect snow, you can bet that 73,000 fervent fans will fill Cleveland Browns Stadium every home game. Built in 1999, the contemporary stadium offers unobstructed views of the field and places fans closer to the action. Tickets are not cheap, and are not easy to get. Online ticket prices range

ARTS AND LEISURE

$75–300 and higher depending on the opposing team and position in the playoff race. For the truly rabid Browns fans, a bleacher section known as the Dawg Pound, located at the east end zone, is home to hooting, hollering, and, yes, woofing. No matter where you end up sitting, it is imperative that you dress as if you were preparing to scale Mt. Everest. Completely open to the elements, the stadium can be quite insufferable for the ill-equipped. Again, alcohol helps.

Fans don't have to wait until the first game to inspect their team. Training camp normally opens in mid- to late July at a training facility in Berea, Ohio, not too far from downtown. All practices are open to the public and free of charge.

Eight regular-season home games are played September–December. Tickets for games can be purchased through Ticketmaster (www.ticketmaster.com), or through the online ticket exchange Viagogo (www.viagogo.com).

### CLEVELAND GLADIATORS

One Center Court, 216/685-9000,
www.clevelandgladiators.com
Map 1

When former Browns quarterback and Cleveland sports legend Bernie Kosar relocated the Arena Football League's Gladiators from Las Vegas to Cleveland, he all but promised a post-season appearance in the first year. Considering that the team's record the prior year was a dismal 2–14, it was a bold statement to be sure. To get there, Kosar retooled the team and hired a new coach. In 2008, the team's first year in Cleveland, the Gladiators came up one win shy of the ArenaBowl. Under the leadership of coach Mike Wilpolt, and behind the arm of quarterback Ray Philyaw, the squad went 9–7 in the regular season, and beat Orlando in the wild-card round and Georgia in the division round. They lost the AFL National Conference title game to Philadelphia. In fitting tribute, coach Wilpolt was selected Arena Football League coach of the year. The 16-game season runs from early March through late June, with eight

home games played at Quicken Loans Arena. Attendance averaged 14,000 people per game in 2008. Tickets range $15–70 and are available at www.clevelandgladiators.com, www.ticketmaster.com, and the Quicken Loans Arena box office. **NOTE:** The 2009 season of the Arena Football League has been suspended league-wide, thus the Cleveland Gladiators will have no 2009 season.

## Hockey
### LAKE ERIE MONSTERS

One Center Court, 866/997-8257,
www.lakeeriemonsters.com
Map 1

Pro hockey fans can enjoy the fast-paced puck action of the Lake Erie Monsters, a team in the American Hockey League and affiliated with the NHL's Colorado Avalanche. Home games are played in Quicken Loans Arena, with roughly 40 dates between mid-October and mid-April. During the team's inaugural 2007–2008 season, they averaged a more-than-respectable 6,000 fans per game. The season closer drew some 15,400 spectators, the largest that year in the American Hockey League. Tickets can be purchased at the Quicken Loans Arena box office, all Ticketmaster (www.ticketmaster.com) locations, or by calling 866/99-PUCKS (866-997-8257).

## Horse Racing
### NORTHFIELD PARK

10705 Northfield Rd., Northfield, 330/467-4101,
www.northfieldpark.com
Map 7

For over 50 years there has been live harness racing at this half-mile track located about a half-hour south of downtown. Also called "trotters," the horses in harness racing maintain a specific gait while pulling a two-wheeled cart called a sulky. Races go off approximately every 20 minutes, at least three days per week year-round, depending on the season. Grab a racing form, pick your race, place your wager, and root for your chosen sulky from the comfortable grandstand. The slightly more upscale Trackside Lounge and Sports Bar boasts dozens of flat-screen televisions that broadcast live races from other tracks.

### THISTLEDOWN

21501 Emery Rd., N. Randall, 216/662-8600, www.thistledown.com

`Map 7`

This mile-long track about 20 minutes southeast of Cleveland is closing in on 85 years of live thoroughbred racing. While nowhere near the glamorous setting of a Las Vegas casino, the track does offer glimmers of the same action. Betting on a horse to win, place, or show creates a sense of drama that lasts much longer than a dozen blackjack hands. And when you get into the bolder bets like exactas, perfectas, and trifectas, the payouts soar in relation to the odds. Visitors can choose to sit in various locations throughout the large, dated facility, but there is no better spot than right along the rail near the finish line. There is live racing Friday–Monday May–October, with simulcasted races every day of the week. Admission and parking are free.

### Roller Derby
### BURNING RIVER ROLLER GIRLS

31515 Lorain Rd., N. Olmsted, www.burningriverrollergirls.com

`Map 7`

Fans of the fast-paced sport of roller derby have a new friend in the Burning River Roller Girls, Cleveland's first all-female flat-track derby league. The league consists of four teams of elbow pad–clad bruiser babes that jam, block, and pivot their way around an 88-foot oval track. Points are scored for each player lapped on the opposing team. Half the fun is just reading the names on the scorecard: Pain Austen, Ivanna Destroya, and Mommy's Little Monster sound like nightmares on wheels. Matches are lively, fun, and chock-full of kitsch. They are played monthly from April through August at the North Olmsted Soccer Sportsplex. Tickets are $10 in advance, $15 at the door, and can be purchased online at Brown Paper Tickets (www.brownpaper tickets.com).

### Soccer
### CLEVELAND CITY STARS

E. 9th St. and Chester Ave., 216/916-6586, www.clevelandcitystars.com

**COST:** $12 adult, $10 child

`Map 1`

While not Major League Soccer, the Cleveland City Stars is professional outdoor soccer. Part of the United Soccer League's Second Division, the Stars are affiliated with the Columbus Crew. The season runs April–August and consists of 10 home games. Matches take place on Cleveland State University's Krenzler Field, a FieldTurf-equipped sports facility. In 2007, its first year out, the team posted a more-than-respectable 10–3–7 record. In its second year, the team shot to the top and captured the USL-2 Championship, ensuring an increase in both attention and attendance.

## WATER ACTIVITIES
### Rowing and Kayaking
### CLEVELAND KAYAK TOURS

22449 Lake Road, Rocky River, 440/289-9911, www.school.clevelandkayak.com

`Map 7`

Knowing how to roll a kayak is an invaluable skill, to be sure. This school will teach you how it's done indoors or out, depending on the season. They provide the boat and gear; you show up and learn. Other outdoor classes offer instruction in everything from basic fundamentals to whitewater kayaking. Longer tours are also offered.

### 41° NORTH KAYAK ADVENTURES

Rocky River Reservation, 1500 Scenic Park Dr., Lakewood, 866/529-2541, www.kayak41north.com

`Map 6`

Paddlers of all skill levels will find what they're looking for at this great local outfitter. For beginners, 41 Degrees offers paddling courses taught by certified instructors. Those with even the littlest bit of paddling experience can sign up for an unforgettable sunset kayak tour, which takes participants into North Coast Harbor along Lake Erie's shore, right by the Rock and Roll Hall of Fame. More adventurous half-, full-, and multi-day trips are also available to those who make arrangements ahead of time. More advanced paddlers can rent their own rig and glide into Lake Erie alone or with friends. The rental center is located at the Boat Barn in the Rocky River Reservation of the Cleveland Metroparks, just south of the public boat ramps and marina. Kayak rentals are available from Memorial Day weekend through October and range from $15 per half hour to $50 for a full day. Dress appropriately.

### WESTERN RESERVE ROWING ASSOCIATION

1948 Carter Rd., 216/621-9772, www.wrra.cc

**Map 1**

Adults, college students, and high school athletes come here to learn how to row from some of the best talent around. Classes range from basic fundamentals programs to pro-level competitive rowing, and they take place on the Cuyahoga River. Fun and social summer and fall rowing leagues are very popular for both casual and serious scullers. The WRRA also fields teams at many regional and national regattas, offering truly competitive scullers an opportunity to test themselves against a larger field. Learn-to-row classes cost $30 and take place throughout April. Check the website for dates, fees, and information.

## FISHING AND HUNTING
### Lake Fishing

Lake Erie offers anglers some serious fishing opportunities, with championship walleye and tasty yellow perch coming in at the top of the list. However, those without their own boat have relatively few options when casting for dinner. The easiest and cheapest is simply dropping a line in the water off a pier or breakwall. Edgewater State Park is a popular site for shore-bound anglers, offering a generous fishing pier. A little east of town is the East 55th Marina (5555 N. Marginal Rd.), another nice spot to spend a few hours casting. The next most economical alternative is to hop aboard a party boat, sometimes called a "head boat" because passengers are charged per head. Unlike pricey charter boats, head boats accept singles and couples for a modest fee. One of the few to depart from within the city, Discover Dive Charters (16975 Wildwood Dr., 216/481-5771, www.wildwoodmarina.com) operates out of Wildwood State Park Marina, just a few miles east of downtown. Majestic Charters (440/244-2621, www.walleye.com/majestic) departs from the Lorain Spitzer Lakeside Marina (301 Lakeside Ave.), located about 25 miles west of town in Lorain. Average head-boat rates are around $35 per person plus another $5 to $10 for equipment rental. All necessary equipment is usually included on higher-end charters. Then again, prices jump to between $400 and $600 for a full-day trip on a chartered boat. Granted, that money is split between all members of the fishing party, and it is still way cheaper than owning and maintaining one's own boat. Red Eye Charters (440/238-9736, www.ohiowalleye.com) departs from the East 55th Marina and charges about $250 for a half day, $400 for a full day. Trump-Tight Fishing Charters (216/581-7619, www.trump-tight.com) charges between $300 and $450 for a full day of fishing, departing from nearby E. 72nd Street. For a totally unique fishing experience, consider signing up for an evening or nighttime walleye trip with FishCrazy Charters (216/408-0404, www.fishcrazycharters.com). The evening trip runs most days 5–11 P.M., while the weekend-only night trips run 11:30 P.M.–5 A.M. Rates are about $300 for up to five people.

Regardless of which option he or she chooses, every angler must possess a current Ohio Fishing License, available through the Ohio Department of Natural Resources (www.dnr.state.oh.us) or at bait shops near the docks. Cost is $11 for a one-day license, $19 for a year. When fishing, it is imperative to bring an ice-filled cooler to protect your catch. Many of the better charter companies will provide one for you. Also, be prepared for the weather.

### River Fishing

The well-stocked rivers and streams of

Northeast Ohio provide some of the best steelhead trout fishing in the country. Fly fishers from throughout the Midwest make their way to Lake Erie tributaries from fall through spring hoping to catch and release one of the most beautiful sport fish of all. The rivers that offer the best fishing are the Rocky, Chagrin, and Grand, though gaining access isn't always easy due to private-property restrictions. The Rocky River and Mill Stream Run Reservations of the Cleveland Metroparks enjoy miles of access to the Rocky River, making those parks a favorite destination for anglers. On the other side of town, the North and South Chagrin Reservations provide access to the bountiful Chagrin River. When it comes to fly-fishing for steelhead, sometimes it's best to call in the pros. Professional guides know the rivers better than anybody, and they will take you to the fish. Plus, many offer lessons in casting before setting out. One such guide is Screaming Reels (440/487-8111, www.screamingreels. net), which charges about $220 for four hours or $360 for eight hours. Other guides of note include Chagrin River Outfitters (440/247-7110, www.chagrinriveroutfitters.com) and Reel River Guide Service (216/533-7488, www.reelriver.com), both of whom charge about $275 for a half day.

## HUNTING

Ohio's dense forests, lush wetlands, and grassy prairies provide the ideal breeding ground for a whole host of elusive game. Depending on the season, Ohio hunters might be after whitetailed deer, wild turkey, waterfowl, squirrel, grouse, pheasant, quail, and coyote. It would take an entire chapter to cover the myriad rules, laws, and restrictions that govern hunting in Ohio, with each game having its own season dates, bag limits, and check-in requirements. For up-to-date information on hunting, visit the Ohio Department of Natural Resources' website (www.ohiodnr.com), which has a wealth of resources on the topic. It goes without saying that a hunting license is required for most pursuits.

## WINTER ACTIVITIES
### Cross-Country Skiing, Ice Skating, and Snowshoeing
### HALLORAN ICE SKATING RINK
3350 W. 117th St., 216/664-4187,
www.city.cleveland.oh.us
**Map 6**

What this rink lacks in luxury it makes up for in sheer curiosity. Run by the City of Cleveland's Department of Parks and Recreation, Halloran is one of the only outdoor refrigerated rinks in the region. In summer, the ice melts and the spot is opened up to roller skaters. Winter skating begins mid-November and runs until spring. If you don't mind weaving your way through exuberant youths, this rink can offer a nostalgic charm that borders on romantic. And because it costs all of $1.25 to skate, including rental fees, this trip will leave you with plenty of cash for that après-skate dinner-date. Open daily except Sundays and holidays.

### KENDALL LAKE WINTER SPORTS CENTER
Truxell Rd., Peninsula, 216/524-1497,
www.nps.gov/cuva
**Map 7**

Tucked deep within Cuyahoga Valley National Park, a cozy stone-and-chestnut shelter serves as the nucleus of winter activities in the park. In addition to the breathtaking scenery, the lodge offers cross-country ski instruction, equipment rental, and priceless information. Sign up for a weekend cross-country ski lesson on your skis or theirs, followed by a vigorous miles-long expedition down the Towpath Trail. For a slower, simpler pace, don a pair of rented snowshoes and head into the majestic backcountry. When nearby Kendell Lake is adequately frozen, take your ice skating to the great outdoors. Don't have your own skates? No problem, the shelter rents them. Even if you prefer to pull on nothing more than a pair of hiking boots, come to this lodge for maps, hot chocolate, and like-minded companionship. Call for snow and ice reports before you visit.

ARTS AND LEISURE

### SERPENTINI ARENA

14740 Lakewood Heights Blvd., 216/529-4400, www.serpentiniarena.com

Map 6

Formerly Winterhurst Ice Rink, this popular Lakewood city rink has been leased by a private operator and received about $1 million in improvements. With two ice rinks, the arena is busy most days of the week with open skating, drop-in freestyle, youth hockey, and speed skating. The arena is also home to three separate high school varsity ice-hockey teams. The facility is open year-round and offers lessons, rentals, and concessions. Hours vary by day, week, and month, so check the website before dropping in. Admission is around $6, less for Lakewood residents.

## Skiing, Snowboarding, and Tubing
### ALPINE VALLEY SKI RESORT

10620 Mayfield Rd., Chesterland, 440/285-2211, www.alpinevalleyohio.com

Map 7

Located smack dab in the middle of the Snowbelt, Alpine Valley gets pounded by snowfall. With average yearly totals around 120 inches, the resort receives double that of Boston Mills and Brandywine. While compact, this charming resort has the look and feel of a quaint little ski village. But modern features like state-of-the-art snowmaking machines, a snow-tube park, and Ohio's longest half-pipe keep this place popular with winter enthusiasts. There are 11 trails covering 72 skiable acres, with a range of easy, moderate, and difficult runs. Lessons, equipment rental, and food service is available. Adult lift passes run about $32 for a full day and $27 for a half day. A complete equipment rental package will cost about $22. Tubing costs $13 for two hours. Check the website for months, days, and hours of operation.

### BOSTON MILLS/BRANDYWINE

7100 Riverview Rd., Peninsula, 330/657-2334, www.bmbw.com

Map 7

The sister resorts of Boston Mills and Brandywine might not offer the best skiing in the country, but they do provide a surprisingly good downhill experience. And their location just 20 miles from town makes them all

COURTESY OF BOSTON MILLS AND BRANDYWINE

Check out Boston Mills for some real, live ski action.

the more appealing. Combined, the two parks boast 18 trails covering 85 skiable acres. Both offer a nice mix of bunny runs, intermediate trails, and challenging black diamonds for skiers and snowboarders. When Mother Nature isn't cooperating, snow-making machines keep the slopes in business. Well-synchronized chairlifts can shuttle 20,000 skiers an hour while preventing overcrowding of the slopes. Boston Mills and Brandywine are two separate parks located five minutes apart by car. Lift tickets and passes are valid at both, however, since they are owned by the same company. Lessons, equipment rental, and food service is available at both resorts, while inner tubing is offered only at Brandywine. Lift passes run about $40 for a full day and $32 for an evening pass, which begins at 3:30 P.M. A complete equipment rental package will cost about $26. Check the website for months, days, and hours of operation.

## Tobogganing
### MILL STREAM RUN RESERVATION
Cleveland Metroparks, 440/572-9990,
www.clemetparks.com
Map 7

Twin refrigerated chutes whisk adventurers 70 feet down and 1,000 feet out on toboggans built for four. This seasonal tradition kicks off the day after Thanksgiving and runs through the first weekend in March. Apart from really warm or really wet days, the chutes are open Thursday through Sunday and holidays. Be prepared to hike up 110 steps to the top to earn your exhilarating 15-second descent. Riders must be at least 42 inches tall and wear mittens or gloves. Passes cost about $8 and net multiple runs. A $3 one-ride ticket is also available. When you've had enough of the frosty freefalls, head into the chalet to enjoy the warm glow of two fireplaces and a large-screen television.

## Winter Surfing
### EDGEWATER PARK
6500 Memorial Shoreway, 216/881-8141,
www.ohiodnr.com/parks
Map 3

If you can tolerate the near-freezing water

temps, Lake Erie can actually provide a pretty decent surf experience. Winter's steady winds whip across the lake, stirring up waves that routinely hit the 10-foot mark. Swells as large as 20 feet have been reported. Only a fool would hit these waters without a wet suit, and it's wise to grab your longest, fattest board for increased buoyancy. Edgewater certainly isn't the O.C.'s Newport Beach, and for that, Cleveland's cultish surfers can be thankful. You better hurry up, though; once the lake freezes, it's either Cali or wait 'til next year.

## BOWLING
### THE CORNER ALLEY
402 Euclid Ave., 216/298-4070,
www.thecorneralley.com
**HOURS:** Mon.-Thurs. 11:30 A.M.-midnight,
Fri.-Sat. 11:30 A.M.-2 A.M., Sun. 4 P.M.-2 A.M.
Map 1

Knocking down pins in rented shoes hasn't looked this cool since Jeff "The Dude" Lebowski did it in his pajamas. This gleaming hipster bowling emporium is located right downtown in the hopping East 4th Street area. Combining 16 lanes, computerized scoring, oversized video screens, and comfy lounge areas, this alley is a far cry from the smoke pits found in two-bit shopping centers. The lanes are located within a larger complex that features a restaurant, martini bar, and pool tables, and bowlers are waited on hand and foot. Weekend rates can seem steep at $35 per hour, but divided by four or six bowlers, it becomes more palatable.

### MAHALL'S TWENTY LANES
13200 Madison Ave., 216/521-3280
Map 6

A beloved Lakewood institution for over 85 years, this 20-lane bowling alley is clean, safe, and family-friendly. In fact, the alley seems more geared to families than leagues. Bowlers had better know how to score a frame the old-fashioned way, because there are no machines to do it for them. Low-tech scoring translates into affordable bowling, with games costing around $3 and shoes $2. Rounding out the

ARTS AND LEISURE

conventional bowling experience is above-average food and a full bar to boot. Call for hours, leagues, and specials.

## GYMS, HEALTH CLUBS, AND YOGA STUDIOS
### THE ATMA CENTER
2319 Lee Rd., 216/371-9760, www.atmacenter.com
**Map 5**

This warm and welcoming studio in Cleveland Heights has been introducing stiff novices to the practice of yoga for over a decade. Free introductory classes are a regular occurrence here, where patient instructors promote holistic health practices. Atma offers a complete range of classes, from the basic fundamentals to lengthy and intensive multi-week programs. New moms and moms-to-be can enlist in pre- and post-natal stretching classes that incorporate breathing and meditation. Always wanted to learn the full 12-pose sun-salutation sequence? A few classes at the Atma and you'll be saying, "Good morning, Mr. Sun." The on-site bookstore stocks a full catalogue of yogic studies materials, required reading for some of the more serious programs. Check the website for classes, times, and prices.

### FITWORKS
530 Euclid Ave., 216/344-9267, www.fitworks.com
**HOURS:** Mon.-Thurs. 5 A.M.-9 P.M., Fri. 5 A.M.-8 P.M., Sat. 8 A.M.-5 P.M.
**Map 1**

This Midwest chain of health clubs has six locations in the Greater Cleveland area. The downtown branch is tucked into the Colonial Marketplace and offers a full lineup of fitness equipment and amenities. Lauded for its laid-back atmosphere and top-notch service, Fitworks is popular with both downtown workers and residents. Fitness buffs will find state-of-the-art cardio equipment like treadmills, elliptical trainers, stair-climbers, and rowers, plus upright and recumbent bikes. In addition to the individual televisions on much of the cardio equipment, this gym boasts a cardio cinema room that projects movies onto a 15-foot screen. Check the website for yoga, boot camp, and power classes.

### KARMA YOGA
1382 W. 9th St., Ste. 300, 216/621-7085, www.karmayogacleveland.com
**Map 1**

One of the only dedicated yoga studios located downtown, Karma has become an oasis of serenity in an otherwise chaotic environment. Led by serious-minded yogis who are well schooled in the eight-limb path, the classes here can be a little intense for the casual practitioner. But those looking for enlightenment in the form of chanting, meditation, and thoughtful movement would do well to enlist. Classes are held every day of the week at various times throughout the day. Despite the deeply experienced talent, individual classes cost just $14. Frequent and repeated hands-on alignment is included at no additional charge.

### THERE'S NO PLACE LIKE OM
5409 Detroit Ave., 216/409-4161, www.buckharris.com/likeom
**Map 3**

Not very long ago, a studio that offered classes in chanting, meditation, and yoga had as much chance of survival in Detroit Shoreway as did a sushi restaurant. Well, the sushi restaurant still hasn't arrived, but There's No Place Like OM has garnered the support of the community and then some. Proprietor and instructor Buck Harris endeavors to unite body, mind, and spirit into a sort of harmony that is often impossible in the "real world." In this studio, regardless of yogic prowess, we are all brothers and sisters. Sisters, however, are not welcome at every class. Buck's surprisingly popular Buck Naked Yoga is for men only. And as the name implies, it is practiced without the confinement of clothing. OM my!

### YMCA OF GREATER CLEVELAND
2200 Prospect Ave., 216/344-0095, www.clevelandymca.org
**HOURS:** Mon.-Fri. 5:30 A.M.-9 P.M., Sat. 7 A.M.-5 P.M., Sun. 10 A.M.-5 P.M.
**Map 1**

The YMCA operates about a dozen branches in Northeast Ohio, including a lovely and convenient location just 20 blocks east of Public

Square. In return for a membership, visitors have access to individual fitness assessments, certified trainers, even massage therapists. There are free weights, cardio machines, racquetball and basketball courts, and a swimming pool. Add to that roster of amenities a hot tub, sauna, and steam room, and you'll wonder why folks bother to spring for pricey health clubs. Members have the right to use facilities at every other Greater Cleveland YMCA. Adult fees are about $55 a month, plus a one-time $100 registration fee.

## GUIDED AND WALKING TOURS
### CITYPROWL
www.cityprowl.com

Jennifer Coleman recalls how exciting it was as a child to explore the nooks and crannies of her downtown. Now an adult, Coleman has figured out a way to share that excitement with other residents and visitors. Through her website, CityProwl.com, Coleman offers free downloadable audio tours for use in any MP3 player. Each covers about a mile in distance and takes around 40 minutes to complete. Loaded with historical, architectural, and anecdotal information, the tours are an easy, cheap, and entertaining way to squeeze more into a leisurely stroll. At least five different downtown tours, or prowls, are available, including ones covering Public Square, the Warehouse District, and the old arcades. Simply visit the site, download the file, print out a map, and make your way to the starting point.

### CUYAHOGA VALLEY SCENIC RAILROAD
800/468-4070, www.cvsr.com
**Map 7**

One of the longest scenic railroads in the nation, the CVSR stretches a full 51 miles, from just south of Cleveland all the way down to Canton. And "scenic" is the operative word. For much of the journey, the tracks bisect the majestic Cuyahoga Valley National Park while hugging the Cuyahoga River and paralleling the popular Towpath Trail. Passengers ride in authentic climate-controlled coaches built in 1940. More than just a tour train, the railroad is a

Take a ride on the Cuyahoga Valley Scenic Railroad through the Cuyahoga Valley National Park.

COURTESY OF POSITIVELY CLEVELAND

ARTS AND LEISURE

key resource for visitors to the valley. Many hop aboard just to travel to their favorite park spot, while bicyclists take advantage of the popular bike-and-ride program, which offers them and their rig a $2 lift back home. But you don't need to bike, hike, or climb to enjoy this train. Sign up for a lengthy scenic expedition through the park and watch as nature unfolds outside your window. The lush forests, wetlands, and prairies of the park teem with flora and fauna. White-tailed deer and wildflowers, songbirds and snapping turtles, cattails and coyotes—it's all on display in the Valley. The trains operate all year long and offer dozens of different excursions, from mid-winter charmers to evening wine-tasting trips. Without question, this railroad is one of the brightest gems in Northeast Ohio. Check the website for more information.

### GOODTIME III

E. 9th St. Pier, 216/861-5110, www.goodtimeIII.com
**Map 1**

If it weren't for the *Goodtime III*, tens of thousands of locals and visitors would never get to view Cleveland from the water, which many assert is her best side. In the 50-plus years that the *Goodtime* has motored these waterways, that view has only improved. Passengers still journey up the Cuyahoga River, past the remnants of the city's mighty industrial past. But the landscape is cleaner, brighter, and more varied than ever before, with attractive new condos, promising development, and actual wildlife. Shutterbugs are afforded some of the very best vantage points from which to capture Cleveland's skyline and its matchless assortment of bridges. The sheer romance of the setting inspires a number of couples to wed aboard this 1,000-passenger ferry each summer. Various tours are offered from Memorial Day through the end of September, including narrated lake and river cruises, lunch and dinner-dance cruises, and the ever-popular rush-hour party cruise. Prices range from $13 for the adults-only party cruise up to $50 for the dinner cruise. Reservations are always recommended.

Take a sightseeing trip up the Cuyahoga River on the *Goodtime III*.

COURTESY OF POSITIVELY CLEVELAND

ARTS AND LEISURE

## TROLLEY TOURS OF CLEVELAND

2000 Sycamore St., 216/771-4484,
www.lollytrolley.com

**COST:** One-hour tour $11 adult, $8 child, $10 senior;
two-hour tour $17 adult, $12 child, $16 senior

**Map 1**

The clang, clang, clang of Lolly the Trolley is a familiar sound for locals, who for years have observed these bright red open-air carriages shuttle the curious about town. Despite the hokiness factor, these trolleys provide a wonderful prospective on a city that often obscures its assets, with seasoned guides weaving historical, architectural, cultural, and political tidbits into a memorable excursion. General one- and two-hour tours hit the major sights of North Coast Harbor, Warehouse District, Ohio City, PlayhouseSquare, Millionaire's Row, and University Circle, while numerous specialty tours focus on Little Italy and Lake View Cemetery, ethnic markets of Cleveland, unique churches about town, and the trail of Eliot Ness. Tours, which leave from the Powerhouse at Nautica Entertainment Complex in the Flats, take place year-round, but occur more frequently from Memorial Day to Labor Day. It is required that all customers reserve a spot by calling in advance. Also, children under five are not permitted on the two-hour tour.

## VETERANS MEMORIAL BRIDGE TOUR

W. 25th St. and Detroit Ave., 216/348-3824,
www.cuyctyengineers.org/subway_tour

**COST:** Free

**Map 2**

Judging by the steady increase in attendance at these rare tours, interest in the past grows stronger every year. Though Cleveland's streetcar lines and subway stops have been dormant since 1954, vestiges of those times remain hidden in plain view. While the main platform of the Detroit-Superior (Veterans Memorial) Bridge was and is devoted to auto traffic, the lower level once linked the east and west sides of town via trolley tracks and tunnels. Three times a year, usually on the Saturdays before Memorial Day, Independence Day, and Labor Day, the Cuyahoga County Engineer's Office opens up the 2nd level for self-guided

tours. There, in a sort of elevated grotto, visitors can enjoy a modest museum dedicated to Cleveland's outmoded transportation system. While the ephemera are cool, it's the views out and down that tickle the most. The museum is open 9 A.M.–3 P.M. on tour days.

# OTHER RECREATION
## Rock Climbing
### CLEVELAND ROCK GYM

21200 St. Clair Ave, Bldg. B3, Euclid, 216/692-3300,
www.clevelandrockgym.com

**HOURS:** Tues.-Fri. 4-10 P.M., Sat. noon-8 P.M.,
Sun. noon-6 P.M.

**Map 7**

For nimble-fingered folks itching to scamper up a wall, this indoor climbing gym will more than satisfy the urge. What once was a light-industrial warehouse in Euclid has been converted into a more-than-acceptable winter substitute for rock climbing. The facility is comprised of 30-foot top-rope walls and numerous bouldering areas, some featuring near-horizontal overhangs. Climbers who have no prior climbing experience must make reservations for an introductory class. Those with enough knowledge to pass a basic belay test, however, are free to plan their routes up the tall walls. A one-day pass is around $12, a five-day pass is $50, and a one-month pass is $65.

## Skateboarding
### CHENGA WORLD

14700 Snow Rd., Brook Park, 216/433-7588,
www.chenga.cc

**HOURS:** Mon.-Fri. 4-10 P.M., Sat. 1-10 P.M.,
Sun. noon-7 P.M.

**Map 7**

Folks with real wheels—a car, that is—will want to make tracks to this monster indoor park, located a couple miles from Cleveland Hopkins Airport. Skaters, BMX riders, even bladers seem to peacefully coexist here thanks to the sheer magnitude of the place. There are plenty of ramps, rails, wall rides, verts, and jumps offering numerous paths and lanes through the park. Owned by flatlander Scott Powell, you know there is plenty of open space to practice your spins, stalls, and hops. An on-site pro shop is well stocked with merch for that last-minute repair or a brand new deck. Rates are around $10 for an all-day pass. Helmets are required and can be rented for about $3 a day. Folks under 18 years of age need a release signed by a parent.

### CLEVELAND SKATE PARK
Northern Terminus of E. 9th St. (beyond Rock Hall)
**Map 1**
This free city-run park may not win awards for its size and scope, but it does offer a pretty decent (and legal) playground for skaters. Located at North Coast Harbor, the 54-by-120-foot modular skate park was donated to the city by the Gravity Games following the 2003 competition. In addition to the street-course kicks, which include quarter-pipes, grind rails, a pyramid, and a launch box, skaters score killer views of the Rock Hall, Science Center, and Lake Erie.

## Swimming Pools
### CITY OF CLEVELAND
216/664-3018, www.city.cleveland.oh.us
**HOURS:** Mid-June–mid-August, Wed.–Sun. noon–8 P.M.
The City of Cleveland operates about 22 indoor and outdoor swimming pools throughout the city. All of the outdoor pools follow the seasonal schedule listed above. Many neighborhood pools offer learn-to-swim programs in addition to general open swim time. Check the City website for locations around town.

## Beaches
Visitors are often surprised to learn that Cleveland has beaches—you know, those sandy stretches of coastline perfect for lazing away a warm summer day. In fact, a number of very fine ones dot the North Coast from Toledo to the Pennsylvania border. The ones closest to Cleveland tend to be either state parks or part of the Cleveland Metroparks system. All have lifeguards on duty during summer, and most of the parks feature party shelters, picnic areas, grills, playgrounds, and shower facilities. The closest is Edgewater State Park (6500 Memorial Shoreway, 216/881-8141, www.ohiodnr.com/parks), which is located just a couple miles west

of downtown. Visitors to this beach can expect more working-class families and bookish loners than bikini-clad hotties. For that, consider heading west to Huntington Beach, which services the posh West Side communities of Bay Village and Rocky River. Located within the Cleveland Metroparks' Huntington Reservation (Lake Rd. at Porter Creek, 216/635-3200, www.clemetparks.com), this smallish beach is overrun in the summer with idle teens and the boys who love them. While there, stop by Honey Hut (28624 Lake Rd., 440/871-7699) for an unbelievably good shake, malt, or sundae. Clear across town is Headlands Beach State Park (9601 Headlands Rd., Mentor, 216/881-8141). Without question, this is the largest beach in the area, boasting a mile-long stretch of natural sand perfect for people-watching and navel-gazing. During summer, the beach attracts scores of folks from throughout the region, all eager for a little vacation close to home. Bird-watchers flock to adjacent Headlands Dunes State Nature Preserve, a native dune environment that sees a steady stream of migratory birds. Whatever beach one chooses, care must be taken before actually entering the water. High bacteria counts in Lake Erie are common, and throughout the season, certain beaches are placed under bacterial advisory. Check the posted signs.

## Ultimate Frisbee
### CLEVELAND DISC ASSOCIATION
www.cleveland-disc.org
Cleveland-based devotees of the fast-moving sport of Ultimate Frisbee are blessed to have the organizing talent of the CDA. Literally hundreds of players and dozen of teams play in competitive spring and summer leagues at parks and school ball fields all over town. There is even a winter league, played indoors at a domed sports complex, for those who never want the fun to stop. The summer action culminates with the annual No Surf in Cleveland Tournament, a monster two-day event that draws players and teams from all across the region. For those who have always wondered what Disc was all about, simply check the website to find out where the next matches will be held.

# SHOPS

It is not too difficult in Cleveland to find places to part with one's hard-earned cash. Stroll through any of the city's most popular neighborhoods and you're likely to unearth a treasure trove of independent shops, many found nowhere else on Earth. Tremont and Little Italy each boast scores of galleries and boutiques stocking one-of-a-kind fashions, fine art, and funky accessories. Coventry Road in Cleveland Heights is a stroller's dream, dotted with incense-filled import shops, used record depots, and wacky novelty-filled toy stores. Lorain Avenue running from Ohio City into Detroit Shoreway has more vintage, antiques, and secondhand shops than a sane shopper can visit in a single weekend. West 25th Street just west of downtown is a patchwork of ethnic shops, hidden gems, and bin-filled thrift stores.

Numerous universities in the area seem to keep the demand for books high, as reflected by a relatively high number of new and used bookstores. Fans of old vinyl and comics have a friend in C-Town, as do lovers of hand-crafted specialty foods. Perhaps it's the cold winters, but folks here appear to enjoy holing up with a good book and a dish of fine chocolates.

Cleveland's proximity to the East Coast means that trend-conscious shoppers have little trouble finding a great pair of designer jeans, a hot bag, or the perfect little black dress. Upscale malls like Eton Chagrin Boulevard and Beachwood Place contain not only the best national retailers, but a surprisingly fresh crop of indie boutiques. And when getting dolled up for that night on the town, guys and girls have their pick of top-talent salons and spas for their mani, pedi, or waxing. Even the furriest of Clevelanders—the dogs and cats, that is—seem to have at their disposal the finest in grooming, day care, and overnight boarding.

© DOUGLAS TRATTNER

# HIGHLIGHTS

LOOK FOR  TO FIND RECOMMENDED SHOPPING.

🄲 **Best Used Vinyl Shop:** When a shop features a cat named Vinyl, it must take music seriously. Fortunately, the friendly folks at **Music Saves** are serious only about the selection of used indie rock. About everything else they are refreshingly genial (page 139).

🄲 **Best Place to Discuss Kerouac:** **Visible Voice Books** owner Dave Ferrante can discuss Boho lit with the best of them. And because his shop is just 2,200 square feet, he likely has the time and inclination to do so (page 140).

🄲 **Easiest Place to Buy a Hostess Gift:** If it's cheesy postcards you seek, **Banyan Tree** will likely disappoint. But if you're looking for home-decor gifts that will be appreciated and adored, this modern boutique will make short order of your gift list (page 141).

🄲 **Weirdest, Wackiest, Nerdiest Novelties:** Coventry Road has always been home to eccentrics, and thanks to **Big Fun,** those wackdoodles have a shop to call their own. For decades, Big Fun has tickled us silly thanks to its cosmic collection of vintage toys, campy gifts and nerd-approved clothing (page 141).

🄲 **Best Place to Sweat:** Apart from the neighborhood around it, little has changed at the **Russian-Turkish Baths** since it opened in the late 1920s. Known simply as "the Schvitz," this is where in-the-know men come to steam, sweat, kibbutz, and eat steak (page 148).

🄲 **Best Shop for your Drama Queen Teen: Nicky Nicole,** an oh-so-hip kids' boutique, sells merchandise for girly girls, fashion mavens, and drama queens. With tie-dyed tees, designer jeans, and hot bags, tweens will be in glam heaven (page 149).

🄲 **Best Place to Mortify Your Pet:** Pet-**Tique** carries all matter of ridiculous doggie

*© DOUGLAS TRATTNER*

Visible Voice Books

duds, making it super easy to embarrass the little ones. Of course, most of the giggles will be directed toward the other end of the leash, especially if the outfits match (page 150).

🄲 **Fanciest Multiplex:** Most malls are as unique as a McDonald's hamburger. But **Eton Chagrin Boulevard** is loaded with scores of independent fashion-forward shops that are found nowhere else on the planet, and the national stores that are here are actually worth checking out (page 151).

🄲 **Best Chocolatier:** Willy Wonka has nothing on Amanda Montague. At her urban confectionary emporium, **Lilly Handmade Chocolates,** she crafts delicious works of art from fine chocolate and fresh ingredients. Handmade truffles, bars, and candies all seem to come with a golden ticket (page 153).

🄲 **Best Source for New-Old Things:** The folks at **Reincarnation Vintage Design** don't just resell old stuff, they transform it into cool new home furnishings. Visit this two-level New York-style loft showroom to see what's currently on display (page 156).

# Arts and Crafts

### EYE CANDY GALLERY

2173 Professor Ave., 216/241-2740,
www.eyecandy-gallery.com
**HOURS:** Wed.-Thurs. 1-6 P.M., Fri. 1-9 P.M.,
Sat. 12:30-9 P.M.
**Map 2**

Funky doesn't begin to explain some of the unique accessories for sale at this popular Tremont gallery. Showcasing the work of numerous artists, the eclectic shop stocks a wide range of sculpture, jewelry, bags, wearable art, ceramics, and fine art. Delicate watercolors share wall space with wild mixed-media collages. The husband-and-wife owners are artists themselves, so customers will find her handmade jewelry and his eye-catching photography. A must-stop on the monthly Tremont ArtWalks, Eye Candy is, as the name implies, a treat for the eyes.

### FINE POINTS

12620 Larchmere Blvd., 216/229-6644,
www.finepoints.com
**HOURS:** Tues., Wed., Fri., Sat. 11 A.M.-6 P.M.,
Thurs. 11 A.M.-8 P.M., Sun. noon-5 P.M.
**Map 5**

Knitters and crocheters make journeys short and long to come to this distinctive shop. Inside this charming Victorian house on artsy Larchmere Boulevard is a kaleidoscope of today's hottest fibers, yarns, and textiles. Shoppers can purchase yarn to go, commission a one-of-a-kind garment, or snag one of the owner's hand-crafted knit fashions. The boutique also stocks a full panoply of knitting supplies, including books, patterns, needles, and accessories. Newbies can sign up for an informal class here to learn the ropes, so to speak.

### GLASS BUBBLE PROJECT

2421 Bridge Ave., 216/696-7043,
www.glassbubbleproject.com
**HOURS:** Mon.-Sat. 10 A.M.-6 P.M.
**Map 2**

Chances are you've never experienced a gallery

© DOUGLAS TRATTNER

**Need some yarn? Hit Fine Points on Larchmere Boulevard.**

like this one. It's an absolute blast—with a blast furnace, to boot. Tucked into a cramped garage, which itself is secreted away behind a block of buildings, Glass Bubble Project is a glass-blowing studio run by remarkable—and remarkably peculiar—artists. An open-studio policy means that visitors can stroll in anytime and catch the artists dipping blowpipes into glory holes. (That's glass-blowing lingo, by the way.) Impromptu demonstrations are fine for most, but the Bubble also offers private lessons, easily scheduled with a phone call. Gift ideas abound, from one-of-a-kind blown-glass bowls and glassware to Christmas ornaments and found-art sculpture.

### PASSPORT TO PERU

1806 Coventry Rd., 216/932-9783
**HOURS:** Mon.-Wed. 10 A.M.-8 P.M., Thurs.-Sat.
10 A.M.-9 P.M., Sun. 11 A.M.-6 P.M.
**Map 5**

Coventry was hippie central in the 1960s, and this store is a lasting legacy of those heady times. Incense fills the air and permeates all matter of imported merchandise, from downy alpaca sweaters and hats to trippy-dippy tie-dyes. Long the go-to source for Birkenstocks and Naot sandals, Passport is also a gift-hunter's best friend. Fine ethnic jewelry, embroidered handbags, wooden wind chimes, and natural skin drums are just a sliver of the hippie-chic shwag on tap. Grab an incense burner and satchel of sticks for the road. It'll keep fresh the memory of Coventry's rich past.

### UTRECHT ART SUPPLIES
1798 Coventry Rd., 216/371-3500, www.utrechtart.com
**HOURS:** Mon.-Fri. 10 A.M.-8 P.M., Sat. 10 A.M.-7 P.M., Sun. 11 A.M.-6 P.M.

Map 5

Sure, this store is not unique to Cleveland. But when Cleveland Institute of Art students need to stock up on quality art supplies, they come to the Coventry Road outpost of this great chain. Utrecht carries one of the largest inventories of oil, acrylic, and watercolor paints, plus the canvases, brushes, and easels to go with them. Sculpture artists will find numerous types of clay and stone and the implements to carve them. Simply painting a dorm room? Come here for tapes, straight edges, and templates to get the job done right. Curious about a specific genre? Grab an instructional manual and, perhaps, change your destiny.

# Books and Music

### BENT CRAYON RECORDS
11600 Detroit Rd., 216/221-9200, www.bentcrayon.com
**HOURS:** Tues. 11 A.M.-7 P.M., Wed.-Thurs. 11 A.M.-6 P.M., Fri.-Sat. 11 A.M.-7 P.M., Sun. noon-5 P.M.

Map 3

You won't find Top 40 music at this focused West Side shop. What you will find is scads of electronica, house, experimental, and lounge music. Obscure labels and imports draw a select demographic to be sure, but for these fans, Bent Crayon is a lifesaver. Special orders satisfy requests for sludge rock, space disco, and primitive techno, genres one isn't likely to come across at Best Buy or Wal-Mart. Don't know your emo from your trance? No problemo—the enthusiastic staffers will not only point you in the right direction, they'll likely pop some on the sound system for an auditory explanation.

### CAROL & JOHN'S COMIC BOOK SHOP
17448 Lorain Ave., 216/252-0606, www.cnjcomics.com
**HOURS:** Mon.-Fri. noon-8 P.M., Sat. 10 A.M.-7 P.M., SUN. NOON-5 P.M.

Map 6

This mom-and-son operation is approaching the 20-year mark thanks to its super-friendly,

customer-oriented approach to sales. Owners pledge to read everything they stock so as to provide an honest, informed opinion when asked to do so. Anybody interested in new and used comics will have a field day at this tidy, well-organized shop, with weekly deliveries of both big-name and small-run publications. While at its heart a hardcore comic depot, Carol & John's also stocks a nice selection of graphic novels, action figures, posters, and apparel. Located in a West Side strip mall, there is plenty of easy and free parking.

### LOGANBERRY BOOKS
13015 Larchmere Blvd., 216/795-9800, www.loganberrybooks.com
**HOURS:** Mon.-Sat. 10 A.M.-6 P.M., Thurs. 10 A.M.-8 P.M.

Map 5

Established in 1994, this cozy book nook specializes in children's and illustrated books, women's history titles, and art and architecture tomes. Along with these genres, plus popular fiction, shoppers can find used rare books, including leather-bound first editions. Fans of traditional bookstores will adore Loganberry, which sports warm oriental rugs, wood floors, and row upon row of open shelving.

© DOUGLAS TRATTNER

**Find a great title at Mac's Backs Books on Coventry.**

Loganberry's popular "Stump the Bookseller," a web service where readers post often-sketchy details in hopes of identifying an old favorite book, has been featured in the *New York Times* and on NPR. Strong Bindery, an outfit that restores and repairs old books, is located on-site.

### MAC'S BACKS BOOKS

1820 Coventry Rd., 216/321-2665,
www.macsbacks.com
**HOURS:** Mon.-Thurs. 10 A.M.-9 P.M.,
Fri.-Sat. 10 A.M.-10 P.M., Sun. 11 A.M.-8 P.M.

Map 5

It makes sense that Mac's carries works by adult-comic artists like Harvey Pekar and Robert Crumb: Both authors spent formative years tooling around this bohemian neighborhood. (Pekar still does.) This delightfully cramped tri-level shop has an unrivaled selection of literary journals, hard-to-find magazines, classics, and nonfiction. Those looking for a lighter read can pore over thousands of new and used fiction, mystery, and science fiction titles. Equal parts town hall

and bookseller, Mac's is the site of frequent neighborhood meetings, readings, discussions, and workshops.

### MUSIC SAVES

15801 Waterloo Rd., 216/481-1875,
www.musicsaves.com
**HOURS:** Tues.-Thurs. 2-10 P.M., Fri. 2-11 P.M.,
Sat. noon-11 P.M., Sun. noon-6 P.M.

Map 7

Though the name might lead you to believe otherwise, Music Saves does not specialize in Christian rock. What this shop does carry is new and used indie rock, in all its blessed forms. Down-to-earth civility is a rare find at many indie record shops, where vast stores of knowledge often can come across as dweeby condescension. Everything here, from the fat cat named Vinyl to the very flexible closing time, is refreshingly genial. Located in artsy Collinwood, the store is bright, festive, and outfitted with comfy furniture. While dedicated largely to vinyl—hence the feline's moniker—Music Saves also deals in CDs and music-related DVDs. Stop here before concerts at the nearby Beachland Ballroom. Not only can you buy the performers' tunes; you can buy your tickets to the show.

### MY MIND'S EYE RECORDS

13723 Madison Ave., 216/521-6660,
www.mymindseyerecords.com
**HOURS:** Mon.-Sat. noon–9 P.M., Sun. noon-7 P.M.

Map 6

Vinyl junkies rejoice at the sight of this small but jam-packed Lakewood shop. Two rooms house an ever-changing catalogue of new and used LPs, CDs, and DVDs. Hardcore music fans know to stop by regularly for the best chance to snag a rare gem, especially in the early-heavy-metal and garage-rock genres. Dusty collections from the recently departed seem to arrive daily. If we didn't know better, one might assume store owner Charles Abou-Chebl had a hand in the process. But no, he merely dispenses an encyclopedic knowledge of music trivia while possessing an almost stereotypic indie-record-store persona. Heck, it's a joy to shoot the breeze with the dude, whether shopping or not.

### RECORD REVOLUTION

1832 Coventry Rd., 216/321-7661
**HOURS:** Mon.-Sat. 11 A.M.-8 P.M., Sun. noon-6 P.M.

Map 5

This Coventry Road institution boasts a basement filled with new and used vinyl and CDs. The underground setting suits the shop to a T considering the place was ground zero for the cultural revolutions that erupted some five decades ago. Vestiges of that counter-culture remain today, largely in the form of all matter of smoking paraphernalia, incense, and hippie clothing. Young alternative types visit the main-floor boutique to stock their wardrobes with funky vintage clothing, jewelry, and accessories. Rounding out the inventory are obscure rock videos, posters, and DVDs.

### $2 RARE BOOKS

6820 Euclid Ave., 216/881-1800
**HOURS:** Mon.-Sat. 11 A.M.-6 P.M.

Map 7

This amazing book warehouse will devour more of your time than money thanks to a charitable pricing structure that places most items in the $1 to $2 range. The downside? Searching the towering stacks for a specific title can be akin to unearthing the Holy Grail. But that's part of the fun at this independently owned retailer/wholesaler. A massive personal collection was the origin for the shop; today, that catalogue is augmented by frequent estate sales and acquisitions of private inventories. As a warehouse and wholesaler, Rare Books typically sells in lots of 1,000 or more. But that doesn't mean you can't come in and spend one buck on a classic science fiction title. Meticulous collectors might even stumble across rare editions by Henry Miller or Mary Shelley.

### ◖ VISIBLE VOICE BOOKS

1023 Kenilworth Ave., 216/961-0084,
www.visiblevoicebooks.com
**HOURS:** Tues.-Fri. 2-10 P.M., Sat. noon-10 P.M., Sun. 12-8 P.M.

Map 2

At this sweet little indie bookstore in hip Tremont, fine literature shares shelf space with a vast collection of pop culture titles. The eclectic catalogue is hand chosen by owner Dave Ferrante and it strongly reflects his personal tastes, which lean toward the bohemian and erudite. At 2,200 square feet, the store is small enough to lavish individual attention yet large enough to accommodate approximately 7,000 titles. Kerouac fans will find here not just words on a page but a kindred beatnik spirit of adventure as well. Bonuses include frequent poetry readings and book signings, a large local-author section, plus a new wine bar and alfresco courtyard for sipping. Live acoustic music is also on tap some nights.

# Gift and Home

## ( BANYAN TREE

2242 Professor Ave., 216/241-1209,
www.shopbanyantree.com
**HOURS:** Mon.-Wed. 11 A.M.-7 P.M., Thurs.-Sat.
11 A.M.-9 P.M., Sun. 11 A.M.-4 P.M.
Map 2

In a neighborhood littered with boutiques, Banyan Tree rises to the top of the pack thanks to its well-edited and ever-evolving catalogue of inventory. Blessed with a keen eye for fashion, home decor, and accessories trends, the owner has created one of the best go-to places for appreciated gifts. Once purchased, those gifts are lovingly and fashionably wrapped at no charge. Sleek and modern, this urban shop carries hand-made textiles, season-appropriate designer garments, vintage jewelry, and funky home furnishings. Sorry, no kitschy postcards or T-shirts here.

## ( BIG FUN

1814 Coventry Rd., 216/371-4384
**HOURS:** Mon.-Thurs. 11 A.M.-8 P.M.,
Fri.-Sat. 11 A.M.-10 P.M., Sun. 11 A.M.-7 P.M.
Map 5

For those among us who refuse to grow up, Big Fun offers relief in the form of cool stuff and kinship. It's hard to not act a wee bit juvenile perusing the over-the-top greeting cards, gag gifts, and campy 1980s TV lunchboxes. Old is new here, with a monster selection of vintage toys, retro candy, and nerd-friendly clothing. Atari T-shirts, *Star Wars* collectibles, and an entire section devoted *The Wizard of Oz* (look for

## COMIC CLEVELAND

From Mr. Natural to Superman, Cleveland has had a hand in creating some of the most lasting comic characters. And judging by the comic-book and novelty shops in town, people around here prefer to never grow up.

**Jerry Siegel** and **Joe Shuster** were just kids when they met at Glenville High in Cleveland. But these whiz kids soon found themselves writing and illustrating comics, including those of the popular Doctor Occult, for big-time mags like *New Fun*. Despite a few earlier failed attempts, Siegel and Shuster finally sold a story they had been working on for years about a mild-mannered reporter with superhuman abilities. In 1938, Superman debuted on the cover of Issue #1 of *Action Comics*. The Man of Steel soon found his way into newspapers, radio programs, television shows, motion pictures, and, if you can believe it, a Broadway musical.

In the 1960s, Coventry Road in Cleveland Heights was a counter-culturist's dream. The bohemian strip with a tie-dye vibe was home to **Harvey Pekar** (and still is). With the neighborhood as his backdrop, he began writing his cur-mudgeonly autobiographical comic *American Splendor*. The long-running strip was adapted into a successful film of the same name starring Paul Giamatti.

One of Pekar's earliest illustrators was **R. Crumb,** a friend who would go on to create such infamous characters as Fritz the Cat and Mr. Natural. Crumb's sexually and politically charged comics made him the darling of the anti-establishment crowd. This work was a far cry from the greeting cards he illustrated at Cleveland's American Greetings. Crumb's squeaky-clean boss at the time was Tom Wilson, the creator of Ziggy. Wilson stayed on at American Greetings for 35 years.

To browse thousands of new and used comic books, locals hit **Carol and John's Comic Book Shop.** This mom-and-son operation has been chugging along for close to 20 years thanks to superhuman customer service and personal attention. Coventry Road is still space central thanks to **Big Fun,** a novelty shop for the kid in all of us. Vintage toys, zany collectibles, gag gifts, and hipster clothing packs this amazing trip of a store.

© DOUGLAS TRATTNER

Big Fun is a riot for kids of all ages.

the spinning model of Dorothy's farmhouse) are just some of the things kitsch shoppers will find here. Grab a seat in the old-timey photo booth and leave with a strip of black-and-white memories. Big Fun truly is big fun.

### CITY BUDDHA

1807 Coventry Rd., 216/397-5862,
www.citybuddha.com
**HOURS:** Mon.-Thurs. noon-8 P.M., Fri. noon-9 P.M.,
Sat. 10 A.M.-9 P.M., Sun. noon-6 P.M.
Map 5

Follow the Buddha's teachings and you may buy nothing here but a carved wooden Buddha. But where's the fun in that? Like a street bazaar airlifted from Indonesia, this fragrant shop deals in imported exotica, mostly from Southeast Asia. Jammed with handmade furniture, hand-carved figurines, hand-painted pottery, and hypnotically beautiful textiles, City Buddha makes home design easy, cheap and fun. What began as an open-air stand over a decade ago is now a bustling Coventry Road shop frequented by hippies, yuppies, and well-heeled travelers. As the Buddha might say, "Fill

your mind with compassion, but fill your home with really cool stuff."

### DUOHOME

6507 Detroit Ave., 216/651-4411, www.duohome.com
**HOURS:** Tues.-Sat. 11 A.M.-7 P.M., Sun. noon-5 P.M.
Map 3

Located in the up-and-coming Gordon Square Arts District, duoHOME is one of the entities helping to reshape the Detroit Shoreway neighborhood. At this smart-dressed storefront shoppers will find a selection of sophisticated yet comfortable furnishings, mostly in traditional, transitional, and modern styles. A full line of carefully chosen lifestyle products and accessories will doubtless brighten one's home while adding affordable functionality to boot. Come here for DIRT sootless soy candles, stylish ARCHITEC kitchenware, and colorful adjustable scatter tables. The "duo," by the way, comes from the store's dual personality as both retail shop and interior design studio, which is run by the owners in the back.

### KITSCH CITY

6511 Detroit Ave., 216/651-2489, www.kitschcity.com
**HOURS:** Tues.-Thurs. 11 A.M.-7 P.M., Fri.-Sat.
10 A.M.-8 P.M., Sun. noon-6 P.M.
Map 3

Looking for a cowboy rubber ducky keychain? (And who isn't?) Stop by this quirky little Detroit Shoreway gift shop for these bandana-clad floaters plus scads of other odd and adorable novelties. What began as a web-based business has blossomed into a brick-and-mortar bazaar. If easily offended by scandalously funny quips, including those that often skew gay, liberal, and blasphemous, you best walk on by. But if you're looking for a Hillary Clinton car air freshener that reads "I'm Your Man," well, now you know where to go.

### THE ONLY CLEVELAND STORE

230 W. Huron Rd., 216/241-2011,
www.theonlyclevelandstore.com
**HOURS:** Mon.-Sat. 10 A.M.-7 P.M., Sun. noon-6 P.M.
Map 1

When you want to take a little piece of Cleveland

COURTESY OF ROOM SERVICE

**eco-friendly wares at the snazzy Room Service**

back home, this unabashedly passionate souvenir shop in Tower City Center will fill your shopping bags. As the area's only authorized retailer for the Rock and Roll Hall of Fame, Cleveland Museum of Art, and Cleveland Museum of Natural History, this store will make short work of your gift list. This likely is the only place in the world that stocks Rock Hall guitar picks, Cleveland Browns pennants, authentic Stadium Mustard, and beautifully framed skyline photos all under the same roof. Returning Clevelanders nostalgic for the "good old days" can score items bearing long-gone celebrities like Mr. Jingeling and Ghoulardi.

### ROOM SERVICE

6505 Detroit Rd., 216/281-4221,
www.roomservicecleveland.com
**HOURS:** Tues.-Thurs. 11 A.M.-7 P.M., Fri.-Sat. 11 A.M.-9 P.M.,
Sun. noon-4 P.M.
**Map 3**

Described by its interior designer owners as a lifestyle shop, this elegant storefront stocks products that enhance life through quality design. Classic bones including tall ceilings, exposed-brick walls, and poured-concrete floors serve as the backdrop for a small but sharp collection of stationery, jewelry, home accessories, and fashions. Form meets function in a sleek lime-green citrus reamer. An ice tray with valentine-shaped hollows makes cubes that are simultaneously cold and heartwarming. There is a decidedly "green" approach to both the space and the product line, with books like *How to Reduce Your Carbon Footprint* alongside organic all-purpose household cleaner. Despite its high styling, this shop boasts budget prices.

### SOMETHING DIFFERENT

1899 W. 25th St., 216/696-5226,
www.somethingdifferentgallery.com
**HOURS:** Mon.-Sat. 10:30 A.M.-6 P.M.
**Map 2**

When tooling around the West 25th Street area of Ohio City, make a quick detour into this wildly eclectic shop. Slightly chaotic and cramped, Something Different carries all matter of gifts, souvenirs, fashions, jewelry, even toiletries, some admittedly more "different" than others. Knickknacks abound, like colorful glassware, greeting cards, and wine carriers. But fine art and sculpture can be found here, too, and the gallery is a great outlet for local artists. Reasonable price points and complimentary designer gift wrapping add to the allure of this fun diversion.

### SURROUNDINGS HOME DÉCOR
850 W. St. Clair Ave., 216/623-4070, www.shdecor.com
**HOURS:** Tues.-Fri. 11 A.M.-6 P.M., Sat. noon-6 P.M.
Map 1

Urban pioneers looking to furnish their modern downtown lofts know to come here for all matter of sleek home furnishings. Like many of the condos it outfits, Surroundings is housed in an open-plan Warehouse District showroom with support columns and exposed HVAC systems. A favorite of designers, architects, and consumers alike, the gallery stocks high-end European lines for both home and office, with numerous pieces for every room, need, style, and budget. This is also the place to come for the latest in lighting technology and design. For those who lack a sharp eye, Surroundings offers interior design consultation.

# Clothing

### ANNE VAN H. BOUTIQUE
2026 Murray Hill Rd., Ste. 106, 216/721-6633
**HOURS:** Mon.-Thurs. and Sat. 10 A.M.-6 P.M., Fri. 10 A.M.-8 P.M.
Map 4

Owner Anne van Hauwaert describes her salon as "the most Parisian boutique this side of New York." She is being modest. Her art gallery–like shop, located in the super-cool Murray Hill School House, would be at home not just in the Big Apple, but also Los Angeles, Montreal, or Brussels, the owner's home turf. Well-traveled shoppers come here for Anne's own sleek fashions as well as those from other top European designers. Truly wearable, the clothes feature bold, artistic prints, modern cuts, and high-quality fabrics. Vintage fans may score an old Pucci, Dior, or Gaultier. Stunning jewelry, bags, shoes, scarves, and hats are also sold here.

### CHRISTOPHIER CUSTOM CLOTHIER
10435 Clifton Blvd., 216/961-5555,
www.christophier.com
**HOURS:** Tues.-Fri. 10 A.M.-5:45 P.M., Sat. 10 A.M.-4 P.M.
Map 3

When the time comes to man-up in terms of fashion—you know, swap the snarky tees for a big-boy suit—shoppers would do well to visit Maurice Christopher. For years, this well-

© DOUGLAS TRATTNER

**Anne Van H. Boutique in the Murray Hill School House**

dressed haberdasher has outfitted clients in timelessly classic apparel, much of it custom made, all of it flawlessly tailored. Bespoke shirts and suits are this shop's bread and butter, but a guy can also pick up a smart off-the-rack blazer and a pair of the world's most comfortable

# CHAGRIN FALLS: WORTH THE TRIP

It might take a good 35 minutes to reach Chagrin Falls from downtown Cleveland, but the destination makes the journey worthwhile. Reminiscent of a quaint New England town, this charming burg boasts a village square (triangle, actually), bustling Main Street, and the namesake waterfalls. Make the trip in early October and you may never again pine for a fall foliage trip to New Hampshire.

Wear comfortable shoes and you can easily hit all the popular spots on foot. Park your car near the centrally located square and you'll even be able to drop off shopping bags as they accumulate.

Every small town needs an independent bookstore, and in Chagrin Falls it's **Fireside Book Shop** (29 N. Franklin St., 440/247-4050, www.firesidebookshop.com). For over 45 years, this cozy bookshop has kept locals well read thanks to its new and used titles. Fireside also carries an uncharacteristically large selection of children's toys, puzzles, and games. Music buffs make the trek to **Warren Henry Music** (49 W. Orange St., 440/247-0300, www.warrenhenrymusic.com) for high-quality musical instruments (especially guitars), sheet music, books, and accessories.

Chagrin Falls residents take pride in their lovely Western Reserve–style homes, and they have no shortage of shops to keep them well furnished. **Tonic Home** (22 N. Main St., 440/893-9800, www.tonichome.com) enables home-decor addicts with a unique line of modern furnishings and embellishments. Gift givers know to come here to cross entire columns off their lists. Arty vases, bookends, candlesticks, and glassware are just some of the items in stock at this sharp shop. Shabby-chic freaks are in heaven upon entering **Stash Style** (46 N. Main St., 440/247-2550, www.stashstyle.com), a 3,200-square-foot shop loaded with trend-conscious treasures. Antique crystal chandeliers, Parisian textiles, and architectural-salvage items adorn this roomy boutique; the in-store bakery turns out delish cupcakes. **Three Home** (67 N. Main St.,

440/247-8425, www.threehome.net) is a creatively decorated home-furnishings boutique where vintage and contemporary furnishings are arranged as one might find them in a home. For those with more traditional tastes, **Chagrin Antiques** (516 E. Washington St., 440/247-1080) stocks high-end collectibles like 19th-century English furniture, rare jewelry, and porcelain.

Clothes-obsessed ladies can lose track of entire afternoons in Chagrin Falls. **Juicy Lucy** (31 W. Orange St., 440/247-5748) attracts women from all over the region thanks to its high-end collection of New York and European fashions and jewelry. **Nola True** (15 N. Franklin St., 440/247-8980) caters to a slightly younger clientele with its fresh and current fashions. The more sophisticated gal hits **Find Me!** (24 N. Main St., 440/247-3131) to shop for clothing, shoes, and accessories in an elegant antique setting. Men are well taken care of at **Cuffs** (18 E. Orange St., 440/247-2828, www.cuffsclothing.com), an old-fashioned gentlemen's outfitter housed in a brick 19th-century home. When Cuffs customers tire of shopping for timeless Italian, French, and American designs, they can enjoy a glass of wine at the in-store wine bar. If you prefer to purchase an entire bottle, stop by **Chuck's Fine Wines** (23 Bell St., 440/247-7534, www.chucksfinewines.com) for matchless selection and service.

You can't travel to Chagrin Falls and not stop for an ice-cream cone at the **Popcorn Shop** (53 Main St., 440/247-6577, www.chagrinfallspopcorn.com). Housed in a 150-year-old building just steps from the roaring waterfalls, the store is a local institution. For a full meal, hit **Rick's Cafe** (86 N. Main St., 440/247-7666, www.rickscafeandcatering.com) for burgers and ribs, or **Gamekeeper's Tavern** (87 West St., 440/247-7744, www.gamekeepers.com) for upscale pasta, seafood, steaks, and wild game in a lodge-like setting.

To turn your daytrip into an overnight stay, book a room with a fireplace at the charming Inn of Chagrin Falls (see listing in chapter).

khakis. To finish the polished look, this West Side boutique maintains an unmatched collection of socks, belts, and cufflinks.

### CLOTHING BRIGADE

1785 Coventry Rd., 216/932-0700,
www.clothingbrigade.com
**HOURS:** Mon.-Sat. noon-9 P.M., Sun. noon-6 P.M.
**Map 5**

On a street long famous for ponchos and sandals, Brigade has introduced a new generation of young men to the cool of the day. Slim denim from brands like Nudie Jeans and Good Society keeps the trend-conscious looking current and sharp. This chic boutique goes well beyond jeans, carrying hot tees, hoodies, sweaters, and blazers, most from labels you won't find anywhere else in town. Shoes, bags, belts, and sunglasses complete the ensemble in appropriate fashion. Luxe skin-care products will keep your skin looking young even when it no longer is.

### GENTLEMAN'S QUARTERS/ FROG'S LEGS

12807 Larchmere Blvd., 216/229-7083
**HOURS:** Tues.-Thurs. 11 A.M.-7 P.M., Fri. 11 A.M.-6 P.M., Sat. 10 A.M.-4:30 P.M.
**Map 5**

Style-conscious men and women have been coming to this upscale clothier for some 40 years. Stocking mostly high-end European fashions, the Larchmere store caters less to hipsters than to upwardly mobile hautesters. An in-house tailor will make sure that those new threads from Italy, France, Sweden, and Germany fit like a glove. Frog's Leap, the women's accessories shop located within GQ, carries custom jewelry, purses, and scarves.

### KILGORE TROUT

28601 Chagrin Blvd., 216/831-0488,
www.kilgoretrout.com
**HOURS:** Mon.-Sat. 10 A.M.-6 P.M., Thurs. until 8 P.M.
**Map 7**

For decades, Kilgore Trout has been recognized as one of Cleveland's finest menswear providers. These days, women don't just tag along

to help outfit their guys; they come to build their own wardrobes. With exclusive lines like Tory Burch and Catherine Malandrino, it's clear why. This handsome East Side boutique is flush with 10,000 square feet of top-quality men's and women's clothing and accessories. In addition to scrupulously tailored suits by Ermenegildo Zegna, men can find belts, cufflinks, English-made socks, and fine shaving products. Gals go gaga over Paul Smith bags, Yummiglass jewelry, and Diptyque perfumes and scented candles.

### KNUTH SHOES

30619 Pinetree Rd., 216/831-9606
**HOURS:** Mon.-Sat. 10 A.M.-6 P.M., Thurs. 10 A.M.-8 P.M.
**Map 7**

Knuth sells shoes, no surprise there. They've got gals well covered when it comes to sandals, sneaks, slides, slings, and stilettos. But this trendy women's fashion boutique goes well beyond footwear, providing one of the sharpest selections of clothing and accessories. Styles run the gamut from young and flirty to classy and sophisticated. All the hottest brands are represented here, with lofty prices to match the au courant threads. Smart shoppers swear by the sales, though, which make room for new inventory by slashing prices. Shopping for someone else? Knuth is a great source for last-minute gifts, with a glut of hip bags, hats, sunglasses, and jewelry.

### PINKY'S DAILY PLANNER

2403 Professor Ave., 216/402-2536,
www.pinkysdailyplanner.com
**HOURS:** Thurs. 5-8 P.M., Fri. 6-10 P.M., Sat. 5-8 P.M., other hours by appt.
**Map 2**

Designer and seamstress extraordinaire Stephanie Fralick calls her shop a "modern clothes-closet for spirited girls." The peculiar name Pinky's Daily Planner refers both to Fralick's Tremont boutique and her line of playful and distinctive skirts and dresses. In addition to those on display, many garments are made-to-order based on past and current collections, or simply custom-made from scratch.

Kilgore Trout: high-end men's and women's styles

Pinky's also carries fashions from independent designers rarely represented in the region. The look is decidedly retro-meets-modern, with throwback-inspired threads mingling with gently worn vintage pieces. This "closet" is also stocked with belts, boots, bags, and bling.

### POWTER PUFF BOUTIQUE
2671 W. 14th St., 216/274-1220,
www.powterpuffboutique.com
**HOURS:** Mon.-Thurs. noon-7 P.M., Fri.-Sat. noon-8 P.M.
**Map 2**

The look owner Brooke Nieves is going for, she says, is "Punky Brewster's palace." As shockingly pink as the hair on a pixie's punk little head, this shabby-chic Tremont boutique straddles the line between rock and frock. Sassy and whimsical '60s-inspired party dresses, bought and sold in limited quantities, are the shop's raison d'être, but fun skirts, tees, under-things, and jewelry abound as well. A well-stocked extended-size section makes Powter Puff magical for free-spirited plus-size shoppers too.

### STYLE LOUNGE
1273 W. 9th St., 216/664-1104,
www.styleloungelive.com
**HOURS:** Tues.-Wed. noon-9 P.M., Thurs.-Fri. noon-10 P.M., Sat. 11 A.M.-10 P.M., Sun. 11 A.M.-6 P.M.
**Map 1**

When it comes to fashion, downtown isn't what it used to be. But this Warehouse District boutique, which caters to the spry and hip, is a bright spot in a seemingly lackluster retail landscape. It isn't just the complimentary beer and wine that attracts female shoppers; high-end lines like "hip-haute" House of Dereon, buzz-worthy People's Liberation, and shoes by Kenzie keep traffic flowing steadily. Situated in the heart of a hopping entertainment district, SL comes straight to its biggest demographic: club-crazy kids.

# Health and Beauty

## FULL CIRCLE STUDIO

3620 Walnut Hills Rd., Beachwood, 216/464-8822, www.full-circle-studio.com

**HOURS:** Tues. 10 A.M.-7 P.M., Wed. 9 A.M.-5 P.M., Thurs. 10 A.M.-7 P.M., Fri.-Sat. 9 A.M.-5 P.M.

Map 7

Run by nationally renowned hairdresser Scott Metzger, this salon likely contains more talent behind the chairs than any other in the region. As former creative director for Vidal Sassoon, Metzger was literally the hairdresser to the stars, with his work appearing on the covers of *Rolling Stone* and *People* magazines. Hip, hot, and relevant, the cuts are both in demand and pricey. While Metzger gets about $175 for his time, other stylists are more reasonably priced. The contemporary salon is warm and sophisticated and features top-notch colorists, extension artists, and manicurists.

## MARENGO LUXURY SPA

401 Euclid Ave., 216/621-4600, www.marengospa.com

**HOURS:** Tues.-Sat. 10 A.M.-8 P.M.

Map 1

Located in the Hyatt Regency at The Arcade, Marengo is one of the only full-service luxury day spas in the downtown area. The plush digs strike the right tone for a half or full day of premium pampering. While a tad pricey, the services offered are top-notch and professionally administered. Massage services include those geared specifically to pregnant woman and sore-muscled athletes. Men's and women's facials, manicures, and waxing are available here, as are traditional hair cutting, coloring, and styling services. This dreamy spa is popular with wedding parties getting their makeup and up-dos before the big event.

## QUINTANA'S BARBER SHOP

2200 S. Taylor Rd., 216/321-7889, www.quintanasbarbershop.com

**HOURS:** Tues.-Thurs. 8 A.M.-9 P.M., Fri. 8 A.M.-6 P.M., Sat. 8 A.M.-4 P.M.

Map 5

Owner Alex Quintana takes the art—and he does consider it an art—of barbering very seriously. His domain is a charming renovated colonial in Cleveland Heights, divided upstairs and down by his barbershop and his wife's day spa. Guys looking for a great cut, or possibly a close shave, would do well to book a chair here. Look for the spinning barber pole, then head inside for a cup of hot coffee, a stack of great mags, and a pleasantly masculine environment. Call the same number to book a massage, facial, or waxing.

## REAGLE BEAGLE

17617 Detroit Ave., 216/228-9677, www.reaglebeagle.net

**HOURS:** Mon. 4-8:30 P.M., Tues.-Fri. 10 A.M.-8:30 P.M., Sat. 9 A.M.-5 P.M.

Map 6

If it weren't for the Beagle, hairy dudes would be roaming the streets of Cleveland like Bigfoot's kin. This men's-only "hair saloon" specializes in manscaping services for those men who are less than enthusiastic about visiting girly salons. Seduced by cold beer, fruity wine, and a pinball machine, among other dude-tastic diversions, guys easily relinquish their superfluous eyebrow, neck, and back hair. Each styling station boasts its very own flat-screen so the chord to SportsCenter never needs to be severed. Sign up for the popular House Cut, a veritable menagerie of post-pubescent primping. Plus a shoeshine!

## ◖ RUSSIAN-TURKISH BATHS

E. 116th St. and Luke Ave., 216/561-0578

**HOURS:** Vary; Oct.-June

Map 7

Known simply as "The Schvitz," this old-school bathhouse remains virtually unchanged since it opened in the late 1920s, when Jewish fathers took their sons for a steam before the start of the Sabbath. Today it serves as a sort of underground men's club, a place where buddies of all religions meet up after work for a steam, a rub, and a steak. Though it's called the Schvitz, the real draw here is the steak, which is cut to order on an old band saw before getting a good broil and dousing of chopped garlic. Men eat in bed sheets, sip ice-cold beer, and *kvetch* about women and work. Would-be patrons will not find a listing for the place in the phonebook, and the club is in a dicey part of town, so it is wise to come with a regular who knows the way.

# Kids

### BACI
2101 Richmond Rd., Beachwood, 216/896-1111,
www.bacikids.com
**HOURS:** Mon.-Sat. 10 A.M.-6 P.M.
**Map 7**

At the rate kids outgrow clothing, you might not expect parents to shell out $50 for a tot's T-shirt. But well-to-do moms and pops who like their progeny as sharp-dressed as themselves come here for Euro-inspired duds. Of course, much of the cash is spent by doting grandparents who can't resist the adorable onesies, twosies, skirts, and dresses. This tasteful children's boutique offers fashions for male and female infants, toddlers, and youngsters, including chi-chi accessories like knit caps, tights, and colorful flip-flops.

### ◖ NICKY NICOLE
28601 Chagrin Blvd., 216/464-4411,
www.nickynicole.com
**HOURS:** Mon.-Sat. 10 A.M.-6 P.M., Thurs. until 8 P.M.,
Sun. noon-5 P.M.
**Map 7**

This oh-so-hip kid's boutique sells merchandise for girly girls aged from 4–14, stocking tie-dyed tees, designer jeans, and hot bags. The selection here is varied enough, says management, to appeal to "soccer players, drama queens, fashion mavens, and equestrians." Just as you'd expect for a tweener glam fest, the vibrant shop is pink, sparkly, and cheerful, making it the perfect roost for a Webkinz party, dress-up bash, or plain-old shopping spree. Killer service lands Nicky Nicole on numerous "Best Of" lists.

### PLAYMATTERS TOYS
13214 Shaker Sq., 216/752-3595,
www.playmatterstoys.com
**HOURS:** Mon.-Thurs. 10 A.M.-6 P.M., Fri. 10 A.M.-8 P.M.,
Sun. noon-5 P.M.
**Map 5**

Indie-minded parents who like to sidestep the big-box chains love this small home-grown toy shop. Like the other four Northeast Ohio locations, the Shaker Square outpost is best known for educational and classic toys. Playmatters holds its own against the giants by offering high-quality products and great customer service. Replacing the sea of plastic play palaces are non-toxic wooden toys, snuggly plushies, and hard-to-find retro games. Thanks to plenty of hands-on displays and fully functional models, kids have just as much fun shopping as they do buying. But Playmatters' tagline is "Toys that teach, challenge, and inspire," so you know you'll find a million new ways to enlighten the little ones.

### SUNBEAM, A SHOP FOR CHILDREN
3469 Fairmount Blvd., 216/397-3929,
www.vgsjob.org/sunbeam.asp
**HOURS:** Mon.-Fri. 10 A.M.-5:30 P.M., Sat. 10 A.M.-5 P.M.
**Map 5**

You *can* do good and shop at the same time. For decades, all proceeds taken in at this chic little kids' boutique in Cleveland Heights has gone to Vocational Guidance Services, a nonprofit agency that provides vocational training and job placement for people with physical, mental, and economic disabilities. They carry the same high-quality children's apparel, toys, and accessories as the other guys—Lilly Pulitzer, for example—but purchases here also include the warm satisfaction of doing a good deed.

# Pets

## BARKLEY PET HOTEL AND DAY SPA

27349 Miles Rd., Orange Village, 440/248-2275,
www.thebarkleypethotel.com

**HOURS:** Mon.-Fri. 7 A.M.-7 P.M., Sat. 9 A.M.-5 P.M.,
Sun. 11 A.M.-4 P.M.

**Map 7**

With amenities like daily linen service, dips
in the pool, and nightly tuck-in tummy rubs,
pooches at this posh doggie hotel and day
spa truly have it better than at home. The
15,000-square-foot state-of-the-art complex
can comfortably board 150 dogs and 18 cats.
Accommodations range from poolside villas to
quiet private suites with plasma TVs. Owners
can ogle their babies 24 hours a day via web-
cam. Barkley also offers cage-free doggie day
care, grooming services, and wellness treat-
ments such as hydrotherapy and acupuncture.
Over the top? Best save that question for Fido.

## CLEVELAND METROBARK

3939 Payne Ave., 216/881-3644, www.metrobark.com

**HOURS:** Mon.-Fri. 6:30 A.M.-7 P.M.

**Map 1**

MetroBark's location and hours makes it popular with East Side commuters, who drop off their
charges on the way to work and pick them up
on the way home. The facility has begun boarding dogs, but the method—sending them home
with an employee—may not sit well with some
parents. Pets who spend the day romping in the
6,000-square-foot indoor and 14,000-square-
foot outdoor pens come home good and tired,
meaning they are less likely to chew your new
Jimmy Choos. Grooming is limited to a quick
bath and towel dry. Campers must be at least
three months old, nonaggressive, and current
with their vaccinations. Rates are approximately
$13 for a half day and $20 for a full day.

## COVENTRY CATS

1810 Coventry Rd., 216/321-3033,
www.coventrycats.com

**HOURS:** Mon.-Sat. 10:30 A.M.-8 P.M., Sun. noon-5 P.M.

**Map 5**

Notwithstanding the name, this Coventry
Road shop features a cornucopia of both dog
and cat paraphernalia. They don't stock live
animals, but they do carry a fine selection of
holistic pet food, toys, clothing, and bedding.
Deck out your pooch in a new collar, some
winter booties, maybe the latest Halloween
costume. Jewish or not, your feline will look
sharp in a stylish yarmulke. If he or she deserves it, buy your kitty friend a stash of fresh
catnip and a cat-friendly video to groove on,
featuring frolicking mice, birds, and squir-
rels. Good dogs get meaty rawhides, annoying
squeaky toys, and fresh-baked goodies.

## INN THE DOGHOUSE

10237 Berea Rd., 216/651-0873,
www.innthedoghouse.com

**Map 3**

If you're looking for a place to stash your pooch
for an hour, afternoon, or evening, this well-
run doggie daycare and boarding house is a
godsend. The lucky dogs have their run of a
roomy 5,000-square-foot indoor playpen with
an attached 1,600-square-foot outdoor pen.
Boarded dogs spend the days with the day-
campers before retiring to individual kennels
for dinner and a nap. While here, dogs can sign
up for grooming services like a brush and blow,
nail clipping, and, er, anal gland expression.
Rates are approximately $12 for a half day, $20
for a full day, and $25 for an overnight. Proof
of current vaccinations is required.

## ◖ PET-TIQUE

10906 Clifton Blvd., 216/631-2050, www.pettique.com

**HOURS:** Sun. 11:30 A.M.-4 P.M., Mon. 3-8:30 P.M.,
Tues.-Fri. 11:30 A.M.-8:30 P.M., Sat. 10 A.M.-6 P.M.

**Map 3**

This smallish near-west shop is filled to the
rafters with—you guessed it—dog and cat supplies galore. Going well beyond the usual grab
bag of treats, toys, and embarrassing clothing,
Pet-Tique stocks a fabulous array of breed-spe-
cific dog-training books, the latest and greatest

pet mags, and a full line of try-to-understand-your-cat books. Bring Fido and Tabby in for a romp around the tiled space, allowing them to pick out their own shwag. Cool sunglasses? Check. Spiky collar? Check. New lead? Check. Clean up in aisle five? Check.

# Shopping Centers and Malls

### BEACHWOOD PLACE

26300 Cedar Rd., Beachwood, 216/464-9460,
www.beachwoodplace.com
**HOURS:** Mon.-Sat. 10 A.M.-9 P.M.,
Sun. noon-6 P.M.
**Map 7**

It may be a mall, and it may be loaded with mostly chain stores, but Beachwood Place still ranks as one of the premier shopping destinations in Ohio. Where else will shoppers find under one glorious roof H&M, bebe, Lucky Brand, and BCBG? Origins and Sephora are here, as are L'Occitane and Lush Cosmetics. Gap, Pottery Barn, and Banana Republic are anchored by Saks Fifth Avenue, Nordstrom, and Dillard's. Far from just another depressing indoor mall, Beachwood Place is bright, airy, and surprisingly cheerful.

### CROCKER PARK

25 Main St., Westlake, 440/871-6880,
www.crockerpark.com
**HOURS:** Mon.-Sat. 10 A.M.-9 P.M.,
Sun. 11 A.M.-6 P.M.
**Map 7**

Encompassing 12 "city" blocks, Crocker Park is much more than just a shrine to capitalism; it is becoming a bona fide village. People actually choose to live at this mall, snatching up apartments and condos so as to be close to the Gap and Smith & Hawken. Seemingly every major chain store is present here, including Abercrombie, Guess, Talbot's, J. Crew, and Victoria's Secret. On warm days, the cafés along "Main Street" throw open their doors and arrange alfresco seating on the generously proportioned sidewalks. A few indie spots like 87 West wine bar and Hyde Park steakhouse can be found among the chains.

### ◖ ETON CHAGRIN BOULEVARD

28601 Chagrin Blvd., Woodmere, 216/591-0544,
www.etonchagrinblvd.com
**HOURS:** Varies by shop and restaurant
**Map 7**

Rarely does a mall get a second chance. But when developers added on to this fading mall, essentially giving it more of a street-side feel, they infused it with fresh life. Today, the mall has grown into an attractive indoor/outdoor multiplex boasting numerous independent clothing shops, most not found elsewhere. This is where you'll find Kilgore Trout, Nicky Nicole, Audrey's Sweet Threads, and Bonnie's Goubaud—all unique to this locale. This is the only place within 120 miles where you can shop at Anthropologie and Design Within Reach, and Eton is the only place on the globe where you can enjoy Nuevo Latino food at Paladar.

### LEGACY VILLAGE

25001 Cedar Rd., Lyndhurst, 216/382-3871,
www.legacy-village.com
**HOURS:** Mon.-Thurs. 10 A.M.-8 P.M.,
Fri.-Sat. 10 A.M.-9 P.M., Sun. noon-6 P.M.
**Map 7**

Euphemistically billed as a "lifestyle center," Legacy Village is essentially an outdoor mall. But built at a cost of $150 million, at least it is an attractive outdoor mall. Constructed to resemble a faux Main Street setting, complete with centrally located village green, the 80-acre complex boasts monster attractions like Crate & Barrel, The Apple Store, and Restoration Hardware. Popular chain restaurants like The Cheesecake Factory, The Melting Pot, and California Pizza Kitchen are represented here. While mostly stocked with national brands, the mall has a couple local shops like Contessa Gallery and Heather's Heat & Flavor.

# SHOPS OF OLD RIVER

Immediately west of Lakewood is the affluent suburb of Rocky River, and shopaholics from all over Northeast Ohio come here for the unique collection of independent upscale shops, boutiques, and salons. Set back from busy Detroit Road are the Shops of Old River, an attractive assemblage of stores arranged in a walkable outdoor district. Park your car and stroll the area.

Fashion-conscious girls will want to make a stop at **Girl Next Door** (19034 Old Detroit Rd., 440/331-4025), a trendy boutique that carries designer labels like Rebecca Taylor, Tibi, and Tom K. Nguyen. Also worth a visit for women's clothing, jewelry, and accessories is **Innuendo** (19144 Old Detroit Rd., 440/333-0365). There is even a shop devoted to mother-of-the-bride (or groom) fashions. **Peneventures** (19102 Old Detroit Rd., 440/356-4188, www.peneventures.info) makes it easy to shop for the big day. If you don't find the perfect accessory to match your outfit, make it yourself at **Embellish** (19055 Old Lake Rd., 440/333-8885, www.embellishaccessories.com). With help from the staff, inexperienced crafters can walk away with beaded necklaces, bracelets, and earrings.

Men are hardly left out of the fashion fun. **Adesso** (19071 Old Detroit Rd., 440/333-4778, www.adessofashions.net) stocks fine-quality fashions for stylish men. Selected for inclusion in *Esquire* magazine's Top 100 Men's Store in the United States, Adesso carries suits, sport coats, formal wear, custom shirts, shoes, ties, and skin-care products.

Custom home furnishings is the name of the game at **Devout Home** (19032 Old Detroit Rd., 440/333-8307, www.devouthome.com), an indispensible resource for interior designers and do-it-yourself decorators. Tastes here run to both modern and spare and earthy and devotional. Equally broad in its design appeal is **Mitchell Sotka** (19071 Old Detroit Rd., 440/333-1735, www.mitchellsotka.com), an

elegant antiques shop with a diverse inventory. Blending various periods and styles is the hottest trend in design, and this gallery is the perfect source for pieces. For the finishing touches, hit **Solari** (19036 Old Detroit Rd., 440/333-9600, www.solarihome.com), a cheery shop loaded with colorful hand-painted Italian ceramics, linens, tableware, flatware, and gourmet food products. Check the website to see which local chef is scheduled to do an in-store cooking demo.

To keep your home clean while being green, visit **Planet Green** (19056 Old Detroit Rd., 440/333-9333). This lifestyle shop carries a wide range or organic, eco-friendly, and recycled products for your home. Find organic bedding, fair-trade supplements, health-conscious dog snacks, and the owner's own line of all-natural cleaning supplies. To go well beyond those healthy dog treats, stroll into **Style Mutt Dog Boutique** (19136 Old Detroit Rd., 440/409-0454, www.stylemutt.com) with or without Fido in tow. This dog boutique and day care sells care and cleaning products and clothing for both humans and canines, and has a snack bar with doggie ice cream.

Stationery fans will go nuts over **Paper Trails** (19146 Old Detroit Rd., 440/333-0033, www.papertrailstoyou.com), a specialty paper boutique. By stocking beautiful, elegant, and artful stationery, cards, wrapping paper, and supplies, the shop keeps letter writers and gift givers well stocked.

At some point even shoppers need a break to refuel. Fortunately, a couple of Cleveland's finest restaurants are also located here. For wonderful Italian food, including ethereal homemade gnocchi, visit **Stino da Napoli** (19070 Old Detroit Rd., 440/331-3944, www.stinodanapoli.com). Stop by charming **Tartine Bistro** (19110 Old Detroit Rd., 440/331-0800, www.tartinebistro.com) for French-inspired small plates, pizza, and a great selection of wines by the glass.

## TOWER CITY CENTER

230 W. Huron Rd., 216/623-4750,
www.towercitycenter.com
**HOURS:** Mon.-Sat. 10 A.M.-7 P.M., Sun. noon-6 P.M.
`Map 1`

You may not find the latest fashions at this mall, which is located in the belly of the Terminal Tower, but that doesn't mean it should be wholly overlooked. When built, the mall was stocked to its gleaming glass roof with world-class stores. These days, the selection is more commonplace than one-of-a-kind, with the likes of Bath & Body Works, Foot Locker, and Johnston & Murphy. Chic et Mode and The Cleveland Store are located here, as is a multi-screen movie theater, food court, and numerous kiosks. Morton's Steakhouse and Hard Rock Cafe call this mall home. And kids still go gaga over the majestic central fountain, which spouts water in rhythmic and dramatic sequences. Tower City Cinemas is the site of the Cleveland International Film Fest.

# Specialty Foods

## B.A. SWEETIE CANDY COMPANY

7480 Brookpark Rd., 216/739-2244,
www.sweetiescandy.com
**HOURS:** Mon.-Fri. 9 A.M.-7 P.M., Sat. 10 A.M.-6 P.M.,
Sun. 11 A.M.-4 P.M.
`Map 7`

With some 300,000 pounds of candy on stock at all times, it's safe to assume that this confection warehouse can satisfy any sweet tooth. Around since the 1950s, Sweetie has grown into a major player in the candy wholesale business, buying and selling ridiculous amounts of the stuff. Lucky for sugar junkies, they also run a retail shop, well stocked with the same dizzying array of treats, including a pretty awesome Pez display. With rows and rows of bulk, retro, and hard-to-find gems like Moon Pies and Mary Janes, this place is like the Sam's Club of sourballs.

## HANSA IMPORT HAUS

2701 Lorain Ave., 216/281-3177
**HOURS:** Mon.-Sat. 9 A.M.-5:30 P.M.
`Map 2`

Located in a kitschy faux Swiss chalet, Hansa Import Haus provides a culinary lifeline for Cleveland's sizeable German immigrant population. This quirky gingerbread shop has survived for over 40 years thanks to its deep selection of German, Swiss, and Austrian imports, ranging from hard-to-find spreads, meats, and cheeses to harder-to-find beers, including Bavarian smoke beer. Rows of store shelving sag beneath the weight of enough cookies, cakes, and chocolates to make even the most stoic national weep with longing. And if that homesickness becomes too unbearable, there is an on-site travel agency to book a hasty return visit.

## HEATHER'S HEAT AND FLAVOR

24687 Cedar Rd., Lyndhurst, 216/291-3450,
www.heatandflavor.com
**HOURS:** Mon.-Thurs. 10 A.M.-8 P.M.,
Fri.-Sat. 10 A.M.-9 P.M., Sun. noon-6:30 P.M.
`Map 7`

You can continue buying those jars of grocery-store spices, despite their dubious origins and ages. Or you can come to Heather's, where some 150 herbs, spices, and custom blends are packaged to order like loose tea in a fine shop. If you're looking to, as some might say, "kick things up a notch," this small, bright, and tidy space stocks over 300 varieties of hot sauce, salsa, mustard, and barbecue sauce. Searching for that final fillip for your perfect martini? Consider a jar of pickled garlic or pickled green beans, both of which have the uncanny ability to make gin taste even better. Located at Legacy Village, the store is graced with easy access and parking.

## ◖ LILLY HANDMADE CHOCOLATES

761 Starkweather Ave., 216/771-3333,
www.lillytremont.com
**HOURS:** Tues.-Sat. noon-7 P.M., Sun. 10 A.M.-2 P.M.
`Map 2`

© DOUGLAS TRATTNER

Lilly Handmade Chocolates crafts to-die-for sweets.

At this urban confectionary emporium owner and culinary school grad Amanda Montague transforms the world's finest chocolate into handmade truffles, bars, and candies. Like delicious works of art, the sweets are nearly as much fun to look at as they are to gobble. Chocolate rich in cocoa butter is paired with fresh ingredients like pistachio, raspberry, Vietnamese cinnamon, even lemongrass or bacon, to create treats that leave a lasting impression. Done up in hot pink and black, the shop would not be out of place on L.A.'s Melrose Avenue. Lilly also stocks chocolate-friendly wine and beer, such as Champagne, big reds, dessert wines, and Belgian-style ales, making it a one-stop shop for gluttonous epicures.

## THE SAUSAGE SHOPPE

4501 Memphis Ave., 216/351-5213, www.sausageshoppe.com

**HOURS:** Wed.-Thurs. 10 A.M.-5 P.M., Fri. 9 A.M.-6 P.M., Sat. 9 A.M.-4 P.M.

**Map 7**

Anthony Bourdain knows his smoked meats, and made sure to visit this Cleveland institution while filming an episode of his award-winning Travel Channel show *No Reservations*. As Old School as a hand-powered egg beater, this Old Brooklyn butcher shop sells German-style meats cured in the traditional Old World fashion. Shops like this, where meats are ground and mixed by hand—with zero preservatives, fillers, or additives—and smoked on premises, are literally a dying breed. Come with a cooler and load up on 15 kinds of bratwurst, garlic bologna, fresh or smoked liverwurst, killer beef jerky, and natural-casing wieners. You may never again come this close to porcine perfection.

# Sporting Goods

## GEIGER'S CLOTHING & SPORTS

14710 Detroit Ave., 216/521-1771, www.shopgeigers.com/lakewood

**HOURS:** Mon.-Thurs. 9:30 A.M.-8 P.M., Fri. 9:30 A.M.-6 P.M., Sat. 9:30 A.M.-5 P.M., Sun. noon-5 P.M.

**Map 6**

At this 75-year-old shop, a guy can walk in and purchase a fashionable necktie, a ridiculously flimsy Speedo, and a pair of cross-country skis. (Let's just hope he doesn't wear them all home.) Despite this seemingly slapdash approach to haberdashery, Geiger's has earned a serious reputation as the place to go to get your skis edged, your tennis racket restrung, and your snowboard waxed baby-smooth. Look good as you play hard in apparel by North Face, Patagonia, and Marmot, all available here. Folks visiting during winter might be happy to learn that this Lakewood shop rents skis, snowboards, and snowshoes by the day and weekend. (Speedo not included.)

# Vintage and Antiques

## ANTIQUES IN THE BANK
4125 Lorain Ave., 216/281-6040
**HOURS:** Wed.-Sun. noon-5 P.M.
**Map 2**

Along with the adjacent Antique Arcade, this delightfully congested shop often stocks complete furniture sets from the eras of Victorian and Art Deco to mid-century, with period-appropriate light fixtures to match. But it is the wide array of architectural salvage that keeps this joint humming with home decorators. Squat porcelain sinks, antique wrought-iron fencing, stately wooden doors, and the occasional claw-foot tub can all be found here. Old-home owners visit the hardware room for hard-to-find escutcheons, crystal doorknobs, and brass switch plates. Even the shop's floor enjoys a tale of revival; it was salvaged from an old bowling alley.

## CLASS ACT RESALE SHOPPE
12404 Mayfield Rd., 216/707-9000,
www.classactresale.com
**HOURS:** Tues.-Wed. noon-7 P.M., Thurs. noon-8 P.M.,
Fri.-Sat. noon-10 P.M., Sun. noon-5 P.M.
**Map 4**

Located in the heart of charming Little Italy, this two-level storefront boutique indeed returns the "class" to resale shopping. Don't expect to thumb through dusty crates of old vinyl at owner Sharon Neura's upscale locale, which is more Martha's Vineyard than Mötley Crüe. A collection of fine designer clothing, much of it supplied by high-end consignors, is augmented by estate jewelry, original artwork, and men's and women's accessories. Enjoy a glass of complimentary wine while weekend browsing, or visit during the summer to stroll through the European-style courtyard.

## THE CLEVELAND SHOP
11606 Detroit Ave., 216/228-9725,
www.clevelandshop.com
**HOURS:** Mon.-Sat. 11 A.M.-6 P.M.
**Map 3**

Around since 1979, Cleveland Shop is one of the oldest and best-known vintage shops in the region. The store's claim to fame is authentic period costumes, which it both sells and rents. Folks looking to get dolled up for a Victorian murder mystery or hippie-themed love-in know to come here for their getups. While half the fun is the hunt, Cleveland Shop makes it easy to snag the booty thanks to its tidy arrangement and wonderful service. Located on the Cleveland-Lakewood border, this secondhand shop is first with bargain hunters.

## ELEGANSIA
1873 W. 25th St., 216/861-2553
**HOURS:** Mon.-Sat. 12:30-5:30 P.M.
**Map 2**

Owner Eva Cirjak combs through countless tag sales, estate sales, and flea markets so you don't have to. All you have to do is amble into her elegant, modern, and well-organized store and spend like it's 1969. Among the gently worn designer and vintage women's clothing lucky shoppers will unearth labels from Gucci, Giorgio Armani, and Lilly Pulitzer. Vintage gowns from Yves Saint-Laurent and Emilio Pucci go fast. Shoppers won't find basic needs here, but if you don't dawdle you might score that one-of-a-kind ostrich cape that Cirjak just got in.

## FLOWER CHILD
11508 Clifton Blvd., 216/939-9933,
www.flowerchildretro.com
**HOURS:** Tues.-Wed. noon-7 P.M., Thurs. 1-7 P.M.,
Fri.-Sat. noon-8 P.M., Sun. noon-5 P.M.
**Map 3**

Shoppers keen on a particular vintage era have it easy at Flower Child thanks to period-specific displays, which are arranged precisely as they might have been at department stores decades ago. This super-popular multi-room shop moves through inventory quickly, meaning that frequent visits net frequent scores. Expect furniture, clothing, jewelry, lighting, and accessories from the 1930s through the 1970s, all artfully displayed. A great source for mid-century furniture, vintage jewelry, including Bakelite and men's cufflinks, and all matter of floor, wall, and ceiling lighting.

### HEIDE RIVCHUN CONSERVATION STUDIOS

12702 Larchmere Blvd., 216/231-1003, www.conservationstudios.org
**HOURS:** Mon.-Sat. 9 A.M.-5 P.M.
Map 5

This Larchmere shop has a dual identity. It is the site of owner Heide Rivchun's renowned furniture conservation and restoration business, and it is the storefront where she displays her wonderful collection of antiques for sale. Stocking fine furniture largely from the 18th and 19th centuries, as well as striking architectural items, the store is popular with designers, decorators, and informed homeowners. Old globes, full fireplace mantels, stained-glass windows, portly earthenware casks—these are just some of the unique items on hand.

### OPEN AIR IN MARKET SQUARE

Market Square Park, corner of Lorain Ave. and W. 25th St., 216/781-3222
**HOURS:** Memorial Day weekend-Labor Day weekend Sat. 10 A.M.-4 P.M.
Map 2

Like a New York City flea market, this weekly summer gathering attracts enthusiastic bargain hunters and accidental tourists. Though one is not very likely to score a future family heirloom, as much of the stock falls into the bric-a-brac category, there are plenty of interesting, kitschy, and just plain odd items up for sale. In addition to the requisite candles and incense, used vinyl and CDs, beaded jewelry and textiles, there is original art and photography, homemade soaps, and vintage clothing. One vendor fashions light-switch plates from recycled roofing slate, while another sells all matter of eyeball art. Live music, food, and community outreach stations add even more character to this exuberant neighborhood block party where locals and their dogs catch up with their mates and playmates.

### PLAY IT AGAIN, SAM

14311 Madison Ave., 216/228-7330, www.playitagainsam.com
**HOURS:** Mon.-Tues. and Thurs.-Sat. 10 A.M.-6 P.M.
Map 6

There has been an undeniable uptick in the demand for old-school vinyl records, and few shops have been positioned to take advantage of that trend like Play it Again, Sam. This West Side institution doesn't sell records, but a bewildering selection of vintage two-channel stereo equipment. Audiophiles come here for both new and used tuners, preamps, receivers, turntables, cassette recorders, CD players—even reel-to-reel tape recorders. If you have a vinyl collection in need of a little TLC, bring it here for a trip through Sam's deep-cleaning machine. Those old platters will come out looking and sounding as good as new.

### ◖ REINCARNATION VINTAGE DESIGN

7810 Lorain Ave., 216/651-9806
**HOURS:** Sat.-Sun. noon-5 P.M.
Map 3

Owner Ron Nicolson doesn't just resell old furniture, he repurposes it into hip home furnishings and accessories. By staying abreast of the latest home-decor trends, Nicolson and wife Cyndy know what to look for while traveling their never-ending circuit of estate sales, auctions, antiques swaps, and demo sites. An old wooden door is transformed into a funky dinette table; a long-forgotten industrial workbench becomes a stainless-steel kitchen island; galvanized wire conveyor belting is segmented into durable and distinctive doormats. This two-level New York–style loft showroom is a must-visit when hitting the antiques and resale shops of Lorain Avenue. Being open only on weekends allows him time to find new cool stuff, says Nicolson.

### SUITE LORAIN

7105 Lorain Rd., 216/281-1959, www.suitelorain.net
**HOURS:** Wed.-Mon. noon-5 P.M., Sat. until 6 P.M.
Map 3

Easily one of the best vintage shops in Cleveland, Suite Lorain is 8,000 square feet of retro fun. The former bowling alley digs are an appropriate setting for the well-tended collection of clothing, home furnishings, small appliances, and accessories from the 1920s through the mid-20th century. Numerous vendors keep the place uber-stocked with cool kitsch and collectibles, including old records, magazines, and posters. A favorite among designers, touring musicians, and fashion-savvy ladies, this West Side shop knows the difference between trash and treasure.

**UNIQUE THRIFT**

3333 Lorain Ave., 216/631-0205,
www.uniquethriftstore.com

**HOURS:** Mon. 7 A.M.–9:30 P.M., Tues.-Thurs. 9 A.M.–9 P.M., Fri. 9 A.M.–9:30 P.M., Sat. 9 A.M.–9 P.M., Sun. 11 A.M.-7 P.M.

**Map 2**

Part of a small Midwest chain of thrift stores, Unique feels a lot like a Salvation Army. This location is large, bright, and occasionally messy, but those with a keen eye and a soft touch can score anything from a rare LP to a bunny-plush cashmere sweater. Shoppers will find a wealth of clothing, furniture, tableware, and outdated electronics. Visit on Mondays for a 25–50 percent discount on every item in the store. Unique's off-label use is as the best source for last-minute Halloween costumes. Oh, the horror.

# HOTELS

Greater Cleveland is blessed with enough chain hotels, independent inns, and charming bed-and-breakfasts that almost every budget, style preference, and location requirement can be met with relative ease. Granted, it does tend to be easier to find a pricey three-star affair than it is to score that perfectly placed budget hotel. But with a little research, compromise, and advance booking, even the most frugal traveler should be able to find a bed that's just right.

Apart from those downtown, hotels in Greater Cleveland are not necessarily clustered where a pleasure traveler might want them to be. Predictably, there is a large contingent of rooms near Hopkins International Airport, but there are precious few in and around University Circle. For some reason, suburban Beachwood is home to about 2,000

rooms, but good luck finding a rentable bed in Tremont. A flurry of commercial development has turned Independence into a sort of hotel nirvana, while inner-ring suburbs like Lakewood, Detroit Shoreway, Cleveland Heights, and Shaker Heights are largely devoid of inns.

The good news, though, is that downtown's central location makes it a fine jumping-off point for most major sights, attractions, and neighborhoods. If you don't have a car it makes sense to compare likely excursions with available public transport before booking a room.

## CHOOSING A HOTEL

For most business and pleasure visits, a downtown address is the most logical option. There are approximately 4,000 rooms in the city

COURTESY OF THE RITZ-CARLTON

# HIGHLIGHTS

LOOK FOR ( TO FIND RECOMMENDED HOTELS.

( **Most Gay-Friendly Digs:** Housed in a renovated bus terminal, **Flex Baths** is an upscale gay bathhouse that maintains dozens of overnight accommodations for men. Included in the price of a room is access to the outdoor heated pool, which stays open even in the dead of winter (page 161).

( **Finest Reuse of a Really Old Mall:** The Arcade is likely the most magical interior space in Cleveland, and now you can sleep there. One hundred years after it was built, the attractive Victorian atrium was converted into the sharp-dressed **Hyatt Regency at The Arcade.** At least now those gargoyles have something to guard come nightfall (page 162).

( **Schmanciest Lobby:** Carved of marble pulled from the same quarry as Michelangelo's *David*, the central fountain in the lobby of the **Renaissance Cleveland Hotel** is truly a work of art. The rest of this grand entrance hall is nothing to sneeze at either (page 162).

( **Best Pad for Pooches:** It isn't just the human guests who get pampered at **The Ritz-Carlton**; pooches are treated with the same white-glove service as their masters. Call ahead and your pet will have his or her own water bowl, toy, and treats waiting in the room (page 163).

( **Best Bed for Bicyclists:** The **Inn at Brandywine Falls** is tucked into Cuyahoga Valley National Park, literally steps from its namesake falls. Better yet, the lengthy and

COURTESY OF THE RENAISSANCE HOTEL

**the grand lobby of the Renaissance Cleveland Hotel**

scenic Towpath Trail is only a mile and a half from the front door (page 169).

HOTELS

---

center, meaning that vacancies abound except in the rarest instances. And downtown is manageable enough in size that lodging decisions need not be based solely on proximity to a sight, event, or organization. Options range from very basic budget inns on the fringes of town to ritzy four-star gems right on Public Square. How you ultimately decide will likely be a combination of availability, location, budget, and occasion. Two buddies backpacking across America may not require

the same level of comfort and elegance as, say, that honeymooning couple from Apalachicola. When staying downtown and traveling by car, it almost always makes financial sense to find overnight parking outside the hotel.

Despite the fact that 2.5 million people visit University Circle each year, you'd be hard-pressed to stumble across a hotel there. InterContinental operates two large hotels nearby on the Cleveland Clinic campus, and there is a smattering of small inns in the area, but that is about the extent of

HOTELS

## PRICE KEY

$ Under $150
$$ $150-250
$$$ Over $250

Due to its bounty of charming century homes, Ohio City has become a happy little breeding ground for bed-and-breakfasts. Four well-run inns can be found within blocks of one another, and each offers the sort of personality and personal attention that fans of the genre seek (see sidebar).

There are also options for those who prefer to stay close to the airport, Cleveland Metroparks, Cuyahoga Valley National Park, or Chagrin Falls.

it. Fortunately, thanks to RTA's Silver Line and light rail system, getting to the Circle from downtown is a snap.

# Downtown

Map 1

### BROWNSTONE INN $

3649 Prospect Ave., 216/426-1753,
www.brownstoneinndowntown.com

If you are the sort of budget-minded traveler who appreciates personal attention and doesn't bristle at the thought of conversing with other guests, consider booking a stay at the Brownstone Inn ($65–95). Run by the impeccable Robin Yates, this 19th-century Victorian bed-and-breakfast has charm and personality to spare. The lovingly restored townhouse offers five rooms, two of which feature sitting areas. All but one has its own bath. Breakfast is taken in the formal dining room, where other visitors might be on hand to share their recent sightseeing experiences. If not, you can count on the amiable Yates to recommend the very best sights, restaurants, and shopping excursions. If all else fails simply pore over the accumulated maps and tourist literature. The Brownstone is located a short five-minute drive from downtown on an oft-traveled thoroughfare into town. While far from bustling, the immediate neighborhood is mostly safe, quiet, and worry-free. Access to all major highways is a few blocks away. To find this attractive inn, simply look for the massive elm tree, which is one of the oldest living specimens in the region.

### COMFORT INN DOWNTOWN $

1800 Euclid Ave., 216/861-0001, www.choicehotels.com

If you're searching for a basic hotel at a great rate, the Comfort Inn Downtown ($85–110) may be the best option. Situated just blocks from Public Square, this hotel is far cheaper than its location would have you believe. Granted, the bargain-basement rates tend to attract a more boisterous crowd, including those visiting for rock concerts and sporting events. Invest in a good pair of earplugs, however, and your stay may indeed be comfortable. Included in the rate is complimentary continental breakfast, wireless Internet, and local phone calls.

### CROWNE PLAZA CLEVELAND CITY CENTRE $$

777 St. Clair Ave., 216/771-7600,
www.clevelanddowntownhotel.com

With its spacious rooms, convenient location, and reasonable rates, it's no wonder that Crowne Plaza is a popular choice for lodging. Within easy walking distance to the Rock Hall, Browns Stadium, and Progressive Field, the hotel serves as a handy home base for downtown adventures. Renovated rooms are designed around cozy "Sleep Advantage" beds, plush pillow-top nests with upscale linens. All rooms feature free high-speed wireless Internet access. The hotel has a lobby lounge with bar, a full-service restaurant, and a level of personal service commensurate with pricier inns. A popular choice with visiting football fans, the hotel can get a bit rowdy before and after home Browns games, especially at the

# THE BED-AND-BREAKFASTS OF OHIO CITY

The singular arrangement of restored Civil War-era homes, a walkable neighborhood with a wealth of attractions, and proximity to downtown and public transportation have made Ohio City fertile ground for bed-and-breakfasts.

Despite its petite size, this picturesque neighborhood boasts four privately operated urban inns, each with its own charms, quirks, and stories to tell. Less than a mile from Public Square, Ohio City is close to downtown's major offerings. But the area's narrow lanes, leafy canopies, and distinctive architecture can make it feel a million miles – and years – away from big-city life. A nearby light rail stop makes for a breezy trip to the airport, downtown, or points east.

The largest of the bed-and-breakfasts is **Stone Gables,** a roomy Queen Anne Victorian with a welcoming double-stair front porch and festive color scheme. Partners Richard Turnbull and James Hauer do triple duty as hosts, chefs, and tour guides at this gay-friendly inn.

Bridge Avenue is one of the most aesthetically pleasing stretches of Ohio City, and it is home to two of the area's four inns. **J. Palen House,** the newcomer, gracefully straddles the line between antiquity and modernity. Long a flophouse, the 1872 Victorian features original floors, doors, and stained-glass windows. Yet, it also boasts Wi-Fi, a fully outfitted business center, and an eager-to-please innkeeper. A half a block away, David and Emily Dennis's **Glendennis Bed & Breakfast** is quite possibly the street's most attractive house. A dusty-rose brick facade evokes the feel of a Georgetown townhouse, while the immaculate urban garden is like a hidden oasis for guests. Thanks to a fully self-contained suite, this inn also offers the most privacy. Just around the corner, **Clifford House** may be the homiest of them all. Innkeeper Jim Miner lives here with his Siamese cat and dog, and there is nothing like a warm slobber from a happy puppy to remind us why we sidestepped that big, anonymous hotel.

---

lobby bar. Request a high-floor room for the best views of Lake Erie and the city. Parking is about $18 for 24 hours.

### ◖ FLEX BATHS ⑤
2600 Hamilton Ave., 216/812-3304, www.flexbaths.com

Flex operates about a half-dozen upscale gay bathhouses around the country. Cleveland's is situated in a sprawling complex just east of town that once housed a bus terminal. Now renovated, the facility attracts men from throughout the region thanks to its laundry list of deluxe amenities. The outdoor heated pool is open year-round. Real sand forms the base of the secluded second-story sundeck. Inside is another pool, 20-person hot tub, two saunas, massive steam-room maze, state-of-the-art fitness center, and full-service restaurant. Male guests looking to spend the night have a number of options with prices ranging $20–240. Over a dozen well-equipped hotel rooms

feature four-poster beds, walk-in closets, private baths, and fridges. If one is willing to relinquish the private bathroom, smaller rooms are available for $30 per night. A measly $20 lands you a private cabana for a full 12 hours. Everybody who enters the facility must pay a membership fee ($9/day, $22/six months, $40/year), which includes use of the amenities and secure off-street parking.

### HILTON GARDEN INN ⑤⑤
1100 Carnegie Ave., 216/658-6400, www.clevelanddowntown.stayghi.com

If you're in town to catch a Cavs or Indians game, it's tough to book a room much closer to the action. In fact, you can see Progressive Field from many of Hilton Garden Inn's 240 guest rooms. Prices tend to fluctuate alongside the activity at the nearby stadiums and arenas, starting as low as $100 and climbing to $200 and up. To save some cash, check the website for packages built around sporting

HOTELS

events, museum passes, and musical performances that include breakfast, parking, and admission. Like most modern hotels, this one offers complimentary high-speed Internet, microwave, refrigerator, and coffee maker in every room. There is also a casual restaurant, fitness center, and small pool on-site. Located adjacent to highway on-ramps, this hotel also provides easy access into and out of the city.

### HOLIDAY INN EXPRESS HOTEL AND SUITES $

629 Euclid Ave., 216/443-1000,
www.ichotelsgroup.com

Perhaps the best union of location, price, and good looks, this Holiday Inn Express ($90–140) often pleasantly surprises first-time guests who are expecting a plain-vanilla property. In a retrofitted 19th-century bank, the hotel may be one of the most architecturally striking Holiday Inns around. From the gorgeous former bank lobby to the spacious, high-ceilinged rooms, nothing is standard-issue budget hotel. Guests can choose between single rooms or suites, but all have free high-speed Internet, mini-fridge, and coffee maker, while some even boast hardwood floors and whirlpool tubs. Stays also include free hot breakfast, access to the recently renovated fitness center, and use of a game room with pool tables and pinball machines. For killer views, request rooms on the upper floors of this 15-story building. The hotel is conveniently located six blocks from Public Square.

### ◖ HYATT REGENCY AT THE ARCADE $$

420 Superior Ave., 216/575-1234,
www.cleveland.hyatt.com

In 1999, Hyatt spent approximately $60 million to retrofit the upper floors and adjoining towers of the stunning 1890 Arcade into a comfortable, modern hotel ($125–225). Most rooms are generously proportioned and feature vaulted ceilings, original artwork, and stellar views of either the Arcade or the city. Guests enjoy wireless Internet access, fitness center, and easy access to the Arcade's shops, services,

and restaurants. This hotel is conveniently located near the East 4th Street entertainment district.

### MARRIOTT DOWNTOWN AT KEY CENTER $$

127 Public Sq., 216/696-9200, www.marriott.com

One of Cleveland's premier accommodations, this 25-story, 400-room property is attached to Key Tower and is within easy walking distance to Browns Stadium, the Rock and Roll Hall of Fame, and the Great Lakes Science Center. Upscale all the way, with prices to match ($180–250), this sharp hotel has undergone a $10 million renovation. Rooms all boast top-of-the-line bedding, flat-screen TVs, wireless Internet access, CD players, and updated bathrooms. Guests have use of an indoor pool, sauna, and fitness center, and an on-site restaurant serves breakfast, lunch, and dinner. The hotel also features a bar, snack shop, and loads of meeting and banquet space. For special occasions, consider booking one of the luxurious guest suites with spectacular city views.

### ◖ RENAISSANCE CLEVELAND HOTEL $$$

24 Public Sq., 216/696-5600, www.marriott.com

Originally opened in 1918 as the Cleveland Hotel, this Beaux Arts gem exudes opulence, grace, and beauty. More reminiscent of a major museum than a hotel lobby, the entrance hall features a soaring barrel-vaulted ceiling, massive marble fountains, and high arched windows that perfectly frame the city outside. The upmarket address right on Public Square comes with a price, of course, with rates generally ranging from $185 to $300 depending on the size of the room or suite. After a long day touring the city, settle into the classy Lobby Court Bar for a classic cocktail. Also in this 500-room property is a wonderful French bistro, an indoor pool, and a well-stocked fitness center. With the RTA located just steps away, transportation to and from the airport, University Circle, and Shaker Square could not be simpler.

## 📧 THE RITZ-CARLTON 💲💲💲

1515 W. 3rd St., 216/623-1300,
www.ritzcarlton.com/hotels/cleveland

While admittedly below par compared to others in this illustrious hotel chain, The Ritz-Carlton Cleveland ($220–300) still deserves props for service, elegance, and location. Though some rooms could use updating, the hotel's common areas sparkle with sophistication, and the in-room amenities are close to what one might expect of the Ritz, with marble tubs, terry robes, pool and hot tub, and the matchless Muse restaurant and ritzy Lobby Lounge. Located just off Public Square, the Ritz is close to public transportation and has covered access to both Quicken Loans Arena and Progressive Field. Adjacent Tower City Center is no Rodeo Drive, but the physically attractive mall has more than enough diversions to kill a few hours of down time. To ease those lofty prices, explore the hotel's packages, such as the Fresh Market package, which includes a chef-guided tour of the West Side Market followed by a meal constructed from those just-purchased items.

## WYNDHAM CLEVELAND AT PLAYHOUSESQUARE 💲💲

1260 Euclid Ave., 216/615-7500, www.wyndham.com

A recent top-to-bottom overhaul freshened up this already attractive downtown hotel. In addition to the upscale public areas, spacious guest rooms, and attentive staff, this hotel boasts a stellar location in the heart of PlayhouseSquare. Just steps from the theaters, the hotel makes a stress-free home base for seeing shows in the area. The hotel's position on Euclid Avenue also makes trips to University Circle via the HealthLine an absolute breeze. Rooms feature comfy beds, high-speed Internet access, and Herman Miller desk chairs. A high-quality restaurant and bar means that guests needn't leave the building for a decent pre- or post-curtain meal.

# Ohio City and Tremont    Map 2

## CLIFFORD HOUSE BED AND BREAKFAST 💲💲

1810 W. 28th St., 216/589-0121, www.cliffordhouse.com

Innkeeper Jim Miner describes his house as eclectic—and that may be an understatement. Built in 1868, added onto in 1890, and renovated in the 1970s, the building features architectural elements as varied as Tuscan, Queen Anne Victorian, Georgian Colonial, and Louis XIV. Despite the mishmash, the result is a cozy home with space enough for privacy. Accommodations range from a single room that shares a bath to a self-contained mother-in-law suite ideal for longer stays and families. A private 3rd-floor suite includes a queen bed, private bath, and fridge. The inn also features Wi-Fi and cable. Miner, who lives on-site, has a dog and a cat, so those with relevant allergies should take note.

## J. PALEN HOUSE 💲💲

2708 Bridge Ave., 216/664-0813, www.jpalenhouse.com

Ohio City's newest bed-and-breakfast, J. Palen House seems to try a little bit harder to please its guests. Once a 14-room flophouse, this 1872 Victorian has been gently converted into a comfortable three-suite urban inn. Thankfully, architectural highlights like original parquet wood floors, pocket doors, and a two-story stained-glass window have withstood multiple remodels. While historic touches remain, including the quirky skeleton-style room keys, modern amenities like guest-controlled thermostats, Wi-Fi, and a fully outfitted business center make this inn a best-of-both-worlds proposition. In the morning, chat with house guests over fresh-squeezed orange juice, stuffed French toast, and Belgian waffles. Free off-street parking.

HOTELS

© DOUGLAS TRATTNER

**the cozy and eclectic Clifford House Bed and Breakfast**

### GLENDENNIS BED & BREAKFAST $$

2808 Bridge Ave., 216/589-0663,
www.glendennis.com

There is only one suite available for rent in this gorgeous brick colonial, but what a suite it is. Nearly 1,000 square feet of private space on two floors contains a bedroom, living room, dine-in area, and private full bath. One full bed and a full-size futon provide room enough for four to sleep. A 2nd-floor deck that overlooks innkeeper Emily Dennis's immaculate urban garden is the ideal place to enjoy a breakfast of fresh-squeezed juice, eggs, and fruit. Guests come and go as they wish thanks to a separate stairway and entrance. This charming inn also features Wi-Fi, garage parking, and an ideal location. Glendennis is a bona fide bed-and-breakfast, meaning that the innkeepers own the property and live on-site.

### STONE GABLES BED AND BREAKFAST $$

3806 Franklin Blvd., 216/961-4654,
www.stonegables.net

Partners Richard Turnbull and James Hauer spent years restoring the 1883 Queen Anne Victorian that is now Stone Gables Bed and Breakfast. With 6,000 square feet of living space, this charming inn boasts two suites and three rooms, each with king beds, private baths, and Wi-Fi. Breakfasts are gourmet, with fresh fruit, eggs Benedict, and French toast the order of the day. Turnbull takes his job as innkeeper seriously and provides guests with local maps, travel info, and recommendations for area restaurants and galleries. This bed-and-breakfast is family-, gay-, and pet-friendly.

# Detroit Shoreway and Edgewater    Map 3

### DANES GUEST HOUSE ⑤
2189 West Blvd., 216/961-9444,
www.bedandbreakfast.com

Joan and Ken Danes love company so much that they open up their elegant West Side home to travelers. In a lot of ways, staying with the Danes is like visiting one's grandparents. The 1920s two-and-a-half-story home is situated on a tree-lined residential boulevard, and the Danes live right upstairs. Guests stay in one of two 2nd-floor suites with sitting rooms and balcony. One bath is shared by both rooms, so families looking for a little more privacy would be wise to book both. Rates are typically $65 to $85 per night, but can go as low as $50 for multi-night stays. Included in the cost of the room is a full hot breakfast and off-street parking. From here, it is only a 20-minute walk to Edgewater State Park and a 10-minute drive downtown.

HOTELS

# University Circle and Little Italy    Map 4

### CLEVELAND CLINIC GUESTHOUSE ⑤⑤
9601 Euclid Ave., 216/707-4200,
www.clevelandclinic.org

Budget-minded families with loved ones receiving treatment at the Cleveland Clinic are this 230-room hotel's bread and butter. The location is every bit as close to the health-care facility as the nearby InterContinental hotels, but the short- and long-term room rates are considerably more affordable. Renovations have given this property a much-needed facelift, but guests looking for luxury would do well to stay elsewhere. For longer stays, make sure to request a room with kitchenette and fridge. Stays do include free parking and Internet access in the lobby.

### GLIDDEN HOUSE ⑤⑤
1901 Ford Dr., 866/812-4537, www.gliddenhouse.com

For forays into the cultural playground that is University Circle, there may be no better jumping-off point than the Glidden House ($139–199). Once you park your car at this 1910 French Gothic mansion, you can rely solely on foot power to get to the orchestra, museums, and institutions that dot the circle. Located on the campus of Case Western Reserve University, the inn also is convenient for appointments at the school. If there is a consistent complaint about the Glidden House, it is that some rooms do not live up to the grandeur of the building's exterior and common areas. In fact, some rooms have little more appeal than a standard chain experience. Like at many off-brand hotels, rooms, suites, and experiences can vary widely. A continental-style breakfast buffet is served each morning in a lovely interior chamber. For a delightfully cosmopolitan meal, book a table at the adjacent Sergio's in University Circle, which is housed in the Glidden's original carriage house. Check the hotel's website for various packages that combine a room with theater tickets and museum passes.

### INTERCONTINENTAL HOTEL AND CONFERENCE CENTER ⑤⑤
9801 Carnegie Ave., 216/707-4100,
www.ichotelsgroup.com

It's understandable that travelers have difficulty making sense of the InterContinental hotels situation in Cleveland, since there are two separate properties located five blocks apart on the Cleveland Clinic campus. The far grander sibling in this hotel family is unquestionably the InterContinental Hotel and Conference Center. Completed in 2003 at a cost of around $100 million, this luxury 330-room hotel wows visitors from the get-go thanks to a 3,000-piece granite mosaic world map that serves as the

the French Gothic-style Glidden House in University Circle

© DOUGLAS TRATTNER

lobby floor. Modern, well-appointed rooms feature high-speed Internet connections, 27-inch flat-screen televisions, mini-bars, coffee makers, and CD players. The on-site fitness center is equipped with state-of-the-art cardiovascular and strength-training machines, plus locker rooms, showers, and sauna. Hungry guests can dine at the world-class Table 45 or the more casual North Coast Café. Of course, as the style, service, and amenities rise, so too does the price. Rooms at this hotel are consistently more expensive than those at the Suites, with rates ranging from $160 to $220 and up per night. Both InterCons are less than two miles from University Circle, Case Western Reserve University, and Little Italy. Downtown is about a 10-minute drive away.

### INTERCONTINENTAL SUITES HOTEL ❸
8800 Euclid Ave., 216/707-4300,
www.ichotelsgroup.com

Around since 1999, the InterContinental Suites Hotel is the older and smaller of the two InterContinentals. It also tends to be the more economical option. Room deals often can be had for as low as $85 through online travel sites, while typical rates hover in the $150 range. Guests can expect mostly one- and two-bedroom suites with all the usual amenities, including high-speed Internet access, refrigerators, microwaves, and coffee makers. This hotel also features a newly renovated fitness center, contemporary restaurant, and festive bar with outdoor patio. Both InterCons are less than two miles from University Circle, Case Western Reserve University, and Little Italy. Downtown is about a 10-minute drive away.

### UNIVERSITY CIRCLE BED AND BREAKFAST ❸
1575 E. 108th St., 216/721-8968, www.ucbnb.com

"This is not the romantic-getaway-type bed-and-breakfast," admits innkeeper William Bowman. "You won't find hot tubs in all the rooms." What you will find at University Circle Bed and Breakfast ($80–125) is a clean, professional, and well-placed inn less than a mile from University Circle's major cultural attractions. As a short-term corporate-stay facility, the renovated century home is popular with professionals visiting the nearby universities, hospitals, and institutions. Typical guests here stay about a week and some even come from overseas. Most rooms have private baths and rates include breakfast, morning paper, Wi-Fi, and free off-street parking. Additional accommodations are available at Bowman's sister operation, The Place on Larchmere (12404 Larchmere Blvd., 216/721-8968), which is located near Shaker Square.

# Cleveland Heights and Shaker Heights Map 5

### THE ALCAZAR ⊙
2450 Derbyshire Rd., 216/321-5400, www.thealcazar.com

Modeled after a similar Alcazar hotel in St. Augustine, Florida, this historic Cleveland Heights landmark ($90–199) exudes architectural charisma. The building's remarkable five-story pentagonal shape frames a sequestered urban garden. Whether spending the night here or not, folks in the vicinity would be wise to poke their heads into the grand lobby to catch sight of the mosaic stone floor, extraordinary Spanish tile work, and fish pond with fountain.

As is the case with the nearby Glidden House, rooms sometimes have a tough time living up to the expectations created by the building's exterior and common areas. Today's Alcazar guests are a mix of frugal pleasure travelers, short-term business guests, and long-term independent senior residents. Rooms range from bare-bones efficiency to fully furnished multibedroom suite. The Alcazar is just steps from a main street lined with a coffee shop, bookstore, wine shop, and restaurants. Nighttown, one of the world's best jazz supper clubs, is less than a block away.

HOTELS

## COUCHSURF YOUR WAY TO A GOOD NIGHT'S REST

Clevelanders have always been generous, and despite present economic challenges, the city is among the most philanthropic in the nation. So it's no surprise that so many locals participate in the **CouchSurfing Project.**

The CouchSurfing craze helps to remove financial barriers from domestic and international travel, but that's not all. Participants open up their homes to travelers, asking for nothing in return apart from a thank you. Many go well beyond simply providing a roof, offering to pick folks up from public transport, preparing a home-cooked meal, and showing guests around the city. The benefits, in addition to the cash savings, are a more personal experience, heightened cultural exchange, and quite possibly a new friend.

A recent search of Cleveland members offering a free stay resulted in over 85 hits. The list includes people with such occupations as paramedic, chef, student, teacher, journalist, photographer, and musician. They are young and old, male and female, attached and single. The only universal quality among them seems to be a spirit of adventure, philanthropy, and camaraderie.

Surf your way over to www.couchsurfing .com to read more about this fun and frugal way to travel.

HOTELS

# Lakewood
Map 6

## DAYS INN $

12019 Lake Ave., 216/226-4800, www.daysinn.com

Lakewood is a beautiful tree-lined community about five miles west of downtown. When it comes to commercial lodging, however, options are few. For the price, this Days Inn ($55–75) offers a clean, comfortable, and efficient place to rest your head. No, it's not the Ritz, and yes, it can get noisy, but this locale provides a decent home base for exploring Cleveland and its western suburbs. Included in the cut-rate price is complimentary continental breakfast, free Wi-Fi, free off-street parking, and cable, making it a sensible, albeit nondescript, temporary address.

## EMERALD NECKLACE INN $$

18840 Lorain Rd., Fairview Park, 440/333-9100, www.emeraldnecklaceinn.com

If plans call for hitting the bike paths of the Rocky River Reservation, consider this inn your cozy home base. Literally steps from the park, this charming Victorian bed-and-breakfast ($119) is close to golf, tennis, fishing, and cross-country skiing. Or simply enjoy the inn's impeccable gardens and surrounding green space. The inn offers guests a choice of three rooms, all with private bath, some with views of the lush Cleveland Metroparks. Stays include complimentary full breakfast, free Wi-Fi, and off-street parking. Have the staff pack a picnic lunch for your travels through the park. Better yet, arrange to have an in-room massage waiting when you return. Reminiscent of days gone by, the snug little country inn also runs a tea parlor that is open to the public.

# Greater Cleveland
Map 7

## CLEVELAND AIRPORT MARRIOTT $

4277 W. 150th St., 800/228-9290, www.marriott.com/cleap

When an early flight out of town awaits, it might be wise to stay near the airport. This nicely appointed Marriott ($80–210) is located five minutes from Hopkins International, and the hotel offers free round-the-clock shuttle service. While nothing to write home about on the outside, this 370-room property is actually quite attractive inside. There is an elegant terrazzo lobby, a surprisingly good steakhouse and lounge, indoor pool, and 24-hour fitness center. The comfortable guest rooms all offer wireless Internet service, crisp new linens, and a workstation outfitted with an ergonomic chair. Not only is this location situated by the airport, it is close to the I-X Center and a highway that offers a straight shot to downtown.

## EMBASSY SUITES CLEVELAND ROCKSIDE $

5800 Rockside Woods Blvd., Independence, 216/986-9900, www.embassysuites-rockside.com

Independence is a popular stop for business travelers; the city includes a thriving economic corridor home to numerous Northeast Ohio companies. Situated at the crossroads of I-77 and I-480, the location also puts travelers about 15 minutes from downtown and 10 minutes from the airport. Like other Embassy Suites, this one features a roomy central atrium around which are the balconied hotel floors. Rooms ($90–120) in the all-suite hotel include separate spaces for sleeping and living, with an additional sleeper sofa, armchair, and TV. Rooms offer wired high-speed Internet access, while wireless is available only in the lobby. All stays include a full breakfast, nightly Manager's Receptions with free snacks and beverages, and complimentary transportation to the airport. Other amenities include indoor pool, fitness center, business office, and free parking.

## HAMPTON INN BEACHWOOD $$

3840 Orange Pl., Beachwood, 216/831-3735,
www.hamptoninn.com

There are times when staying in the eastern suburbs just makes sense. Perhaps you are visiting family or friends who reside in Beachwood, Pepper Pike, or Shaker Heights. Or maybe you want to hit the shops of Beachwood Place, Eton Chagrin Boulevard, or Legacy Village. With the Hampton Inn ($120–180) you know you'll find reliable comfort, service, and value. All 139 rooms feature cushy Cloud Nine beds, complimentary high-speed Internet access, and cable TV. Included with the price of the room is Hampton's complimentary breakfast buffet. The modern hotel has a business center, indoor swimming pool, whirlpool spa, and fitness center. Travel to downtown is a snap thanks to nearby highway access.

## HILLBROOK INN $$

14800 Hillbrook Dr., Chagrin Falls, 440/247-4940,
www.clubhillbrook.com

Mention Hillbrook Club to most East Siders and you're bound to receive some oohs and ahhs. The tony private club is located in the densely forested Chagrin River Valley, and it is the preferred wedding site of the area's wealthiest socialites. But you needn't be a Rockefeller to experience this 40-room English Tudor mansion. The Hillbrook Inn ($155–215) allows guests to live like a member for a fraction of the cost. Included with a night's stay is access to the private dining room, swimming pool, fitness center, and tennis courts. Approximately seven different suites are available, each with private bathrooms and Wi-Fi. Most feature original architectural accents like leaded-glass windows, black-walnut moldings, and stately fireplaces. A continental breakfast is included in the price of the room.

## ◖ INN AT BRANDYWINE FALLS $$

8230 Brandywine Rd., Sagamore Hills, 888/306-3381,
www.innatbrandywinefalls.com

This 160-year-old farmhouse estate is tucked into the Cuyahoga Valley National Park, literally steps from scenic Brandywine Falls, a 65-foot gem. Guests who book a room or suite at this charming inn ($140–250) likely do so because they plan on taking advantage of the wealth of recreational pursuits in the area. The Towpath Trail and Cuyahoga Valley Scenic Rail are both about a mile and a half from the front door. Ohio's best ski resorts are around the corner. And Blossom Music Center, the summer home of the Cleveland Orchestra, is just down the road. Rooms range from cozy 2nd-floor nooks to spacious suites with wood-burning Franklin stoves. Vertically gifted guests are advised to avoid the low-ceilinged Anna Hale's Garret. Despite the historical nature of the house and property, all rooms feature private baths and free Wi-Fi.

## INN OF CHAGRIN FALLS $$

87 West St., Chagrin Falls, 440/247-1200,
www.innofchagrinfalls.com

Though located only 35 minutes from downtown Cleveland, Chagrin Falls has enough charms to warrant an overnight stay. Situated around the town's village square are scores of independent boutiques, galleries, shops, and restaurants, not to mention the namesake waterfall. Granted, as the town's only hotel, the Inn of Chagrin Falls ($145–250) has a bit of a lock on the local lodging. But this graceful Western Reserve building has charms all its own. Many of the 15 rooms boast gas fireplaces, and some of those also have a whirlpool tub. Guests can expect a certain country-style decor, and the finishes may not be the most up-to-date. But calm, comfort, and service seem to make up for the inn's lack of panache.

HOTELS

# EXCURSIONS FROM CLEVELAND

Ohio is a state of remarkable contrasts. Tucked alongside metropolitan areas like Cleveland, Akron, and Columbus is the world's largest Amish community. A day or two spent exploring these scenic back roads is like a trip back in time. Jimmy Buffett may have Key West, but North Coasters have Put-in-Bay, an island town with similar hedonistic sensibilities that attracts a million revelers each summer. And thanks to peculiar micro-climates, scores of modern winemakers continue to set up shop along the southern shores of Lake Erie, where they produce intensely flavored fruit and high-quality wines—and cozy tasting rooms to sample them in.

## PLANNING YOUR TIME

While visits to Akron, Ashtabula County, and Amish Country can conceivably be accomplished as part of a day trip, if you spend the night you can experience more of these region's attractions. Cedar Point Amusement Park is possible as a day-long outing from Cleveland, but because visits to the Lake Erie islands require a ferry trip from the mainland, an overnight stay is all but a necessity.

Amish Country is prettiest in the fall when the landscape changes color from verdant green to crimson and gold. It is also the busiest time here, when shops, restaurants, and hotels get crowded. The Lake Erie islands all but shut down after Labor Day, so schedule your visit between Memorial Day and early October to enjoy the festive atmosphere. The same is true about Geneva on the Lake, a seasonal lakeside community. Akron, Canton, and the wineries and covered bridges of Ashtabula County can be enjoyed all year long, so these areas make ideal off-season destinations.

COURTESY OF THE HOLMES CTY CHAMBER COMMERCE

# HIGHLIGHTS

LOOK FOR ◖ TO FIND RECOMMENDED SIGHTS, ACTIVITIES, DINING, AND LODGING.

◖ **Best Place to See Chuck Close Up Close:** The renovated **Akron Art Museum** has one of the most impressive collections of 20th-century art. Fans of Chuck Close's large-scale photorealistic paintings can ogle at his mesmerizing *Linda* here as well as works by Andy Warhol and Frank Stella (page 174).

◖ **Most Complete Collection of Super Bowl Rings:** Gridiron fans make the pilgrimage to Canton from points afar to wallow in the memorabilia at the **Pro Football Hall of Fame.** The museum's Super Bowl Room contains collectibles from every championship game played to date (page 176).

◖ **Longest Covered Bridge in America:** Ashtabula County is home to 17 covered bridges, including **Smolen-Gulf Bridge,** the longest in the United States. Bridge buffs come here to admire the craftsmanship and charm of these handsome overpasses (page 180).

◖ **Most Interesting Souvenir from the Ice Age:** When a massive glacier rubbed its way across the northern tip of Kelleys Island about 18,000 years ago, it etched striking **Glacial Grooves** into solid bedrock. Measuring 10 feet deep, 35 feet wide, and 400 feet long, the furrows are remnants of the Pleistocene Ice Age (page 188).

◖ **Most Appropriate Place to Scream:** Thanks to its matchless collection of the world's tallest, fastest, steepest roller coasters, **Cedar Point Amusement Park** is consistently heralded as the world's best amusement park. Hop on Top Thrill Dragster to zip to a speed of 120 miles per hour before climbing to a height of 420 feet (page 190).

◖ **Best Place to Buy a Goat:** When a gentleman farmer needs to buy livestock, he heads to the **Kidron Auction.** This lively Amish Country auction is open to the public, making the weekly event a popular albeit unconventional tourist attraction (page 194).

© ROLAND HALBE/FOTOGRAFIE

the Akron Art Museum

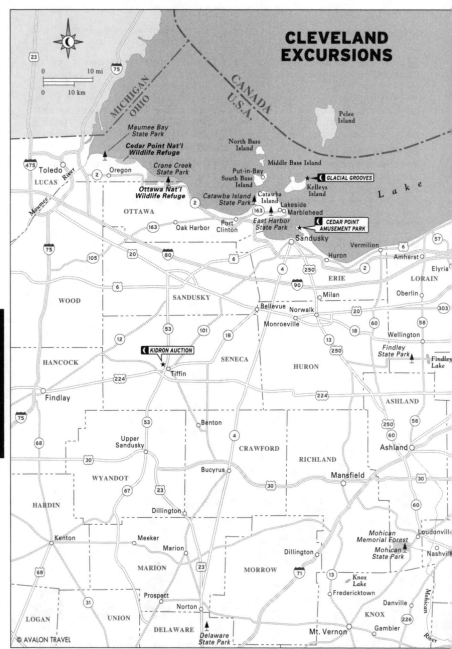

# CLEVELAND EXCURSIONS

0    10 mi
0    10 km

MICHIGAN
OHIO
CANADA
U.S.A.

Pelee
Island

Maumee Bay
State Park

**Cedar Point Nat'l
Wildlife Refuge**

North Bass
Island

Middle Bass Island

Crane Creek
State Park

Put-in-Bay
South Bass
Island

★ ◀ *GLACIAL GROOVES*

Kelleys
Island

L a k e

Toledo

LUCAS

Oregon

**Ottawa Nat'l
Wildlife Refuge**

OTTAWA

*Catawba Island
State Park*

Catawba
Island

Lakeside

Marblehead

★ ◀ *CEDAR POINT
AMUSEMENT PARK*

Oak Harbor

Port
Clinton

*East Harbor
State Park*

Sandusky

Vermilion

Amherst

Elyria

LORAIN

Huron

ERIE

WOOD

SANDUSKY

Bellevue    Norwalk

Milan

Oberlin

303

Monroeville

Wellington

58

◀ *KIDRON AUCTION*
★

HANCOCK

Tiffin

SENECA

HURON

*Findley
State Park*

Findley
Lake

Findlay

Benton

ASHLAND

Upper
Sandusky

53

CRAWFORD

RICHLAND

Ashland

WYANDOT

Bucyrus

Mansfield

HARDIN

Dillington

Kenton

Meeker

Marion

MARION

23

Dillington

*Mohican
Memorial Forest*

*Mohican ▲
State Park*

Loudonvill

Nashvill

Knox
Lake

MORROW

Prospect

Fredericktown

Danville

Norton

KNOX

LOGAN    UNION

DELAWARE

*Delaware
State Park*

Mt. Vernon

Gambier

Mohican
River

© AVALON TRAVEL

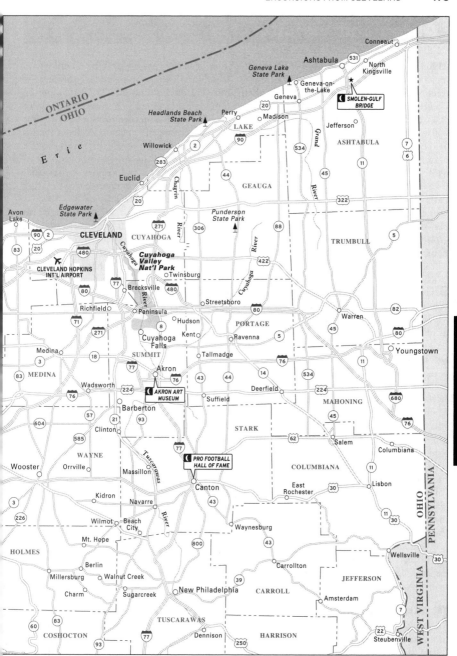

# Akron and Vicinity

Akron, located a short drive south of Cleveland, presents travelers with a number of enticing attractions. Smaller and more manageable than Cleveland, the city can assuredly be the site of a wonderful day trip. But an overnight stay will accommodate a more vigorous exploration of the city's treasures. Art fans will doubtless plan a stopover at the Akron Art Museum, while minor league baseball buffs will want to take in an Akron Aeros game at lovely Canal Park. Garden and architecture aficionados absolutely must discover the grandeur of Stan Hywet Hall. If there are football fans in the group, a stop in Canton to explore the Pro Football Hall of Fame on the way to or from Akron is required.

## SIGHTS
### Akron Aeros

Many fans of America's favorite pastime hold minor league ball in higher regard than the big leagues. Citing cheaper outings, a more manageable setting, elevated player passion, and better in-park promotions, true baseball fans are wild about the minors. As the Cleveland Indians' AA affiliate, the Akron Aeros (300 S. Main St., 330/253-5153, www.akronaeros.com, $10 reserved, $9 bleachers) outfit is a proving ground for the big-brother team to the north. And the Aeros' home, newly built **Canal Park,** is an absolute gem of a ballpark. Designed by the same firm behind Progressive Field and Camden Yards, the park is modern, intimate, and integrated within its downtown environment. The park seats 9,000 and treats fans to the largest free-standing scoreboard in minor leagues. The 70-game home season runs from early April through August. Single-game tickets can be purchased over the phone, online, or in person at the box office.

### ◖ Akron Art Museum

To much fanfare, in 2007 the 85-plus-year-old **Akron Art Museum** (1 S. High St., 330/376-9185, www.akronartmuseum.org, Tues.–Sun. 11 A.M.–5 P.M., Thurs. until 9 P.M., $7 adult, $5 senior and student) unveiled the opening of the new John S. and James L. Knight Building, which combines with an original 1899 structure to more than triple the size of the gallery. Upon its debut the ultramodern glass-and-steel edifice was the talk of the art and architecture world. With "floating" gallery spaces and exaggerated cantilevered overhangs, the contemporary building rivals its contents for attention.

While smaller than many major museum holdings, Akron's 3,700-work collection is a tightly curated sampling of important 20th-century art, with particularly close attention to postmodern painting, photorealism, surrealism, and Pop art. Chuck Close's mesmerizing *Linda* is here, as is Andy Warhol's *Elvis* and Ohio-native Elijah Pierce's *The Wise and Foolish Virgins and Four Other Scenes*. Works by Frank Stella, Claes Oldenburg, and Donald Judd are also on display. Akron Art Museum also maintains a choice photography collection, with whole galleries devoted to the medium. Ironically, cameras are prohibited in the galleries.

### American Toy Marble Museum

While spherical marbles were made as far back as 5,000 years ago, Akron was the site of the first mass-produced clay marble. Big deal, right? Well, Akron's American Marble & Toy Manufacturing Co. didn't just manufacture marbles, it created an affordable children's toy that swept across the landscape like a whirling dirt devil. At its peak in the late 1800s, the factory was cranking out a million orbs a day, making it the first mass-producer of toys in the nation. Located on the very site of that old marble factory is the American Toy Marble Museum (200 S. Main St., Lock 3 Park, 330/869-5807, www.americantoymarbles.com, Sat. 10 A.M.–1 P.M., free), a shrine to all things round and roly. Here, visitors can track the evolution of the game, the toy, and the craft that

## WHY CANTON IS HOME TO THE FOOTBALL HALL OF FAME

By the 1900s, organized football had become a popular American pastime. Many cities fielded teams, but they largely remained individual entities. Ohio was a particular hotbed of football activity, with numerous teams spread throughout the state. In 1920, the American Professional Football Association (now the NFL) was founded in Canton with 11 teams in the league. Football legend Jim Thorpe was selected as president. Five of the league's teams were from Ohio, including the Canton Bulldogs, Cleveland Tigers, and Akron Professionals. In 1961, the City of Canton made an official bid to the NFL to be the site of the hall. Acceptance soon followed and the Hall of Fame opened to the public two years later.

COURTESY OF POSITIVELY CLEVELAND

Football fans are powerless to resist the Pro Football Hall of Fame.

is marbles. Kids can even pick up the sport and play for "funsies." The museum is also the site of a popular annual marbles tournament.

### Blossom Music Center

Fans of the Cleveland Orchestra might consider adding a summer Blossom Music Center visit to their Akron excursion (or building an Akron itinerary around a trip to Blossom). Built in the late 1960s as the summer home of the symphony, this amphitheater (1145 W. Steels Corners Rd., Cuyahoga Falls, 888/225-6776, www.clevelandorch.com) is tucked into the leafy Cuyahoga Valley National Park. Pack a picnic and a blanket and find a space on the sweeping lawn to enjoy the orchestra under the stars. To insure a dry night, it might be wise to invest in sheltered pavilion seats. Blossom is also the site of rock, country, and alternative music performances spring to fall.

## Hale Farm & Village

Want to show your children what life was like before cell phones, computers, and refrigerators? Hale Farm & Village (2686 Oak Hill Rd., Bath, 800/589-9703, www.wrhs.org, Memorial Day–Labor Day Wed.–Sat. 11 A.M.–5 P.M., Sun. noon–5 P.M., $14.50 adult, $12.50 senior, $7.50 child) is a town trapped in the mid-1800s, when things like electricity, automobiles, and iPhones were still a few years down the road. This living history museum employs historical interpreters dressed in period costume to recount the story of the Western Reserve, the Civil War years, and life in the middle of the 19th century.

The land originally belonged to Jonathan Hale, a Connecticut farmer who relocated in 1810 to the Western Reserve. Today, skilled artisans demonstrate the very same techniques used to construct the buildings, tools, and crafts of Hale's day. Brick makers fire air-dried bricks the old-fashion way; blacksmiths forge farm and household implements by hand; glassblowers keep Ohio's rich glass-making history alive. In fact, at the farm you can buy primitive hand-blown glass objects in their characteristic amber, cobalt, and green tints.

## National Inventors Hall of Fame and Museum

In 1995, a well-established inventors museum relocated from the U.S. Patent and Trade Office in Alexandria, Virginia, to Akron, Ohio. Since that time, the National Inventors Hall of Fame and Museum (221 S. Broadway St., 800/968-4332, www.invent.org) has paid tribute to the hundreds of men and women whose inventions "make human, social, and economic progress possible." Some, like the creators of recipes for Campbell's green bean casserole and Hidden Valley dressing, just make life taste better. All are on display at this museum. (Currently, the museum is undergoing construction and is closed to the public. It is projected to open in fall of 2009. Check the website for updates.)

## ◖ Pro Football Hall of Fame

For over 45 years, the Canton-based Pro Football Hall of Fame (2121 George Halas Drive NW, 330/456-8207, www.profootballhof.com, daily 9 A.M.–5 P.M., Memorial Day–Labor Day daily 9 A.M.–8 P.M., $16 adult, $13 senior, $10 child) has been attracting gridiron fans with its shrine to the legends of the game. This museum of football history has expanded three times to accommodate its growing collection and its burgeoning attendance figures. Nearly a quarter of a million visitors travel to sleepy Canton, Ohio, to pay tribute to football's past and present superstars. Most popular on the must-see list likely is the Hall of Fame Gallery, where bronze busts of all enshrinees are on permanent display. Cleveland Browns fans might want to bypass the Super Bowl Room, which exhibits memories and memorabilia from every championship played to date.

Real football fans strive to attend the annual Pro Football Hall of Fame Enshrinement Festival, a days-long event that includes the Enshrinement Ceremony, dinner, parties, and the NFL Hall of Fame Game. Tickets are hard to come by, so phone early (888/310-4255).

## Stan Hywet Hall

Akron's Stan Hywet Hall (714 N. Portage Path, 330/836-5533, www.stanhywet.org, Apr. 1–Dec. 31 Tues.–Sun. 10 A.M.–4:30 P.M., $8 adult, $4 student, more for tours) is widely considered one of the finest examples of Tudor Revival architecture in the region. The moniker (pronounced STAN HEE-WIT) is Old English for "stone quarry," a fitting name for this stunning American country estate built in 1912 by F. A. Seiberling, founder of Goodyear Tire & Rubber. Akron's only National Historic Landmark, the magnificent manor house, outbuildings, and gardens are open to the public for self-guided and guided tours.

The Manor House alone boasts 21,000 panes of glass, 23 fireplaces, and 65 rooms. Guided one-hour tours take visitors throughout the house, paying special attention to the Great Hall, Music Room, and Billiards Room. Well preserved and brimming with original fixtures, furnishings, and priceless antiques, the house was a model of modernity when it was completed. Tours begin on the hour most days.

While considerably smaller than its original 1,000 acres, the lush estate surrounding the home is filled with botanical treasures. Perched on the precipice of the Cuyahoga Valley, the 70 acres feature English and Japanese gardens, an apple orchard, and a stately birch tree allee. Throughout the year, the grounds are the site of outdoor theater, musical performances, and food and wine festivals. Check the website for special events.

## RESTAURANTS

Located in the heart of downtown Akron, **Crave** (59 E. Market St., 330/253-1234, www .eatdrinkcrave.com, Mon.–Thurs. 11 A.M.– 10 P.M., Fri. 11 A.M.–11 P.M., Sat. 5–11 P.M.) is a boldly contemporary bistro that specializes in eclectic, affordable comfort food. The menu features a raft of creative small plates, sandwiches, and entrées. Wildly unconventional-sounding combinations invariably work to create unforgettable tastes. Cumin-scented fried pickles, Guinness-glazed steak skewers, and sour cherry–infused duck breast are just some of the 50 or so dishes available on the all-day menu. Wine and beer fans will dig Crave's lengthy and equally affordable roster of great finds. When booking a table, it might be helpful to know there is an airy dining room, a long communal table, and a lively barroom, so choose accordingly.

From the curb, the **Diamond Grille** (77 W. Market St., 330/253-0041, Mon.–Fri. 11 A.M.– 11 P.M., Sat. 5 P.M.–midnight) looks more like a shuttered shot-and-a-beer joint than a popular steak house. In fact, if it wasn't for the dimly illuminated neon sign, you'd swear the place was toast. But this clubby Akron landmark is beloved precisely for that understated elegance. This is where professional golfers like Tiger Woods and Vijay Singh come to protein-load before hitting the links at nearby Firestone Country Club. Nationally recognized as the place to come for stiff martinis, thick slabs of prime beef, and, perhaps, a heaping serving of nostalgia, the Grille can be tough to get into on a busy night, so call in advance. And don't expect cushy leather banquettes when you do

score a table—the interior matches the exterior. As one might expect, the food's not cheap, with steaks priced well north of $30. To sample this anachronistic steak sensation, you can leave the charge cards at home: The Grille accepts only cash.

Any way you slice it, **Luigi's** (105 N. Main St., 330/253-2999, www.luigisakron .com, Mon.–Thurs. 11 A.M.–2 A.M., Fri. 11 A.M.–4 A.M., Sat. 4:30 P.M.–4 A.M., Sun. 4 P.M.–2 A.M.) is an Akron institution. Since 1949, folks have been coming here for what many believe is the city's best pizza, lasagna, and Italian comfort food. The setting is casual, lively, and fun, with walls of old black-and-white photos to keep you occupied during the (sometimes lengthy) wait for a table. Readers of the comic Funky Winkerbean will recognize Luigi's as the uncanny inspiration behind Montoni's, a recurring location owing to the cartoonist's fondness for the place. Perhaps unique to this family-run eatery are the late-night hours, which on Friday and Saturday stretch well into the next morning. Bring cash or a bank card; Luigi's doesn't accept credit cards (but there is an ATM machine on-site).

When Pretenders singer Chrissie Hynde went back to Ohio, she built an upscale vegan restaurant that even carnivores can get behind. **VegiTerranean** (21 Furnace St., 330/374-5550, www.thevegiterranean.com, Mon.–Sat. 7:30 A.M.–10 P.M.), located on the fringe of downtown Akron, uses no meat, eggs, or dairy products when crafting its surprisingly delicious menu items. Set into a sleek, modern shell, the restaurant is as far removed from those 1970s twig-and-berry hippie cafés as one might imagine. How can a diner possibly miss meat when chowing chewy pizza topped with banana peppers, wild mushrooms, and spicy marinara sauce? Tomatoes are stuffed with grilled veggies and orzo pasta. Risotto is slow-cooked with grilled artichokes and saffron. Even the typically unsavory meat-replacement items like tofu, Gardien, and vegan sausage (oxymoron?) come out of the kitchen tasting great.

The **West Point Market** (1711 W. Market St., 800/838-2156, www.westpointmarket.com,

EXCURSIONS

Mon.–Sat. 8 A.M.–7 P.M., Sun. 10 A.M.–5 P.M.) has blossomed from a third-generation grocery store into a world-class specialty foods market, with over 25,000 square feet of wine, cheese, meat, seafood, produce, prepared foods, and bakery departments. With the market as its larder, it is no surprise that the quality of food served at the in-store **Beside the Point Café** is impressive in its own right. Diners can expect an upscale cafeteria-style operation featuring house-made soups, create-your-own salads and sandwiches, and hearty home-style comfort foods. Beverage choices include fine beer and wine by the glass.

## NIGHTLIFE
With a name like **69 Taps** (370 Paul Williams St., 330/253-4554, www.69taps.com, daily 4:30 P.M.–2:30 A.M.), it is no stretch to assume that this bar stocks a nice selection of draft ales and lagers. And they do—69 of them to be precise. While not exceptional in its range, the list includes plenty of tasty suds. This unpretentious bar is a favorite of young professionals and of-age college students who flock here for the daily happy hours featuring $2 drafts. Plenty of TVs, a couple pool tables, and a foosball table give this den a mild sports-bar feel, but it rarely gets as rowdy as the others.

Next door to Luigi's you'll find **The Northside Grille** (111 N. Main St., 330/434-7625, www.northsideclub.com, Mon.–Fri. 11 A.M.–1 A.M., Sat. 5 P.M.–1 A.M.), a popular booze and live-music roadhouse beloved for its good-natured yet rambunctious spirit. The club's motto is "Loud Food and Spicy Music," and it's true that folks come here to fill up on both. Great for lunch or dinner, the chow includes affordable Italian-style salads, sandwiches, and pastas. Those who prefer a more tranquil setting should wander to the adjacent **Snook's Wine Side** (same contact info and hours), an organic eatery and lounge. Here, visitors can enjoy art-filled walls, candlelight, and numerous wines by the glass. Snook's also holds regular wine tastings every Friday and Saturday night. Be sure to check out the nearby art galleries and studios.

## SHOPS
### Don Drumm Studios and Gallery
Artist Don Drumm has made a name for himself by pioneering the use of cast aluminum as an artistic medium. His distinctive sculptures have been commissioned by fans worldwide, but Ohio natives appear to be most smitten. Art lovers flock to Don Drumm Studios and Gallery (437 Crouse St., 330/253-6268, www.dondrummstudios.com, Mon.–Fri. 10 A.M.–6 P.M., Sat. 10 A.M.–5 P.M.), home to two wonderful galleries that showcase works not just by Drumm but also some 500 other North American craftsmen, artists, and designers. To wipe out your holiday gift lists in one fell swoop, come here to shop the huge inventory of handcrafted jewelry, glass, crafts, and sculptures. Large alfresco courtyards are stocked with unique outdoor home accessories like wind chimes, water fountains, and sculptural wall hangings.

### Hartville MarketPlace and Flea Market
Located roughly halfway between Akron and Canton, the Hartville MarketPlace and Flea Market (1289 Edison St., Hartville, 330/877-9860, www.hartvillemarketplace.com, Mon., Thurs.–Sat. 9 A.M.–5 P.M.) is a 100,000-square-foot building stuffed to the rafters with over 100 independently owned and operated 10-foot-by-10-foot shops. For the sheer sake of brevity we'll simply call the variety staggering. While live animals are no longer proffered here, shoppers can still walk away with pet-related items like treats and collars. Vendors come and go, but you can always count on finding books, clothing, antiques, cheese, fudge, nuts, coins, jewelry, sports memorabilia, and hardware. There is an equally large outdoor flea market, arranged on more than 20 acres of blacktop, that bursts with additional vendors during the summer months (though it is open year-round). When you're hungry for some biscuits and gravy, sidle on over to Sarah's Grille, the on-site restaurant.

## Harry London Candies

Chocolate lovers might want to pull off I-77 for an emergency confection on the way to or from the Akron-Canton area. Harry London Candies (5353 Lauby Rd., N. Canton, 800/321-0444, www.londoncandies.com, Mon.–Sat. 9 A.M.–6 P.M.), founded by a steelworker turned chocolatier, has been handcrafting fine candies in the European tradition since 1922. This shiny new chocolate factory and retail shop sells over 500 varieties of sweets, from truffles and pralines to peanut butter joys and dark chocolate–covered pretzels. One-hour factory tours are offered Monday–Friday 10 A.M.–3 P.M. Reservations are required and can be made by phone.

## HOTELS

Set inside a magnificent 1923 Tudor Revival mansion, the **O'Neil House** (1290 W. Exchange St., 330/867-2650, www.oneilhouse.com, $75–200) is not your run-of-the-mill bed-and-breakfast. Once the home of William O'Neil, founder of Akron's General Tire Company, the museum-quality residence now offers discerning travelers a choice of four glorious suites, each with private bath. The 19-room property boasts oak-paneled walls, leaded-glass windows, and Oriental rug–clad wood floors. Gourmet breakfast, served in a lovely sunroom, is included in the room price. Innkeeper Gayle Johnson maintains pets of her own, so none are welcome.

Winning the award for the most unusual rooms, **Quaker Square Inn at The University of Akron Hotel** (135 S. Broadway, 330/253-5970, www.quakersquareakron.com, $109–189) houses guests in the perfectly circular silos left over from when Quaker Oats used them for grain storage. While oddly shaped, those concrete bunkers are remarkably quiet, a good thing now that half of the historic property is home to student dorm rooms. Though the hotel shows its age, its location is within walking distance of the Akron Art Museum and Canal Park, and is five miles from Stan Hywet Hall and the Akron Zoo. Many rooms feature balconies and the hotel has a business center, indoor swimming pool, and fitness center.

For a clean, comfortable, convenient, and affordable night's stay in Akron, the **Radisson Hotel City Centre** (20 W. Mill St., 330/384-1500, www.akronradisson.com, $85–110) is a good bet. Guest rooms include all the usual amenities, including Wi-Fi, coffee makers, large TVs, and in some cases in-room whirlpool tubs. There is an indoor swimming pool on the 20th floor with impressive views, a hotel restaurant and bar, and a fitness center. Travelers in search of five-star lodging, 24-hour room service, and 800-thread-count Egyptian cotton sheets should keep looking. But those who desire a reasonably priced room within walking distance to The Akron Art Museum, Canal Park, and downtown bars and restaurants will find that here.

## PRACTICALITIES
### Tourist Information

The **Akron/Summit Convention & Visitors Bureau** (77 E. Mill St., 330/374-7560, www.visitakron-summit.org, Mon.–Fri. 8 A.M.–5 P.M.) is located inside the John S. Knight Center, Akron's convention center. By phone, online, or in person, the CVB helps potential visitors with all aspects of their trip, including accommodations, planning excursions, suggesting attractions, and locating discounts.

You'll find the **Canton/Stark County Convention & Visitors Bureau** (222 Market Ave. N., 800/552-6051, www.cantonstarkcvb .com, Mon.–Fri. 8:30 A.M.–5 P.M.) inside the Millennium Centre office building in downtown Canton. Or simply visit their website, which has all the information a visitor to Stark County might need when planning a short or extended stay in the area.

For information on a host of Ohio sights, attractions, and activities, contact the **Ohio Division of Travel and Tourism** (800/ BUCKEYE, www.discoverohio.com).

### Media

The main daily newspapers in the Akron/Canton

region are the *Akron Beacon Journal* (www
.ohio.com) and the *Canton Repository* (www
.cantonrep.com).

## Getting There

From Cleveland, getting to Akron and Canton
is a relatively straight shot south on I-77. Akron
is approximately 45 minutes by car, while
Canton is closer to an hour and 10 minutes.
Many frugal travelers to Akron, Canton, and
Cleveland choose the **Akron-Canton Airport**
(888/434-2359, www.akroncantonairport
.com) over Cleveland Hopkins Airport because
of cheaper fares and fewer hassles. Discount
carriers like AirTran Airways (800/247-8726)
and Frontier Airlines (800/432-1359) operate

flights from here. For less than $25, travelers
can hop a Greyhound (www.greyhound.com)
in Cleveland and travel south to either city.

## Getting Around

A traveler abandoned in Akron or Canton
without wheels could manage, but it would
be difficult to experience all these cities had
to offer. Many of the attractions listed in this
section are miles apart and neither city has the
most comprehensive public transportation system. Plus, it would be hard to move from one
city to the other. Do yourself a favor and rent
a car or hire a cab (Yellow Cab, 330/253-3141,
Akron Checker Cab, 330/535-6273) if you really want to experience both cities.

# Ashtabula County

A short ride east from Cleveland lands travelers in one of the most scenic patches of the
state. Out here, there is a closer connection to
the landscape, with much of the tourist industry hinging on proximity to Lake Erie. Geneva
on the Lake is a century-old lakeside resort,
complete with old-time strip, cozy rental cottages, and family-friendly activities. Ashtabula
County boasts 170,000 farmed acres, and agri-
tourism is big business. Farm stands dot the
scenic country lanes and corn mazes and apple
orchards fill the fields. There are 17 covered
bridges in this one county, elevating a pleasant
autumn drive to an unforgettable experience.
And when it comes to wine, this northeastern
corner of the state is king. Thanks to the mod-
erating temps of Lake Erie, wine grapes thrive
here, and the wine they produce is no joke.
An overnight stay is recommended, especially
when enjoying multiple wineries!

## SIGHTS
### Adventure Zone

Kid fun is priority one at Adventure Zone (5600
Lake Rd., Geneva on the Lake, 440/466-3555,
www.adventurezonefun.com, Memorial Day–
Labor Day daily 11 A.M.–10 P.M., weekends

only in May and September), a family-friendly
entertainment center. Pay-as-you-go attractions
like go-karts, climbing walls, batting cages, a
restored merry-go-round, and a rather challenging 18-hole mini-golf course will keep the
little ones occupied for hours. In operation for
over a decade, this independently owned and
operated amusement center takes pride in its
cleanliness, its well-mannered staff, and the af-
fordability of entertainment. Adults can rent
street-legal golf carts here to cruise up and
down the famous Geneva on the Lake strip.

### ◖ Smolen-Gulf Bridge

They are still building **covered bridges** in
Ashtabula County, if you can believe that. The
latest, the Smolen-Gulf Bridge, is the longest
covered bridge in the United States at 613 feet.
For those keeping track, that makes 17 covered
bridges in the county, more than any other in
Ohio. Most are far older than the Smolen-Gulf,
with some dating all the way back to 1867.
Bridge fans come to admire the craftsmanship
of the various construction methods, which include Pratt truss, Howe truss, and Town lattice
designs. Self-guided auto tours of the bridges
are very popular, especially in the picturesque

# OHIO WINE

It surprises folks to learn that Ohio winemakers produce great wine. And not just the sickly sweet stuff, either. Currently, there are over 100 licensed wineries in the state. Each year they produce over 750,000 gallons of wine valued at $75 million. Most have tasting rooms and welcome visitors to sample the latest vintages.

In 1860, Ohio led the entire nation in wine production. Growers learned early on that areas near Lake Erie enjoyed unique microclimates that provided long growing seasons. Wineries were first established on the Lake Erie Islands, but soon they began popping up along the entire southern shore of the lake. This area was long referred to as the Lake Erie Grape Belt.

Prohibition shuttered most Ohio wineries. And when production did again become legal, most operations set up shop in California. But over the years there has been a steady resurgence in Ohio grape growing, and new wineries continue to open throughout the state. Most are located along Lake Erie in Northeast Ohio, where long, dry autumns give the grapes plenty of time to mature and ripen.

Ohio has a deserved reputation for producing sweet wine, and many wineries do still concentrate on those styles. Catawba, a domestic variety first planted in the 1820s, is still a popular choice for sweet-wine fans. But more and more, sophisticated winemakers are planting classic European varietals such as cabernet franc, chardonnay, and pinot noir, which thrive in the cool climate. The wines these vintners make routinely earn awards and garner national attention.

While visiting all 100 wineries would be admirable, most people choose to arrange more reasonable expeditions. The Ohio Wine Producers Association has divided the state into six wine-producing regions, each with its own wine trail. Stretching from Cleveland to the Pennsylvania border is the **Lake Erie Vines and Wines Trail,** a strip of 40 some wineries. To sample some great juice, visit Markko Vineyard, Tarsitano Winery, and Harpersfield Vineyard. When hunger strikes, stop by the lovely Ferrante Winery & Ristorante for Italian fare or the uber-casual Hil-Mak's Seafood for killer fried lake perch.

If you are in the area over the first weekend in August, consider hitting **Vintage Ohio** (www.visitvintageohio.com), a huge wine and food festival held at Lake Metroparks Farmpark.

autumn months. The routes are well marked and maps can be obtained by contacting the **Ashtabula County Covered Bridge Festival** (25 W. Jefferson St., 440/576-3769, www.coveredbridgefestival.org). Paddlers might choose to experience the bridges from below while cruising along the lovely Grand River. Contact **Raccoon Run Canoe Rental** (1153 State Rd., Harpersfield, 440/466-7414, www.raccoonruncanoerental.com) to rent a canoe or kayak for a two- to eight-hour trip. One flat fee includes equipment, shuttles to and from drop-off points, floatation devices, river maps, litter bags, and safety demonstrations. They are open from May through October.

## Geneva on the Lake

Ohio's oldest summer resort district (800/862-9948, www.visitgenevaonthelake.com) has, since the turn of the 20th century, enticed well-heeled vacationers from nearby cities to take in the beaches, burgers, and big bands. While "progress" has tarnished some of this historic town's old-timey charm, there is still plenty to do, see, and enjoy in and around this lakefront village. Charming cottages and bed-and-breakfasts still dot the shoreline, along with glitzy new hotels and condos. Like a Jersey Shore midway, the famous strip is lined up and down with fast-food snack bars, ice-cream parlors, arcades, bars, and nightclubs. Cars, motorcycles, and golf carts prowl the road in search of adventure, camaraderie, and entertainment. The **Cove** (5326 Lake Rd., 440/466-8888) is the strip's oldest rock-and-roll joint, with live music all weekend long, while the **Swiss Chalet** (5475

Lake Rd., 440/466-8650) is geared more toward the Top 40 set. All summer long, Geneva on the Lake is home to seasonal festivals, outdoor concerts, flea markets, and celebrations. Most businesses, sights, and attractions keep different hours depending on the season, so it is wise to call before visiting. Check the visitors bureau's website for detailed information.

## Geneva State Park

This 700-acre lakefront park (4499 Padanarum Rd., 440/466-8400, www.ohiodnr.com) offers a wealth of recreational pursuits. There is a 100-yard sandy beachhead, boat marina, ramps for launching watercraft into Lake Erie, and numerous all-purpose trails that snake through the terrain. The park is popular with hunters, cross-country skiers, and fisherman who angle for walleye, yellow perch, and even salmon. Stop by the park's **Geneva Marina** (440/466-7565) to get your fishing license, bait and tackle supplies, and boating accessories. When you've reached your daily limit, come back and take advantage of the marina's fish-cleaning services. For overnight visitors to the area, the park offers campsites and cedar cottages, and is also the site of the Lodge at Geneva on the Lake, a well-appointed 100-room hotel.

## Kiraly's Orchard

If it's autumn when you visit Northeast Ohio, stop by Kiraly's Orchard (6031 S. Ridge West, Ashtabula, 440/969-1297, Aug.–Oct. daily 9 A.M.–5 P.M.) to pick your own apples straight from the tree. Yellow delicious, granny smith, rome, fuji, and other varieties are grown on-site in the family's 70-acre orchard. Apples are typically ready for harvest beginning early September and running through October. Bring your own bags and the apples cost about $16 a bushel, roughly the size of a clothes hamper. The retail shop also sells already-picked apples, fresh apple cider, and other seasonal produce. The farm also grows its own peaches, nectarines, and plums.

## Lake Metroparks Farmpark

Agrarian-minded parents may wish to make a stopover at Lake Metroparks Farmpark (8800 Chardon Rd., Kirtland, 800/366-3276, www .lakemetroparks.com, daily 9 A.M.–5 P.M., closed major holidays, $6 adult, $5 senior, $4 child) on their way to or from Ashtabula County. At this 235-acre working farm, city folk can experience all matter of country life, from milking a cow to enjoying a wagon ride or corn maze. Demonstrations cover such agricultural activities as sheep herding, cheese making, maple syrup tapping, and crop harvesting. Over 50 breeds of livestock, including a dozen endangered breeds, are on hand to inspire future PETA members. Solar- and wind-power exhibits show off the future of sustainable energy production. A farmers market selling locally grown produce runs here from June through October. Many other interesting seasonal events take place throughout the year.

## WINERIES

Hugging the southern shore of Lake Erie is a microclimate ideally suited to growing wine grapes. The lake's accumulated heat from summer provides warm autumn breezes that extend the grape-growing season well into fall, giving the fruit the opportunity to fully ripen. Ohio is one of the top 10 wine-producing states in the nation, and the lush Grand River Valley is home to more than half of the state's vineyard acres. Like other wine-producing regions, this one is filled with wineries offering tastings, bottle sales, and winery tours. A day or two spent exploring the numerous wineries that populate the landscape is time very well spent. Call ahead as hours change by vineyard, season, and day of the week.

**Debonne Vineyards** (7743 Doty Rd., Madison, 440/466-3485, www.debonne.com) is one of the oldest, largest, and most commercially successful wine producers in the state. The 110-acre vineyard produces Riesling, chardonnay, pinot gris, and cabernet franc. Debonne also produces ice wine, which is unique to very few regions in the world. Vidal Blanc grapes are left on the vine to freeze, then they are immediately picked and pressed and the highly concentrated nectar transforms into a deliciously sweet dessert wine. The large, modern facility

© DOUGLAS TRATTNER

EXCURSIONS

**Wine grapes are a big draw in Ashtabula County.**

offers tours and tastings year-round and an outdoor grill serves food in the summertime. Throughout the year are activities include hot-air-balloon races, Sunday jazz concerts, car shows, and wine and food festivals.

At 18 acres in size, **Harpersfield Vineyard** (6387 Rte. 307W, Geneva, 440/466-4739, www.harpersfield.com) is a moderately sized estate winery, but it boasts charm in spades. Come during winter and you'll sample the vineyard's fine wines by fireside in the rustic tasting room. Imagine sipping gewürztraminer, pinot noir, and late-harvest pinot gris as fresh-baked baguettes are plucked from the wood-fired brick oven. Gourmet cheeses and specialty foods are also served in the tasting room, and there is live entertainment during summer weekends.

**Markko Vineyard** (4500 S. Ridge Rd., Conneaut, 800/252-3197, www.markko.com) just may produce the finest estate-grown wines in Ohio. In fact, their chardonnay and Riesling can hold their own against any in the country.

Using European Vinifera grapes rather than the more popular (and hardy) French-American hybrid grapes was a risk these winemakers were willing to take to make great wine. The employment of a unique vine trellis and canopy system has allowed the grapes not only to survive but flourish, resulting in world-class wines.

Charming **Tarsitano Winery** (4871 Hatches Corners Rd., Conneaut, 440/224-2444, www .tarsitanowinery.com) is located just four miles from the Pennsylvania border, putting it squarely in the picturesque Conneaut Creek growing region. This boutique-style winery maintains just 17 acres of vineyards, but it produces about a dozen different wine varieties. Sample the cabernet sauvignon and chardonnay to taste their best work. An on-farm café is open Thursday–Sundays year-round.

For more information on Ohio wineries visit **Ohio Wine Producers Association** (www.ohiowines.org) and **Ohio Wine Country** (www.ohiowinecountry.com).

## RESTAURANTS

**Eddie's Grill** (5377 Lake Rd., Geneva on the Lake, 440/466-8720, daily from Memorial Day to Labor Day) is rightly famous for its killer cheeseburgers, foot-long chili dogs, and fresh-cut fries. The popular '50s-style diner features open-air counter service, indoor booths with personal jukeboxes, and youthful servers. This place gets super crowded on warm summer nights, but things move quickly. Bring cash or a bank card for the nearby ATM. No credit cards are accepted.

Just down the road from the scenic Harpersfield covered bridge is **Ferrante Winery & Ristorante** (5585 Rte. 307, Harpersfield, 440/466-8466, www.ferrantewinery .com, hours vary by month), an amiable winery and restaurant. Complementing the house-made wines are hearty Italian-style specialties. Pizza, pasta, and chicken and veal dishes rule the menu, and many are made with the winery's award-winning vintages. During summer, a sprawling outdoor patio overlooking the vineyards is host to live music, wine tastings, and light meals. A large gift shop stocks wine and wine accessories.

Folks trek to the Ashtabula Harbor for swimmingly fresh fried perch dinners at **Hil-Mak's Seafood** (449 Lake Ave., Ashtabula, 440/964-3222, www.hilmaks.com, Tues.–Sat. 11:30 A.M.–2:30 P.M. and 5–10 P.M.). Because Hil-Mak's also operates a fish market, the restaurant has access to a full roster of local and regional seafood. They don't do fancy here; what they do specialize in is great clam chowder, perch sandwiches, fried clams, crab cakes, and onion rings. Seafood aficionados will swear they were dining on the East Coast instead of the North Coast.

When you've had all you can take of the touristy crowds, slip away to the comforting embrace of the **Old Mill Winery** (403 S. Broadway, 440/466-5560, www.theoldmill winery.com, Mon.–Thurs. 3–9 P.M., Fri. 3 P.M.–midnight, Sat. 1 P.M.–midnight, Sun. 1–9 P.M.). This cozy neighborhood winery and restaurant treats everybody like regulars, mainly because most of them are. Tucked into a big old red mill, the restaurant grills up a mean steak, but the house favorite is assuredly the loaded wineburger, topped with bacon, mushrooms, and grilled onions. A little snow in winter doesn't stop the intrepid chefs at Old Mill from grilling outdoors all year long. There are live bands most weekend nights.

## HOTELS

If you want to be close to the summer action at Geneva on the Lake, **The Eagle Cliff Inn** (5254 Lake Rd. E., 440/466-1110, www .beachclubbandb.com, $119–149) places you squarely in the thick of things. Located directly on the strip, this elegant inn is steps from Lake Erie and provides easy access to Ashtabula County's best assets. Listed on the National Register of Historic Places, the faithfully restored inn offers six rooms with private baths. Bed-and-breakfast guests take their full breakfast in the parlor or from the comfort of the inn's gracious front porch. The inn also runs the more budget-friendly **Beach Club Cottages,** well-appointed efficiencies located behind the house.

Built at a cost of close to $20 million, the **Lodge at Geneva on the Lake** (4888 Rte. 534, 866/806-8066, www.thelodgeatgeneva. com, $100–250) is located on the grounds of Geneva State Park but is operated by the county. This hotel is the natural choice for travelers who prefer modern amenities over country charm. The 100-room complex offers guests numerous lodging choices, ranging from comfortable standard rooms to premium lake-view rooms with balconies. Multi-room suites are ideal for families. An outdoor pool and kid zone is open during summer, while a glass-enclosed pool and hot tub is available year-round. Other amenities include a great game room, fitness center overlooking Lake Erie, and massage services. Rent a bike from the lodge and hit the trails that hug the Lake Erie shoreline. Folks traveling with pets will be happy to know that the lodge offers pet-friendly rooms with direct access to a grassy expanse.

Romantic getaways are the order of the day (and night) at **Peggy's Bed and Breakfast**

(8721 Munson Hill Rd., Ashtabula, 440/969-1996, www.peggysbedandbreakfast.com, $119–140). Tucked into a leafy landscape, Peggy's one and only cottage is nothing if it isn't private. The snug environment features a full kitchen, loft bedroom, two fireplaces, patio, and screened porch. Breakfast is delivered in the morning right to your residence. And we're not talking cereal and toast: Peggy offers her guests a full menu of gourmet options, including cream caramel French toast, corned-beef hash, and corn muffins with pecans and maple syrup. The location is ideal for hitting the trails, wineries, covered bridges, or Lake Erie shore, and you can even borrow one of Peggy's bikes.

Looking like a vintage city hall transplanted from New England to Geneva, the stately Western Reserve–style building that houses the **Polly Harper Inn** (6308 S. River Rd., 440/466-6183, www.pollyharperinn.com, $95–155) sits proudly atop a bluff in the scenic Grand River Valley. The location is idyllic for winery visits, as the inn literally overlooks vineyards and is close to dozens more. This countrified bed-and-breakfast offers three suites, all with private baths and gas fireplaces. Enjoy the rustic beauty of the nearby Grand River courtesy of a scenic trail that winds right behind the inn.

## PRACTICALITIES
### Tourist Information
Information and maps of Ashtabula County covered bridges can be obtained by contacting the **Ashtabula County Covered Bridge Festival** (25 W. Jefferson St., 440/576-3769, www.coveredbridgefestival.org).

The **Ashtabula County Convention & Visitors Bureau** can be reached by calling 800/337-6746 or by clicking www.visitashtabula county.com.

For information on Geneva on the Lake, contact **Visit Geneva on the Lake** (800/862-9948, www.visitgenevaonthelake.com).

For information on Ohio's wine industry, wine-related events, and wine-trail maps, contact the **Ohio Wine Association** (800/227-6972, www.ohiowines.org).

Another great source for Ohio winery information is www.myohiowine.com.

### Media
Read the *Ashtabula Star Beacon* (www.starbeacon.com) for local news and current events. Gazette Newspapers (www.gazettenewspapers.com) publishes a number of community newspapers throughout the county, including the *Ashtabula County Gazette, Jefferson Gazette, Pymatuning Area News, Shores News,* and *Valley News.*

### Getting There
Expect a non-stop drive from downtown Cleveland to Geneva on the Lake to take just over an hour. The trip is easily accomplished by taking I-90 to OH-2 to US-20. Greyhound (www.greyhound.com) has a station in Ashtabula at 1520 Bunker Hill Road (440/992-7550).

### Getting Around
Serious cyclists can get along just fine on a good bike (depending on the weather, of course), but others will likely need a car to move about since major sights and attractions are located miles apart. Two taxi companies operate in the area, **Premier Transportation** (440/466-1515) **City Taxicab** (440/992-2156), and are available for inter-county trips.

EXCURSIONS

# Lake Erie Islands and Vicinity

Just an hour west of Cleveland is an entirely different landscape. From Memorial Day until Labor Day, typically sleepy lakeside communities transform into seasonal hotspots, teeming with pleasure boaters, nature-loving day-trippers, and hard-partying souls. Comprised of mainland towns like Sandusky, Lakeside, Marblehead, and Port Clinton, and islands such as South Bass and Kelleys, the Lake Erie Islands region is a magnet for summer fun. The epicenter of this party is assuredly Put-in-Bay, but Cedar Point in Sandusky is no slouch either. To reach South Bass and Kelleys Islands you'll need to ride a ferry from the mainland, making a day trip impractical. Many businesses in the area are seasonal, so check before planning a stop.

## SOUTH BASS ISLAND

Home to rowdy Put-in-Bay, South Bass Island often is described as the Key West of the North Coast. While downtown is indeed party central, the island can be extremely accommodating to families, especially during the week and away from downtown. But many come to South Bass precisely for the no-holds-barred party atmosphere, and they are rarely disappointed.

### Sights

If you enjoy the cold comfort of caves, consider a visit to **Crystal Cave** (978 Catawba Ave., 419/285-2811, www.heinemanswinery.com, tours daily early May–late Sept., $6 adult, $3 child), thought to be the world's largest geode. The 55-degree chamber is lined with sky-blue celestite crystals, some sticking out a full foot and a half, and it feels like you're walking through the inside of a paperweight. Non-gemstone fans may not see what all the fuss is about, but crystal collectors might just call this place mecca. When the tour is through, visit the attached **Heineman Winery,** which has been making wine for over a century. Tours of the winery are offered and wine and grape juice tastings are held in a picturesque garden.

Rising 352 feet above Lake Erie, **Perry's Victory and International Peace Memorial** (93 Delaware Ave., Put-in-Bay, 419/285-2184, www.nps.gov/pevi, daily late Apr.–mid-Oct., limited or no hours the rest of the year, $3 adult, free child) is a conspicuous landmark on the shoreline. Established in honor of those who fought in the Battle of Lake Erie during the War of 1812, from the top the monument offers visitors views of the islands, Michigan, and Ontario. However, work is going to force the closure of the observation deck; it will be open until August 2009 and then closed for two years of renovation. Check the website for updates. The memorial is now a national park, and on weekends uniformed rangers do history demonstrations capped off by the firing of flintlock muskets.

Parents in search of a sure-fire way to occupy the kids should plan a visit to **Perry's Cave Family Fun Center** (979 Catawba Ave., 419/285-2283, www.perryscave.com, daily May–Sept., weekends only Apr. and Oct.). This family entertainment center is jam-packed with enjoyable time-killers. Best among them is the War of 18 Holes miniature golf course, which peppers kids with historical facts about the War of 1812 and Commodore Perry along the way. The rather challenging course is surrounded by mature trees and winding (faux) streams. If you can differentiate between a swallowtail and a lacewing you might really enjoy the Butterfly House. This 4,000-square-foot butterfly aviary houses over 500 different varieties of exotic butterflies. For help identifying the species, tap the knowledge of the helpful staff. Kids can strap into a harness and tie onto a safety rope at the 25-foot climbing wall. Varying degrees of difficulty ensure that even the most novice climber should be able to have some degree of success. Pan for gemstones at the Gemstone Mining Sluice, stop by the Antique Car Museum and spelunk in Perry's Cave: there is no shortage of low-impact fun at this place. Because each attraction is separately priced, the fees can quickly add up. To get your money's worth it might make sense to purchase an Island Fun Pack from **Lake Erie Islands Regional Welcome Center** (800/441-1271).

## Recreation

There is little sense visiting the walleye capital of the world only to leave the fishing to everybody else. Get a group of five or six together and contact **Hard Water Charters** (419/285-3106, www.hardwatercharters.com) for a half or full day of chartered boat fishing. All you need to bring is cash, an Ohio fishing license, and a cooler full of snacks: Captain Joe Kostura will handle the rest. Packages range from $300 to $600 and include all bait, tackle, and equipment. Fish cleaning is extra. If you prefer to travel the waterways without a guide, call the folks at **Put-in-Bay Watercraft** (419/285-2628, www.pibjetski.com) to rent fishing and power boats, personal watercraft, and kayaks. They are located within South Bass Island State Park.

## Restaurants

Praised equally for its waterfront views and lobster bisque, the **Boardwalk** (341 Bayview Ave., 419/285-3695, www.the-boardwalk.com, daily Memorial Day–Labor Day, weekends only in Apr. and Oct.) is one of the most popular dining and entertainment spots on the island. Enjoy views of the harbor boat traffic from elevated decks. Meals are casual, affordable, and delicious, and include live Maine lobster, shrimp, and that island-famous bisque. Live music and dancing keeps this joint jumping well into the night.

**Frosty's Bar** (252 Delaware Ave., 419/285-3278, www.frostys.com, daily Memorial Day–Labor Day, weekends only in Apr. and Oct.) is busy morning, noon, night, and late-night thanks to a full slate of tasty offerings. Many island-hoppers start their day here with eggs Benedict or a big plate of blueberry pancakes made with fresh fruit. Others start with a Bloody Mary to clear away the cobwebs. Frosty's pizza has been a Put-in-Bay staple for over 50 years.

Despite the name, **Goat Soup and Whiskey** (820 Catawba Ave., 419/285-4628, daily Memorial Day–Labor Day) is not as crazy as it might sound. In fact, this restaurant's location about three-quarters of a mile from downtown provides a less intense Put-in-Bay milieu. Sit inside or on the amazing outdoor patio while you enjoy numerous homemade soups, perch tacos, and fried walleye fingers.

## Nightlife

Depending on what sort of crowds you can handle, the **Beer Barrel** (441 Catawba Ave., 419/285-7281, www.beerbarrelpib.com, mid-Apr.–Oct.) and the **Roundhouse Bar** (60 Delaware Ave., 419/285-2323, www.theroundhousebar.com, mid-Apr.–Oct.) are notorious nightspots. As such, they can be insufferably loud, crowded, and crass. But given the right time of day and proper frame of mind, they also can be riotously fun. Typically, weekend nights are the craziest times. Beer Barrel claims rights to the world's longest permanent bar, a commendable 400-footer that if placed on its end would best Perry's Memorial. Both bars play host to some of the finest island musicians, so check the schedules to see if Mike "Mad Dog" Adams or Pat Daily is on tap to play.

## Festivals and Events

Plan well ahead if you intend to visit South Bass Island for its popular **Christmas in July** weekend. Hotels, bed-and-breakfasts, and campgrounds fill up early and fast, and some ferry companies require proof of lodging before you can come aboard. But book in advance you'll enjoy a wild weekend filled with Christmas-themed entertainment, anachronistic holiday decorations, and bachelorettes in Santa caps. Look for it in late July.

South Bass Island takes on a whole new charm come October, and many people elect to delay their visit until then so as to enjoy Put-in-Bay sans the crowds. Hence the popularity of mid-October's **Island Oktoberfest,** an annual smorgasbord of German food, drink, and entertainment, complete with beer halls and bratwurst.

**EXCURSIONS**

## Hotels

Host to one million visitors per year, South Bass Island has as many lodging options as there are tastes. From pitching a tent to renting a multi-room luxury cottage, the sleep of one's dreams is easy to land given a little advance planning.

Folks looking for a slower pace and quainter setting should book a night's stay at the **Anchor Inn** (500 Catawba Ave., 419/285-5055, www.anchorinn.info, $79–170). This 1917 bungalow boasts classic front-porch charm and gracious hospitality. Close to the action but far enough away to be peaceful, this romantic getaway is popular with couples, honeymooners, and mature travelers. Lovely gardens attract a multitude of migratory birds and provide a delightful spot for the day's included breakfast. This bed-and-breakfast offers three guest suites with private baths. One has its own balcony overlooking the gardens.

Stay at the **Grand Islander Hotel** (432 Catawba Ave., 419/285-5555, www.grandislanderpib .com, $140–290) if you want a lively pool scene: Splash! is billed as the world's largest swim-up bar. While we can't verify that boozy factoid, we can promise you a pirate ship (with a bar) and an on-site Vegas-style nightclub (without gambling). Comfortable if not glamorous lodging is the order of the day here, but most guests could care less where they pass out after a long night of fun. This festive complex is not exactly what one might call kid-friendly, though during the week things tend to be on the mild side.

Got a crowd? Book a suite at the **Put-in-Bay Resort** (439 Loraine Ave., 888/742-7829, www.putinbayresort.com) and you and seven friends can sleep comfortably. This hotel's three-bed grand suite features a living room, kitchenette with refrigerator, wet bar, and private bath with bathtub. Rates range from $150 for a standard room up to $850 for a multi-room suite.

## KELLEYS ISLAND

If South Bass Island is the Key West of the North Coast, then Kelleys Island is Sanibel. A slower pace and more nature-centric pursuits attract families looking for a true island getaway. Birdwatchers flock here in spring and fall to catch the migratory bird scene. Anglers and water-sports enthusiasts spend hours in and around the lake. Honeymooners and amorous couples hole up in romantic Victorian inns. The above is not meant to imply that Kelleys Island is a snooze; a party is always happening somewhere.

## Sights
### CADDY SHACK SQUARE

Located in downtown Kelleys Island is Caddy Shack Square, a complex with family entertainment, shopping, and food and drink. This is where folks can rent bikes and golf carts, play 18 holes of miniature golf, hit the arcade, or relax with a massage. If you're searching for a souvenir or gift, try the **Booga Shack,** which sells original island wear. No need to divulge what the **Flip Flop Shop** sells. Dessert fans swear by the hand-dipped cones at **Dipper Dan's Ice Cream Stand,** while caffeine junkies line up for a fix at the incomparable **Erie Island Coffee Co.**

## ◖ Glacial Grooves

Trek to the northern tip of the island to see what effects a little ice can have on solid bedrock. Sometime near the tail end of the Pleistocene Ice Age, a massive glacial sheet rubbed its way across this stretch of North America, leaving behind an otherworldly landscape. These deeply etched Glacial Grooves (419/797-4530, dusk–dawn, free), some 10 feet deep, 35 feet wide, and 400 feet long, are striking illustrations of nature's potent force. The immediate area is fenced off, but a walkway takes visitors close to the action, which likely took place 18,000 years ago.

## Kelleys Island State Park

While partiers flock to nearby South Bass Island, nature lovers gravitate to Kelleys. One of the major draws is Kelleys Island State Park (920 Division St., 419/797-4530, dusk–dawn, free), a 677-acre park in the north-central portion of the island. Six miles of hiking trails wind sightseers past scenic lake views and through beautiful nature preserves. Take the

COURTESY OF LAKE ERIE SHORES & ISLANDS

**Glacial Grooves on Kelleys Island are a visible reminder of the Ice Age.**

one-mile North Shore Loop trail to enjoy shoreline vistas, blooming wildflowers, and, in spring and fall, an anthology of migratory birds that use the island as a stopover point in their travels. Bring a towel and plop down at the sandy beach or drop a fishing line into the lake from a pier. Looking for something a little more high impact than pier fishing or birding? Contact **Kelley's Island Kayak Rental** (419/285-2628, www.kelleysisland.info), located within the park, to rent your own craft.

### Restaurants and Nightlife

At night, **Bag the Moon** (109 W. Lakeshore Dr., 419/746-2365, daily in season) turns into a rambunctious saloon, where folks go gaga for booze-filled strawberries with whipped-cream topping. During the day, however, Bag the Moon is a family-friendly restaurant serving reasonably priced American fare. Come here to start your day with one of the best breakfasts on the island. Popular meals include corned-beef hash and strawberry-stuffed pancakes. Enjoying a handcrafted microbrew on the

shores of Lake Erie is a singular joy. **Kelleys Island Brewery** (504 W. Lakeshore Dr., 419/746-2314, www.kelleysislandbrewpub.com, daily in season) brews great small-batch beer just yards from the lake, and a pet-friendly patio means you don't have to enjoy a pint in solitude. Come here for a satisfying lunch of burgers, brats, and beer. For dessert, there are fantastic root beer floats and milkshakes. If you have an action-packed morning planned, call ahead to order the Wake and Bake, a pot of hot coffee and a half-dozen muffins packed up to go with all the fixings.

More than just a restaurant, **Kelley's Island Wine Co.** (418 Woodford Rd., 419/746-2678, www.kelleysislandwine.com, daily in season) is really a family-friendly entertainment destination. Set apart from downtown, the spacious setting has room enough for volleyball courts, horseshoe pits, and plenty of alfresco dining. The wine, like most produced in the area, leans toward the sweet and rosy variety. But the straightforward food seems to be liked by all. Great pizzas, pastas, fish skewers and steak are served by a gracious staff.

For some odd reason, the Brandy Alexander is the official drink of Kelleys Island, and the **Village Pump** (103 Lakeshore Dr., 419/746-2281, www.villagepump.com, daily Mar.–Dec.) is the official supplier. This historic building once housed a post office and then the town gas station, hence the name. On a prime summer weekend, this homey tavern might serve 3,000 hungry guests, an eclectic mix of locals, island-hoppers, and families. Favorites here include textbook fried lake perch, home-style specials, and those addictive ice cream–infused Brandy Alexanders.

### Festivals and Events

South Bass has its wild Christmas in July, while Kelleys throws the more family-friendly **IslandFest.** The event kicks off with dancing, parades, and craft fairs and culminates with a rousing fireworks display. If you plan on visiting the island around the end of July when this popular weekend-long party takes place, you'll want to plan well ahead.

EXCURSIONS

## Hotels

Scenic Lakeshore Drive is sprinkled with attractive Victorian homes. Few are as graceful as **A Water's Edge Retreat** (827 E. Lakeshore Dr., 800/884-5143, www.watersedgeretreat.com, $200–280), a three-story beauty that houses a luxury bed-and-breakfast. The impeccable inn offers six suites with private baths and views of Lake Erie, Cedar Point, and Marblehead Lighthouse. Book a sailing trip on the owner's 35-foot yacht or just kick back with a glass of wine on the sweeping front porch. Prices include a gourmet hot breakfast, use of a bicycle, and a discount on golf-cart rentals.

Campers have it made on Kelleys Island. **Kelleys Island State Park** (920 Division St., 419/746-2546, $25–100) offers numerous shaded campsites, many with electric hookups. For something a little more out of the ordinary, put in a reservation for one of the park's yurts. These large circular canvas tents provide a nice middle ground between roughing it and luxury. Each has a kitchen, living area, and private bath.

# MAINLAND

You don't have to hop a ferry to enjoy the mainland communities of Lakeside, Port Clinton, Marblehead, and Sandusky. Home to major tourist attractions and out-of-the-way finds, these seaside locales buzz all summer long with activity.

## Sights

### AFRICAN SAFARI WILDLIFE PARK

We assume camels don't drive, but judging by the way these beasts of burden inspect automobiles at African Safari Wildlife Park (267 Lightner Rd., Port Clinton, 800/521-2660, www.africansafariwildlifepark.com, daily late May–early Nov., hours and admission vary), you'd swear they were in the market for a new ride. This 100-acre wildlife preserve is a must-do adventure for families with children. During the drive-through portion of the park, animals literally poke their heads inside the car to snack on grain and carrots. Gentle zebras, alpacas, camels, and elands all approach the

cars, absolutely thrilling the youngsters within. A walk-through portion has a number of other animal-related activities, including pony and camel rides. Pig races are a popular daily diversion. Come to the park early, bring your own carrots (much cheaper than at the park), and leave the Ferrari at home—cars routinely endure bumps, occasional bruises, and plenty of slobber. Check the website for "carload" discounts.

### C CEDAR POINT AMUSEMENT PARK

Thanks in no small part to its collection of the tallest, fastest, steepest roller coasters, Cedar Point Amusement Park (1 Cedar Point Dr., Sandusky, 419/627-2350, www.cedarpoint.com, daily mid-May–Aug., weekends only Sept.–Oct., $43 adult, $16 child under 48" and senior) is widely recognized as the world's best thrill park. Top Thrill Dragster zips to a speed of 120 miles per hour before climbing to a height of 420 feet. The newest ride, Maverick, is a mile-long ride through

COURTESY OF CEDAR POINT AMUSEMENT PARK

**Only the bravest riders hop aboard Wicked Twister at Cedar Point.**

COURTESY OF LAKE ERIE SHORES & ISLANDS

Picturesque Marblehead Lighthouse is an oft-photographed site.

canyons, dark tunnels, and around embankments. Tamer children's rides, live entertainment, and food options abound at this massive 370-acre amusement park. To avoid the longest lines, try scheduling your visit between Sunday and Wednesday. It is helpful to know that rides do shut down due to rain, high winds, or lightning, and no, rain checks and refunds are not awarded. Located next to Cedar Point is **Soak City** (daily late May–Aug., $29 adult, $16 child under 48" and senior), an 18-acre waterpark with dozens of waterslides, a sizeable wave pool, inner tube river rides, and sun-soaked spots for kicking back. Season passes, Ride & Slide tickets good for both Cedar Point and Soak City, and AAA passes all can save considerable money on admission. Parking is $10.

### KALAHARI WATERPARK
One of three in the nation, this 880-room African-themed resort (7000 Kalahari Dr., Sandusky, 877/525-2427, www.kalahariresort. com/oh, Sun.–Thurs. 10 A.M.–9 P.M., Fri.–Sat. 10 A.M.–10 P.M., $39, $42 weekends) is Ohio's largest indoor waterpark. Regardless of the weather outside, families can hit the beach all year long at this ginormous all-in-one entertainment complex. A FlowRider offers surfable waves everyday; the Zip Coaster is a wet-and-wild roller coaster; a 12,000-square-foot wave pool keeps the swells steady despite the tide. An equally enjoyable outdoor waterpark, open Memorial Day through Labor Day, adds a whole new dimension of fun come summertime. Hotel stays include admission to the parks.

### MARBLEHEAD LIGHTHOUSE
The view from the top of Marblehead Lighthouse (110 Lighthouse Dr., Marblehead, 419/734-4424, www.dnr.state.oh.us, tours late May–mid-Oct., free) includes Kelleys Island, South Bass Island, and the beautiful Sandusky Bay. This landmark lighthouse has guided sailors since 1822, making it the oldest continuously operated lighthouse on the Great Lakes. Selected for inclusion on a United States postage stamp, the classic form rises to a height of 65 feet and is one of the most photographed structures on the lake. The picturesque grounds also make a great location

for a family picnic, filled with scenic vistas, room to relax, and massive stones that kids can scramble up and over. An old lighthouse-keeper's house now serves as a museum operated by the Marblehead Lighthouse Historical Society. It is open whenever the tower is open.

## Restaurants

For over 20 years, **Chez Francois** (555 Main St., Vermillion, 440/967-0630, www.chezfrancois.com, Tues.–Thurs. 5–9 P.M., Fri.–Sat. 5–10 P.M., Sun. 4–8 P.M., closed Jan.–mid-Mar.) has offered incomparable French cuisine in a romantic post-and-beam structure. Classics like escargot, veal sweetbreads, and beef Wellington are freshened up by seasonal ingredients and matchless execution. The restaurant maintains a dress code (jackets for men, no flip-flops, etc.), but the more casual riverfront café serves the same food without the fuss. Pleasure boaters can tie up at the nearby Vermilion Public Guest Docks (440/967-7087).

In an area festooned with fried fish shacks, **Jolly Rodger Seafood House** (1737 E. Perry St., Port Clinton, 419/732-3382, mid-Feb.–late Nov., Sun.–Thurs. 11 A.M.–8:30 P.M., Fri.–Sat. 11 A.M.–9:30 P.M.) stands out for its quality, consistency, and value. Baskets overflowing with fresh-fried perch, walleye, onion rings, and hush puppies stream out of this busy little kitchen. As it should be, Jolly Rodger is a no-frills operation, with disposable plates, plastic cutlery, and paper napkins.

Know going in that **Mon Ami** (3845 E. Wine Cellar Rd., Port Clinton, 800/777-4266, www.monamiwinery.com, daily, hours vary by season) has changed considerably since its days as a quaint winery restaurant. This operation seems to grow each year, making it one of the busiest attractions in the region. Depending on the season, visitors can expect crowds of hungry day-trippers lining up for the popular all-you-can-eat buffet. Folks in search of peace, quiet, and romance would do well to pick out a spot in the dining room, while those looking for a party should make a bee line to the Chalet, a massive bar area with live entertainment.

Mon Ami shines on warm summer nights as the food and party spill outdoors.

## Festivals and Events

Times Square has its fancy-schmancy LED-powered crystal ball. Port Clinton has a 20-foot-long, 600-pound fiberglass walleye named Wylie. Each New Year's Eve, the tiny town of Port Clinton doubles in size from 6,000 to 12,000 when enthusiastic crowds brave frigid temps to experience the **Walleye Drop** (Madison St. in downtown Port Clinton, www.walleyemadness.com). Festivities begin at 3 P.M. and climax at the stroke of midnight, when Wylie makes the plunge from his comically large rod and reel. Like a viral video clip, this event has been featured on David Letterman and NPR.

## Hotels

With the rugged good looks of a northwest lumberjack, **Great Wolf Lodge** (4600 Milan Road, Sandusky, 888/779-2327, www.greatwolflodge.com, $150–350) is a wilderness-themed resort and indoor waterpark. The 271-suite hotel is loaded with family-friendly attractions and activities. There are two casual restaurants, game arcades, a rock climbing wall, and fitness center, not to mention one of the largest indoor waterparks in the nation. In the summer, an outdoor pool joins the list.

If you want a short two-minute walk to Cedar Point, stay at the historic **Hotel Breakers** (1 Cedar Point Dr., Sandusky, 419/627-2350, www.cedarpoint.com, $150–350). This beachside hotel is located on Cedar Point Peninsula and features two outdoor pools, an indoor pool, and beach access. Prices can vary widely based on room size and location within the complex, so do your research before booking. Guests get to enter the amusement park an hour before the general public, making roller coaster lines short and sweet.

Lakeside is an enlightened community of progressive types—a true chautauqua where seasonal residents seek to nurture mind, body, and spirit through intellectual, cultural, and recreational pursuits. Many summertime visitors own pricey Victorian cottages, but travelers can simply book a room at **Hotel Lakeside** (150 Maple Ave., Lakeside, 866/952-5374, www.lakesideohio.com, Memorial Day–Labor Day $80–200), a 130-year-old landmark. Sign up for lectures, seminars, and classes at nearby Lakeside or simply unwind on the hotel's gracious porch and take in the views.

## PRACTICALITIES
### Tourist Information
For more information on Lake Erie's shores and islands, visit the **Lake Erie Islands Welcome Center** (800/255-3743, www.lake-erie.com). Other helpful websites include the **Port Clinton and Put-in-Bay Travel Guide** (www.portclinton.org), the **Put-in-Bay Chamber of Commerce** (419/285-2832, www.put-in-bay.com), and **Kelleys Island Chamber of Commerce** (419/746-2360, www.kelleysislandchamber.com).

### Media
Check out the *Sandusky Register* (www.sandusky register.com) and *Port Clinton News Herald* (www.portclintonnewsherald.com) for up-to-the-minute news and information in the area.

Dig up a copy of Norman Hills' *A History of Kelleys Island, Ohio* originally published in 1925, for a historical look at Kelleys Island.

### Getting There
#### ISLANDS
If you've got your own boat, just dial 41° 39' 15" N, 82° 49' 15" W into the GPS to find Put-in-Bay, otherwise you'll need to hop a ferry. The **Jet Express** (800/245-1538, www.jet-express.com, $12–16 one-way) is the fastest way to the islands, but it is also the most expensive. The Jet Express departs from two locations: Port Clinton and Sandusky. The **Kelleys Island Ferry** (510 W. Main St., 419/798-9763, www.kelleysislandferry.com, $8 one-way) goes back and forth between Marblehead and Kelleys Island. **Miller's Boat Line** (800/500-

2421, www.millerferry.com, $6 one-way) operates a ferry between Catawba and South Bass Island. Free overnight parking makes this option a great choice.

Regardless which option you choose, make sure you are familiar with the ferry's return schedule before booking passage; some operate later than others.

#### MAINLAND
To get to Sandusky, Marblehead, Lakeside, and Port Clinton from Cleveland, simply take I-90 west to OH-2 west. Greyhound (www.greyhound.com) will drive you from Cleveland to Sandusky for about $15 with advanced purchase.

### Getting Around
The preferred modes of transportation on Kelleys and South Bass Islands include golf carts, mopeds, bicycles, and stumbling. Wise visitors know to leave their cars on the mainland. To rent a golf cart on South Bass Island contact **Delaware Golf Carts** (266 Delaware Ave., 419/285-2724, www.putinbayrentals.com), which rents four-, six-, and eight-person gas-powered carts by the hour, day, or week. Prices range from $50 to $100 a day based on cart model and day of the week. For bicycles stop by **Island Bike & Cart Rental** (419/285-2016, www.perryscave.com/island_transportation) as you disembark in downtown Put-in-Bay. This outfitter stocks nice-quality singles, tandems, trailers, and tag-alongs for around $15 a day.

On Kelleys Island, contact **Caddy Shack Rentals** (Caddy Shack Square, 419/746-2518, www.caddyshacksquare.com) or the **Casino Restaurant & Marina** (104 Division St., 419/746-2773, www.kelleysislandcasino.com) for a full range of bike and golf-cart rentals. Call for pricing and to reserve in advance.

To move from South Bass Island to Kelleys Island and vice-versa, contact **Jet Express** (800/245-1538, www.jet-express.com).

# Amish Country

The world's largest Amish community resides in a five-county area of rural Ohio, and Holmes County is home to about half of them. A day or two spent exploring the scenic backroads of this unspoiled landscape can be pure magic. Filled with blazing red barns, fertile fields, and horse-drawn buggies, the scene is one visitors often cherish for a lifetime. Despite what you may have read or heard about the Amish, they are a graceful, gentle community that welcomes visitors into their villages, shops, even homes. They support themselves largely by crafting furniture, foodstuffs, and handicrafts that they sell to "English" folk like you and me. Make sure to explore the historic Main Streets of Millersburg, Berlin, and Charm. Autumn, when visitors are treated to the tail end of the harvest, colorful fall foliage, and cooler temps, is the busiest time in Amish Country. Most Amish businesses are also closed on Good Friday, Thanksgiving, and Christmas.

## SIGHTS
### Amish & Mennonite Heritage Center

Your very first stop in Amish Country should be the Amish & Mennonite Heritage Center (5798 County Rd. 77, Berlin, 877/858-4634, www.behalt.com, Mon.–Sat. 9 A.M.–5 P.M., June–Oct. Fri.–Sat. 9 A.M.–8 P.M.). Start with an informative video on the local Amish and Mennonite community, then immerse yourself in *Behalt*, a 265-foot cyclorama, or cylindrical panoramic painting. Observers standing in the middle have a 360-degree view of the painting, which depicts the heritage of the Amish people from 1525 Zurich to the present day. This is a good place to stock up on area maps, brochures, and books about the Amish written by the Amish.

### Holmes County Balloon Rides

Hot-air balloons seem uniquely suited for scenic Amish country. Holmes County Balloon Rides (330/473-7444, www.holmescountyballoons.com, $200 adult, $110 child 8–14)

entertains brave souls with an unforgettable trip over a lush rural landscape. Drift lazily over Amish farms as awestruck children wave and give pursuit with barking dogs in tow. Fall is the best time, when leaves change from green to yellow, orange, and fire-engine red. The one-hour flights include a post-flight celebration. Sunrise and sunset flights are available. Bring along a camera for once-in-a-lifetime shots.

### ◖ Kidron Auction

When a farmer needs to buy or sell a farm animal, he visits his local livestock auction. Lucky for you, the experience is open to the public. The oldest and largest livestock auction in the state, the Kidron Auction (4885 Kidron Rd., Kidron, 330/857-2641, www.kidronauction.com, Thurs.) has been in operation from 1924, with weekly events since 1932. Gentleman farmers or the just plain curious are welcome to sit in and observe the lively action. The event opens with a hay and straw sale at 10:15 A.M. before moving on to dairy cattle, feed pigs, sheep, and goats. Get here early to grab a good seat in the selling ring; it fills up fast.

### Yoder's Amish Home

Eli and Gloria Yoder have made a living by sharing with outsiders the unique culture of their Amish past. They open their 116-acre Yoder's Amish Home (6050 Rte. 515, Millersburg, 330/893-2541, www.yodersamishhome.com, mid-Apr.–Oct. Mon.–Sat. 10 A.M.–5 P.M., $5 adult, $3 child) to visitors and along the way convey interesting facts about the history and lifestyle of the Amish people. Tour a 120-year-old barn constructed in the old-fashioned peg-and-beam design. The barn is filled with bunnies, lambs, horses, and puppies. Take a ride around the farm in a horse-drawn buggy ($3.50 adult, $2 child).

## RESTAURANTS

The granddaddy of Amish restaurants, **Amish Door** (1210 Winesburg St., Wilmot, 888/264-7436, www.amishdoor.com,

# NEGOTIATING AMISH BUGGIES

Holmes County is Amish Country, and this picturesque rural region looks, sounds, and smells different from any other place on Earth. The Amish believe in simplicity, hard work, and religion, and their old-fashioned customs are designed to foster strong family bonds. Because they eschew modern technologies like automobiles, the Amish travel by horse and buggy.

Almost every road in Holmes County is a designated National Scenic Byway, and motoring along these gorgeous country lanes is a thing of beauty. But beauty quickly can turn to tragedy when a fast-moving car collides with a slow-moving buggy. Buggies travel at speeds of just 5 mph and seemingly can appear out of nowhere. Drive slowly and cautiously at all times, but especially at night and when approaching a hill. And if you do approach a buggy, do not tailgate or honk, which can spook the horse. Simply pass by slowly, making sure to leave plenty of room between car and buggy. Keep in mind that it is considered disrespectful to stare, take photographs, or enter one's private property.

COURTESY OF THE HOLMES CTY CHAMBER COMMERCE

**Amish horse and buggy in Holmes County**

Mon.–Sat. 7 A.M.–8 P.M.), has been serving stick-to-your-ribs comfort food for over 30 years. What began as a small eatery has ballooned into an entire complex, complete with dining, shopping, and lodging. Dinners are filling, fabulous, and wallet-friendly. The menu is loaded with Amish kitchen classics like meatloaf, roast turkey, and chopped steak. Folks travel miles out of their way to tuck into plates of "broasted" fried chicken. Dinners include salad bar, vegetable, real mashed potatoes with gravy, and stuffing. If that doesn't push you over the edge, stop by the amazing bakery on your way out this Amish door.

For traditional Swiss, Austrian, and Amish cuisine, hit **Chalet in the Valley** (5060 OH-557, Millersburg, 330/893-2550, www.chalet inthevalley.com, Tues.–Sat. 11 A.M.–8 P.M., closed Jan.–mid-Mar.). Since it's located next to Guggisberg Cheese, it is only natural that one of the house specialties is bubbly cheese fondue. Move on to one of five different schnitzel entrées or the Amish sampler overloaded with roast beef, ham, fried chicken, mashed potatoes, and gravy. Cap off the meal with fresh-baked fruit pie. This is hearty home-style comfort at its best.

When you've had your fill of old-country dining, head to **South Market Bistro** (151 S. Market St., 330/264-3663, www.southmarket bistro.com, Tues.–Sat. 11 A.M.–2 P.M., Tues.– Sat. 5:30–10 P.M.) in nearby Wooster. Tucked into the fertile farmland of Wayne County, South Market Bistro attracts diners from as far afield as Cleveland and Columbus with its sustainable, seasonal cuisine. A full three-quarters of the food served in this cosmopolitan bistro comes from local farms and producers, including the meat, poultry, and dairy. I guess you could call the place Wooster's answer to Chez Panisse.

## SHOPS

Calling themselves "The Grandma of bulk foods," the **Ashery Country Store** (8922 OH-241, 330/359-5615, Mon.–Sat. 8 A.M.–5 P.M.) specializes in bulk sales of spices, nuts, candy, dried fruit, pasta, and baking supplies. This old-fashioned general store stocks over 1,200 items, with a matchless inventory of spices, cheese, meats, and fresh-baked goods. Home cooks and bakers used to high grocery-store prices will be in happy disbelief when they shop at the Ashery.

Located about two miles from downtown Berlin, in the picturesque Doughty Valley, **Guggisberg Cheese** (5060 OH-557, Millersburg, 800/262-2505, Apr.–Dec. Mon.–Sat. 8 A.M.–6 P.M., Sun. 11 A.M.–4 P.M., Jan.–Mar. Mon.–Sat. 8 A.M.–5 P.M.) is home to the original Baby Swiss. Founded by a cheese maker of Swiss origin, the factory and retail store stocks a vast array of dairy and meat products, plus imported Swiss cuckoo clocks. Buy a four-pound wheel of the cheese that made Guggisberg famous, or select others from the amazing variety of distinctive cheeses. On weekday mornings visitors can peek through a window to watch cheese being made.

Concerned that the Amish community would begin to have trouble finding the non-electric tools they needed to survive, Jay Lehman founded in 1955 **Lehman's Hardware** (1 Lehman Cir., Kidron, 330/857-5757, www .lehmans.com, Mon.–Sat. 8 A.M.–5:30 P.M.). Of course, it isn't just the Amish who crave old-fashioned, high-quality non-electric merchandise. Survivalists, environmentalists, victims of natural disasters, and nostalgia buffs all have needs that are satisfied by this amazing store. Filled with anachronistic items like wood-burning cook stoves, steel-cut nails, wooden wheelbarrows, and American-made children's toys, the 32,000-square-foot retail store is quite the adventure. Ironically, it is now the Amish themselves who are stocking the store with their high-quality handmade products.

## HOTELS

Folks who relish the homey atmosphere of a bed-and-breakfast while enjoying the amenities of a contemporary hotel will appreciate the **Barn Inn Bed & Breakfast** (6838 County Rd., Millersburg, 877/674-7600, www.thebarn inn.com, $110–220). Clean, comfortable, and gracious, the inn offers 11 well-appointed rooms, all with private entrances, private baths, and wireless Internet. Rooms also include a full country breakfast. The location is ideal for exploring Amish Country and the innkeepers will be glad to provide guests with recommendations.

Perched on a hilltop overlooking the beautiful Holmes County countryside, **Holmes with a View** (3672 Township Rd. 154, Millersburg, 877/831-2736, www.holmeswithaview.com, $135–245) truly does offer stellar vistas. Stacked into a trio of unique round buildings, six circular suites come fully equipped with kitchen, living, and dining areas, gas fireplace, whirlpool tub, and entertainment center. The location is close to many Amish Country sites yet the inn is sheltered away in a quiet corner of the county.

The serene and stunning **Inn and Spa at Honey Run** (6920 County Rd. 203, Millersburg, 800/468-6639, www.innathoney run.com, $120–320) fits well into its attractive landscape. Surrounded by 70 natural acres, this private retreat offers a number of wonderful accommodations. The Main Lodge has rooms with views of nearby bird feeders that attract a wealth of avian activity. In the unique earth-sheltered Honeycomb, guests stay in rooms carved into a hillside. Small families or couples looking for solitude will appreciate the cabins, which are tucked into the woods and feature a kitchen, living area with stone fireplace, and whirlpool tub. The spa's top-notch therapists and world-class treatments are worth a visit to Honey Run on their own.

## PRACTICALITIES
### Guided Tours and Maps
To experience the Amish way of life that is hidden beneath the surface, it is imperative to sign up for a guided tour. **Amish Heartland Tours** (330/893-3248, www.amishtoursofohio.com) offers a wide range of informative and captivating excursions, from half-day trips to overnight adventures. Participants are granted entry into private Amish homes for dinner, taken for a ride in a horse-drawn buggy, or whisked away on a narrated drive through the backroads of Amish Country. This outfit will even custom design a multi-day voyage, with all arrangements for lodging, meals, and attractions mapped out in advance.

The next best thing to a well-versed insider is a good map. When in Amish County, pick up a copy of the **Amish Highways and Byways Map**, which is available at most shops for around $4. (Or visit www.experience-ohio-amish-country.com to order one in advance.) This invaluable resource contains detailed maps of Holmes County, Millersburg, Berlin, Walnut Creek, and Sugarcreek, allowing tourists to get lost on out-of-the-way backroads without ever really getting lost.

## Tourist Information
There are a number of particularly helpful organizations and websites to help plan your visit to Amish Country. Perhaps the best recourse is the **Holmes County Chamber of Commerce** (877/643-8824, www.visitamishcountry.com). Their website is jammed with all sorts of wonderful info on area sights, shops, restaurants, hotels, and maps. While not an official tourism site, **Experience Ohio Amish Country** (www.experience-ohio-amish-country.com) is one of the best out there, especially when it comes to detailing the Amish way of life. It is written by passionate fans of the area. Also check out www.berlinohio.com and www.millersburgohio.com.

## Getting There
Holmes County is about 80 miles south of Cleveland. To get here involves a bit of backcountry driving, so get a good map and plan your route accordingly. Also, there is more than one way to get here, so decide what stops you might like to make on the way to or from Amish Country and plan a route around those.

## Getting Around
While rural Holmes County has plenty of scenic country roads, it has zero interstate highways. Getting around requires a car and a very good map. (GPS wouldn't hurt either.) Towns, attractions, and sights are spread apart by miles of farmland, making an automobile or motorcycle one's best bet for experiencing as much as possible.

# BACKGROUND

## The Setting

### GEOGRAPHY AND CLIMATE

The dominant natural feature of Cleveland isn't land but water. Lake Erie, the southernmost of the Great Lakes, occupies a none-too-subtle position due north of the city. The lake's freshwater supports local industry, sustains sport fish populations, irrigates regional crops, flows through kitchen faucets, and falls as winter precipitation. Yet, despite the importance and proximity of this sizeable body of water, Clevelanders largely ignore it. It isn't their fault: A shoreline freeway thwarts easy access, a municipal airport gobbles up prime real estate, and exclusive marinas snub the masses.

The city's second most defining physical feature is likely the Cuyahoga River, which slices through town, dividing Cleveland into two distinct and distinctive sides. To locals, east and west are not merely points on a compass, they are lifelong labels affixed at birth. Here, you are either an East Sider or West Sider, and as such possess a certain assemblage of stereotypical characteristics, accurate or otherwise. In the old days, it was rare for folks to venture from one side to the other, as odd as that sounds. These days, those traditions are as outdated as the aforementioned stereotypes.

Much fuss has been made of Cleveland's weather, but apart from the six months of winter (okay, that's a joke), the region possesses a

© DOUGLAS TRATTNOR

# LAKE ERIE MIRAGE EFFECT

Imagine standing on the banks of Lake Erie in Cleveland and suddenly the Canadian shore comes into perfect view, as though the 50-mile divide was whittled down to one mile. A rare optical phenomenon known as the Lake Erie Mirage Effect can do just that, making buildings, cars, and even people seem like they were close enough to reach out and touch.

Mirages occur all the time. Whether it's the proverbial oasis in a desert or a shimmering highway on a sun-soaked day, the optical trickery is the result of light refracting as it passes through layers of variously heated air. But while highway mirages are an everyday occurrence, the Lake Erie Mirage is not. Still, there have been numerous reports by people on both sides of the lake that have experienced this remarkable spectacle.

During an atmospheric inversion, cold dense air hovers near the lake's surface and warm air floats in layers above. As light travels through these layers, it refracts, or bends, acting like a magnifying lens that brings distant objects into clear view. So if you find yourself by the water's edge on a calm day, glance across the lake; you may just spot a Canadian flag.

---

fairly typical continental climate. Spring can provide a loathsome late-season snowfall before warming up to a seasonable 70 degrees by June. Summers are hot, occasionally humid, and punctuated by spectacular thunderstorms. Don't worry, they pass through briskly, leaving cooler, clearer, and drier weather in their wake. Fall is Cleveland's most brilliant season, boasting warm, dry days, crisp, cool evenings and a backdrop of luminous fall foliage. In Northeast Ohio, smart brides skip the June wedding in favor of early October. Winters start slower around here than in other parts of the Midwest thanks to the lake, its accumulated warmth acting as a sort of down blanket. Cleveland's impressive snow totals can be blamed—or credited, depending on one's point of view—on a phenomenon know as the Lake Effect. As cold arctic air passes over the relatively warm lake water, it picks up evaporated moisture and dumps it as shovelfuls of snow on area driveways. The largest snow accumulations occur well south and east of downtown in an area appropriately dubbed the Snow Belt, and rare are the occasions when road crews don't immediately clear it from the streets.

## ENVIRONMENTAL ISSUES

In many ways, the environmental challenges faced by Cleveland and Cuyahoga County mirror those found elsewhere in the nation. Unchecked urban sprawl has seen the creation of numerous exurban communities, along with the requisite big-box shopping centers, all at the expense of once-fertile farmland. What do we have to show for all that progress? How about lengthy commutes, increased air pollution, and deteriorating inner-ring neighborhoods and infrastructure. Add to that Cleveland's proximity to coal-fired power plants, soot and sulfur dioxide–spewing steel mills, and other heavy industry and you get a city with elevated levels of ozone and particle pollution.

But the news is not all bad. Ambitious downtown development projects show promise in stemming the outward migration and already are bringing thousands of new residents into the city center. Better still, many of these new structures are taking advantage of ecologically friendly green-building techniques. The recently completed $200 million HealthLine links Public Square and University Circle, Cleveland's two most dynamic employment centers, with a shiny fleet of environmentally friendly hybrid-electric buses. Bike lanes allow nearby commuters to pedal to work. And a national study in 2008 recognized Cleveland as the country's 14th most walkable city, with special nods to the neighborhoods of downtown, Ohio City, Tremont, and Detroit Shoreway.

Cleveland was the butt of innumerable jokes

when, in 1969, the Cuyahoga River burst into flames thanks to layers of oily industrial run-off. That shameful fire brought national attention to environmental issues everywhere, eventually leading to the passage of the Clean Water Act. While nobody dips their canteen into the Cuyahoga, wastewater treatment improvements have brought the river within accepted water-quality standards, and it's not uncommon to spot snapping turtles, great blue herons, and red-tailed hawks along the banks. Lake Erie, once a pea-green cesspool of fetid decay, is far cleaner, clearer, and teeming with sport fish. There are still water-quality issues, and swimmers are advised to keep apprised of no-swim advisories at area beaches (check www.ohionowcast.info), but even those appear to be decreasing from year to year.

Best of all, perhaps, is a 2008 study that recorded wind speeds off Lake Erie's shoreline as well above those necessary to support energy-producing turbines. Such promising reports could very well translate into jobs, clean energy, and a progressive new image for Cleveland.

# History

Long before there were the Cleveland Indians there were Indians in Cleveland. The area's first settlers, members of various Native American tribes, gave the twisty, turny Cuyahoga River its name: Cuyahoga is the Indian word for "crooked river." In 1796, Moses Cleaveland departed his vessel at the mouth of that very river to begin surveying the Western Reserve, a three-million-acre tract of land governed by Connecticut. In the process, he established the city that would become the territory's capital. Cleaveland became Cleveland, anecdotal lore will have one believe, when the village newspaper dropped the "a" in order to squeeze the name onto the paper's masthead.

The swampy Flats on either side of the Cuyahoga River, which served as a trading post and pioneer hangout, soon became the epicenter of commerce and industry. It was on the banks of this river that Cleveland generated its fortunes, with steel mills, shipyards, oil refineries, breweries, and assembly plants springing up like shitakes. The Ohio & Erie Canal opened up Cleveland and the interior of Ohio to the Ohio River and points east and west, providing a massive new market for its goods. The rapidly developing city was the first to employ electric streetlights, streetcars, and traffic signals. Cleveland was the site of the first automobile sale and offered free home mail delivery before any other American city.

John D. Rockefeller, "the richest man in America," transformed the Flats into the nation's oil capital. By the late 1800s, Standard Oil controlled most of the nation's refining capacity. Rockefeller's unlawful monopoly was broken up soon after the turn of the 20th century, but his largess lives on in named buildings, parks, and through generous donations and endowments.

By 1920, Cleveland was the nation's fifth-largest city. That same year the Cleveland Indians defeated the Brooklyn Dodgers to win the World Series, no doubt helped along by the first unassisted triple play in a world championship game. Despite the nationwide Depression, Cleveland, for two summers in 1936 and 1937, hosted the elaborate Great Lakes Exposition. Similar in size and scope to a World's Fair, the event saw the construction of 200 art deco–style buildings, stretching from Public Square to the lakefront. Literally millions of people traveled far and wide to experience exotic cultures, theatrical performances, and spectacular attractions. Billy Rose's Aquacade was a floating extravaganza filled with singers, dancers, and swimmers, including Olympic gold medalist Johnny Weissmuller. General Electric debuted the nation's first 50,000-watt lightbulb, a glowing achievement to be sure.

Following its peak in 1950, Cleveland's

# MAD BUTCHER OF KINGSBURY RUN

When two boys playing in the Kingsbury Run area of Cleveland stumbled across a decapitated body, it was the beginning of a city-wide reign of terror that would last for years. What police discovered when they arrived on the scene was not one but two decapitated bodies.

It was September of 1935, and over the next three years a dozen other victims would turn up, all decapitated and most dismembered. The Mad Butcher of Kingsbury Run, as he would soon be called, was one of the most depraved serial killers in our nation's history. Officially, the case has never been solved, despite having Eliot Ness in charge of the investigation.

When Ness accepted the job of Cleveland Safety Director, he intended to focus on greed, corruption, and fraud. But soon, the lawman found himself in charge of one of the most heinous killing sprees in history. He personally interviewed witnesses, placed 20 of his best men on the case, and rounded up every bum in Kingsbury Run for questioning.

Because the heads and hands were removed from the bodies, identifying the victims was nearly impossible. Many remain nameless to this day. In an attempt to identify one of the latest victims, Ness ordered a plaster cast be made of the severed head. This "death mask" was then displayed during the 1936 Great Lakes Exposition, a Cleveland-based World's Fair that attracted four million visitors in a single summer. Nobody recognized the face. This mask and three others are on display at the Cleveland Police Historical Society and Museum.

As a profile emerged, it was believed police were looking for a killer with a firm grasp of anatomy and a private place to perform the messy business. Butchers, hunters, and even doctors were considered likely suspects. But an almost complete lack of clues made finding him extremely challenging.

Attention soon turned to Dr. Frank Sweeney, a big, strapping man who grew up in the Kingsbury Run area and had an alcohol problem. Despite overwhelming confidence that Sweeney was the killer, a lack of direct evidence prevented a conviction. Two days after he was interrogated, Sweeney voluntarily admitted himself to a hospital. The murder spree stopped at the same time.

population began a slow and steady decline. Industrial production waned, white residents fled the city for neighboring suburbs, and the once-mighty Flats conflagrated into a national disgrace. Racial unrest visited many U.S. cities in the 1960s, and Cleveland was not immune. For six days in 1966, the 20-block neighborhood of Hough was the scene of fires, gunplay, and looting. When all was said and done, four were dead and another two dozen were severely injured. Just one year later, however, Carl Stokes was elected as the first black mayor of a major American city. His victory made the cover of *Time* magazine.

Cleveland's darkest days, perhaps, were in the late 1970s, when it became the first major American city since the Depression to default on its financial obligations. Yet, by the bicentennial celebrations of 1996, the "mistake on the lake" had begun its transformation into "The New American City." Ambitious new downtown projects saw the construction of three new professional sports venues, a state-of-the-art science center, and the Rock and Roll Hall of Fame. The Flats was reborn once again, this time as a nationally recognized adult playground with nightclubs, restaurants, and brewpubs. More than just something to do on a weekend, this compilation of civic triumphs buoyed the spirit of an entire city, signaling brighter days ahead. Some were even calling it a renaissance.

As present-day Cleveland deals with the serious issues of employment, education, inner-city crime, and balancing the books, ambitious new projects once again point to a brighter future. The just-completed HealthLine project is spurring over $4 billion in supplemental development up and down Euclid Avenue. Cleveland Clinic, University Hospitals, Case Western Reserve University, and scores of other University Circle startups continue to generate cutting-edge jobs in biotech at an unprecedented pace. Presently, there is a mini-boom of downtown residential and commercial projects, including a green-lighted $500 million makeover of the east bank of the Flats. A new convention center and medical mart may someday get built, which will showcase medical devices, inventions, and discoveries.

# Government

Cleveland is the county seat of Cuyahoga County, Ohio's most populous county as of the last census. The historically progressive district has voted Democrat in all but one presidential election since the 1960s. Despite a record 227,000-vote advantage over President Bush in the 2004 election, Kerry went on to lose the state of Ohio, and thus his bid for the White House. Many in politics contend that voting irregularities in Ohio clinched Bush's victory in the Electoral College. Some will go so far as to say that Bush, with help from then secretary of state Kenneth Blackwell, flat out stole the election. Issues included the use of outmoded punch-card voting machines, the purging of tens of thousands of eligible voters from the rolls, the refusal to process new voter registration cards, understocking likely democratic polling sites with voting machines, and barring people from voting in the wrong precinct. The story ends on an even more troubling note when, against state and federal law, two-thirds of Ohio's 2004 ballots were lost or destroyed, making it impossible to ever fully determine the accuracy of that year's vote count. (No, folks in Cuyahoga County are *not* over it.) Vowing reform, the incoming Democratic secretary of state Jennifer Brunner forced the resignation of numerous Board of Elections officials.

Every city has problems that shape and define it; Cleveland and Cuyahoga County seem to be suffering from governmental bloat that threatens to drag the entire region down. Thanks to 200 years of business as usual, the 16 counties that make up the economic region known collectively as Northeast Ohio has become a fragmented web of independent cities, villages, and townships, most with their own school system, city hall, and police and fire station. This redundancy in service has lead to an aggregate cost of government that has risen at a level more than twice the rate of inflation. These days, the watchword on local editorial pages is "regionalism." Leaders, finally seeing the negative effects on the region's economy that this unchecked waste causes, have begun endorsing plans for reform. By consolidating services, surrendering some autonomy, and coming up with appropriate tax-sharing strategies, the region may yet work its way of the muck, mire, and mess of the status quo. On a slightly smaller scale, equally fervent attempts are being made to reform Cleveland's overstuffed city council. With 21 members representing just 445,000 residents, the council employs more members than those of Cincinnati and Columbus combined. In predictable fashion, most of the aforementioned governing bodies agreed that the ideas are so beneficial they warrant further study.

To further complicate matters, numerous county officials, including the commissioner and auditor, are currently under investigation by the FBI and IRS. During a massive raid in mid-2008, the Feds executed search warrants inside the county administration building, engineer's office, and the homes and businesses of numerous officials and construction companies. The mess could take years to sort out.

# Economy

If you look in the right places, there is plenty to be optimistic about when it comes to the economic future of Cleveland and Northeast Ohio. Despite its Rust Belt roots, the region is fast becoming a hotbed of high-tech activity in the areas of bioscience, aerospace, information and health-care technology, and alternative energy solutions. While overall employment in manufacturing has undoubtedly taken a hit, the industry still accounts for about a fifth of the jobs in the region. But these days, in addition to rolling out steel, rubber, and automobile parts, area factories are beginning to focus on next-gen polymers, innovative medical devices, and tomorrow's fuel cell components.

Spurred on by initiatives like the Third Frontier Project, a 10-year $1.6 billion cash infusion, and grants from the Cleveland Foundation, one of the country's most generous philanthropic organizations, area institutions continue to expand and spin off new startups. Building upon partnerships with the Cleveland Clinic, Case Western Reserve University, and University Hospitals, Northeast Ohio companies attracted $318 million in venture capital in 2007, double the amount of the previous year. Technology leaders like NASA Glenn Research Center, Case Western, Cleveland State University, and Parker Hannifin are helping to cultivate a "green collar" workforce centered on the field of renewable energy. The state is poised to become a leader in fuel cells, biofuels, and wind-turbine-component manufacturing.

## HEALTH CARE AND EDUCATION

Cleveland is home to a number of top hospitals, medical schools, and universities, and it appears these days that health care is becoming the economic engine of this ship. The epicenter of this activity is University Circle, a one-square-mile cluster of cultural, educational, and medical institutions. The district is the second-largest employment center in Cleveland. Each day, approximately 40,000 people go to work at 50 or so organizations, pulling down a collective $850 million per year.

In addition to being among the most respected health-care facilities in the world, the Cleveland Clinic is an economic powerhouse, with revenues topping $4 billion annually. The immense hospital system employs 38,000 people, making it Ohio's second-largest private employer. It even maintains its own police force. The Clinic continues to expand its Midtown footprint, steadily replacing deserted brownfields and neglected warehouses with new medical buildings and parking garages. Built at a cost of over $600 million, The Miller Family Pavilion and the adjacent Glickman Tower are the latest additions to the sprawling campus. Meanwhile, nearby University Hospitals is on track to invest more than $1 billion over the next few years, a good portion of that going to the construction of a 375,000-square-foot cancer hospital.

To further capitalize on Cleveland's successes in health care and bioscience technologies, city and county officials are attempting to fund and build a medical mart and convention center. The mart would feature showrooms filled with health-care equipment and products while the convention center would provide a venue for trade shows and conferences. Issues over construction budget, site selection, and management agreements have delayed the project launch.

## LEGAL

Home to the founding offices of Jones Day, Squire, Sanders & Dempsey, Baker Hostetler, and Thompson Hine, among other firms, Cleveland has long been a legal powerhouse. There are over 10,000 registered attorneys in Greater Cleveland, giving the region a lawyer density on par with Chicago, Atlanta, and New York. The legal profession is one of the city's largest employment sectors, following closely behind health care and education.

## RTA HEALTHLINE

This massive infrastructure project took two years to complete and cost $200 million. But supporters say it has already spurred over $4 billion in new investment along the seven-mile route.

What some deride as simply a fancy new bus system is being billed by others as the rebirth of Euclid Avenue. Once called "Millionaire's Row," Euclid was known the world over for its unparalleled beauty and unrivaled concentration of wealth. Prosperous industrialists like John D. Rockefeller, Charles Brush, and Marcus Hanna all had stately mansions along the tree-lined avenue. Famous department stores like Higbee's, May Co., Halle Bros., and Sterling-Linder-Davis attracted well-heeled shoppers from all over the region and beyond. But thanks in large part to suburban sprawl, once-great Euclid Avenue crumbled like a sand castle at high tide.

These days, Euclid is making a comeback. This major artery connects Cleveland's two most dynamic employment zones, Public Square and University Circle. It bisects Cleveland State University, PlayhouseSquare, Cleveland Clinic, and the region's burgeoning Midtown tech sector. And the Euclid Corridor Project, now called the RTA HealthLine (www.rtahealthline.com), is making life a whole lot better for everybody along the way.

In addition to new roadways, bike lanes, sidewalks, transit stations, and streetscaping, the most noticeable newcomers are the buses themselves. Called rapid transit vehicles (RTVs), these extra-long hybrid-electric buses produce 90 percent less emissions than a traditional bus and zip passengers from downtown to University Circle in 20 minutes flat. To accomplish that feat, the RTVs travel in dedicated bus lanes down the middle of the street and GPS systems communicate with traffic signals. Also, riders pay fares before boarding, resulting in faster pick-ups.

Because of the unconventional traffic arrangement caused by the dedicated bus lanes, drivers need to be hyper-aware when traveling along Euclid Avenue. To avoid traffic tickets and collisions with large moving objects, drive only in the marked car-only lanes. There are close to 60 new stations, also located in the middle of the street, and crosswalks are everywhere, so keep a vigilant eye out for pedestrians. To make a left turn, look for the marked left-turn lanes. When you see the green left arrow it is safe to turn, even in front of a bus.

To ride the HealthLine, use the crosswalk to reach the station. Some dual-purpose stations service both east and west routes, while others are dedicated for only east or west travel; they are marked. Vending machines at all stations dispense single-trip, all-day, seven-day, and monthly passes. They are good for use throughout the RTA public transportation system. When boarding, there is no need to show your ticket to the driver – just enter through either door and sit down.

The HealthLine runs 24 hours a day, seven days a week. During peak times, buses comes every five minutes. Between 11 P.M. and 5 A.M. they slow to one every half-hour. Fares are $2 for a single trip.

## FINANCIAL

Up until the recent economic meltdown, Cleveland was home to two of this nation's biggest banks, National City and KeyCorp. Early advances in steel, oil, and auto industries, coupled with favorable banking laws, turned Cleveland into a major financial center. Finance still plays a major role in the local economy, with one of the country's 12 Federal Reserve banks, plus sizeable offices for money giants JPMorgan Chase and Fifth Third, calling Cleveland home.

## FORTUNE 500

Northeast Ohio is home to a number of Fortune 500 companies, including Progressive Insurance, Goodyear Tire, Eaton Corporation, Sherwin-Williams, KeyCorp, and American Greetings.

## EUCLID CORRIDOR PROJECT

Cleveland has suffered terribly from the foreclosure crisis, with as many as 12,000 homes now vacant in and around Cleveland neighborhoods. But thanks to one massive infrastructure project, there is some good news to counter the bad. Greater Cleveland Regional Transit Authority's $200 million undertaking saw the rehabilitation of seven miles of Euclid Avenue, paving the way for speedy transit service along dedicated bus lanes between Public Square and University Circle. According to some estimates, close to $4 billion is being invested along the refurbished HealthLine route. Piggybacking off those sporty new buses, streetscapes, and transit stations are renovated apartment buildings, fashionable restaurants, and fresh tech startups. Ever-expanding Cleveland State University, which is bisected by Euclid Avenue, is spending $300 million alone on new academic buildings and student housing.

## LOOKING AHEAD

Water helped make Cleveland an industrial powerhouse decades ago, and it may play an even more important role in the city's economic future. While Southern and Southwestern U.S. cities are battling over access to freshwater, Ohio, along with seven other U.S. states and two Canadian provinces signed the Great Lakes Compact. The Great Lakes–St. Lawrence River Basin Water Resources Compact was then signed into federal law, preventing thirsty outsiders from diverting water from the Great Lakes, the largest source of freshwater outside the polar icecaps. As freshwater becomes an increasingly sought-after resource, one necessary for business and development, not to mention that thing called life, some foretell a reverse migration back to Midwestern cities with access to that water.

# People and Culture

Located roughly equidistant from Chicago and New York City, Cleveland is described as the point where the East Coast meets the Midwest. The city is close enough to the heartland to reap the hospitable sensibilities of that region—hence the saying: "Winters here may be harsh, but never the people." Quick jaunts to the Big Apple are easy as pie, creating locally a demand for the same products, fashions, restaurants, and nightlife enjoyed out of town. Cleveland's best-of-both-worlds situation tanslates to hurried commuters, dressed to the nines, stopping to point a misguided soul in the right direction.

If any word accurately describes the people of Greater Cleveland, it is diverse. After the initial settling of transplanted British colonists, Cleveland enjoyed numerous waves of ethnic-specific immigration. By the late 1800s, a full 10 percent of the population was Irish. Most lived in Ohio City and worked at the docks unloading cargo. A comparatively larger contingent of German immigrants followed, some coming from as near as Pennsylvania, others straight from the motherland. Other significant migrations

included large contingents of Italians, Russians, Jews, Slovenians, Slovakians, Poles, Hungarians, and Ukrainians. Much later, the city welcomed Asian immigrants, specifically Chinese, Korean, and Vietnamese, but also Thai, Laotian, and Indian. Hispanics came in equally impressive numbers too. Walk into the West Side Market on a busy Saturday morning and you might be able to pick out a dozen different languages.

Cleveland's present-day population is just under a half million, down about 8 percent from the late 1990s. The city suffered its biggest losses in the 1970s, when almost 25 percent of its residents fled town, many simply relocating to suburban environs. Today, the five-county Greater Cleveland area contains well over two million people, making it one of the most densely populated regions in the country.

There are signs that this outward migration may slow, even reverse, in the coming years. Massive new investment in University Circle–area hospitals, spurred by a surging knowledge economy, coupled with a mini-boom of downtown housing projects, show promise in stemming the tide.

# The Arts

Cleveland has always been a leader in the cultural arts. Its impressive collection of world-class institutions would be a boon for a city of any size, let alone one of only a half million. Supported by a long-standing tradition of generous arts philanthropy, the city's theaters, museums, music ensembles, dance companies, and independent galleries enjoy relatively strong footing despite rocky economic times.

For close to 100 years, the Cleveland Museum of Art has been regarded as one of the finest repositories of visual art in the world. Generous donations and a sizeable endowment have made possible an ongoing $260 million makeover. For just as long, the Cleveland Orchestra—"the Best Band in the Land," according to *Time* in 1994—has regaled listeners from its majestic perch in Severance Hall. Established at the same time, the Cleveland Play House was the nation's first professional theater company. PlayhouseSquare is the second-largest arts district in the country, bested only by New York's Lincoln Center. All five of the district's 1920s-era theaters have been carefully restored.

University Circle, just one square mile, contains the country's greatest concentration of cultural and educational institutions. In addition to Severance Hall and the Cleveland Museum of Art, the dense enclave is home to the Botanical Garden, Western Reserve Historical Society, Museum of Natural History, Institute of Music, Institute of Art, and the Children's Museum. The Museum of Contemporary Art is presently building there a multimillion-dollar showcase for cutting-edge art. Many of these institutions are enjoying financial support thanks to a voter-supported cigarette tax, with 1.5 cents per cigarette going to numerous arts and cultural organizations.

Now in its fourth decade, the Cleveland International Film Fest is an 11-day event featuring more than 130 films and 160 shorts from 60 countries. As many as 50,000 viewers attend screenings at Tower City Cinemas. The Ingenuity Festival returns annually with a

Founded in 1915, Cleveland Play House is one of America's oldest regional theatres.

weekend-long celebration of art and technology, filling the streets with live and interactive exhibits in visual art, music, dance, and video.

Art has and continues to be a driving force in the resurrection of urban neighborhoods. Tremont is buoyed by a vast array of independent galleries, studios, and boutiques, and its monthly ArtWalks keep the area's shops, restaurants, and bars hopping year-round. Little Italy has carved a sort of double-sided niche for itself, with art and food sharing equal billing. Up-and-comer Detroit Shoreway can credit theater as one the main reasons for its present-day resurgence.

Cleveland has music in its blood, plain and simple. The "Rock and Roll Capital of the World" loves its live music, and countless clubs around town regularly attract yesterday's, today's, and tomorrow's hottest acts. Meanwhile, the Rock and Roll Hall of Fame attracts everybody else, with millions flocking to the museum to take a stroll down musical memory lane.

All of these quality-of-life amenities combine to create a city that is vibrant, relevant, intelligent, and fun, which is one of the reasons Cleveland regularly finds itself near the top of lists ranking livability, literacy, and places to raise a family.

# ESSENTIALS

## Getting There

Cleveland is serviced by a major international airport, a Greyhound bus terminal, an Amtrak station, numerous interstate highways and a turnpike, making travel to and from the city a relative breeze.

### BY AIR

Cleveland Hopkins International Airport (CLE, 216/781-6411, www.clevelandairport.com) is the largest commercial airport in Northeast Ohio, serving around 12 million passengers annually. Most major airlines and regional jets operate into and out of the airport. CLE is a major hub for Continental Airlines (www.continental.com, 800/231-0856), often making that airline

the best and most affordable option. Other major carriers include Delta (800/221-1212, www.delta.com), Northwest (800/225-2525, www.nwa.com), Southwest (800/435-9792, www.southwest.com), United (800/864-8331, www.united.com), and U.S. Airways (800/428-4322, www.usairways.com).

CLE offers more than 320 daily nonstop flights to over 80 destinations, with direct international service to cities in England, France, Mexico, and Canada. The busiest times at the airport are between 6:00 and 7:30 A.M., and between 4:30 and 6:30 P.M. Parking is available 24 hours a day, 365 days a year in short- and long-term garages.

COURTESY OF POSITIVELY CLEVELAND

Ground transportation to downtown Cleveland is cheap, easy, and efficient thanks to a light rail service that transports passengers from an airport train station directly to Public Square. The Greater Cleveland Regional Transit Authority (216/566-5100, www.riderta.com) Red Line operates Monday through Saturday approximately every 15 minutes from 4:29 A.M. until 7:45 P.M., and approximately every 20 minutes from 7:45 P.M. until 1:05 A.M. On Sunday, the train operates from 4:32 A.M. until 1:14 A.M. The train costs $2 for the one-way trip and takes approximately 25 minutes to travel from the airport to downtown.

To hail a cab, travelers need to make their way to the taxi stand located at the southern end of the lower-level baggage claim area. The journey to town takes between 20 and 30 minutes and costs approximately $40. Most area hotels offer complimentary shuttle service to and from the airport, and like the taxi cabs the shuttles are accessed on the lower-level baggage claim area. Call your hotel from the lower-level courtesy phones to verify service times.

To arrange private ground transportation, call Hopkins Transportation Service (800/543-9912). The company offers door-to-door service for all travelers, including those with disabilities.

## BY TRAIN

Cleveland is serviced by Amtrak (200 Cleveland Memorial Shoreway, 216/696-5115, www.amtrak.com) but arrival and departure times are anything but convenient. The Capitol Limited runs daily between Washington, D.C., and Chicago, stopping in Cleveland around 3 A.M. The Lake Shore Limited travels daily between Chicago and New York City, stopping in Cleveland around 6 A.M.

## BY BUS

Travelers can leave the driving to Greyhound by visiting what once was a flagship terminal for the bus line. Built in 1948, the building (1465 Chester Ave., 216/781-0520, www.greyhound.com) is one of the finest examples of Streamline Moderne design in the nation. The terminal is conveniently located downtown and is accessible by foot, car, and cab from most area hotels.

# Getting Around

## PUBLIC TRANSPORT

The Greater Cleveland Regional Transit Authority (216/566-5100, www.riderta.com), known locally as the RTA, operates buses, light rail, community circulators, and downtown trolleys throughout Greater Cleveland. Fares are $2 for buses and trains, $1.25 for trolleys and circulators. Four rail lines make up the Rapid Transit System. With Tower City as the center, lines take riders as far west as Cleveland Hopkins International Airport, north to the lakefront and North Coast Harbor, and east to East Cleveland and Shaker Heights. Fares on trains are typically paid when entering or exiting at Tower City station.

All of RTA's buses are equipped with external bike racks. To use the service, riders should visually signal the bus driver before loading his or her bike onto the rack. Additionally, bikes are permitted on all RTA trains at all times. Just cautiously roll your bike onto the train and stand with it. In 2007, RTA was named by the American Public Transportation Association as North America's Best Public Transportation System.

Completed in the fall of 2008, RTA's HealthLine offers quick and efficient transit service between Public Square and University Circle, with stops in between, on electric-hybrid buses.

## DRIVING

To take advantage of most of the attractions and activities in this book, a comfortable pair of shoes and access to the RTA is all that is required. The trains quickly and safely move people between the airport, downtown, and University Circle, and the city center isn't so large that walking between destinations is a marathon. Toss in some inclement weather, however, and those leisurely strolls can become rather unpleasant. When weather or distance prevents walking or riding, a car might come in handy. If renting one, make your life easy and spring for GPS; Cleveland's East Side contains more roundabouts than straight roads. Do your wallet a favor and obey posted speed limits and traffic signals; Cleveland has installed a slew of automated cameras that snap speeders and red-light runners. For those drivers with AAA memberships, emergency roadside assistance is available 24 hours a day, seven days a week by calling 800/AAA-HELP.

## TAXIS

To put it bluntly, hailing a cab in Cleveland can be like waiting for Godot: Hope quickly fades to frustration. If you want a cab and you are not at the airport or a hotel, call one on the phone. A few popular companies are Ace Taxi (216/361-4700), Americab (216/881-1111), and Yellow Cab (216/623-1550).

## BICYCLING

While far from two-wheeled nirvana, Cleveland is beginning to see the light when it comes to providing access for riders. New bike lanes, bike racks, and bike-awareness programs are converging to make the city much more conducive to pedal power. After much debate, bike lanes were added to the final design for the Euclid Corridor Project. A new city law requires all downtown parking lot operators to install bike racks. And the RTA installed bike racks on all of its buses, making bike-and-ride commuting a reality.

## MOTORCYCLING

Like many states in the nation, Ohio requires only riders under the age of 18 years old, or riders in their first year of motorcycle licensure, to wear a protective helmet. Passengers riding with such young or novice drivers must also wear helmets.

## DISABLED ACCESS

RTA is one of the first transit authorities in the country to operate a bus fleet that is 100 percent wheelchair accessible. Buses have a low-floor design that makes it easier for senior citizens, persons with disabilities, and everybody else to board and exit the vehicles. They also feature an easy-to-use ramp that works faster than traditional wheelchair lifts found on other buses. Ace Taxi (216/361-4700) operates wheelchair-accessible vans that can accommodate one wheelchair passenger and three other riders, or two wheelchair passengers and one additional rider. Call for reservations. Hopkins Transportation Service (800/543-9912) offers door-to-door service to the airport for everyone, including travelers with disabilities.

# Tips for Travelers

## SMOKING

Despite the state's relatively high number of smokers, Ohio voters approved a comprehensive smoking ban that went into effect in late 2006. The sweeping ban covers most public spaces and places of employment, including bars, restaurants, and bowling alleys. What does this mean for smokers? It means they spend a lot more time standing around on sidewalks, for starters. Bars and restaurants with patios have become popular with smokers as they are one of the few remaining public places to puff. Some restaurants, especially those that offer more upscale dining, do not allow their patios to become smoke havens. It's always wise to seek permission before lighting up.

## TIPPING

Considering that restaurant servers earn $3.50 an hour, it is reasonable to assume that most rely on tips as their major source of income. It is customary to tip between 15 and 20 percent of the pre-tax total for competent service. And it is never fair to penalize a server for the faults of a kitchen. If the food is poor, send it back and get something else. Don't stiff the waiter because the cook is lousy. At bars, the going rate is about a buck per drink when ordering one or two, less when picking up a round. Cabbies expect a tip; no surprise there. A good rule of thumb is to round up to the nearest dollar and then add another dollar or two, depending on the distance. For long trips, 10 percent of the fare may be appropriate, assuming you ended up at the proper destination.

## GAMBLING

Ohio is surrounded by states that offer full-scale legal gambling, and trips to their casinos is a favorite pastime for local residents. Despite this, Ohio voters continually strike down casino ballot initiatives come election day. But gamblers aren't totally shut out. Folks can play the ponies at two race tracks, **Northfield Park** and **Thistledown.** The first offers year-round live harness racing, the second offers live thoroughbred racing May through October. But glitzy casinos they are not. In an attempt to raise revenue without crossing the "gambling" line, the state lottery recently introduced Keno, where players wager up to $20, hoping to match 1–10 numbers from a pool of 80. Drawings take place every four minutes at some 2,000 bars, restaurants, bowling alleys, and clubs. On most weekends, card sharps can find a legal game at the Nautica Charity Poker Festivals (2000 Sycamore St., www.nauticacharitypoker.com). Held at the Powerhouse at Nautica Entertainment Complex in the Flats, the events feature blackjack and Texas hold 'em tournaments for players of at least 21 years of age. Rotating charities host the events and take 100 percent of hourly seat fees plus all losses. Players keep their cash winnings. There is no alcohol permitted at these festivals.

## GAY AND LESBIAN

Thanks to a thriving arts and culture scene, Cleveland enjoys a robust gay and lesbian population. Lakewood likely contains the largest concentration of gay residents, and thus it boasts many gay-owned and gay-friendly businesses. Cleveland's annual Pride Parade and Festival, held in June, is well attended by both gay and straight revelers. Some bed-and-breakfasts, like Ohio City's Stone Gables, are both gay-owned and gay-friendly. For more information contact the Lesbian, Gay, Bi-sexual and Transgender Community Center of Greater Cleveland (216/651-5428, www.lgcsc.org).

# Health and Safety

While the rates of homicides and other violent crimes are down overall across the city compared with previous years, there is no shortage of danger lurking in and around Cleveland. But by and large, the bulk of the hazardous activity is confined to a handful of impoverished and gang-riddled neighborhoods well outside the scope of most visits. That doesn't mean that care should not be taken everywhere, especially at night. Whenever possible, travel in groups, stick to well-lighted and well-traveled lanes, and know your route. Need an escort? Call the Downtown Cleveland Alliance (216/621-6000) and they will send out one of their ambassadors to lend a hand.

Downtown is very safe, even at night. Most parts of Ohio City and Tremont are well traveled and thus safe, but as one ventures towards the fringes, things get a bit dicier. Same goes for Detroit Shoreway. Neighborhoods to avoid include those east of East 55th Street and south of Shaker Heights, and east of MLK Jr. Drive and north of Superior Avenue.

## EMERGENCIES, HOSPITALS, AND PHARMACIES

Dial 911 for all fire, police, or medical emergencies. The Greater Cleveland Poison Control Center can be reached at 800/222-1222. The Cleveland Clinic (800/223-2273, www.clevelandclinic.org) operates dozens of regional hospitals, family health centers, emergency rooms, and surgery centers throughout Cuyahoga County and beyond. When traveling in the University Circle area, visit the main campus at 9500 Euclid Avenue. If downtown or in Ohio City, visit Lutheran Hospital (1730 W. 25th St., 216/696-4300). When in Lakewood consider Lakewood Hospital (14519 Detroit Ave., 216/521-4200). Other hospitals of note include St. Vincent Charity Hospital (2351 E. 22nd St., 216/861-6200) and University Hospitals Case Medical Center (11100 Euclid Ave., 216/844-1000). Most hospitals offer emergency treatment.

# Communications and Media

## PHONES AND INTERNET ACCESS

For the most part, Cleveland telephone numbers fall within the 216 area code. As one travels west or east, 216 gives way to area code 440. Well south of town, 330 is the name of the game. When calling from one area code to another, it is necessary to dial a "1" before the 10-digit phone number. Time and weather reports can be accessed by calling 216/931-1212 or #622 on Verizon Wireless phones.

Cleveland is served by all major cellular carriers, including Verizon, Sprint, and ATT.

Free Wi-Fi service is available at most Cleveland Public Library branches, including the main branch downtown and those in Tremont and Ohio City (and all branches have public computers with Internet access). Free wireless Internet also blankets much of the University Circle area. Countless coffee shops, restaurants, and hotels offer free Wi-Fi as well, guaranteeing that a hotspot is never far away.

## POSTAL SERVICES

Those who need to send mail or set up a P.O. box can do so throughout town at numerous United States Postal Service locations. Call 800/275-8777 or click www.usps.com to find the closest one. For additional mail and shipping services, contact The UPS Store (800/789-4623, www.theupsstore.com) or FedEx (800/463-3339, www.fedex.com), both of which maintain numerous Cuyahoga County outposts. To speedily move items from one location to another within the city, it might make sense to employ a courier service. Some popular companies include Bonnie Speed Delivery (216/696-6033) and BOBCAT Same Day Delivery (440/458-5374).

## NEWSPAPERS AND MAGAZINES

Cleveland's one major daily newspaper (Ohio's largest) is the *Plain Dealer* (www.cleveland .com). The Sun News (www.cleveland.com/ sun) publishes approximately 20 different community-specific weekly newspapers that come out on Thursdays. For some of the best arts, entertainment, and political coverage, grab a copy of *Cleveland Scene* (www.clevescene. com), a free alternative weekly that is available all over town. For a more in-depth look into the goings on in and around Northeast Ohio, purchase the latest issues of *Cleveland* magazine (www.clevelandmagazine.com) and *Northern Ohio Live* (www.northernohiolive. com), two great glossies. For all the latest business news, Crain's *Cleveland Business* (www. crainscleveland.com), a weekly news magazine, is tough to beat. Owned by the famous boxing promoter Don King, the *Call and Post* (www.call-post.com) is a 90-year-old newspaper that covers African-American events and affairs. The *Gay People's Chronicle* (www.gay-peopleschronicle.com) is a biweekly publication covering Ohio's lesbian, gay, bisexual, and transgender community.

## RADIO AND TV

All major television affiliates are present and accounted for in Cleveland, while public television fans are serviced by WVIZ/PBS (www .wviz.org). The Cleveland radio dial has a little bit of everything when it comes to sports, news, talk, and music. For classic rock tune into WMMS 100.7 FM and WNCX 98.5 FM; for Top 40 try WQAL 104.1 or WMVX 106.5; for hip-hop and R & B hit WENZ 107.9 FM; for country music tune into WGAR 99.5 FM; for news, talk, and sports visit WTAM 1100 AM and WKNR 850 AM; for talk and oldies hit WMJI 105.7 FM; for Christian go to WFHM 95.5 FM; for classical and public radio WKSU 89.7 FM or WCPN 90.3 FM.

# RESOURCES

## Suggested Reading

### HISTORY AND GENERAL INFORMATION

Cayton, Andrew R. L. *Ohio: The History of a People.* Columbus, OH: Ohio State University Press, 2002. This contemporary text covers a lot of ground, from the attainment of statehood in 1803 all the way to the new millennium. Way more than a dusty history book, this entertaining read relies on letters, fiction, art, architecture, and sports to tell the story about this complicated state in the heartland.

Grabowski, John J. *Cleveland, Then and Now.* Berkeley, CA: Thunder Bay Press, 2002. Serving as a sort of visual narrative, this unique book juxtaposes historical photographs with modern color images of the identical scene. In order to know who we are, we must know from whence we came, and this book offers a unique vehicle to get there.

Miller, Carol Poh. *Cleveland: A Concise History, 1796–1996.* Bloomington, IN: Indiana University Press, 1997. While indeed concise, this thorough book spans 200 years of Cleveland history, from the moment Moses Cleaveland stepped off his dinghy in the Flats to the city's bicentennial celebration. Augmented by wonderful illustrations and photographs, this methodical book brings people up to speed in record time.

Nickel, Steven. *Torso: The Story of Eliot Ness & the Search for a Psychopathic Killer.* Winston-Salem, NC: John F. Blair, 2001. Most know only about Eliot Ness through his dealings with Al Capone and his depiction on the TV series *The Untouchables.* But as Cleveland's safety director, Ness was placed in charge of tracking down one of the most heinous serial killers of all time, the Mad Butcher of Kingsbury Run. This book tells the tale.

Van Tassel, David. *The Encyclopedia of Cleveland History.* Bloomington, IN: Indiana University Press, 1996. There may be no more comprehensive historical text of any city than this exhaustive tome. This 1,100-page hardback covers seemingly every aspect of Cleveland's first 200 years, with entries on industry, philanthropy, art, music, and flight. Add to that hundreds of photos, numerous maps, and the sharp writing of over 200 journalists, and you get an encyclopedic digest that makes others in the genre look like tourist pamphlets.

Woods, Terry K. *Ohio's Grand Canal: A Brief History of the Ohio & Erie Canal.* Kent, OH: Kent State University Press, 2008. The Ohio & Erie Canal was so influential in the development of Cleveland and the entire state of Ohio, it is no wonder there are so many titles on the subject. Few, however, can match the level of detail captured in this thoroughly researched and well-penned account of the events surrounding Ohio's most ambitious infrastructure project.

### RECREATION, MUSIC, AND SPORTS

Adams, Deanna R. *Rock 'N' Roll and the Cleveland Connection.* Kent, OH: Kent State University

Press, 2002. Weighing in at over 600 pages, this comprehensive tome leaves no doubt as to why Cleveland landed the Rock and Roll Hall of Fame. The book tracks the history of rock as it applies to Cleveland, touching on early musicians, local DJs, trend-setting radio stations, and the lead up to acquiring the Rock Hall.

Gorman, John. *The Buzzard: Inside the Glory Days of WMMS and Cleveland Rock Radio.* Cleveland: Gray & Co., 2008. Gorman, who served as WMMS's program director in the 1970s, offers readers a salacious glimpse into life at one of the most influential rock radio stations in the country. No surprise: This one includes tales of sex, drugs, and rock and roll.

Hoskins, Patience Cameron. *Cleveland on Foot: 50 Walks & Hikes in Greater Cleveland.* Cleveland: Gray & Co., 2004. Walkers, hikers, and outdoors enthusiasts will have a field day with this guide, which points folks in the direction of some of the most picturesque walks around town. Northeast Ohio is blessed with great parks and this handy book will help you explore them.

Latimer, Patricia. *Ohio Wine Country Excursions.* Cincinnati: Emmis Books, 2005. Few people outside Ohio realize just how much quality wine production goes on in the state. For those who are eager to learn more, this great guide offers detailed info on over 60 Ohio wineries. In addition to some historical context, the indispensible book contains maps, photos, and tasting guides.

Pluto, Terry. *The Curse of Rocky Colavito: A Loving Look at a Thirty-Year Slump.* Cleveland: Gray & Co., 1995. Pluto, who covers sports for the Cleveland *Plain Dealer,* is one this country's best sports reporters. He has penned a number of books on Cleveland sports, including those on the Browns and the Cavs. This one links the Cleveland Indians' lengthy championship drought to the fateful day in 1960 when the team traded away beloved slugger Rocky Colavito.

Taxel, Laura. *Cleveland Ethnic Eats: The Guide to Authentic Ethnic Restaurants and Markets in Greater Cleveland.* Cleveland: Gray & Co., 2006. In this helpful guide, Cleveland-based food writer Laura Taxel documents hundreds of ethnic restaurants and markets in and around the Cleveland area. Adventurous foodies would do well to grab a copy.

## FICTION, POETRY, AND CHILDREN

Holbrook, Sara. *What's So Big About Cleveland, Ohio?* Cleveland: Gray & Co., 1997. When a well-traveled 10-year-old is dragged by her parents to dull old Cleveland, she expects to be bored to tears. And she is—until she discovers a secret about the city that changes her outlook. What better way to get your kids excited about C-Town than with this illustrated children's book?

Lax, Scott. *The Year That Trembled.* Forest Dale, VT: Paul S. Eriksson, 1998. This coming-of-age novel by Cleveland writer Scott Lax is set in Northeast Ohio and tracks a close-knit group of friends in the days leading up to the Vietnam draft. In 2002, the book was adapted into an independent film.

Roberts, Les. *Pepper Pike.* Cleveland: Gray & Co. Roberts, the recipient of the prestigious Cleveland Arts Prize for Literature, is a mystery writer with dozens of novels under his belt. He is best known for his Milan Jacovich series, which revolve around a likable blue-collar private eye of the same name. In addition to the above title that kicks off the series, other books include *Full Cleveland, The Lake Effect,* and *Deep Shaker.* No surprise that the novels are set in and around Cleveland.

Swanberg, Ingrid (ed.). *D. A. Levy and the Mimeograph Revolution.* Huron, OH: Bottom Dog Press, 2007. Underground poet d. a. levy used his relationship with Cleveland as the fuel for his stirring poetry, prose, and art. Modern readers walk away with a unique and moving perspective of 1960s Cleveland. Levy used his own photocopier to self-publish his works, essentially kick-starting the local alternative press movement. This anthology of his work is supplemented with interviews, essays, and letters.

Winegardner, Mark. *Crooked River Burning.* Orlando: Harcourt, 2001. In this ambitious American novel, Winegardner weaves fictional and non-fictional events into a patchwork tale of a once-great city in decline. The stars of this drama hail from opposite sides of town—he from blue-collar Old Brooklyn, she from affluent Shaker Heights—but fate has a way of bridging divides. In spite of its negative circumstances, Cleveland somehow shines through it all.

# Internet Resources

## GENERAL INFORMATION

### About.com
### www.cleveland.about.com

Like other About.com sites, this one compiles a broad swath of information on a host of Cleveland-related topics. Good for the casual visitor and the potential relocater, the site melds info on tourist attractions, specific neighborhoods, dining and nightlife, and current events.

### City of Cleveland
### www.city.cleveland.oh.us

The official City of Cleveland website is intended as a portal to government services, residential information, and city jobs listings. This is also where folks pay their parking tickets online.

### Cleveland.com
### www.cleveland.com

This online version of the Cleveland *Plain Dealer* tracks local, regional, national, and international news, but also sports, weather, entertainment, and seasonal events. There are scores of bulletin boards where lively discussions on every conceivable topic take place 24/7. This is also the online home for *Sun News,* a family of community newspapers that cover the Greater Cleveland area.

### The Cleveland Memory Project
### www.clevelandmemory.org

Get lost in the Special Collections archives of the Cleveland State University Library at this beautiful website. Compiled here are over 500,000 newspaper photographs, covering decades of Cleveland history, architecture, and events. There are 6,000 images documenting the construction of the Terminal Tower alone. Bridge fans will go nuts over the vast catalogue of historic bridge pics. Also here is the full text of hundreds of rare books.

### Cleveland Plus Living
### www.clevelandplusliving.com

Hosted by area chambers of commerce, regional business-growth associations, and travel and tourism professionals, Cleveland Plus Living is designed to attract skilled residents to Northeast Ohio. More stuff than fluff, the site contains hard info on the region's top employers, housing and cost of living, and education from kindergarten through post-grad. There is also a comprehensive listing of visitors' sites for nearby counties, cities, and attractions.

### Cuyahoga Valley National Park
### www.nps.gov/cuva

This is the official U.S. National Park Service site for Cuyahoga Valley National Park, a 33,000-acre sanctuary 15 minutes south of Cleveland. The well-organized site includes information on the park's history, its diverse flora and fauna, and the numerous recreational activities that exist throughout the park. The downloadable PDF maps of the park, its trails and waterfalls, and the popular Ohio & Erie Canal Towpath Trail make this site an indispensable resource.

## EcoCity Cleveland
## www.ecocitycleveland.org

For followers of the green movement, the smartly written content from this nationally recognized nonprofit serves as a how-to guide for modern times. Promoting environmentally friendly redevelopment, stemming the tide of urban sprawl, and improving the quality of life for all residents are the breezes that propel this organization. Visit this site to read about living sans car in Cleveland, where to find green housing, and why moving to cornfields is bad for everybody.

## The Encyclopedia of
## Cleveland History
## http://ech.cwru.edu

This is the online version of the book listed in the previous section, which is the authoritative text on historical information about Cleveland. In addition to all the articles from the print version of *The Encyclopedia of Cleveland History,* this easy-to-search website also includes revised text, tons of new content, and high-res photos and documents.

## Ohio Division of Travel and Tourism
## www.discoverohio.com

This official travel and tourism site covers the great state of Ohio from border to border. In addition to information on where to go, what to do, and when to do it, the well-designed site also features interactive maps, glossy publications, and special deals and discounts. Here travelers also will find listings for every local tourism organization throughout the entire state.

## Positively Cleveland
## www.positivelycleveland.com

The official website for the Convention and Visitors Bureau of Greater Cleveland, Positively Cleveland is extremely useful for tourists, potential new residents, travel professionals, and meeting planners. Chock-full of info regarding attractions, accommodations, shopping, transportation, and excursions from town. Suggested itineraries take all the guess work out of planning a short stay.

## University Circle Inc.
## www.universitycircle.org

University Circle is the epicenter of arts, culture, education, and health care in Northeast Ohio, and this official website is a great place to begin your exploration. Geared both to visitors and job seekers, this thorough site has information on major cultural attractions, seasonal events and exhibits, dining and nightlife, accommodations, career listings, and real estate.

# EVENT LISTINGS

## Cleveland.com
## www.cleveland.com/events

This helpful tool searches upcoming events by day, week, or month. Further sorting by event type, location, and entertainment genre makes it easy to pinpoint your way to fun.

## Cleveland Scene
## www.clevescene.com

Cleveland's premier alternative weekly publishes comprehensive entertainment listings covering art, music, dance, theater, film, dining, and nightlife.

## Cool Cleveland
## www.coolcleveland.com

Tens of thousands of Clevelanders get a weekly email newsletter from this organization detailing all the cool stuff going on around town. One of the most complete listings of arts and culture events around, it is worth checking out before stepping out.

## Plugged In Cleveland
## www.pluggedincleveland.com/events

Check out this site for a decent listing of upcoming events in a broad range of entertaining pursuits.

# BLOGS

## Brewed Fresh Daily
## www.brewedfreshdaily.com

This group-effort blog compiles comments

from leading Cleveland voices on news, politics, and current events.

## Working with Words
### www.workingwithwords.blogspot.com

This sharply written blog by Cleveland-based journalist John Ettorre casts a wide, humorous net around topics as varied as local politics, business, fiction, sports, and current events.

## Writes Like She Talks
### www.writeslikeshetalks.com

Cleveland blogger Jill Zimon is a regular contributor to radio-show panels and she was pegged by *WE* magazine as one of their 101 Women Bloggers to Watch. She writes about politics, among other topics, at her award-winning site.

# Index

# Restaurants Index

# Nightlife Index

# Shops Index

# Hotels Index

# Acknowledgments

It has been said that writing a book is a lot like giving birth. While that statement likely is an affront to every mother who has ever been, the process truly is a monumentally challenging but ultimately rewarding one. Not only was *Moon Cleveland* the most demanding gig of my professional writing career, it also was the most gratifying. And for that I'd like to thank those who had a hand in the year-long gestation.

My sincere appreciation goes out to Avalon Travel acquisitions director Grace Fujimoto, who "graciously" permitted me to jump into the selection process so late in the game. Ms. Fujimoto's faith in my competence and enthusiasm for the project served me well for the months of hard work to come. Thanks also are due to editor Tiffany Watson, whose seemingly infinite patience and encouraging outlook inspired in me the desire to produce a product of which we could both be proud. Deserving, too, of my heartfelt appreciation are production coordinator Tabitha Lahr and map editor Albert Angulo, who together transformed the potentially maddening task of corralling photos and maps into a less-than-unobjectionable activity.

Had it not been for Samantha Fryberger, another writer's name would be splashed across the front of *Moon Cleveland*. It was Sam who tipped me off that Avalon Travel was searching for a writer to attach to the project in the first place. And, as director of communications for Positively Cleveland, Sam served as a sort of silent partner throughout the entire process. Her only motivation: a genuine desire to show off the city she calls home.

As my indefatigable research assistant, Janelle Rooker tracked down the bits of information not easily accessible through traditional means. She approached her work with a level of seriousness and professionalism commensurate with much grander endeavors. I'd also be remiss not to single out the good folks at the Cleveland *Plain Dealer,* who on a daily basis keep me well informed about the city's goings-on.

Most notably, I want to thank my beautiful wife, Kim. There is much more to being supportive than simply picking up dinner or doing the dishes. One of Cleveland's biggest boosters, Kim infused the project with consistent gusto, even when I found it difficult to do the same. If I worked half as hard as my wife does on a consistent basis, I'd have finished the book twice as fast. Glad we're on the same page, literally and figuratively.

And just because they'd kill me if I didn't mention them, thanks to Mom and Dad. See what good things can happen when you give up the practice of law?

# www.moon.com

DESTINATIONS | ACTIVITIES | BLOGS | MAPS | BOOKS

**MOON.COM** is all new, and ready to help plan your next trip! Filled with fresh trip ideas and strategies, author interviews, informative blogs, a detailed map library, and descriptions of all the Moon guidebooks, Moon.com is all you need to get out and explore the world—or even places in your own backyard. As always, when you travel with Moon, expect an experience that is uncommon and truly unique.

# MAP SYMBOLS

| | | | | | | | |
|---|---|---|---|---|---|---|---|
| ▦ | Expressway | ◖ | Highlight | ✗ | Airfield | ⚲ | Golf Course |
| | Primary Road | ○ | City/Town | ✈ | Airport | ℗ | Parking Area |
| | Secondary Road | ◉ | State Capital | ▲ | Mountain | ⬟ | Archaeological Site |
| ▫▫▫▫ | Unpaved Road | ⊛ | National Capital | ✛ | Unique Natural Feature | ⚑ | Church |
| ------- | Trail | ★ | Point of Interest | | | ⛽ | Gas Station |
| ·········· | Ferry | • | Accommodation | 🮲 | Waterfall | | Glacier |
| ▬▬▬ | Railroad | ▼ | Restaurant/Bar | ▲ | Park | | Mangrove |
| | Pedestrian Walkway | ■ | Other Location | ⓣ | Trailhead | | Reef |
| �🮋🮋🮋 | Stairs | ⋀ | Campground | ⛷ | Skiing Area | | Swamp |

# CONVERSION TABLES

°C = (°F - 32) / 1.8
°F = (°C x 1.8) + 32
1 inch = 2.54 centimeters (cm)
1 foot = 0.304 meters (m)
1 yard = 0.914 meters
1 mile = 1.6093 kilometers (km)
1 km = 0.6214 miles
1 fathom = 1.8288 m
1 chain = 20.1168 m
1 furlong = 201.168 m
1 acre = 0.4047 hectares
1 sq km = 100 hectares
1 sq mile = 2.59 square km
1 ounce = 28.35 grams
1 pound = 0.4536 kilograms
1 short ton = 0.90718 metric ton
1 short ton = 2,000 pounds
1 long ton = 1.016 metric tons
1 long ton = 2,240 pounds
1 metric ton = 1,000 kilograms
1 quart = 0.94635 liters
1 US gallon = 3.7854 liters
1 Imperial gallon = 4.5459 liters
1 nautical mile = 1.852 km

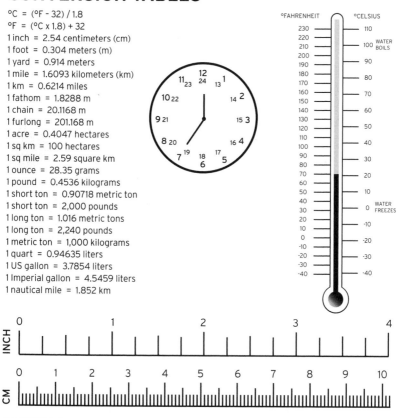

**MOON CLEVELAND**

Avalon Travel
a member of the Perseus Books Group
1700 Fourth Street
Berkeley, CA 94710, USA
www.moon.com

Editor: Tiffany Watson
Series Manager: Erin Raber
Copy Editor: Amy Scott
Graphics Coordinator: Tabitha Lahr
Production Coordinator: Tabitha Lahr
Cover Designer: Kathryn Osgood
Map Editors: Albert Angulo, Brice Ticen
Cartographer: Chris Markiewicz

ISBN-10: 1-59880-206-2
ISBN-13: 978-1-59880-206-1
ISSN: 1947-9174

Printing History
1st Edition – June 2009
5 4 3 2 1

Text © 2009 by Douglas Trattner.
Maps © 2009 by Avalon Travel.
All rights reserved.

Some photos and illustrations are used by permission and are the property of the original copyright owners.

Front cover photo: © Jeremy Woodhouse/Alamy
Title page photo: Rock and Roll Hall of Fame, courtesy of Positively Cleveland

Interior color photos: page 3, skyline, courtesy of Positively Cleveland; page 19, detail of the Hope Memorial Bridge © Douglas Trattner; page 19, St. Theodosius Russian Orthodox Cathedral © Douglas Trattner; page 19, Parade the Circle, courtesy of Positively Cleveland; pages 20–25, courtesy of Positively Cleveland; pages 26 and 27 © Douglas Trattner; page 28, courtesy of Fire Food Drink

Printed in the U.S.A. by RR Donnelley

## KEEPING CURRENT

If you have a favorite gem you'd like to see included in the next edition, or see anything that needs updating, clarification, or correction, please drop us a line. Send your comments via email to feedback@moon.com, or use the address above.